GREAT BRITAIN
AND THE
CREATION OF YUGOSLAVIA

James Evans completed his D.Phil at Oriel College, Oxford. He now works as an Associate Producer on historical and political documentaries and as a freelance writer.

GREAT BRITAIN AND THE CREATION OF YUGOSLAVIA

Negotiating Balkan Nationality and Identity

JAMES EVANS

BLOOMSBURY ACADEMIC
LONDON • NEW YORK • OXFORD • NEW DELHI • SYDNEY

BLOOMSBURY ACADEMIC
Bloomsbury Publishing Plc
50 Bedford Square, London, WC1B 3DP, UK
1385 Broadway, New York, NY 10018, USA

BLOOMSBURY, BLOOMSBURY ACADEMIC and the Diana
logo are trademarks of Bloomsbury Publishing Plc

First published in Great Britain by I.B. Tauris 2008
Paperback edition published by Bloomsbury Academic 2020

A catalogue record for this book is available from the British Library.

A catalog record for this book is available from the Library of Congress.

ISBN: HB: 978-1-8451-1488-6
PB: 978-1-3501-7145-9
ePDF: 978-0-8577-1307-0
eBook: 978-0-7556-2939-8

Series: International Library of Twentieth Century History, vol. 13

To find out more about our authors and books visit
www.bloomsbury.com and sign up for our newsletters.

Contents

Acknowledgements

This monograph had its remote origin in a Masters thesis I wrote on British attitudes to the emergence of Tito's regime in Yugoslavia in 1944-45. The central theme of that work was the manner in which British observers interpreted the new Communist regime's proclaimed democratic credentials, particularly as concerned the tightly-controlled 'election' of November 1945. A subsidiary theme was the way in which Tito's seemingly 'progressive' and 'democratic' treatment of Yugoslavia's national question – the federal, six-state solution which endured, with minor modifications, until the state's collapse in the early 1990s – secured him the esteem of the British political mainstream, in spite of his illiberal ideology and authoritarian instincts.

My initial intention with my doctoral thesis was to look further into British attitudes to the Yugoslav national question during the period of Tito's rise to power. I gradually became conscious, however, that attitudes and preconceptions prevalent during the Second World War tended to have their origin in the period of the First, when the demise of Austria-Hungary paved the way for 'Yugoslavia' and obliged British observers to attend closely for the first time to questions of South Slavic history and nationality. Since there existed no detailed study of British attitudes to the formation of the Yugoslav State in 1918, to the notion of a single Yugoslav 'nationality' which underpinned it, or to the process of internal political wrangling which preceded the state's first constitution of June 1921, there seemed reason to transfer my focus to the earlier period. This monograph is based substantially on my doctoral thesis as it was then written, although I have looked since at a range of French sources – primary and secondary – which provide useful additional context.

I would like to thank my PhD supervisor, Mark Almond, for reading numerous drafts and for all his help and encouragement, and Mark Cornwall, my examiner, who has been very generous with advice. I want to pay special tribute to my parents, for their constant love and support – particularly during the early stages of my postgraduate career when ill-health would have made productive research impossible without their selfless assistance. And finally I would like to thank my wife Nicola, both for her practical help – printing, proof-reading and assisting with my bibliography – and more importantly for being a sympathetic ear and an unfailing source of love and encouragement.

Abbreviations and Orthography

The following abbreviations are used:

DMI	Director of Military Intelligence
EPD	Enemy Propaganda Department
IB	Intelligence Bureau
PID	Political Intelligence Department
HMG	His Majesty's Government
SCS	Serb-Croat-Slovene
HSK	Serbo-Croat Coalition (*Hrvatsko-Srpska koalicija*)
DS	Democratic Party (*Demokratska stranka*)
NRS	National Radical Party (*Narodna radikalna stranka*)
HPSS/HRSS	Croat People's Peasant Party (*Hrvatska pučka seljačka stranka*)/ Croat Republican Peasant Party (*Hrvatska republikanska seljačka stranka*)
SSP	Starčević's Party of Right (*Starčevićeva stranka prava*)
HZ	Croat Union (*Hrvatska zajednica*)
JMO	Yugoslav Muslim Organisation (*Jugoslavenska muslimanska organizacija*)
SLS	Slovene People's Party (*Slovenska ljudska stranka*)
KPJ	Communist Party of Yugoslavia (*Komunistička partija Jugoslavije*)

In the early 20th century it was common for 'Yugoslav' to be used in Britain in the forms 'Yugo-Slav', 'Jugo-Slav' and 'Jugoslav'. When the hyphenated form is used in quoted text it is reproduced here unchanged. For the sake of consistency, however, Js are changed to Ys throughout unless in the titles of cited works.

The common pre-war forms 'Servia'/ 'Servian' are likewise rendered as 'Serbia'/ 'Serbian'.

Introduction

This is a study of British attitudes towards the emergence of the Yugoslav State in 1918, as well as towards the chronic unrest and acrimonious debates which preceded the Yugoslav constitutional settlement in June 1921. Scholars have long dismissed the notion that the shape of post-war Europe was simply decreed by the Council of Four sitting at Versailles. Before that conference even convened, Yugoslavia had emerged from the wartime chaos, and the Powers could do little to alter the fact. The allied chancelleries 'created' Yugoslavia only in the negative sense that they approved its existence, accorded it legal recognition, and cast judgement on the controversial fine-tuning of its frontiers.[1]

But this does not mean that British observers of South Slav unification were purely passive, or that British attitudes had no bearing on the events themselves. It is largely (if not exclusively) true that those whose views are analysed here merely watched, and wrote, rather than contributing directly to the developments they discussed. But during the war in particular, Yugoslav activists monitored opinion in Allied countries, convinced – unduly, as it turned out – that their plans depended upon Great Power sponsorship. (A united Yugoslavia, maintained Frano Supilo, would be possible only 'if strongly supported by England').[2] At crucial moments the behaviour of Yugoslav politicians was governed by a desire to influence opinion in the Allied countries, and publicists purveyed (often successfully) a misleading impression of the region's history and culture.

Nor, in any case, should a study of British attitudes be justified with reference only to their influence on contemporary events. The manner in which one 'nation' or similar circumscribed group perceives another is apt to endure. Patterns form, and assumptions ossify, often regardless of their basis in fact, sheltered by semi-porous linguistic barriers, bequeathed by senior diplomat to junior official or by seasoned correspondent to apprentice, lodging in the cultural discourse. If such ideas do not influence events at the moment of their conception, they may yet. And what is paramount about the period in question is that it was then, for the first time, that the great upheaval of the war compelled Britons to study the Slavs of east-central Europe as independent actors. It was a formative period, in other words, in which patterns of perception first acquired a concrete and lasting form. One cannot study later episodes in British-Yugoslav relations – the dealings in occupied Yugoslavia during World

War II, the Stalin-Tito rift of 1948, or the demise of Yugoslavia in the 1990s – without marking the longevity of western stereotypes and preconceptions dating from the early 20th century. And it is clear that British (and more generally western) attitudes *did*, in these subsequent crises, contribute actively to the shaping of events.

Any historical study claiming to analyse the attitudes of a nation, or of 'public opinion', begs a question: whose attitudes precisely? Lacking the space to attempt a theoretical discussion of the nature of public opinion in an age before scientific polls, the answer here must be pragmatic: the attitudes examined are not those of 'Britons' in general, but those only of people in Britain who contemplated the situation of the Yugoslavs, and who left a record of what they thought. From the attempts such people made to interest government or public (and from assessments of their success), from the frequency and the prominence of relevant publications, from Government sensitivity to parliamentary or perceived wider opinion, and from other similar indications, one can at least estimate the impression made by the fate of the South Slavs upon what is vaguely termed the 'national consciousness'.

One can talk, of course, of 'intellectual', 'elite' or 'educated' opinion, and most of those quoted or discussed here fit that loose categorisation (if only because 'intellectuals', almost by definition, are more prone to leave records of their views). But the labels are not wholly satisfactory. For one thing, ordinary soldiers and relief workers who found themselves in south-east or east-central Europe published their experiences and reflections. For another, one cannot assume, by any stretch of the imagination, that those in Britain who were 'intellectual', 'educated' or members of the 'elite' (however this term be defined) necessarily had any acquaintance with the problems of the South Slav region.

Far from it. Historians have often remarked upon the 'abysmal ignorance of English society' regarding continental or world affairs, noting that late 19th century British travellers approached the Austrian territories south and east of Vienna 'in much the same state of mind as to the heart of darkest Africa'.[3] (One contemporary writer who did venture into south-eastern Europe suggested that it was 'no exaggeration to say that many regions of Africa are more familiar to the cultured Englishman [...] than the lands which lie beyond the Adriatic').[4] A long-sighted imperial vision left parts of the continental middle-ground decidedly out of focus so far as Britons were concerned, and this was certainly as true of the Yugoslav region as anywhere. 'There is scarcely any race in Europe of which most people in England know less than they do of the Serbs', one Slav specialist observed.[5] Even the British Government, a historian has claimed, only a little unfairly, 'knew little and cared less' about the subject nationalities of Eastern Europe on the eve of the First World War.[6] Pre-war British diplomacy, focused upon the great capitals of Berlin, Paris, Vienna,

St.Petersburg and Constantinople, was certainly not closely acquainted with political tendencies in Belgrade, Zagreb, Sarajevo or Ljubljana.[7]

A small number of dedicated publicists attempted during the war to raise the profile of the South Slavs and other national groups, often with considerable success. But while younger Foreign Office officials often became enthusiastic supporters of the hitherto suppressed nationalities of East-Central Europe, certain senior members of Whitehall remained bluffly cynical. (Wickham Steed, foreign editor of *The Times* and close ally of Robert Seton-Watson's *New Europe* campaign, was, Lord Derby noted suspiciously, an 'idealist', even if he did know more than most 'about these weird people the Czecho-Slovaks and Yugo-Slavs').[8] And if Seton-Watson felt that public opinion in Britain was 'far ahead of the British government' on the idea of Yugoslav unity, general levels of awareness nevertheless remained well below those to which idealistic publicists aspired.[9] 'I am more and more appalled', J.L.Garvin, editor of *The Observer*, told Seton-Watson in October 1917, 'at the ignorance of foreign affairs even amongst people who are supposed to be intelligent'.[10] Such disillusion only increased after the war, as the public's interest in hitherto little-known allies or grand ideas of a reformed diplomacy withered amid a renewed preoccupation with domestic issues.[11]

While it is important to bear this context in mind, however, my purpose in this monograph is not a comprehensive survey of British public opinion and the Yugoslavs. For one thing, studies exist which treat the question at some length, particularly with regard to the wartime period. (Harry Hanak, for instance, has dealt thoroughly and well with the spectrum of British attitudes towards the demise of Austria-Hungary, a subject encompassing the Yugoslav question).[12] Nor is it my purpose simply to study diplomatic attitudes to the creation of a Yugoslav State as a factor in international affairs.[13] Rather, I intend to focus particularly on the concept of the 'Yugoslav' nation as it was understood in Britain in the early 20th century, and to explore the ways in which Britons reacted to the idea, suddenly and forcefully propagated, that various groups with apparently distinct ethnic identities – Serbs, Croats, Slovenes, Montenegrins, Dalmatians and others – were in fact a single racial and national group, with aspirations to a corresponding political unity.[14]

Furthermore, in addition to analysing British attitudes towards the notion of Yugoslav 'nationality', and towards its component national or sub-national identities, I mean to analyse the way a united Yugoslavia was conceptualised constitutionally in Britain: how, in other words, Britons supposed the constitutional structure of the new state should reflect the varied history, culture and identities of its component parts, how they reacted to the constitutional debates which did take place in Yugoslavia in the lead-up to the 1921 settlement, and how they responded to the form that settlement took.

Essentially, therefore, this monograph attempts to answer two questions: firstly, what did British observers think of the idea of Yugoslav nationality during the period of the creation of the Yugoslav state? And secondly, how did they relate the conclusions they drew on this score to the putative and then to the actual political structure of the state? The first question I want to address thematically, exploring in isolation those factors which contemporary theorists commonly identified as 'objective' contributors to 'subjective' national feeling – racial kinship, linguistic unity, religious background, and secular history and mythology. In each case I have attempted to present a generalised theoretical context before looking at the ways in which underlying assumptions were related to the specific and complicated case of the South Slavs. In these thematic chapters I have drawn from a wide range of contemporary source material dating from the late 19th century through to the early interwar period on the basis that, while attitudes to a specific group like the Yugoslavs could shift quite dramatically in response to short-term circumstances, background assumptions about the theory and practice of nationality were less mutable. (They were also, of course, not certain to be voiced explicitly in material dealing specifically with the Yugoslav case). With British analyses of the Yugoslavs in particular I have tried to be more careful with chronology, exploring, for instance, the impact of the war on the way their national identity was presented.

It is hoped that this first, thematic section of the monograph provides a valuable backdrop for the second: a more conventional survey of the constitutional debate leading up to the first Yugoslav constitution of 1921 as it was portrayed and understood in Britain. A chapter is devoted to the controversy surrounding the incorporation of Montenegro into Yugoslavia, because this issue's peculiar diplomatic complications cast light on the broader problems of amalgamation, as well as being worthy of study in their own right. Subsequent chapters survey firstly the wartime evolution of British attitudes towards a Yugoslav State and towards the political structure which such a state would be likely to adopt, and secondly the post-war coverage of the wranglings in Yugoslavia before and immediately after the controversial centralist settlement. Necessarily, these chapters are chronological rather than thematic in approach. They rely much more heavily upon official British diplomatic records, since few outside the Foreign Office had detailed knowledge of the internal situation in Yugoslavia during or after the war, and as such they amount effectively to a study of British Government thinking on the subject.

In general, then, I have preferred to discuss what the minority did know than what the great majority did not. It has been necessary at times to draw attention to mistakes and misconceptions. But, particularly as far as those private individuals who took an interest in the South Slavs are concerned, it is not forgotten that these were pioneers in the study of a region remarkably little known or understood before this period.

And if we acknowledge hindsight's advantages, moreover, no less should we be alert to its dangers. Inevitably, the events of the early 1990s have affected the way in which Yugoslav history is perceived. Wherever the balance is struck in explaining that crisis, between deep socio-economic forces and cynical political manoeuvring, it plainly revealed profound tensions within the Yugoslav system. Observing the fervent nationalism of Serbs and Croats at the end of the 20th century has made it hard to empathise with an earlier conviction that the two peoples were really one, and would quickly fuse, within a single state, into a homogeneous Yugoslav nationality.

It must be right, of course, to question the faith many British observers had that Yugoslav racial and linguistic kinship not only made a united Yugoslav state inevitable, but would submerge ethnic varieties within a shared national consciousness. But, equally obviously, one should not assume, on the basis of subsequent history, that the unification project was necessarily misconceived, or naively idealistic, or the state itself the 'doomed creation' it has seemed in much modern writing.[15] That serious tensions existed within the Yugoslav population in 1921, unresolved and probably exacerbated by the constitution of that year, is evident. But who can say that they might not have been resolved, or that Yugoslav ideology was any more 'artificial' than other, successful national projects? Yugoslavia's history as a state, from the instability of the interwar years and the desperate hardships of Nazi occupation to the authoritarian one-party 'federalism' of the Tito era, has been far too sinuous and complex (and shaped far too often by events and influences outside its borders) to be reduced to such crude inexorability. My intention here is not to draw such sweeping lessons, but merely to study the period in question on its own terms. Such broader relevance as may fairly be drawn will, in any case, be more likely to emerge on that basis.

And as in time, so in space: the emergence of Yugoslavia must be seen now as an element in the wider, revolutionary settlement of 1919, as must British attitudes towards the Yugoslavs be understood within the context of the wider war and its aftermath. I can only endeavour, however, to highlight, where relevant, the ways in which it impinged upon the narrower subject; and hope that perhaps, in a small way, this detailed study may cast light back out upon the wider picture of Britain and Europe at the end of World War I.

I have said that my approach to public opinion will be pragmatic, and that this will be a survey of those in Britain who – for whatever reason – chose to record their views of South Slav politics, history or culture. It may help at the outset, however, to comment briefly on the backgrounds and propensities of those various categories of observers whose testimonies recur most frequently in the pages that follow – to highlight, where possible, some of the respects in which they tended to be representative, or unrepresentative, of the wider population. The assigning of an array of witnesses to neat compartments must inevitably be procrustean. Often the details of a life rail against such simplification, and examples may easily be found of individuals who shifted, over time, from one category to another, or who produced simultaneously works which would assign them to different categories. Nevertheless, with the caveat that boundaries were in practice graduated and porous, we may perhaps consider British observers in four principal categories:

i.   Travel writers and other non-expert protagonists who recorded first-hand experiences in the South Slav lands;

ii.   Serious scholars of the South Slav region, or of the Ottoman Empire or the Habsburg Monarchy and their various subject peoples;

iii. Students of the theory of nationality, whose interest in the Yugoslav case was as an interesting and controversial instance of a general phenomenon;

iv.   Career diplomats.[16]

Exotic places and peoples, rendered in easy-going, colloquial traveller accounts, were a staple of the Victorian reading public, and remained popular in the Edwardian period. If south-eastern Europe was, geographically, less remote than Africa or Central Asia, it nevertheless possessed – particularly in the case of those territories with a strong Ottoman heritage – an aura of oriental mystique which travel writers did little to play down. In the hands of writers like Harry de Windt and P.E. Henderson, this region of 'savage Europe' was one of vivid and heady sensory perception, but 'wild and lawless' and swarming with 'strange nationalities'.[17] It possessed 'the attraction and glamour of the East, its gorgeous colouring, its brilliant costumes, sense of mystery'.[18] To many of these writers the region seemed 'more part of the extraordinary and exotic world of Asia than of Europe'.[19] 'Everything', wrote William Miller, 'is the exact opposite of what it might reasonably be expected to be; the traveller finds himself in the realms of romance, where all his wonted ideas are turned topsy-turvy'.[20] The last quarter of the nineteenth century witnessed, as Barbara Korte has noted, a marked rise in attempts to travel 'unconventionally' – to walk on paths untrodden and away from what seemed the mixed blessings of western civilisation.[21] In pre-war accounts of places like Montenegro, Serbia and Bosnia-Hercegovina one notes a common quest and admiration for those primitive, atavistic virtues which seemed to survive only in the remotest regions.

During the war, of course, such travel accounts dried up. They were superseded, however, by narratives of personal involvement in Serbia in particular, as that country's embattled resistance won it considerable coverage and sympathy in the British press. Soldiers who had experienced the Serbian defence and ultimate retreat of 1915-16, and/ or the fighting return through Macedonia in 1918, recorded their impressions of Serbia and the Serbs – almost invariably and understandably tinted with romanticised admiration for their former brothers-in-arms.[22] As important were the vivid testimonies of those who had been involved in Serbia in a relief capacity, working in military hospitals to cope with the wounded and the victims of the typhus epidemic that decimated the Serb forces.[23]

Most of those involved in relief work were women – Lady Paget, Mabel St.Clair Stobart and Elsie Inglis became revered figures in Serbia, and numerous others worked in anonymity for organisations like the Women's Emergency Corps or the Scottish Women's Hospital for Foreign Service. Significantly, many of them also had strong suffragette or suffragist connections or sympathies – a cause whose righteous indignation on behalf of a long-disfranchised community translated easily into a passionate support for Europe's beleaguered smaller nations.[24] A similar empathy may perhaps also explain the disproportionate representation of individuals and organisations from non-conformist (often Methodist) religious backgrounds, and from Britain's own smaller, historically marginalised nations – Scotland in particular (a question we will return to shortly). Though non-political in its direct aims, the charity work sponsored, organised and carried out by British relief organisations was, as Harry Hanak points out, often initiated and publicised by individuals strongly sympathetic to the creation of a single, Yugoslav state, who tended naturally to reflect this sympathy in their fund-raising and educational writings.[25]

A number of these individuals, in fact – men like Robert Seton-Watson and Sir Arthur Evans – had become sincerely and deeply engaged with the history, culture and political development of the South Slavs to the extent that they must be considered within our second category of observers: the serious British scholars of the region. Also among this group, with a variety of individual caveats, may be considered such influential writers as William Miller, Edith Durham, Harold Temperley, A.H.E. Taylor, Neville Forbes, H.N. Brailsford, J.A. Marriott, Sir Charles Eliot, G.M. Trevelyan and Wickham Steed. As we will discover during our discussion, their perspectives and attitudes towards the South Slavs as a whole, and towards relationships within the South Slav group, differed in some important respects. But it is worth briefly considering here some characteristics they broadly shared.

Most importantly, perhaps, it should be borne in mind that the majority of those who wrote extensively about the South Slavs (and who therefore loom large in the ensuing pages) were inclined to be favourably disposed towards them, and towards the project of a united, independent state – their enthusiasm for the cause of Yugoslav unity motivating their in some cases prolific writing and research.[26] Those in Britain who were unsympathetic on intellectual grounds to a Yugoslav cause which entailed the dismemberment of the Habsburg Empire, or who were instinctively contemptuous of these seemingly new-fangled, conglomerate nationalities of East-Central Europe (and of those British campaigners who adopted them), may be under-represented in this monograph. Put bluntly, a lack of interest was less likely to speak its mind.[27]

The idea that the group of writers who wrote at length about the South Slavs were not a representative sample of British political and intellectual life seems confirmed by a glance at their political affiliations and sympathies. As Robert Evans has observed, those British historians drawn to write about Europe's emergent, hitherto-suppressed nationalities were overwhelmingly Liberals, commonly with a Radical tinge: 'they were inspired by a sort of Gladstonian moral crusade to rectify abuse […] and by sublime confidence in the ability of the constitutional and parliamentary process to sustain liberty and social justice'.[28] (Robert Seton-Watson had himself toyed with standing as a Liberal candidate before the war).[29] Interestingly, of those with Balkan or Habsburg expertise, it was only those like Brailsford or Charles Buxton who tended towards more radical, socialist politics who were less enthused by the politics of national liberation, prioritising instead bonds of economic subjection and the need for large, federal entities.[30]

The label 'expert', of course, is a subjective one. There were, as we mentioned, caveats in individual cases regarding the validity of claims to be regarded as such. One general caveat, however, is worth mentioning here because of its wide application – admittedly, in varying degrees – to almost all the scholars under discussion. The historic, civilisational divide which separated the Habsburg realm from the territories of the present and former Ottoman Empire was one seldom convincingly straddled by British scholars, who tended to approach the problems of south-eastern Europe from a perspective either distinctively Habsburg or distinctively 'Balkan'. As a result, many of the writers in question were markedly more sure-footed on one side of this divide than the other, with significant consequences for their perspective on the history and future alignment of the broader region. Thus, for example Seton-Watson's familiarity with pre-war independent Serbia was – as he himself later confessed – markedly weaker than his knowledge of the South Slav lands of the Austrian empire. Meanwhile his close ally Wickham Steed was, much more so, an expert of Central Europe rather than the Balkans. By contrast, writers like Henry Brailsford and Noel Buxton were Balkan specialists, deeply knowledgeable about Bulgaria and Macedonia, but relatively unversed in the history and politics of Habsburg Central Europe.[31] Edith Durham, likewise, had travelled in Serbia and had a sophisticated understanding of highland society in Montenegro and Albania, but was scarcely the authority on all of central and south-east Europe she purported to be. At times the demand in wartime Britain for 'expert' commentary on hitherto unknown regions exceeded the supply.

In the case of our third category of observers the same caveat more obviously applies. Themes of national identity and its relationship to political organisation, widely discussed since the days of Mazzini and the movements of Italian and German unification, became again during World War I a focus for intellectual discussion. Numerous theoretical works attempted to define nationality in general terms and to analyse its likely significance for a future peace settlement. For their authors the Yugoslavs were of obvious interest, both as a long-suppressed but increasingly assertive national group within the Habsburg Empire, and as a purported single nationality comprising various component identities grounded in differences of language, religion and historical tradition. Writers like Alfred Zimmern, James Bryce, Arnold Toynbee, J.Holland Rose and Sidney Herbert found in the Yugoslavs a telling test-case for their more general ideas about nationality and the future political disposition of Europe. Ranging widely in their discussions, however, they were all of them reliant for the specifics of the Yugoslav case on the more specialist authors we have discussed.[32]

Not a few of these writers (as well as those who focused more specifically on the South Slavs) had in their personal histories, it may also be noted, elements which seem to have fostered an interest in the vexed question of national identity and its relationship to the modern state. For some, like Alfred Zimmern or Lewis Namier, a Jewish heritage and strong Zionist sympathies, combined with a migrant's preoccupation with roots and rootedness, bequeathed a wider interest in the themes of nationality and identity.[33] For a significant number of others, allegiance to one of Britain's historically marginalised nations seems to have encouraged an identification with peoples struggling to assert their identities in the shadow of dominant neighbours. Some, like James Bryce or the Leeper brothers, were Protestant Irish in background. A disproportionate number of the individuals and organisations involved in wartime relief work in Serbia were Scottish.[34] Most notably, perhaps, Robert Seton-Watson ('Scotus Viator') displayed a proud and romanticised conception of Scottish history and of the union with England which influenced his views on the Habsburg Monarchy and on the post-Habsburg national states.[35]

Our fourth and final category of observers includes those whose careers in government service led them to contribute to the formulation of official British attitudes and policies towards the South Slavs. The pre-war Foreign Office and diplomatic service, as Zara Steiner and others have shown, conducted much of its business in a state of serene and haughty isolation – from the organs of domestic government as well as from the wider British public.[36] (After 1906, in particular, a significant degree of distance developed between the predominantly Eton-educated and conservative diplomatic service and the ascendant Liberal element within the political establishment). There is certainly little evidence that clerks or diplomats were significantly influenced by published accounts of the Yugoslav region written by independent scholars or travellers. As Roberta Warman has pointed out, not before the creation of the Political Intelligence Department in 1918 did the Foreign Office recognise any responsibility to collect and digest miscellaneous information regarding foreign countries.[37] Few diplomats, it may also be noted, chose to convey their experiences or impressions to a general readership.[38]

Even within the official foreign service palpable internal divisions and tensions remained, between the diplomatic corps and the distinct, subordinate consular service. In relation to Austria-Hungary, for instance, the service history of many of the British consuls serving in Sarajevo was levantine: commonly they had served as interpreters in Constantinople. This background was rarely shared, however, by British diplomatic representatives in Vienna or Budapest, and the result, as Robin Okey has noted, was that 'a certain fracture entered the reportage'.[39] As we will see later, this variation of perspectives could be marked and significant: as, for instance, when it came to British attitudes towards the treatment by Serbia of Muslim minorities in Kosovo and Macedonia.[40]

During the war, and during the peace conference which followed, the Foreign Office suffered significant encroachment on its role in the formulation of foreign policy, and was obliged in response to become markedly less insular in its approach. An urgent need for expertise which could not be met from within the service led to the breakdown (temporarily, at least) of the divide between career diplomats and Foreign Office clerks on the one hand, and independent academics and journalists on the other. The erosion of barriers was certainly not complete, and mutual suspicions and rivalries remained. But it does become easier to discuss British official and unofficial attitudes as a related, if by no means homogeneous, whole.

The significance of the role played by independent academics and writers within British Government in the late war period is a question to which we will later return.[41] Let us now turn directly, however, to the question of Yugoslav nationality as it was understood in early 20th century Britain, and first, specifically, to the perceived importance of a shared *racial* ancestry among the South Slavs.

Part I

The Idea of Yugoslav Nationality in British Writing, 1900-1918: Elements and Themes

1

Race: British Attitudes to the Racial Element in South Slav Nationality

In 1906 the Austrian thinker Otto Bauer distinguished three tendencies into which nationality theory had effectively divided. These schools of thought he categorised under the headings 'metaphysical', 'psychological' and 'objective'.[1] In general, British theoretical debate has been dominated by the last two: by questions of conscious identity (the psychological approach) and of external ('objective') characteristics such as language, religion or political tradition. One might easily assume that the 'metaphysical' approach – whether 'spiritualist' (founded on the posited existence of an unchanging racial 'soul') or materialist (assuming hereditary transmission of racial characteristics) – played no substantial role in British thought. After all, British philosophers had tended to distance themselves from the romantic nationalist tradition, associated with German thinkers like Herder, Humboldt and Fichte, which presented the nation in 'organic' or 'primordial' terms as a family with a distinct biological lineage and an inviolable cultural and linguistic heritage.[2] Britain's historians could scarcely deny her people's divergent racial ancestry.[3]

Many British theorists certainly did denounce the notion of racial purity. They insisted that no substantial correlation could exist between 'race' in a scientific sense and 'nationality' as it was then experienced. Any such doctrine had been sharply rejected by British intellectuals of the previous generation like Mill, Buckle and Huxley.[4] Their successors were no less wary of those 'premature exploitations of science' which brought reputable anthropological investigation to the service of 'monstrous doctrines of "racialism"'.[5] Only 'malice and ignorance' could assume national groups were racially homogeneous.[6]

Nevertheless, the vigour of the flogging administered to 'racialism' by British theorists suggests that this was a horse which, however malnourished beside its German stablemate, had not expired altogether. On the one hand, in spite of Mill's insistence on the vulgarity of 'attributing the diversities of conduct and character to inherent natural differences', many scholarly writers were unwilling to dismiss the contribution of racial strain to national character.[7] 'Strange to say', one eminent ethnologist concluded, 'the element that appears to have undergone the least change is the racial temperament'.[8] The respected historian Lord Bryce conceded that the significance of race had been exaggerated; but even his moderate voice insisted that 'in the thought and imagination of every civilised people there is an unquestionable racial strain'.[9] When Alfred Zimmern attempted to define 'nationality', common race seemed 'perhaps the most important factor'.[10] Most notably, the revered figurehead of one school of British nationality theory, Lord Acton, had stated with customary assurance that 'the same race of men preserves its character, not only in every region of the world, but in every period of history, in spite of moral as well as physical influences'.[11]

On the other hand (and more important for our purposes) is the influence these ideas had upon the tacit assumptions of intellectual discourse. To the concept of 'national character', by which was usually meant 'racial character', was attributed an explanatory power which would now be considered quite unwarranted. Lloyd George could still assert in Parliament that the intractability of the Irish question was due to a 'difference of blood'.[12] An eminent (and still-respected) historian considered it an explanation of the comparative failure of state-sponsored Russianisation in the late 19th century to observe simply that 'the Russian nature is averse from system'.[13] Robert Seton-Watson, the foremost British specialist on the Habsburg nationalities, explained the phenomenon of pan-Slavism with reference to a 'deep-seated call of the blood, which rises superior to differences of language, religion, geography and historical tradition'.[14] In his work on Romania he stressed that that country's latinate language and culture was evidence of a *'racial* link with Italy and France'.[15] The political and academic discourse of the period abounds with such examples. 'Anthropologists, ethnologists, sociologists, and historians [...]', one theorist lamented, 'all alike recognise differences of national character as giving meaning and unity to national history'.[16]

It is true that the origin of 'national character', for some who thought carefully about the issue, lay less in *racial* inheritance than in the more tangible influences of physical and cultural environment. (To regard 'complicated social and historical traits as race tendencies', protested one writer, was to overlook 'the importance of environment in the formation of the character and mental make-up of a group').[17] But for most race remained not only an important but also an *unchanging* influence, having long ago solidified into its contemporary divisions. [18] And the attribution to races of traits assumed to be the expression of inherited stock remained a near-universal tendency, of intellectual as well as popular discourse.

To some extent, of course, this broad assumption recurs today.[19] It would be unusual, however, to encounter now the quasi-mystical belief, common in early 20th century Britain, in an unalterable 'soul' or 'spirit', representing the collective consciousness, values and aspirations of each nationality. ('That nations have souls, who can doubt?', asked one writer in 1916 in response to the bravery of Serb, Polish and Belgian resistance).[20] This view, described by one contemporary as 'at once vaguely and tenaciously held by the vast majority of civilised people', was popularised in Britain by the likes of Gustave Le Bon, for whom each national soul possessed 'fundamental characteristics as immutable as the anatomical characteristics of an animal species'.[21] Exposure to wartime German supremacism may have heightened the reaction of British theorists to the 'racial fallacy'.[22] It did not seriously undermine the facile assumption of a racial basis for the national 'soul'. 'Even when it is not expressly asserted', one writer complained, 'it is tacitly admitted as the premise of important conclusions'.[23] A later writer echoed this verdict, noting that while no distinguished British writer had tried to vindicate the racial hypothesis, its influence had permeated the country's literature and politics.[24]

That this was true is more remarkable given that the general term 'race' was applied with startling inconsistency, its meaning, as one recent historian has observed, 'exceptionally amorphous and indeterminate'.[25] Its close association with the concept of nationality extended at times to their demonstrable confusion, as when the influential American adviser George D. Herron described the South Slavs as having recently entered into 'a racial unity that has no precedent in their past'.[26] The concept was routinely attached, furthermore, often by a single writer within the space of a few pages, both to large families of peoples and to any of a series of subdivisions. In popular applications – the 'French race', the 'Slavic race', the 'Latin race' and so on – it was employed with reference rather to nationalities or linguistic groups than to physiological types or relationships.[27] It was not unusual, for instance, for allusion to a single Slavic 'race' to coexist unabashedly with comment on the South Slavic 'race', with further magnification to the component Serb, Croat or Slovene 'races', or even with discussion in racial terms of identities generally regarded as provincial: the 'Dalmatian race', the 'Bosnian race' etc.[28] Lacking the terminological resources and precision of biological classification, as well as the objective means of distinction (human races, unlike animal species, have had a troublesome habit of interbreeding), analysts resorted to 'race' as a flexible label. They did so despite, indeed partly because of, the difficulty in ascertaining which of these multiple identities should be considered provincial, cultural or environmental, and which 'racial' in the sense of entailing a shared congenital inheritance.

We cannot, however, become submerged here in theoretical problems. The important point is that, despite the admonitions and fulminations of a small group of theorists, significance continued to be attached to the concept of race in British discourse about nationality. It is this which makes it necessary to examine the ways in which Britons assessed or preconceived the *racial* relationships of South Slavs with other groups, and particularly with each other. First, however, we must clarify some points of terminology which may otherwise become confusing.

Insofar as the group as a whole was concerned, the labels 'South Slav' (or 'Southern Slav') and 'Yugoslav' (often then written 'Yugo-Slav') were both common in English usage by the war period, though they had been little used before then.[29] Technically, of course, they are precisely synonymous, the latter simply connoting 'South Slav' in the Serbo-Croatian language. Their use in British analysis, however, reveals idiosyncrasies and discrete ambiguities which make it necessary to consider them separately.

The label 'South Slav', as employed in Britain, was generally less clearly defined, potentially more inclusive and certainly less politically loaded than the 'Yugoslav' alternative. Perhaps as a result, its use to describe a specific element of the Balkan population declined during and after the war as 'Yugoslav' became the accepted standard form. In the standard classification of Slavic populations – or rather, fundamentally, of their languages – 'South Slav' was a primary subsection of the Slav group. It was, as the name suggests, a counterpart of 'Western Slav' and 'Eastern Slav', neither of which indicated strictly 'national' groups but were rather collective forms containing their own subset of closely related racial, linguistic and national identities. Though less common, 'South Slav' in this strict sense encompassed not only Slovenes, Croats and Serbs – those groups who would in 1919 acquire their own eponymous South Slavic state – but also Bulgarians and the disputed populations of Macedonia (often labelled simply 'Macedonian Slavs').[30]

The characterisation in Britain of the relation of the Bulgarians to other South Slavic groups illustrates the ease with which the supposedly objective classification of 'race' could be co-opted to suit contemporary political realities and interests – by British observers as well as by the populations concerned. It was all too apparent after the Serbo-Bulgarian war of 1885, the war over the Turkish spoils in 1913, and the alleged atrocities during World War I that feelings of unity and racial brotherhood between Serb and Bulgarian were at a low ebb and prospects of early union remote. For the Allies there was no question of including Bulgarians in a united South Slav bloc viewed as an allied nation. Unlike the Slavs of the southern Habsburg lands, marched (it was assumed) unwillingly into a war wrought by the dominant Germans and Magyars, the Bulgarians had spurned Allied overtures and freely aligned themselves with German imperialism. In the light of this it is striking, but not perhaps surprising, that strong emphasis was placed in Britain on the specifically *racial* dissimilarity between the two peoples, which rendered union as unnatural as it was inexpedient. This emphasis had been less marked before 1878 when the ultimate amalgamation of Bulgaria, Serbia and Macedonia had seemed to some a desirable as well as a probable consummation, and was similarly less marked several years after the war, when hopes of Serbo-Bulgarian unity within a Balkan federation began to revive.[31]

Although by the 19th century feelings of Slavonic solidarity were arguably more potent in Bulgaria than in the lands of her western neighbours, belief in the enduring influence of ancestral blood led British writers to dwell upon the non-Slavic element in the Bulgarian make-up.[32] Serb historians such as Chedo Miyatovich, much respected by scholars like Robert Seton-Watson and Harold Temperley, drew British attention to the fact that Bulgars were 'a Slavonic nation of a quite different type, created by the circulation of Tartar blood in Slavonian veins' – a 'simple fact [which] throws much light on the conflicts between the Serbians and Bulgarians during the Middle Ages, and even in our own days'.[33] In his 1915 study, *The Southern Slavs*, Neville Forbes noted that the Bulgars were 'far from being purely Slav in origin or in temperament'. In peculiarities of the Bulgarian language he discovered the linguistic footprint of a non-Slavic ancestry, and attributed to this racial ingredient an enduring psychological import.[34] Sir Charles Eliot, in his respected history of Turkey in Europe, similarly characterised the Bulgarian tongue as 'a Slavonian language mangled by a non-Slavonic race', and saw in the Macedonian peasantry a look of 'the Finns of the Volga or the hordes of the Steppes'.[35]

After Bulgaria signed up with the Central Powers in 1915, the Bulgarophile element in Britain became subdued, and this alien admixture to the Slavic stock offered a propagandistic backdrop to Bulgarian perfidy. Seton-Watson even noted in 1916 that the Bulgars were being talked about in Britain, along with the Magyars and Turks, as constituting a pan-Turanian threat.[36] The Inter-Allied Commission deputed after the war to investigate claims of Bulgarian atrocities in Macedonia found itself, 'forced to the conclusion that, though the Bulgars wear a thin Slav veneer, they have retained the cruellest and most bestial instincts of their Tartar-Mongol origin'.[37] Such resort to distant racial origins in the service of a contemporary political position was, as we shall see, the similar expedient of those who opposed the narrower 'Yugoslav' project. Even after the war, though some were inclined to re-induct Bulgarians into the project of South Slavic unity, the emphasis remained upon the different nature of this 'amalgam of races' to that of their 'purely Slav neighbours'.[38]

On rare occasions 'Yugoslav' was employed in Britain in the broad sense, encompassing Bulgarian as well as Serb, Croat and Slovene. In his book *The Birth of Yugoslavia* Henry Baerlein condemned the use of this term to describe a state which excluded the Bulgarians.[39] During the war the Serbian Government raised the same objection on the same grounds.[40] But Baerlein's book was not published until four years after the war, and the sincerity of the Serbian Government is open to doubt.[41] In general, usage of the term in Britain reflected the fact that it had entered British vocabulary at a more recent date than the vaguer 'South Slav', and had done so in the service of a unification project which excluded the Bulgarian element. It was, therefore, less explicitly a racial or linguistic label. References to a 'Yugoslav race' were less common than the alternative 'South Slav race'. And, as we will see, 'Yugoslav' (perhaps in small part because of its then composite orthographical form: 'Yugo-Slav') never lost in this period a veneer of artificiality exacerbated by stubborn official use of the form 'Serb-Croat-Slovene'.[42]

The awkward ambiguity of the 'Yugoslav' designation in this period stemmed not from its weak racial implications, which usually embraced precisely those Slavic groups which would constitute the Yugoslav state after 1918, but rather from its particular political associations. Prior to 1914 the notion of an independent state consisting of Serbia and Montenegro on the one hand and the Habsburg South Slav lands on the other seemed fanciful. The Empire might be in decline but it was far from collapse and the most ardent enthusiast for South Slavic unity could not will the conflagration which might bring it to fruition.[43] Commonly envisaged, however, was a reformed 'trialist' monarchy, with an autonomous South Slav unit joining the existing Austro-Hungarian federation. Before the war, it was this hypothetical conglomeration within the Empire which was most commonly implied by 'Yugoslavia'.[44]

After the outbreak of war, as the Buxtons observed, Serbia 'stood forth for the first time distinctly and without equivocation as the champion not merely of Greater Serbia but of the Southern Slavs as a whole'.[45] The term 'Yugoslav' was rapidly co-opted by Serbian officials and publicists in Britain as a direct synonym for 'Serb' or 'Serbian', in accordance with an outlook which conceived the Yugoslav idea as the expansion of Serbia.[46] Thus in late 1914 the Serbian Government released a statement entitled 'Serbian (Yugoslav) War Aims'. In Britain the campaign for a Yugoslav state was an objective of, and was associated with, the 'Serbian Society'.[47] In a period when Serbia's military effort and humanitarian crisis attracted headlines and few knew much of the South Slavs within the Habsburg Monarchy, the terms 'Serbian' and 'Yugoslav' came by repeated juxtaposition to seem interchangeable. The message of Serbian propaganda – that the South Slavs living in Austria and Hungary were unredeemed Serb brethren – was widely accepted.

As the war progressed there emerged in the usage of 'Yugoslavia', however, a further layer of ambiguity and confusion, with the emergence of a self-anointed mouthpiece for the Habsburg South Slavs calling itself the 'Yugoslav Committee'. From 1915 this body conducted a high-profile propaganda campaign, one gradual effect of which was to re-appropriate the label 'Yugoslav' as signifying not the Serbs of Serbia and Montenegro (along with, only secondarily, their 'unredeemed brethren') but, once more, the assorted Serbs, Croats and Slovenes of Austria-Hungary. As the Committee campaigned for the creation of a 'Yugoslav' army distinct from that of Serbia, and then pressed to be recognised as representative body of the 'Yugoslav' (ie Habsburg South Slav) nation, diplomatic notes and published works in Britain began to refer to 'Serbs' and 'Yugoslavs' as distinct groups.[48] In November 1918, as an unexpectedly sudden military victory brought belated attention to political questions, Balfour sought 'reconciliation between the Yugo-Slavs and the Serbs'.[49] In December the noted exponent of Yugoslav unity Arthur Evans reported to Lord Derby from Paris the institution of 'one united kingdom of Serbia and Yugoslavia'.[50] Nor is this an end to the complications. As British observers belatedly appreciated the tension between the unification projects envisaged by the Serbian government on the one hand and by the Yugoslav Committee on the other, 'Yugoslav' became associated with a certain form and ethos of unification – by the federal union of equal parties – which placed it in *opposition* to a 'Serbian' solution.[51]

We must not yet, however, become immersed in those questions of culture and politics with which perceptions of the South Slavic racial make-up became entangled. We will return later to these elements in the difficult question of Yugoslav 'nationality'. Here we must address the extent to which Britons believed in a single, unified South Slav 'race' – bound by deep physical or psychological ties, born of a common ancestry, which existed, at least by implication, independently of any shared cultural, linguistic or sociological heritage.[52] How did observers assess the racial relationships *between* those groups which united to form Yugoslavia?

Without wishing to marginalise Slovenes, Montenegrins or other smaller groups, there is no doubt that the foremost question for British observers, as for the nascent state itself, was that of 'Serbo-Croat' unity. This, as Seton-Watson observed, fundamentally *was* the 'South Slav Question'.[53] The label 'Serbo-Croat' is itself, of course, ambivalent. The combination of two commonly-used existing terms, it carries simultaneous implications both of unity and of difference. To the extent that its composite form implies an amalgamation of distinct identities, it might seem to testify against a single primeval racial identity. While it did partially supersede British references to separate 'Serb' and 'Croat' groups, it was far from doing so entirely. In general the amalgamated form was used with greater frequency by British wartime observers with reference to those areas of the future Yugoslavia which formed part of the Habsburg Monarchy. This is perhaps not surprising given that the population was here considerably more divided between religious confessions and Serb, Croat and Slovene identities than were the broadly homogeneous 'Serb' states of Serbia and Montenegro.[54] For British enthusiasts of Yugoslav unity it was obviously preferable to portray regions like Bosnia, Dalmatia and Croatia as of homogeneous 'Serbo-Croat' race rather than to present, in a patchwork of Serb, Croat and Slovene settlements, a picture of tangled racial miscegenation. (The same, of course, was true for the Yugoslav unitarists by whom they were influenced).[55] The fact that the most reliable information for population distribution in these areas derived from Austro-Hungarian censuses using linguistic data meant that there was, in any case, no means of accurately differentiating groups recorded simply as 'Serbo-Croat'. The dispute between Yugoslavs and Italians in Dalmatia – that 'wearisome Adriatic Question' which bored and exasperated British observers in equal measure – further encouraged this tendency.[56] This mixed region was analysed simply in terms of Slav ('Serbo-Croat') versus Italian for the plausible reason that this seemed the primary and, in the circumstances, the only significant opposition at work.

We shall return often to the ways in which Britons rationalised 'Serb' and 'Croat' identities, and the nature of the divisions between them. What matters here is that they were considered by most in Britain who thought or wrote about them to be *racially* either identical or so closely akin as mattered little. Diplomats and others who had been used to think of the peoples of Austria-Hungary purely in terms of regional identities (in which a 'Croatian' was simply an inhabitant of the narrow administrative region of Croatia) were gradually induced by South Slav and British publicists to think in broader racial terms.[57] By late 1918, when the British representative in Belgrade came to congratulate Serbian Crown Prince Alexander, he was happy to applaud the unification of Serbia with her 'blood kin' of the late Austro-Hungarian Empire.[58]

Serbs and Croats were almost universally perceived as being by origin two kindred Slavonic tribes whose single race had acquired its 'dual nature' through subsequent exposure to different cultural traditions.[59] A.H.E. Taylor, in his study *The Future of the Southern Slavs*, noted that Serbs and Croats were originally distinguished only by 'slight tribal differences'. Similarly, while Neville Forbes observed that 'there must have been some fundamental difference in early tribal days, otherwise the two names would hardly have survived', once again the distinction he drew was *tribal* rather than racial. It was over the subsequent centuries, exposed to contrasting pulls of geography and culture, that these separate identities 'doubtless grew more marked'.[60] Philologists, Seton-Watson noted, had derived the indigenous forms 'Srb' and 'Hrvat' from the same root – testimony, he implied, to the common ancestry of the 'Croato-Serb race'.[61] An assumption of racial homogeneity marks also the account given by the anthropologist A.H. Keane. Serbs and Croats, he implied, had moved south of the Danube under the collective name of 'Sorbs' (or 'Srps'). Croats ('Crovats') derived their appellation not from a distinct ethnic background, but from their previous homeland in the valleys of the Oder and Vistula – an etymology he linked to the 'Carpathian' mountains.[62] Another writer went so far as to insist that, in their original migrations to the Yugoslav region, the ancestors of Serbs, Croats and Slovenes, although subdivided into clans, were all 'simply *Slavs*', the individual labels emerging through subsequent religious and political vicissitudes.[63]

This terminology of tribal rather than deeper ethnic distinctions was, of course, employed by South Slav unitarists themselves. It cannot be overstated that Slavic studies as a scholarly discipline was at an embryonic stage in Britain.[64] Those who studied the background to the South Slav question relied heavily on the work of linguists and historians of Central and Eastern Europe whose perceptions of history were influenced, inevitably, by their attitudes towards contemporary events. British historians, particularly during the war, were similarly caught up in the region's difficult present and uncertain future. In general they dealt only at second hand with key source material for the early history of the South Slav peoples (such as the crucial tenth century *De Administrando Imperio* of Byzantine Emperor Constantine Porphyrogenitus, which told of the arrival of Croats and Serbs in the Balkan Peninsula two centuries earlier).[65]

It is interesting, in relation to British perceptions of the ethnic roots of Serb and Croat identity, that Seton-Watson among others should have credited the influence of that 'greatest living Slavistic scholar', the Croatian philologist Vatroslav Jagić. A professor at Vienna University and editor of 'that mine of Slavonic learning, the *Archiv für slavische Philologie*', Jagić was the leading exponent of a line of thought known as the 'Slavic school' which, significantly, viewed Serbs and Croats as essentially one people.[66] It vehemently denied, however, the apparent implication in Constantine that both peoples were of non-Slavic, possibly Iranian, origin who, like the Bulgars, had assumed political authority over an established Slavic population. Accordingly it undermined Constantine's credibility as a source, and presented the original Serbs and Croats as closely related Slavic peoples who had moved to roughly their contemporary locations in one great migration during the late sixth and early seventh centuries. This was the view which British historians understandably followed.[67]

The question of racial miscegenation of Serb and Croat groups over the subsequent centuries with surviving indigenous populations or other neighbouring peoples was rarely raised and attributed scant significance. A few anthropologists rejected the fundamental distinction of South Slavs into Serbs, Croats and Slovenes and marked out, instead, a division between human types in the region quite unrelated to contemporary identities. From the late 19th century, the South Slavs were sometimes divided into three *racial* rather than national types: the Dinaric, Pannonian and Macedonian.[68] To these groups, whose distribution cut across boundaries of administration and identity (though Montenegrins, for example, were considered typical exemplars of the 'Dinaric' race), were attributed distinct mental and physiognomic characteristics.[69]

In general, however, British writers analysed Yugoslavs' racial background only within the artificial constraints of modern identities and assumed the anthropological unity of 'Serb' and 'Croat' groups. In part this reflected not any British attitude to the South Slavs in particular, but was a symptom of the assumptions about racial ossification which we noted earlier.[70] It is interesting to note, however, the impact which the outbreak of war had upon British analysis. Once the South Slavs were welcomed as an allied people, united in their opposition to German oppression (an opposition freely attributed to the South Slav's innate racial antagonism towards the German and similar affinity with the English), it became much more unusual to encounter admissions of racial confusion.[71] As greys in wartime resolve to blacks and whites, so 'lesser' distinctions within the South Slav population diminished before the long-projected clash between Teuton and Slav in East-Central Europe. Certainly, during the war, it was rare for British commentators to mark the mixed ancestry of Serb populations as the *Encyclopaedia Britannica* had done in 1911:

> The stature and features of the Serbs vary in different regions; but the northern peasantry are generally fairer and shorter than the mountaineers of the south. Those of the Shumadia are blue-eyed or grey-eyed. In many parts the prevailing types have been modified by intermarriage with Bulgars, Albanians and Vlachs; so that, along the Timok, for instance, it is impossible to make physiognomy a test of nationality.[72]

Or as the anthropologist H.J. Fleure would do in 1922:

> In the west of the [Balkan] peninsula, north of the region of Albanian speech, many of the people are Slavonised autochthones rather than real Slav intruders, and this is true of the mountains of Montenegro and of Bosnia.[73]

Naturally enough that minority of observers hostile to the Yugoslav idea did attach much greater emphasis to racial differences. Edith Durham, for example, resolute in her conviction that the Balkan Slavs were turbulent and self-serving, lost no opportunity to expose racial as well as historical divisions within the supposedly homogeneous Serbo-Croat population. The Slav-speaking peasants of Dalmatia, she noted were:

> by no means the same in physical type as the South Slavs of the Bosnian hinterland. It is obvious that they are of other blood. They are known as Morlachs, that is Sea Vlachs, and

historically are in all probability descendants of the pre-Slav native population which, together with the Roman colonists, fled coastward before the inrush of the Slav invaders of the seventh century.

Nor was this purely a matter of ancient history. The 'Slavizing process' – entailing unspecified 'artificial means' as well as natural pressure – had, she stressed, continued until the late nineteenth century.[74] Similarly in relation to the Montenegrins, whose culture she made the object of particular study, she emphasised the heterogeneity of a group drawing its lineage from Bosnia, Hercegovina and Albania. The enduring relevance of this racial diversity she illustrated by observing that the 'Brda group' which had joined Montenegro voluntarily in the eighteenth century and was 'mainly of Albanian blood' was now 'strenuously resisting annexation by Serbia'.[75] Even she, however, while lingering on the South Slav history of religious strife, conceded almost inadvertently that such divisions occurred between 'people of the same race and language' – an admission of overarching racial unity at odds with her previous anthropological survey.[76]

The loose fashion in which the term 'race' was used did, in general, create seemingly irreconcilable ambiguities. At one point A.H.E. Taylor implies fundamental ethnic diversity *within* the Yugoslav region:

> By race the inhabitants of Croatia, a great part of Slavonia with the exception of Syrmia or Srem, and northern Dalmatia are Croat, while the inhabitants of Syrmia, the Serb Vojvodina of Hungary, southern Dalmatia, Bosnia, the Hercegovina, Montenegro and Serbia belong to the Serb stock.

In general, however, he provides a strong impression of racial unity. A future Yugoslav state would be, he noted, 'remarkably homogeneous' because 'the Serbs and Croats are ethnologically one people'.[77] The *Encyclopaedia Britannica*, similarly, had moved from its description of racial interbreeding to stress that Serbs were 'ethnically and by language the same as the Croats'.[78] Neville Forbes was similarly unequivocal. Political divisions in the South Slav territory, he noted, should not hide the fact that 'as regards population, it is homogeneous'; Serbs and Croats were 'identical in kind, but different in name'. And while, as we have seen, the term 'race' was often used loosely to designate divisions within the larger Yugoslav region (as by Harold Temperley for whom 'Serbo-Croats of Croatia', 'Bosnians', 'Montenegrins', 'Serbs of Dalmatia' and 'Serbians of Serbia proper' are all thus described), concurrent references to a broader 'Yugoslav' race display the belief in a fundamental unity.[79] Wartime propaganda accused Austria of cynically masking Yugoslav racial unity behind regional labels promoted as spurious national identities. And this not unjustified claim was helpful, of course, in legitimising the suddenness of British enthusiasm for 'Yugoslavia', which had led opponents to portray it as purely self-interested and exploitative.[80]

Similar confusion in the writings of Seton-Watson – the leading British expert on the South Slavs – does testify to real uncertainty as to the precise racial relationship of Serbs and Croats, as well as to the subtle shifts in presentation wrought by contemporary circumstances. In his pre-war study of the 'Southern Slav Question' he appealed to the broader patriotism which would, he hoped, lead Serbs and Croats to 'transcend the sense of *racial individuality*' and cited the British conception of citizenship, 'creating new nations and combining *an endless diversity of race and type*'.[81] Early in the war the emphasis, at least in public, was markedly on unity rather than diversity. A draft memorandum of May 1915 lamented a 'civil war' that forced Austrian South Slavs to fight their 'bloodbrothers' in Serbia and Montenegro.[82] As the war progressed, and the Yugoslav idea found favour with British and French diplomats and public (and so to seem a plausible contingency rather than a remote aspiration), Seton-Watson's growing concern over Serbian hegemonism influenced his formulation of South Slav relationships. A leader in his journal *The New Europe*, co-written with Wickham Steed at the end of 1916, referred to 'the three sister-races of Serbs, Croats and Slovenes'.[83] By January 1918 a Serbian Society letter to Lloyd George, again drafted with Steed, stressed the importance of equal rights for the 'three Southern Slav races'.[84]

We have seen how Serbian propaganda and the greater British acquaintance with Serbia than with the Slav regions of Austria-Hungary contributed to a widespread assumption, particularly but not exclusively early in the war, that 'Serbia' and 'Yugoslavia' were almost synonyms. It is significant regarding our emphasis on the belief in Serbo-Croat racial unity that the terms 'Serb' and 'Serbian' came, as a result, to be used in Britain in a dual sense.[85] On the one hand, as today, they designated a particular branch of the South Slav group which incorporated also 'Croat' and 'Slovene' identities. On the other, they were commonly used, as almost never today, to refer to this whole, broader racial group. Serbo-Croats of Bosnia and Croats of Croatia were parts of 'the Serbian race'.[86] Simultaneous reference was made to the distinction between Orthodox Serbs and Catholic Croats, on the one hand, and 'the scission of Serbians into three religious groups', on the other. The 'westernmost Serbs', Leon Dominian noted, 'are also known as Croats'.[87] Croats were 'Catholic Serbs'.[88] The whole of the country from the Timok in the east as far west as Istria, bounded on the north by the Danube and Drave, and on the south by the Adriatic, was, Neville Forbes agreed, 'inhabited by the Serb race'.[89] The inhabitants of Croatia and Slavonia, Bosnia-Hercegovina, Dalmatia, Montenegro and the Sanjak were, stressed D.H. Low, all Serbs: 'there is no excuse nowadays for ignorance of this fundamental truth'.[90]

No wonder, Gibbons observed, that Serbia saw in the Austro-Hungarian occupation of Bosnia a fatal blow to her national aspirations:

> The inhabitants of the two Turkish provinces on her west were Serbian; Bosnia-Hercegovina formed the centre of the Serbian race. Montenegro on the south was Serbian. Dalmatia on the west was Serbian. Croatia on the north was Serbian. Everything was Serbian to the Adriatic Sea. And yet Serbia was landlocked.[91]

It is pertinent that the regional-specific form 'Croatian' was commoner in British usage than the broader ethnic label 'Croat' (a semantic distinction which, it is true, was often ignored). At the same time, the juxtaposition of 'Croatian' with other regional designations such as 'Dalmatian', 'Istrian' and 'Slavonian' reflects the former's continued use in reference only to 'narrow Croatia' or 'Croatia proper' – the administrative region around Zagreb, rather than a 'triune', more closely ethnic Croatia consisting of Dalmatia, Croatia proper and Slavonia. In a report to the Foreign Office at the end of the war, the prominent Yugoslav enthusiast Sir Arthur Evans, for instance, divided the ex-Habsburg 'Yugo-Slav' state into regional rather than ethnic identities: 'Slovenes, Croats, Dalmatians and Bosnians'.[92]

This lack of equivalence between Serb and Croat identities had, of course, long been reflected in, and was doubtless partly instigated by, a political reality in which Serbia was an established state and factor in diplomacy while the Habsburg Yugoslavs were merely an oppressed minority. It is therefore perhaps not surprising if Serbian nationalist portrayals of the Austrian South Slavs simply as Serb 'irredenta' were accorded an unquestioning credence. It should be recalled too that Serbia's nineteenth century quests for recognition (of its sovereignty, its Balkan leadership, its interests in Macedonia, and its efforts to expand) had all been carried out in the name of Serbian nationality rather than any broader Yugoslav ideal.[93] It was natural that Serbian claims during the First World War continued, to some extent, to be interpreted in this light.

The influence of Serbian claims is apparent in the fact that, while 'Serb' identity was often at one level associated with Orthodoxy, nevertheless Catholic and Muslim Slavs of Dalmatia, Bosnia, and even Croatia-Slavonia, were routinely described in Britain as 'pure-blooded Serbs'.[94] Dalmatians and Croatians, Viscount Bryce noted, differed in religion from the Serbians, but were nevertheless 'all Serbs'. 'The Bosnians', he continued, 'are also Serbs, mostly Orthodox, though there are some Catholics, and a few Muslims remain'.[95] The geographical distribution of the Bosnian confessional communities, with Orthodox predominant in the north-west, nearest Croatia, seemed confirmation of

Serb claims that Catholics and Muslims enclosed within this Orthodox band were *racially* Serb.[96] (None were persuaded by, or even aware of, similar Croat claims that Bosnian Orthodox and Muslims were converted Croats). The expression 'Great Serbia', which late in the war would become for an observer like Seton-Watson a pejorative allusion to Serbian chauvinism, had often simply connoted the project of racial unification: as when he urged MPs in 1916 that only a complete Allied triumph could 'fulfil the ideal of a Greater Serbia, stretching north to include Croatia'.[97]

In general, of course, it is scarcely surprising if accounts of the ancient origins of the Yugoslav peoples were apt to be conceptually muddled. The task of precisely defining the identities of Serb and Croat and the relationship between the two had long caused antagonism among Slavic intellectuals. It is significant that the specifically *racial* ancestry of the South Slavs was most emphasised and discussed by those Serb and Croat intellectuals on the political extremes who, despite the gulf separating their respective outlooks, largely concurred in the unity of their peoples. Thus while disciples of the Croatian Ante Starčević and the Serb Vuk Karadžić were irreconcilably opposed, their arguments were actually, in their extremist quasi-unitarism, closely aligned. Whether a homogeneous people was regarded as almost entirely 'Croat' in race (Starčević's view) or almost entirely 'Serb' (Karadžić's) could seem to an outsider a surmountable question of semantics: the lasting impression one not of division but of a shared conviction of unity.[98] As the Slovene publicist Bogumil Vošnjak noted, both figures could be considered, despite their narrow extremism, as pioneers of the movement for unity. ('It is distinctly one of history's ironies', he observed, with an appreciation rare in British analyses, 'that this very Idea of Unity gave rise to some of the sharpest conflicts between Croats and Serbs').[99] In Britain these influential but extreme ideologues were among the very few 19th or 20th century South Slav political thinkers whose ideas were familiar to those with an interest in the region.[100]

Equally significant is the fact that this location of the thought of Starčević and Karadžić in a unitarist tradition accorded with the dominant political trends among the Habsburg South Slavs in the early 20th century. The Croat-Serb coalition (HSK) which emerged in 1905 and broadly endured until 1918 testified to the feeling that Croats and Serbs must unite against intensified Austro-Hungarian oppression. Ideologically, it upheld a form of Yugoslavism revived under the label 'Croat-Serb national oneness' (*narodno jedinstvo*). Similarly, in the thought of an influential group known as 'Young Croatians', the difference between the ideas of Starčević on the one hand and of Serb expansionist ideologies on the other was reduced simply to the question of appellation for a single, racially united people.

It was, moreover, largely with leading figures in these groups that influential British commentators had forged links. Seton-Watson, Steed

and others corresponded at length with enthusiasts for *narodno jedinstvo* like
Frano Supilo, Josip Smodlaka, Hinko Hinković, Ivo Lupis-Vukić and the
sculptor Ivan Meštrović.[101] And Meštrović, in fact, exerted through his
work a direct influence in Britain. A unitarist ideologue and Serbophile
Croat, the 'true prophet in stone of the Southern Slav idea', he gained an
international reputation and the ardent admiration of British cognoscenti
with his 'racial art'.[102] Portraying Serbian history and myth as the joint
heritage of a single South Slav race, it appealed to Britons in the emotional
circumstances of wartime. It seemed 'instinct with the suppressed fury of
an oppressed land, and the burning spirit of an unquenchable freedom'.[103]
'Not since the days that Rodin had exhibited his masterpieces', notes
Harry Hanak, 'had London been so impressed by a sculptor'.[104]

It should be remembered, moreover, that South Slavs who had
espoused unitarism were, as a rule, precisely those who were forced to flee
the vengeance of the Habsburg authorities after the outbreak of war.
Many were among those Yugoslavs-in-exile who decisively influenced
British and French public opinion. Then, as now, the inherently
unrepresentative nature of exile opinion, in terms of vehemence if not
basic direction, was too often overlooked by those sympathetic to its
ideals.[105]

We have focused thus far on British views of the Serb-Croat relationship.
We must also, however, consider attitudes regarding the *racial* identity of
other South Slav groups incorporated in the Yugoslav state – notably
Slovenes, Montenegrins and Macedonians. (Whereas it is true that loose,
habitual references occurred, for instance, to 'Dalmatian', 'Bosnian',
'Hercegovinian' or 'Slavonian' races, these were rarely considered to have
any basis in ethnic rather than simply regional identities).

Of these labels the one with the strongest claim to represent a
distinct racial heritage was the Slovene – a claim recognised in the official
nomenclature of the new state. The difficulty in analysing British attitudes
to the Slovenes before and during the war, however, is that despite being
one of the three eponymous 'races', 'nations' (or simply 'names') of the
prospective kingdom, they earned scant consideration.[106] 'Western
Europe', Bogumil Vošnjak chided in 1917, 'at present knows very little of
the most western branch of the Yugoslavs'. If England had only recently
discovered the Serbs and Croats, it was 'fairly safe to say that as yet she
knows not enough about the Slovenes'.[107] 'Very little', Ivan Žolger agreed,
'is known to the general public concerning the Slovenes'.[108] When Harold
Temperley, in his 1917 *History of Serbia*, distinguished 'five great divisions
of the Yugo-Slav race' he separated 'Serbo-Croats of Croatia', 'Serbs of
Dalmatia', 'Montenegrins', 'Bosnians' and 'Serbians of Serbia proper',
relegating the Slovenes to a cursory footnote.[109] A report by the
Department of Enemy Propaganda (in which Steed and Seton-Watson

served under Lord Northcliffe) referred to territories 'ethnographically
Serbo-Croatian (Yugo-Slav)' – evidence of the low priority given to the
Slovenes beside the dominant question of Serbo-Croat unity.[110]

Certainly the Slovenes were much less discussed in Britain than
either Montenegrins or Macedonians, neither of whom were considered
nationalities in the new state. But it would be a mistake to conclude that a
distinct Slovene identity was denied by British observers. The lack of
attention they commanded was the result not only of ignorance but also of
the relative lack of controversy regarding either their incorporation in the
South Slav group or their individual heritage. They seemed to British
observers to have become 'fully possessed of the consciousness of their
race brotherhood with their Serbo-Croat neighbours'.[111] Suddenly and
decisively during the war they had moved from 'timid' loyalty to the
Habsburg state to a desire for 'national' union with Serbs and Croats.
'Before the war', Rumbold informed Balfour in March 1918, '[the
Slovenes] seemed quite satisfied to remain Austrian subjects; now they are
firm in their demand for independence'.[112] More knowledgeable observers
did recognise a longer gestation. Back in 1914 Seton-Watson had advised
the Foreign Office of the Yugoslav feeling of the Slovenes, 'one of the
three kindred races'. But he too was struck by the sudden development of
national allegiance among a 'clerical' people, a phenomenon which was
'perhaps the most remarkable feature of the whole [Yugoslav]
movement'.[113] This dramatic transition seemed aptly symbolised by the
attitude of Prince-Bishop Jeglić of Laibach (Ljubljana) who, having
blessed the Austro-Hungarian soldiers marching to fight Serbia in 1914,
had since been charged with high treason for supporting the South Slav
movement.[114] As with the Habsburg Croats, Slovene destiny now seemed
conclusively bound up with their racial 'kindred'. (The movement for a
Slovene state *within* the Monarchy was thought to have petered out with
the disappearance of its leader Dr Šuštersić into exile and obscurity). 'All
three branches of Yugoslavdom, Serbs, Croats and Slovenes', Allen
Leeper emphasised in 1918, 'are indivisibly bound together, not only by
language and blood, but also by their common life'.[115]

Within the Yugoslav grouping, however, a genuine and enduring
Slovene identity was largely acknowledged in Britain. Indeed, whereas
Slovenes were sometimes incorporated by British analysts within the
broad concept of a 'Serb race', by and large they were more secure in their
racial individuality, so far as Britons were concerned, than the Croats.
Sometimes viewed as the remnant of an old, largely undifferentiated Slavic
population which inhabited the Yugoslav region prior to the arrival of the
Serbs and Croats, little credence was given to the claims of Croat
ideologues like Starčević that Slovenes were in truth only 'mountain
Croats'.[116] (The tendency to regard Croat identity as primarily regional or
religious rather than racial mitigated against the recognition of any such

underlying 'Croat-ness' – much more than was the case with Serb identity). A crucial factor, of course, was their language – a question of central importance in contemporary ideas about national identity. While Yugoslav enthusiasts in Britain were often reluctant to consider Slovene a separate language, and stressed its mutual intelligibility with Serbo-Croatian, few could deny that it was at least a peculiar 'dialect' of the dominant tongue.[117] Importantly, this linguistic consideration influenced the claims of narrower and noisier South Slavic nationalisms in Britain. Serb propagandists in particular, having absorbed Karadžić's argument that Serb identity could be linked to the štokavian dialect used by many Croats as well as Serbs, were obliged to acknowledge the non-Serb heritage of kajkavian Slovene-speakers. Slovene populations were not often, therefore, the object of Serb as opposed to 'Yugoslav' claims. Non-nationalist Serbs like Chedo Mijatović also assumed the Slovenes to be ethnographically as well as geographically more distant from Serbia than the Croats. If the latter were 'twin brothers', the Slovenes were 'cousins'.[118]

If the question of Montenegrin identity and inclusion in a Yugoslav state was, as we will see later, controversial in Britain, this was certainly not due to any informed dispute about racial make-up. It may have been true, as Neville Forbes claimed, that many simply did not know that the label 'Montenegrin' conveyed a regional rather than an ethnic identity.[119] (A similar uncertainty existed for those unacquainted with the area regarding other, particularly Austrian, South Slav regions – 'Bosnian', 'Hercegovinian', 'Dalmatian' etc). But, for those who felt qualified to comment publicly on the Yugoslavs, it was a near-unanimous assumption that, however admirable this small state's tradition of independence, ethnically the Montenegrins were Serbs. Subsequent Montenegrin authors may have claimed that the self-applied label 'Serb' connoted a feeling only of religious (Orthodox) identity with Serbs of Serbia. But there is little doubt that, despite a strong regional consciousness, Montenegrins in the period up to 1918 did consider themselves Serbs in a broader ethnic sense.[120] Outside observers tended, understandably, to take them at their word. 'The little state of Montenegro', Laffan affirmed, 'differs on no test of race, language, or religion from Serbia, and its inhabitants are but an independent and allied portion of the Serbian nation'.[121] Bryce agreed: Montenegro was 'hardly a nationality, for its people are racially identical with those of Serbia, Bosnia, and Dalmatia'.[122] Even a tireless campaigner for Montenegrin independence within a Yugoslav federation did not deny that Serbs and Montenegrins shared an underlying racial identity.[123]

It is true, as we have seen, that an unsympathetic observer like Edith Durham emphasised the recent absorption into Montenegro of groups of non-Serb, even non-Slavic, ancestry. She later pressed on Sir John Myres 'a point of which I am more and more certain viz: that the Montenegrins are not Slavs but Albanian and Vlah [Vlach] by origin'.[124] Paradoxically, however, the acknowledgement of racial divergences between Montenegrin and Serbian was more often used to *affirm* the former's Serb identity. The observation that Montenegrins tended to be more physically impressive than northern Serbs (that they were, indeed, among the most imposing in Europe – 'a race of giants')[125] was combined with the folk history of the flight of independent-minded Serbian aristocracy in the face of the Ottoman incursion. (A poetic account which, fostered by an earlier generation of British admirers including Gladstone and Tennyson, found an emotive parallel in the heroism and suffering of the Serbian retreat in the winter of 1915-16).[126] Montenegrins, therefore, were portrayed as the descendants of this fugitive nobility, as 'pure Serbs, [...] a pure-blooded race, descended largely from the old Serbian nobles'.[127] While the population of northern Serbia was, Eliot sniffed, 'not a good or characteristic specimen of the race', 'the descendants of the least vigorous and enterprising portion of the nation', in Montenegro, 'the refuge of the Serbian aristocracy after the Turkish conquest':

> they are all chiefs and princes, and have that air of well-built, well-mannered aristocracy which is so rare in the plains. A series of brilliant marriages attests that the royal house of Europe consider the blood of the Princes of Montenegro as good as their own.[128]

Durham's killjoy insistence that Montenegro had been created not by refugees from the field of Kosovo but by migrants from Bosnia, Hercegovina and Albania (a fact she related to Montenegrin reluctance to amalgamate with Serbia) little affected the common perception.[129] And of course, here again, British accounts were shaped by the self-projection of South Slavs, absorbing a rationale for Montenegrin feelings of superiority over lowland Serbians seen as corrupted by exposure to alien influences.

If British attitudes to Montenegrin racial identity were broadly unanimous, the same could not be said regarding the peoples of Macedonia, a region central to the Balkans' reputation for impenetrable complexity and ethnic conflict. Needless to say, the question of Western perceptions of race and nationality in Macedonia is a formidable topic. Our concern here is specifically with the population of those regions incorporated into Serbia after the Balkan Wars, which became part of the Yugoslav state and which were – at least insofar as the Slavonic element was concerned – almost invariably treated by the Serbian and Yugoslav regimes as liberated Serbs with no claim to an independent identity or administrative autonomy.[130]

If the Macedonian population was the object of numerous conflicting claims by bordering states and ethnic groups – Serbians,

Bulgarians, Greeks, Albanians, Turks, even Romanians – some individual or organisation popped up in Britain to support each cause (though many more bemoaned the impossibly fissiparous nature of Balkan politics). Certainly the different bases on which claims were made rendered them utterly irreconcilable. While Serbs and Bulgarians traded claims based variously on race, history and language, Greeks focused on religious identity (itinerant Britons during the 18th and 19th centuries had, after all, identified all the Orthodox of the Balkans as 'Greek').[131] The claims of Albanians and Romanians, meanwhile, neither as audible nor as credited in Britain, were premised on racial ancestry (on the assumption, in the Romanian case, that Vlachs were their ethnic kin) and the allegedly involuntary conversion of their racial brothers to other, alien identities.[132]

Insofar as British views of the racial origins of Yugoslav Macedonians were concerned, most commentators hedged their bets. The commonly-used phrase 'Macedonian Slav' was deliberately non-committal about both ethnic identity and national allegiance.[133] Sir Charles Eliot referred to this population as 'intermediate between the Serbs and the Bulgarians'.[134] Seton-Watson scorned Bulgarian claims. 'Every novice in Balkan affairs', he wrote, 'knows that [...] the Macedonian Slavs are neither pure Bulgar nor pure Serb, but something between the two'.[135] The chaotic history of this 'Naboth's Vineyard',[136] two unusually sympathetic observers noted, had 'produced a hybrid race'.[137] Meanwhile H.N. Brailsford, a firm Bulgarophile and believer in the allegiance of most Macedonians to Bulgaria, also admitted that, racially, they represented a primitive Slav stock, akin to both Serb and Bulgarian:

> They are not Serbs, for their blood can hardly be purely Slavonic. There must be in it some admixture of Bulgarian and other non-Aryan stock (Kuman Tartars, Pechenegs, &c). On the other hand, they can hardly be Bulgarians, for quite clearly the Serbian immigrations and conquests must have left much Serbian blood in their veins, and the admixture of non-Aryan blood can scarcely be so considerable as it is in Bulgaria. They are probably very much what they were before either a Bulgarian or a Serbian Empire existed – a Slav people derived from rather various stocks, who invaded the peninsula at different periods.[138]

It was agreed by the impartial, A.H.E. Taylor concluded, that these Slavs were 'neither pure Serbs nor pure Bulgars'.[139] It was when confronted with situations as tangled as that in Macedonia that some British observers were obliged to admit what nationality theorists had often pointed out: that 'race' need not be correlated to national identity at all. The analysis of Sir Charles Eliot, for instance, was unusually clear on this point:

> We can hardly be wrong in considering that the original
> Bulgarian type is preserved in the somewhat Mongolian figure
> and features which are common in the eastern part of the
> Balkans [...]. As the Serbian type may be taken the tall, broad-
> headed men who are found in South Serbia, Bosnia and
> Montenegro. But these two types by no means coincide with
> the people who call themselves Serbians and Bulgarians. The
> Bulgarian type is found all over Northern Serbia as far as
> Belgrade; and the Albanians, though so clearly separated from
> the surrounding Slavs in language and customs, are physically
> indistinguishable from them. The tall, broad-headed men form
> an anthropological but not a political or linguistic unit.[140]

Nor, as we shall see, was the linguistic evidence to which analysts
invariably turned in discussions of racial and national identities conclusive.
The Macedonians seemed, for the most part, to be descendants of
undifferentiated Slavic migrants, while the innumerable subsequent
population movements and cultural pressures experienced in the region
made any anthropological clarification unlikely. In general, however,
British commentators construed the mixture of objective evidence and
subjective national consciousness as indicating that the population in the
vicinity of the Serbian border – those areas north-west of Skopje absorbed
by Serbia in 1913 – either was Serb, or was close enough that, after
cohabiting for a generation or two, it would be considered so. (The town
of Niš, it was noted – seemingly Bulgarian before 1876 – had since the
Serbian occupation become 'thoroughly Serbian').[141] Racially, Eliot
observed, 'the Slavonic population of the vilayet of Kossovo, north-west
of Uskub, is homogeneous with that on the other side of the Serbian,
Montenegrin, and Bosnian frontiers, the mountaineers of South Serbia
being very unlike the tradesmen and farmers of the north'.[142]

Few writers, it must finally be noted, appreciated or considered the
non-Slavonic element in these regions. The name 'Kosovo', as we shall
see, had been so thoroughly appropriated by Serb nationalist
historiography as indicating the historic cradle of Serbian civilisation that it
came as a great surprise to those few intrepid Britons who visited the
region to discover it in fact largely inhabited by Albanians. 'I came
expecting to find', Brailsford admitted, 'as one finds elsewhere in
Macedonia, a population by majority Christian, living under the rule of a
Muslim minority'. But 'in all Old Serbia', he reported, 'there are not as
many Serbian families as there are Albanian families in Ipek and Prizrend
alone'.[143] The liberal weekly *The Nation*, hostile to Serbia as the 'least
scrupulous and the least civilised' of the Balkan allies of 1912, observed
before the outbreak of the Second Balkan War that 'Servia has a mainly

Albanian population to deal with in the country which is already hers'.[144] This information seems not, however, to have permeated the general intellectual awareness of a region which, with the outbreak of the Great War and the dramatic rise in Serbia's esteem, was almost universally accepted as natural Serbian territory.

We must now turn, however, to examine the role in British eyes of an element in the modern phenomenon of nationality which was attributed greater and indeed often paramount importance: language. It is one, as we shall see, which can in any case only with a certain degree of arbitrariness be separated from considerations of 'race' which were often assumed to be directly correlated with linguistic identity. In the case of British perceptions of South Slavic unity in particular, furthermore, language would play an unusually dominant role.

2

Language: Britain and South Slavic Language Questions

Whatever the significance accorded to race in this period, there is no doubt that, among British theorists of the 'objective' school, the primary criterion by which nationality was assessed externally was language. An individual's linguistic identity, more even than his racial origin, was widely regarded as synonymous with his 'nationality'.

It is misleading, however, to imply that race and language were treated as discrete categories (as we would now assume them to be). It is true that, back in 1870, Henry Pelham had noted the lack of correlation between boundaries of physical type and language.[1] But we have seen that in popular usage the term 'race' was often used for groups whose common bond was in fact linguistic. While in part this was simply an inexactitude to which the concept was particularly prone, it would be mistaken to view it solely as a lay corruption of anthropological or linguistic science.

The Herderian tradition which associated race, language and national identity, and regarded language as the profound expression of a particular racial 'soul', certainly had its critics in Britain. We have noted the reaction among British theorists against the equation of race and nationality, and there was no less hostility towards the correlation of language and race.[2] T.H. Huxley, one early opponent of this tendency, denied vigorously that 'what is true of speech is true of the speaker', a facile hypothesis 'as questionable in science as it is in ordinary life'.[3] Viscount Bryce was similarly sceptical of language as a test of *racial* affinity. Known instances in which peoples had lost one tongue and adopted another, he argued, made such a theory untenable. But while it might be true, as he noted, that the scholarly tendency to associate certain political and social institutions with particular linguistic families had lately 'withered up and died', such supremacist assumptions retained a hold on popular thought.[4] ('Correct errors of concrete fact', as J.M. Robertson observed after George Eliot, 'and you leave still lingering the errors of feeling which were their atmosphere, partly cause, partly effect').[5]

And in fact there did exist in the English-speaking world a 'scientific' tradition which treated race and language as coterminous expressions of ancient ethnic identity. Nations, in an essentialist and determinist scheme given little credence today, were viewed as both natural and linguistically determined, or as one recent writer has put it, as 'bounded cultural objects'.[6] Philology might have been, as Eric Hobsbawm has observed, 'the first science which regarded evolution at its very core', but this was no immediate obstacle to a philosophy conceiving language, like race, less as an evolving or exchangeable property than an immutable inheritance.[7] And this position, however flawed, imbued language with unique significance as the encrypted expression of a racial psychology: a window onto the social predilections and mental peculiarities by which it was assumed (though with great difficulty proven) that all races were differentiated.[8] 'From every language', as von Humboldt put the claim in its extreme form, 'we can infer backwards to the national character'.[9]

The belief was certainly widespread in Britain and America as well as in continental Europe that race, culture and language were, as one historian has noted, 'different manifestations of the one inherent entity', an assumption which legitimated 'the use of cultural and linguistic data to delineate racial taxonomy'.[10] The pre-eminent American anthropologist suggested tentatively in 1911 that '[racial] type, language and type of culture, may not be closely and permanently connected', but nevertheless noted in a later edition of the same work the general assumption 'that race and culture must be intimately associated, that racial descent determines cultural life'.[11] This position was fortified by evidence from the Balkans and elsewhere (Franks, Bulgars, Manchus in China, Swedes in Russia) that language reflected majority descent even in cases where a population had been subjugated by an alien aristocracy.[12] For the adopted British writer Alfred Zimmern language and race were one and unchanging, German and Magyar policies of linguistic assimilation equivalent to 'trying by Act of Parliament to whiten the Ethiopian or to change the leopard's spots'.[13] As late as 1939 an anthropologist denounced the continued equation of race and language used in Britain to justify the Munich settlement and other boundary revisions. 'The claim that cultural evidence of such a kind can be taken to indicate that the peoples separated had very different origins is', he complained, 'accepted far too often by writers and speakers who have little sympathy with racial ideology'.[14]

With regard to 'nationality', as opposed to the background question of race with which it was often associated, the role accorded to language was paramount. Exceptions little threatened the assumption noted by Bernard Joseph that 'each nationality speaks one language, and that its own'.[15] This tendency was most marked in theorists with an interest in East-Central Europe and the Balkans, regions in which language and 'fatherland' seemed strikingly coterminous.[16] In the Habsburg Monarchy Czech leaders like František Palacky, and German socialists like Otto Bauer and Karl Kautsky, had considered language *the* essential feature of national identity, and nationality within a multinational empire a linguistic-cultural issue rather than a political one. Some in Britain agreed that nationality was a 'spiritual' question, bound up exclusively with language and culture.[17] In most British discussions of German or Magyar 'oppression' before 1914, it was specifically linguistic oppression which was cited: the imposition of German or Hungarian as languages of administration and restriction of 'the sacred rights of the mother tongue'.[18] It was as readily assumed by British supporters of the Habsburg minorities (few of whom before the war thought the Empire's dissolution likely or desirable), as it was by leaders of the minorities themselves, that the solution to 'national' tensions lay in linguistic freedom in political as well as personal life. The identification of language and nation, noted H.A. Gibbons, 'explains in a nutshell the Austro-Hungarian and Balkan problems': 'to the Slav, there can be no other test of nationality'.[19]

Of course, for those who insisted that nationality was a question of conscious *feeling*, no objective test could determine identity. By stressing the emergence of national consciousness within a previously-existing national group – locating 'nationality', in other words, at the culmination of a process – many theorists had to believe that common language might exist, like other common traditions, without a mature national identity.[20] For Arnold Toynbee national culture was not imparted by the mere possession of a mother tongue but only by its 'consecration' by an effort of will.[21] Nationality, Sidney Herbert insisted after Renan, required active assent: 'to take an outward and material sign as expressing this inward and spiritual will is to run the risk of inflicting grave injustice'.[22] 'Community of language', Pillsbury agreed, 'does not mean community of spirit'.[23]

Given that Britain could itself provide – in Wales, Ireland and Scotland – examples of national identities only in small part attributable to linguistic individuality, it is surprising that such reservations did not run deeper.[24] But while theorists rejected a simplistic equation of language and nationality, invoking the obvious counter-examples from Alsace, Belgium and Switzerland to French Canada and South America, they emphasised language's formative role in the inculcation and consolidation of national identity. Herder, it seemed, had been on the mark: in a people's speech resided 'its whole thought-domain, its traditions, history, religion and basis of life, all its heart and soul'.[25] To realise its full powers, wrote J.H. Rose, a people must wed its thought and aspirations 'to a mother tongue [which] ceases to stammer and learns to sing'.[26] Language above all fostered that 'fancied unity of race' which promoted a feeling of national community.[27]

It was 'the most visible and tangible of the fundamentals of that like-mindedness which is indispensable to a fully developed nationality'.[28]

Philosophy's exploration of the relationship between language-structure and thought had suggested language might succeed where race had failed in providing a firm basis for national stereotype. While language differences 'transcend and run counter to those of colour and physical conformation', noted one writer, 'they coincide, so far as we know, with those of character'.[29] 'There is', agreed wrote, 'a natural and mutual attraction amongst persons who speak the same language'. Language was a 'part of the national soul' whose 'importance in cementing the various elements of a nationality cannot be overestimated'.[30] The obvious import of this analysis for the Southern Slavs, a group seen to share linguistic and racial ties but little political or religious tradition, will be discussed below.

The widespread acceptance of language's role in shaping patterns of nationality led even students of the phenomenon to overlook its deficiencies as a guide to identity. ('The national language', one sceptic later lamented, 'has become one of the idols of a new religion').[31] Deprived of race as a test of nationality, Madison Grant noted in 1917, 'we are compelled to resort to language'.[32] And as Bernard Joseph observed ten years after the Paris settlement: 'if it were not that language serves as a distinguishing mark the political rearrangement of the nations of Europe could not be considered to be other than purely arbitrary'.[33] A 1944 Foreign Office Research Department paper referred to the doubt which plebiscites had cast upon 'the assumption, upon which so much of the distribution of territory in 1919 was based, that language provides an automatic test of national sentiment'.[34]

Only a few had voiced reservations. One, Arnold Toynbee, argued that if all the peoples of Europe were to group themselves on the principle of self-determination, there would be notable departures from the confines of identity of language. He was one of surprisingly few British writers to raise the case of Ireland, a country unified by the almost complete predominance of a single language but divided by religious and historical tradition into what must be deemed separate nationalities (an example whose parallels with the Serbo-Croat relationship make it of particular interest to our study).[35] A few others noticed the fact that, in cases where similar languages merged gradually into one another, linguistic criteria were no more able than those of 'race' to provide clear frontiers.

In general, however, British theorists cautious of 'race' as a primary factor in the process of national amalgamation were obliged to elevate language in its place. Only thus could they rationalise the apparently voluntary union of peoples with little else obvious in common. (And as we have seen, those who embraced or assumed a correlation between race and nationality were happy to refer to language as a mark of racial background). In the framing of the 1919 treaties it was taken for granted, as Frederick Hertz later observed, that 'people of approximately the same language wished to form a common nation, and that no further proofs of their common nationality were required'.[36] Nor did theorists weigh the significance of this 'approximately'. Few asked whether mutual intelligibility alone sufficed for language to operate as a wholly unifying force, or considered, for example, the role in perpetuating feelings of difference which dialectal variation, divergences in written language, or contrasting scripts might exert within a 'single language' area. This oversight would have important ramifications in the Yugoslav case.

'Serbo-Croat': Language, Dialect, Nation

Language unquestionably lay at the heart of the movement for South Slav unity. The sense of common ethnicity which underpinned the tentative progress of Yugoslavism among intellectuals from the late 18th century onwards was founded on awareness of a shared linguistic heritage which (it was assumed in accordance with the prevailing romantic view of nationality) indicated common descent. Educated South Slavs were no less influenced than British commentators by the tradition identifying language as the truest expression of a national 'soul'. Indeed, they were probably more so. The linguistic reforms and standardisation of philologists like Ljudevit Gaj and Vuk Karadžić was motivated by an overt sense of language's significance in paving the way for cultural and political unification. Yugoslavism was derived from ethnicity (a concept more bound up with 'race' than in modern theories of 'constructed' identities) and language was both symptom and agent of this common bond.[37]

The importance of the reforms instituted by Gaj, Karadžić and others in fashioning linguistic unity in the South Slav lands was greatly emphasised by British writers. While Karadžić was credited with creating from a variety of dialects a unified Serbian language, standardising the demotic speech and undermining conservative veneration for Old Church Slavonic, Gaj was associated with the Croat literati's decision (much admired among British pro-Yugoslavs) to abandon a distinctive Croatian form in favour of Karadžić's standard. Both, it seemed, had promoted broader cultural and political amalgamation. 'The linguistic unity which has been wrought by philologists and men of letters', Seton-Watson observed in 1911, 'may be regarded as a happy omen for the achievement of that wider unity upon which the future of the race depends'.[38] In 1915 he was more confident. In bringing the 'various Serbo-Croat dialects' into line, Karadžić ('the Grimm of Serbia') had prepared the way for 'that literary unity which is the sure forerunner of political union'.[39] With the creation of a single Serbo-Croat literature, Taylor agreed, 'the way was now clear for a real Serbo-Croat unity'.[40] (There was an unacknowledged inconsistency here. Analysts recognised the malleability of language in forging a nation-state, yet assumed it to be part of that primordial racial inheritance which underpinned national identity).

For British enthusiasts of Yugoslav unity the question of language was, in any case, fundamental. For those who saw in language 'the most potent ingredient of nationality', it was no less than 'the foundation of modern Yugoslavia'.[41] Even those who adopted a subjectivist position, preferring evidence of shared national feeling to external signposts, could not explain or back the demand for unification without reference to the shared traditions which might underpin it and augur well for its future. With few historical or religious bonds (indeed, in the face of evident divisions in these respects) it is not surprising that the 'Serbo-Croat' language was embraced as demonstrating that shared mentality – widely associated with a common 'racial' and linguistic inheritance – which must underpin a stable nation. Laffan was one of many to stress the unity of the 'Serbian' race on this ground. Croats might be Catholics, but they used the 'Serbian language'. 'Not unnaturally', therefore, Serbia's friends expected her 'to be the nucleus round which a state would grow up, embracing all the Slav peoples of southern Austria-Hungary, as well as the Serbian portions of the old Turkish Empire'.[42] 'By any doctrine of political philosophy', Herbert Vivian had proclaimed some time before the war, 'the whole [Yugoslav] district should be one country'. The 'all-important point' was linguistic unity.[43]

Some, it is true, continued to juxtapose 'Serbian' and 'Croatian' in a linguistic context. The journalist Harry de Windt included both among that 'babel' of tongues he confronted in Mostar in 1907.[44] But this habit reflected that tendency to view the Monarchy in provincial rather than ethnic terms which exasperated Yugoslav enthusiasts, and which declined during the Balkan and 1914-18 wars as the notion of South Slav unity took hold in Britain. As late as 1915 Neville Forbes noted that 'very few people outside Austria-Hungary realise that the Croatians are Slavs and speak the same language as the Serbs'.[45] (During the peace negotiations Lloyd George himself asked the Serbian Prime Minister whether this was so).[46] Seton-Watson later defended Jagić's claim that inhabitants of Bosnia had historically thought of their tongue as 'Bosnian' rather than as 'Serbian' or 'Serbo-Croat', but thought this a sign of their subsequent progression 'from provincial to national consciousness' rather than a defence of Habsburg attempts to foster an 'entirely artificial' Bosnian nationality.[47]

It was, indeed, widely agreed that Serbo-Croat was essentially a single, uniform language and that it represented as such a uniform (if not yet wholly conscious) nation. Serbs and Croats were, Seton-Watson wrote, 'a homogeneous population, speaking a single language';[48] 'Serb' and 'Croat' were 'two names for one and the same language'.[49] Herbert Gibbons referred to the 'Serbian-speaking peoples, known as the

Yugoslavs'.[50] 'Whatever be the name applied to Croats, Dalmatians, Slavonians, Bosnians or Serbs', agreed Dominian, 'all speak the Serbian language'.[51] *Ipso facto*, it was implied, all were in fact Serbs, or 'Serbo-Croats', in the linguistic unitarian's more tactful formulation. (British insensitivity to Croat pride meant that the choice between 'Serbian' and 'Serbo-Croatian' as language label seemed of minor importance, while to Yugoslavs it was 'a great change in emphasis').[52] Provided Bulgarians and Slovenes were excluded, Toynbee agreed, South Slav unity was promoted by shared use of 'an absolutely homogeneous dialect' – an analysis which was misleading, as we shall see.[53] Meanwhile, in Whitehall, a conference paper on South-East Europe by Sir Ralph Paget, Harold Nicolson and Allen Leeper noted, in a telling elision of linguistic and racial identity, that the Yugoslavs were 'indisputably of one race: linguistically the only division that can be made is between the Serbo-Croats, forming the great majority of the race, and the Slovenes'.[54]

Others did show some appreciation of dialectal variations within the 'Serbo-Croat' area. Alfred Stead wrote in 1909 of a 'Croatian language' closely related to the 'Serbian', before noting that 'the two languages are not more different than two dialects of the same language'.[55] Sir Charles Eliot had similarly observed that the Serbian language 'includes Bosnian, Montenegrin, and Croatian, which only differ in slight dialectic peculiarities'.[56] But such variations were granted no significance. The Croatian language, Eliot concluded, 'is indubitably Serbian'.[57] For Herbert Vivian, as for almost every subsequent informed observer up to and including the interwar period, the whole Yugoslav area (excluding the Slovene lands) was characterised by 'one self-same language, whose dialects are as homogeneous as those of Yorkshire and Sussex'.[58] There was, wrote Taylor, no reason to dwell on the existence of dialect forms 'which are to be found in all languages'.[59] 'Slight dialectic differences in pronunciation' were of no import, Forbes agreed: Serbs and Croats 'are of the same race and speak the same language'.[60]

With hindsight these analyses seem deficient. (One must recall the embryonic state of British Slavic studies; Edith Durham had found it almost impossible to find a teacher of 'Serbo-Croat' in London in 1900; Seton-Watson wrote to Ronald Burrows in 1915 that while a Russian department had opened at the University of Liverpool, other Slavonic languages had 'hardly been thought of anywhere').[61] Particularly striking is the failure to appreciate that the dialectal reforms and debates of the preceding generations had played out within a context of intra-Yugoslav rivalries as well as of desire for unification and standardisation. Few in Britain recognised the regional and national sensitivities provoked by language questions in a world of persistent provincialism, substantial illiteracy, and Yugoslav aspirations which remained fragile, nebulous and restricted to a minority intellectual class. Nor was any awareness shown of the narrow nationalism which had motivated much work of linguistic reform and classification, which flourished in its wake, and which ensured that unification campaigns waged (to British eyes) in a generous spirit of compromise proved often in fact divisive and inflammatory.

Most important of the questions facing 19th century Yugoslav philologists and unitarists was the division of the 'Serbo-Croat' linguistic area into three fundamental dialects, labelled 'štokavian', 'čakavian' and 'kajkavian' after their respective words for 'what' (*što*, *ča* and *kaj*).[62] The centuries between the medieval and modern periods saw significant fluctuations. The čakavian dialect, having extended as far south as Dubrovnik, became confined to Istria and the northern Dalmatian islands. Kajkavian was largely restricted to the area around and to the north of Zagreb – early medieval Slavonia or roughly what was known in the early 20th century as 'Croatia proper'. Štokavian, having been divided into western and eastern branches (the former considered close to čakavian), converged into a new dialect – 'neoštokavian' – which was substantially spread by East-West migrations in the wake of the Ottoman conquest.

The question of dialectal consistency was therefore one which weighed more heavily upon Croats, divided between all three branches and with literary traditions in each, than it did upon Serbs. (It should be remembered too that while wide areas of Dalmatia, Croatia 'proper' and Slavonia boasted a literary culture, most Serb intellectuals shared a linguistic heritage as a result of their common provenance from the more affluent Serb regions of southern Hungary). The grand gesture of Ljudevit Gaj and the pro-Yugoslav 'Illyrian' movement, most of whom came from the kajkavian region around Zagreb, was to agree to abandon their exclusively Croat literary heritage in favour of the neoštokavian dialect spoken by almost all Serbs and a substantial body of Croats.[63]

Though most British writers on the South Slavs were, perhaps understandably, little aware of such detailed linguistic questions, some did recognise and admire this move, which chimed with that spirit of tolerance associated with the Illyrian movement and with 19th century Yugoslavist Croats such as the respected Archbishop Strossmayer (known in Britain for resisting the doctrine of Papal Infallibility).[64] British observers did not appreciate, however, the extent to which Croatian Illyrianism had provoked a hostile rather than a warm response among many Serbs. In particular they showed no awareness of the ways in which Serb philologists (most notably Karadžić) had exploited the question of dialectal variation in pursuit of a narrowly Serb nationalist agenda which was anathema not only to all Croats but also to moderate Serbs.

The famous (or infamous) article *Srbi svi i svuda* ('Serbs all and everywhere') in which Karadžić used the mistaken assumptions of Central

European scholars to classify all štokavian speakers as Serbs regardless of religion or conscious identity (in opposition to the conservative tendency in Serbia to tie Serb identity to Orthodoxy) was cited by Bogumil Vošnjak in his English-language work on the Slovenes but was unnoticed in British studies.[65] Text-books in Serbia, Charles Jelavich has shown, 'laid claim to all the Croatian lands – Croatia, Slavonia, and Dalmatia', and based their case 'primarily on a linguistic argument', an element of pan-Serb ideology unparalleled in Croatian nationalism.[66] Language was in some respects:

> the crucial issue in the development of Serbian nationalism. The authors [of Serbian textbooks] accepted the premise held by many nineteenth century European scholars that a nation was defined by its language. Since the Serbs spoke the što dialect of Serbo-Croatian, they concluded that anyone who used it was a Serb.[67]

But even the few British works which did remark on Serb nationalist claims that Catholic Croats were 'really' Serbs, made no mention of the linguistic criterion which was their ideological foundation.[68]

This oversight certainly increased the susceptibility of British writers to Serbian claims. Many, for instance, unquestioningly repeated the assertion made regarding the disputed province of Bosnia that Catholic and Muslim Slavs were actually (racially) 'pure Serbs'.[69] Had it been appreciated that the premise for this claim, formulated by Karadžić and embraced by other Serb maximalists, lay in the province's štokavian dialect which was presumed to demonstrate Serb race, and had it been realised that this claim also encompassed large populations in Dalmatia, Slavonia and Croatia, its extremity and implausibility might have been apparent.[70]

Nor was this tripartite dialectal division the end of the difficulties facing philologists and others of both unitarist and narrower nationalist persuasions. Important too, symbolically and emotionally, and equally ignored by British observers, was the separation of the dominant štokavian dialect (and in part the kajkavian and čakavian) into three sub-dialectal groups known, after their transliteration of a Church Slavonic vowel, as ijekavian, ikavian and ekavian.[71] Again, it was not the variations themselves which mattered, since most languages contain similar discrepancies. And in terms of mutual comprehension this divide was (and is) much less substantial than that between the što-, kaj- and ča- forms. But in the context of the Yugoslav 'national question' they assumed, nevertheless, a definite political significance.

The Croat Illyrianist 'awakeners', with their romantic Yugoslav unitarism, had adopted the ijekavian subdialect despite it being in fact least prevalent among the Croats. They did so in part because it was the idiom of Dubrovnik's great literary heritage (much cherished among Croatian intellectuals despite its subsequent decline), and in part too because its prevalence among Serbs and Muslims of Eastern Bosnia, Hercegovina, southern Dalmatia and Montenegro offered the prospect of substantial harmonisation. Significantly, it had also been favoured by Karadžić himself, who adopted the demotic speech of Eastern Hercegovina as the purest and most euphonious form of the Serbian tongue. Partly as a result of his efforts, in Vienna in 1850 Serb and Croat linguists and literati signed an agreement establishing štokavian ijekavian as the literary standard for both peoples, laying the foundations for full linguistic unity.[72] But while this form *was* standardised in Croatian intellectual and administrative usage (despite opposition from the Magyarophile petty nobility), Belgrade and Novi Sad favoured the ekavian 'eastern dialect' of Šumadija-Vojvodina. 'The Serbs of these politically and intellectually dominant areas', Banac notes, 'understandably preferred their own influential idiom as the basis for literary activity centred on Belgrade'.[73] The result was two literary standards which, however mutually comprehensible, could continue to develop in divergent directions, and which, though imperfectly aligned with the pattern of Serb and Croat populations, could become associated with the rival nationalisms centred on Belgrade and Zagreb.[74]

Naturally one should not overstate the importance of these linguistic variations to the subjective national sense of 'ordinary' early 20th century Serbs and Croats, many of whom remained illiterate, and for whom lofty if acrimonious debates about dialectal norms were remote to say the least. (Though it was the primitive, patriarchal and religiously-intolerant world in which most of the population lived which, as Milorad Ekmečić has argued, ultimately made the linguistic case for unity unrealistic).[75] Some historians, Yugoslavs among them, have denied the significance of language variation within the 'Serbo-Croat' area, insisting that Yugoslavs (excepting Slovenes and Macedonians) 'all speak one language', and that no linguistic barriers separate the ethnic groups.[76] Some modern nationality theory has similarly downplayed the contribution of language to separate Serb and Croat identities. 'The old enmity between Orthodox Serbs and Catholic Croats', a leading scholar has written, 'is, in practice, one of religious community, since language differences are very slight; for all practical purposes, Serbo-Croat represents a unified language which affords no basis for two nationalisms'.[77]

But a lack of 'linguistic barriers' implies only mutual *intelligibility*. It is true that the variations between 'Croatian' and 'Serbian' standards provide no major obstacles in this respect (although the čakavski and kajkavski branches remain markedly divergent). The error made, however, and that invariably made by early 20th century observers, is to assume that intelligibility *per se* is enough for language to act as a unifying force (or at least to prevent it being divisive). The fact that 'Croatian' and 'Serbian' are linguistically very close does not preclude the importance of what are now called 'socio-linguistic' differences.[78] The problem, as one recent writer has expressed it, is that 'language as a cultural, let alone political phenomenon is quite different from philology': 'From this perspective Serbian and Croatian were culturally different languages and culture [...] has a central role in the definition of nationhood through ethnicity'.[79]

As the cases of Britain and the US show, words in the same language, used in discrete communities undergoing different experiences, 'acquire different meanings, carry different emotional charges and evoke different responses'.[80] And such minor variations, overlaid on pre-existing ethnic difference in a context of 'historically conditioned emotionalism', acquire greater importance as markers of identity than is easily appreciated by outside observers.[81] Disputes over grammar and orthography within the Serbo-Croat zone can seem now, as Robert Auty recognised, 'petty, even comic'. But we should recall that the protagonists, 'were not dealing with language for its own sake' since 'even minute questions of orthography reflected attitudes towards wider issues'.[82] As a theorist noted in 1945, while Dutch and Flemish, Czech and Slovak, Serbian and Croatian, Danish and Norwegian, are all in effect sibling *dialects*, 'mere dialectical differences often contribute to national antagonism or are regarded as precious peculiarities'.[83] The 'rather modest range of differentiation in the variants of standard štokavian' implies, as Katičić observes, 'sharp distinctions of identity, stylistic values and cultural affinities'.[84]

From a theoretical perspective, moreover, recent writers have stressed that the very distinction between 'language' and 'dialect' is 'purely relative': ultimately not *linguistic* at all but political.[85] It matters little whether 'Serbian' and 'Croatian' are characterised as distinct dialects of a single language, or as two literary languages of a larger 'diasystem'.[86] What does matter is the degree to which the relationship between politics and language can be seen to operate causally in *both* directions, with politics shaping language as well as being shaped by it. As Stephen May has noted, language and dialect cannot be distinguished on the basis of mutual intelligibility: there are groups of languages which are mutually intelligible, and single languages which encompass dialects mutually incomprehensible:

> Rather, the distinction between language and dialect is primarily a political consequence of the language legitimation process undertaken by nation-states [...]. The boundaries between languages, and the classification of dialects, have invariably followed the politics of state-making rather than the other way around.[87]

The force of this argument in relation to Yugoslavia has become manifest in the last decade, with the drive to establish distinct Serbian and Croatian language varieties in the wake of the country's separation into constituent national units.[88] But this has not only been, as is sometimes implied, a response to the events of the 1990s. Croatian cultural institutions suffered oppression in Communist Yugoslavia for attempting to maintain linguistic differences, unhappy at the imposition of distinctively 'Serbian' dialect for official administration.[89] A declaration issued in Croatia in 1967 rejected the 1954 Novi Sad agreement on a single Serbo-Croat standard, and demanded a constitutional separation of Croatian and Serbian literary languages.[90] Centralist policy, well served by the premise of a single Serbo-Croat norm, and promulgated by linguists of 'pan-Slavic orientation', had only exacerbated 'the smouldering conflict between Croats and Serbs on the linguistic issue'.[91] 'Serbo-Croat', in its official, largely Serbian form, had in Croatia been limited to the armed forces and diplomatic service, and as such was associated with the Belgrade government. The Croatian-Serbian language controversy of the 1960s testified, as Ivo Lederer notes, to the fact that language served 'as the living symbol of a nation's franchise'.[92]

All of which, insofar as it concerns sensitivities in the post-World War II era, is germane to our discussion only as evidence that linguistic issues can acquire political and emotional importance within a near-homogeneous language area. In fact the very process of homogenisation, in a context of pre-existing ethnic identities, can cause 'a passionate clinging to the remaining differences'. As a result, in Yugoslav lands in which Croats, Serbs, Montenegrins and Slavic Muslims shared 'basically one language', this language became 'an important political tool', as Serbs used linguistic criteria to promote assimilation while non-Serbs clung to linguistic idiosyncracies to protect their identity.[93] It was this attachment of closely-related peoples to seemingly insubstantial symbols of individuality that Sigmund Freud termed the 'narcissism of minor differences'.[94]

Particularly pertinent to the early 20th century Yugoslav case is the emphasis put by recent theorists on the social function of language. If, within a given language area, a recognised elite exists with a characteristic vernacular, it is this norm, Einar Haugen notes, which 'will almost inevitably prevail'. Where 'there are socially coordinate groups of people within the community, usually distributed regionally or tribally', however, 'the choice of any one will meet with resistance from the rest'.[95] We must, in other words, heed the *register* of regional language forms, to distinguish between dialects serviceable only in informal and low-prestige situations, and those which, adopted by local or national elites, serve a high-level, literary and official function.[96] In Croatia, as observers knew, an elite existed which considered itself not only equal to any equivalent class in Serbia, but its cultural superior: which had 'never been willing to play understudy to the Serbians' and which considered Zagreb not Belgrade the centre of the Serbo-Croat movement.[97] Most in Britain shared this sense of the cultural superiority of ex-Habsburg Yugoslavia, with its proximity to the intellectual currents of Central Europe. None, however, considered the obstacle this might present to the standardisation of language on a largely Serbian model. It was not appreciated that linguistic disputes mattered because they were 'conflicts involving prestige'; that 'disagreements over language [...] were actually disagreements over its social background'.[98]

The symbolic significance of dialectal questions was missed even by the few British writers who knew of their existence. The modern trend, it was often noted, was for languages to amalgamate in response to economic pressures towards integration and homogenisation.[99] With no grasp of the link between language and national identities in Yugoslavia, it was assumed that variations would rapidly diminish within a single economic and administrative unit. As late as 1941, the most thorough and accurate British treatment of 'Serbo-Croat' dialects hitherto published continued to reject any wider significance. While it might be 'regrettable', it noted, that Belgrade had not followed Croatia's adoption of the ijekevian standard, the difference between literary Croat and literary (Belgrade) Serb remained 'fundamentally nothing more than that between subdivisions of one and the same dialect'.[100] (This is inaccurate, of course, not in what it says but in what it omits to say). Popular and general works continued to state baldly that Serbs and Croats were 'one by race and language'.[101]

Script

In considering dialectal differences, we have ignored thus far the one difference between Croatian and Serbian language usage which could not elude the most superficial observer: that of script. It was, of course, widely observed in Britain that Serbs used the cyrillic, Croats and Slovenes the latin alphabet. This 'curious phenomen[on] of [a] people speaking practically the same language yet using a different alphabet' seemed to many an intriguing instance of Balkan exoticism.[102] Opinion diverged not on whether this difference existed, but on whether it mattered.

In general, not surprisingly, those enthused by Yugoslav unity were disinclined to give weight to this obvious distinction between Croat and Serb, West and East. Neville Forbes was typical in noting simply that Serbs and Croats spoke the same language, 'the only difference' being that of alphabet.[103] Seton-Watson agreed that the 'only' linguistic difference was that of script.[104] A.H.E. Taylor, who unlike Seton-Watson approached South Slav issues invariably from a Serb angle, was particularly bluff. Since moves to introduce cyrillic in Croatia had foundered, he noted, both orthographies would remain on an equal footing. But, he continued:

> The central administrative documents will doubtless continue to be written in the Cyrillic script in order to avoid confusion as the central administration of the enlarged kingdom will be an extension of the present government offices. Any remains of the old jealousy on this score should be assuaged, and the matter regarded as being quite divorced, as naturally it is, from any question of religion or tribal difference, and the field left clear to the eventual predominance of whichever script forms the best vehicle of the common language.[105]

The blindness of this analysis to Croatian concerns that Yugoslavia would be treated as an expanded Serbia is striking. No less so is its unwarranted assurance that script was divorced from religious and 'tribal' sensitivities. In any case the orthographic distinction, Taylor and others were clear, was superficial: a curiosity rather than a factor of moment. The 1917 Corfu Agreement, hailed in Britain as testimony to the appetite among Serbs, Croats and Slovenes for compromise and unity, had specified equality for alphabets as for religions. There, for many, the matter ended.

But the Corfu Agreement had serious flaws. On the one hand it represented rather the aspirations of idealists than prevailing attitudes. On the other, each contracting party – most notably Pašić's government – had been brought to the table more by the pressure of political circumstances than by any genuine desire to cooperate, least of all on an equal basis. It was, in other words, a superficial gloss over the real differences in background and outlook which existed between representatives of the Serbian government and of the Yugoslav Committee.[106] The question of alphabet, it seemed to some, was in reality at least representative of, and might even be a factor in, the great division assumed to split the Yugoslav lands between East and West, Byzantium and Rome, Ottoman and Habsburg, Orthodox and Catholic. It was, in other words, symbolic (literally!) of a cultural gulf stemming from the different historical experiences of the East-looking South Slavs of independent Serbia, Montenegro, Macedonia and (pre-1878) Bosnia on the one hand, and the non-Orthodox of Croatia, Dalmatia, and Slavonia on the other.

William Miller, in his influential survey of the Balkans, had included the difference of alphabet among the '[considerable] difficulties' which stood in the way of union between Croats of Western mentality and Serbs of Eastern.[107] Seton-Watson showed, in his private correspondence, an awareness of linguistic sensitivities which he downplayed or denied entirely in his published work (which sought to promote the Yugoslav cause). Setting up his magazine, *New Europe*, he was unsure whether a translated edition in 'Croat' would suffice for Serbia also. By 'Croat', it is clear, he meant simply the Latin as opposed to the 'Cyrilline' alphabet. Producing separate Serb and Croat editions would, he felt, compel him to produce Bulgar and 'perhaps even Slovene' editions also.[108]

The use of cyrillic script, along with the Orthodox element of Serb identity, often seemed indicative of a psychological bond between Serbs and Russians, an impression reinforced by pan-Slavist ideology and diplomatic history. Fellow-feeling with Russia was an emotion Catholic Croats were not presumed to share. A wartime intelligence report on 'the Yugo-Slav Problem' by Harold Temperley went so far as to describe the division between cyrillic and latin orthography as 'an even more serious difference' than that between Orthodoxy and Catholicism with which it was associated.[109] While the Foreign Office's pre-Conference report considered, as we have seen, that the Serbo-Croat language was entirely uniform, it nevertheless listed the orthographic divide as one of those 'incompletely conciliated rivalries' which made the Yugoslav situation more difficult than that of any other country in South-Eastern Europe.[110]

Nor was such caution unwarranted, for, contrary to Taylor's blithe assurance that a mere question of alphabet need not inflame nationalist pride, it had already shown signs of doing so. The compromise proposal by one Serb writer in 1913 that a standardised language might be achieved by Croats adopting the eastern ekavian dialect in return for Serbs foregoing their cyrillic script, was taken up by 'Yugoslav' enthusiasts in Serbia and Croatia but soon met opposition. Not only did some Croats reject a second linguistic sacrifice, but Serbs, particularly after the outbreak of war (and the Habsburg attempt to suppress cyrillic in Bosnia), came to view their script as a cherished national symbol. While the Serb national existence was endangered, one nationalist averred, the Cyrillic script would remain an '[emblem] that cannot be abandoned, a banner under which we must endure'.[111] For many Serbian Radical politicians during and after the war, cyrillic remained the only truly Slavic and national alphabet.[112] No less did it seem, in the western regions, a symbol of hegemonic tendencies in Belgrade which viewed Croats as liberated members of an expanded Serbia rather than as equal partners in a new state.

As British observers became aware in the immediate post-war period of the conflicts of interest and identity which stood in the way of a harmonious new 'national' state, a few observers began to emphasise factors which seemed representative of the divisions they perceived. For H.J. Fleure, discussing the peace settlement in 1921, Yugoslavia's language divide remained, at root, 'not very deep'. The significance of the divergence in scripts was, however, he recognised, precisely what Taylor had indicated it should not be: language, and (through the central importance of the written word) *alphabet*, were not distinct from but were intimately tied up with the religious divide which still seemed to underpin rival Serb and Croat identities. And whereas dialectal differences were not linked by British observers with this divide, its connection with the pattern of cyrillic and latinate orthography was clear. The dominant view, as Hugh Seton-Watson later expressed it, was that:

> The normal distinction between Serb and Croat was religious. Both spoke the same language (differences of dialect were a matter of regional not of religious division), but Orthodox were Serbs and used the Cyrillic alphabet, while Catholics were Croats and used the Latin alphabet.[113]

Awareness of the complications resulting from 'the association of alphabet difference with religion' has been echoed by some modern theorists of language and ethnicity.[114] They have stressed more explicitly the perennial link between language and religion, the latter conferring on the former a 'sacred' status particularly potent in cultures where religious identity has been strongly linked to ethnicity.[115] In fact the importance of the South Slavic association between alphabet and religion has been illustrated not simply with reference to the modern latin-cyrillic divide. Attention has been drawn to the development by Bosnian Muslims of a significant if modest štokavian literature in the Arabic script.[116] Similarly, examination of orthographic controversies in 19th century Croatia has shown the religious motivation for the opposition by, for instance, the anti-Illyrianist Slovene Jernej Kopitar, to diacritical innovations derived from Czech (and therefore Protestant) usage.[117] Historians of the wider Balkans, meanwhile, have noted a similar alignment of script and religion among Greek Catholics, Turcophone Orthodox, and Catholic, Orthodox and Muslim Albanians prior to imposed latin standardisation.[118]

We will shortly examine the perceived role of religion in Yugoslav national identities. First, however, we must look at British observers' treatment of the clearest challenge to their notion of a South Slavic linguistic unity that had prepared the way for a single 'nation state'.

Slovene: language or dialect?

Most scholars of emerging nationalities now consider that by 1860, if not earlier, three distinct literary languages had crystallised among the South Slavs: Bulgarian, Serbian/Croatian and Slovenian.[119] It is true, as Robert Auty has noted, that the Slovene area had long been characterised by 'extreme dialectal fragmentation [...], no dialect having become sufficiently extensive or influential to form the national written language in its own image'. Nevertheless, the essential features of the modern standard were established in the late 1850s.[120] While the Slovene philologist Jernej

Kopitar followed his predecessors in considering his native tongue a dialect of a single great Slavonic language, he used 'dialect' to mean a written standard within a large linguistic family, and certainly did not imply a status inferior to the written language of Belgrade or Zagreb.[121] On the contrary, the erroneous teaching of early Slavicists that all kajkavians were Slovenes, regardless of their subjective identity, strengthened Slovene faith in their sense of linguistic nationality. 'Separate linguistic traditions', as Ivo Banac observes, 'were at the root of Slovene nationalism'.[122]

Albert H. Putney, head of the US State Department Near Eastern Division assigned to consider the future of the Habsburg Empire, recommended in May 1917 a Serbo-Croat Yugoslav state which *excluded* Slovenes on the grounds of their historical bonds with Austria and their clear linguistic differences.[123] The first official census of the new state, carried out in 1921, offered the Slavic population a threefold choice: 'Serbian or Croatian', 'Slovene' or 'other Slavic'.[124] And although the 1921 Constitution declared the existence of a single official language, 'Serb-Croat-Slovene', this label was deliberately used, as a Foreign Office report later noted, 'to cover the linguistic differences of the Yugoslavs'.[125] Plainly Slovene linguistic traditions offered a challenge, at least, to those observers who considered language the principal argument for Yugoslav unity.

Some commentators – even otherwise informed ones – either ignored this challenge or denied it entirely, maintaining the complete linguistic unity of the Yugoslav region. In the post-war edition of his respected survey of the Balkans, William Miller noted differences in script and culture within the new Serb-Croat-Slovene State, but recorded that, 'the oral speech of all the three contracting parties is the same'.[126] Neville Forbes, treating all western South Slavs as of purely Serb race with only minor dialectal distinctions, entirely overlooked Slovene linguistic individuality.[127] Similarly, Noel Buxton's assertion that Croats and Slovenes were 'akin in race and language', and H.A. Gibbons' statement that the Slavs of the southern Monarchy spoke 'practically the same language' as the Serbs (without referring specifically to the Slovenes), were typical of the vagaries exhibited by enthusiasts for the 'nationality principle', who were often either ignorant of the detail of individual cases or reluctant to admit complexities which muddied the ideological waters.[128] Seton-Watson, though aware of Slovene linguistic individuality, was content to repeat the Prince-Regent's claim that Serbs, Croats and Slovenes were all 'one people' with 'the same traditions' and 'the same tongue'.[129] And similar Yugoslav propaganda was met equally uncritically: the Yugoslav Committee claim that Yugoslavs were a single nation 'alike by identity of language', and numerous other statements that Serbs, Croats and Slovenes were 'a single indivisible people'.[130] The Slovene Bogumil Vošnjak – whose speculation that Slovene might gradually merge back into a single South Slav language may have seemed plausible to British readers – nevertheless expressed pleasant surprise at the rapidity with which British analysts had accepted Yugoslavs as a single 'culture-nation'.[131]

Most British writers on the South Slavs did, of course, acknowledge a degree of individuality in the Slovene linguistic heritage. Toynbee observed that both Slovenes and Bulgarians possessed dialectal characteristics which 'distinguish them sharply' from the main body of South Slavs in between; the Slovene dialect, he continued, was 'distinctly different'.[132] This degree of emphasis, however, was unusual. The majority preferred to acknowledge, but at the same time to downplay, any linguistic frontier between Slovene and Serbian/ Croatian. They talked, like Bernard Joseph, of the 'virtual identity of their languages', or characterised Slovene, like Laffan, simply as 'closely akin to Serbian'.[133] Almost none, among the many who emphasised language's formative role in the modern phenomenon of 'nationality', considered Slovene linguistic individuality a challenge to the much-credited single 'Yugoslav' identity.

3

Religion: Faith, Nationality and the South Slavs in British Analysis

In the assessment of a population's nationality (in the modern sense of 'ethnicity') language was attributed unrivalled pre-eminence in the early 20th century as an indicator of race, or at least of 'sense of race'. Certainly no other objective criterion was treated in isolation as a test of subjective allegiance, and many considered it the sole important catalyst of national consciousness. A few writers did worry, however, that this single factor might be dangerously over-extended. One sceptic feared the vogue for a linguistically-defined conception of race might 'force into common national organisations peoples claimed as belonging to the same race, but separated by different institutions, different laws and customs, [...] different sympathies and different hates'. Hardly one of the 'numerous volumes' dealing with Austria and the Balkan States, he cautioned, was without 'dangerous examples of this fallacy'.[1]

There was substance to this concern. Nevertheless, most commentators, particularly those with a theoretical interest in the concept of 'nationality', were willing to consider the role of other factors in creating and binding the modern nation. Invariably foremost in language's wake were the related themes of religion and historical tradition, both plainly germane to the Yugoslav case.[2] Let us look first, then, at the treatment of religion in British analysis of the South Slavs.

Theorists recognised the paramount contribution that religion had made to the growth and maintenance of national feeling in certain cases. In the Jews they found 'the crowning manifestation of religion as a fundamental factor in nationality', an ethnic identity scarcely separable from a body of religious traditions and beliefs.[3] The separation and distinct national development of Holland and Belgium was commonly attributed to contrasting religious identities. And in Ireland Britain had rather too close at hand a territory united by geography and (overwhelmingly) by language in which it was recognised that 'absence of common tradition combines with religious differences to divide the country into two nationalities'.[4] The formative significance of religion varied, to be sure; unlike 'blood' or language it seemed a contingent rather than a necessary ingredient of ethnic identity. But some influential writers continued, nevertheless, to sell it strong. 'In every case [...]', argued C. Delisle Burns, 'religion seems to have an important influence on the formation of nationality'.[5]

Theorists interested in the nationalities of Central and Eastern Europe particularly emphasised religion's formative role. They observed that the Ottoman 'millet' system, by allowing substantial administrative and judicial autonomy to religious hierarchies, had identified religious affiliation with emergent national consciousness. The Turkish ascendancy, H.N. Brailsford noted, had rested 'not upon race but on religion'; and as such the emergent nationalist opposition of the late 18th and 19th centuries assumed a religious as well as a national coloration. For the Balkan peasant apostasy meant 'a forswearing of his nationality and a treason to the cause of his own race'.[6] 'In the East', observed William Miller, 'ties of religion count for more than anything else'.[7]

The Orthodox Church, lacking the centralised, supra-national structure of its Roman rival, seemed to have a particularly close affinity with nationalism. 'A Christian Greek or Bulgarian who [...] converted to Mohammedanism', it was observed, 'would hardly be deemed to remain a Greek or Bulgarian'.[8] Vatican control of the Catholic Church had discouraged the same alignment of national and ecclesiastical identity. Nevertheless, it was often remarked that in practice Poland or Ireland, for example, displayed a similar elision of religious and 'ethnic' allegiance. Among emerging nations of both confessions religion, it seemed, had provided a rallying cry – had constituted 'the cornerstone in the earliest edifice of nationality'.[9] Even age-old struggles once considered purely religious seemed with hindsight to have been 'a groping after nationality'.[10]

Having said this, however, the work both of nationality theorists and Balkan analysts was pervaded by the assumption that the war marked a watershed in European civilisation, revolutionising the way populations defined themselves and their relations with others. The violent end to *ancién régime* Europe seemed the culmination of a process, quietly at work since the French Revolution, in which 'race' and language (commonly equated, as we have seen) had assumed the pre-eminent formative role which religion had once enjoyed. Linguistic nationality, it was now widely argued, had become to European consciousness what religion had once been – the primary category of personal identity. This sense of change, of a new dawn, meant the revolutionary peace many assumed must follow a decisive Allied victory was compared not with that which was commonly portrayed as reinstating the old order in 1815, but with that of 1648. It was this that seemed the most obvious precedent to the 'new map of Europe' contemplated at Versailles. And it would be Versailles that, after 270 years, would finally supersede the equation of religious and state authority in the famous Westphalian formula, '*cuius regio eius religio*'.

So while religion's historical role in the gestation of nationality was admitted, modern nationalism seemed to have rendered it 'no longer a factor of much consequence'.[11] With the rise of religious toleration and the multi-confessional state, Sidney Herbert wrote, 'the influence of religion in aiding or hindering the growth of nationality grows steadily less'.[12] To many writers (including those enthusiasts for a 'new', ethnically-divided Europe) religion was an element of identity less profound, less *real*, than race or language. The influential theorist Alfred Zimmern stressed that race was an involuntary inheritance: permanent, and thus deeper than religion.[13] And while a few sceptics protested that populations *had* changed their language, and with it their *sense* of race, they remained a minority.

This sense that religion was the defining symbol of a previous, now obsolete age ('byzantine, medieval, reactionary')[14] helps explain why it was, as we will see, largely overlooked in 1918 as a factor of ethnic identity. Perhaps inevitably there was a wistful optimism that the victors could inaugurate, on a post-war *tabula rasa*, a new order of national self-determination. In the Balkans, one British official emphasised, 'we are really out for a comprehensive and permanent, and not merely an opportunist, settlement'.[15] To the sceptical eye of a later observer it seemed that the vogue for nationality had itself become 'a new religion'.[16]

In the case of the Yugoslav populations, of course, commentators could scarcely avoid the question of religious affiliation, or the impact it had upon national or 'ethnic' identity. Though racially united, Seton-Watson noted, the 'true line of cleavage' was religious, every Croat a Catholic and every Serb a member of the Orthodox Church.[17] In fact, long before awareness developed in Britain of the South Slavs' ethno-linguistic affinity, the religious divides separating the Western Church from the Eastern, and Christian rule from that of Ottoman Islam, had been among the fundamental geopolitical facts of European life. (For much of the 19th century the English public had vaguely considered all Muslims in south-east Europe 'Turks', all Orthodox 'Greeks', and Catholics either Austrian, Hungarian or Italian).[18] Once awareness did develop of the kinship of the Serb, Croat and Slovene regions, their position athwart these religious boundaries became, for British observers, a defining characteristic.

John Allcock has argued that only in Yugoslavia did Serbs and Croats become defined as antagonistic groups, and this opposition come to be regarded as 'perpetual'. He is right that other oppositions – Serbs with Turks and Albanians; Croats with Hungarians – had contributed more to the genesis of Serb and Croat identities. A few British observers belatedly noticed the struggle of Croats in particular against Habsburg domination.[19] But in fact well before the war the Serb-Croat relationship had come to seem in Britain one fraught with religious enmity. The two peoples, William Miller had noted in 1898, were separated by 'the wide chasm which keeps the Roman and the Orthodox Greek asunder'.[20] The 'only difference' between Croat and Serb, agreed a pre-war student of the Orthodox Church, was religious: one looked to Austria-Hungary, the other to the Russian Tsar, and the result was a 'great hatred' between the two peoples.[21] And though occasional developments (like the emergence of the Serbo-Croat Coalition) might have seemed to suggest a 'weakening of their religious dissensions', in general pre-war Foreign Office reports likewise stressed the 'bitter hostility' between the confessions.[22] 'The difference of religion', Fairfax Cartwright observed in 1913, 'must always be a bar between the Slavs of Austria and those of the Balkans'.[23]

Allcock's point about a recent rivalry becoming regarded as 'perpetual', however, certainly applies to British attitudes. Despite (or perhaps because of) Britons' short acquaintance with the South Slavs, the confessional tension they observed, in the Zagreb riots of 1902-3 for instance, was rationalised as manifesting an 'age-old' enmity. As with the simultaneous unrest in Macedonia, an appreciation of events based upon traceable political history was eschewed in favour of an assumption of timeless 'Balkan' norms. Before the Habsburg occupation of Bosnia, Noel Buxton averred, Muslim, Catholic and Orthodox had lived 'in perpetual and blood-stained feud'.[24] If Austria-Hungary ever withdrew from the province, William Miller agreed, the different creeds would be immediately at each other's throats: *Pax Austriana* alone prevented a recrudescence of those religious quarrels which had 'stained with blood' the annals of medieval Bosnia.[25] Only in 'most recent times', Harold Temperley argued in his 1917 history of Serbia, had Orthodox and Catholic in Bosnia and Croatia been induced to cooperate as fellow Slavs.[26]

Maria Todorova has made a similar argument to Allcock's in relation to the broader conflict between the Catholic and Orthodox worlds. Only in the inter-war period, she argues, did Westerners embrace the image of a profound cultural 'fault-line' in east-central Europe, between the incompatible mindsets of Rome and Byzantium, Vienna and Constantinople.[27] It is true that obvious tensions in the Yugoslav state during the 1920s and 1930s produced a greater emphasis on this theme. But once again, at least in relation to British observers of the South Slav regions, this post-dates the phenomenon. Already in pre-war works one finds argued a fundamental psychological incompatibility of the major religious cultures, far transcending differences of dogma or ritual. Even an early and sanguine Yugoslavist like Seton-Watson noted the 'eternal strife [...] of two opposing systems of thought and culture' which had lent the Serbo-Croat race its 'dual nature'.[28] That 'insuperable gulf, difference of religion' mattered not only for the superficial symbols of identity dividing

Catholic and Orthodox.[29]   Over the centuries it had engendered a 'profound difference of mentality, rather than of doctrine, between the Western and Eastern Church'.[30] Many in Britain concurred with the eminent German historian whose comparative study found a deep, unbridgeable gulf between Eastern and Western civilisation, attributable to the influence of their churches, more profound even than that which divided the Orthodox and Islamic worlds.[31]

Let us now look at British assumptions about each of the region's major religious communities, before assessing the impact of the war on attitudes towards religion's role in Yugoslav national identities.

The Orthodox Church

Historically, British attitudes to the Orthodox Church had been influenced less by spiritual than by diplomatic considerations. The expansion of Russia – a threat to British interests in India and the Middle East – had nurtured a deep suspicion of the whole Orthodox bloc.[32] Pan-Orthodox ideology, and Russian interest in the 'emancipation' of Orthodox peoples, were considered a smokescreen for an imperialism which deliberately incited dissent to justify intervention. In Britain 'Christianity in the East' seemed to have 'degenerated from a religion into a secret society comparable to Fenianism'.[33] A determination grew, particularly in the Conservative Party, to bolster the seemingly moribund Ottoman Empire.

Insofar as the Yugoslavs were concerned, many in Britain believed that, despite talk of pan-Slavism, Russia was genuinely protective only of the Orthodox Serbs. Some saw her ultimate aim as the assimilation of all Orthodox in one empire. Adrian Fortescue, for instance, argued in his 1907 study of the Eastern Church that Russia's policy was rooted in militant pan-Orthodoxy, which encouraged the Balkan states to consider the Tsar their natural protector in preparation for their absorption. 'All the Orthodox', Fortescue concluded, 'will apparently soon be Russian'.[34] And though the Anglo-Russian Entente of 1907 revolutionised European diplomacy, such deep-rooted suspicions died hard. While a Serb propagandist argued in 1916 that the Franco-Russian alliance had silenced all claims of division between Catholic Croats and Orthodox Serbs, in truth only the 1917 revolutions eased British fears of Orthodox militancy.[35] These (and the Yugoslav Corfu Agreement which they helped to foster by leaving Pašić dangerously isolated) had, Temperley noted, finally removed 'the Russian-Orthodox bogey, which sought to erect a barrier of religious hatred between Serb and Croat'.[36]

This view of pan-Orthodoxy as a screen for secular ambition chimed with a tendency to regard Orthodox communities, particularly those of the Balkans, as scantily religious in any genuinely spiritual sense. The turbulent rivalries in Macedonia between adherents of Bulgarian, Serbian and Greek Churches, separated by no significant points of doctrine, encouraged British observers to regard Orthodoxy in southeast Europe simply as a badge of national allegiance. This battle of 'Churches' was 'simply a political or more properly a racial conflict'.[37] Paradoxically, fears of Russian sway over her Balkan coreligionists coexisted with the observation that, while the Eastern Church was ecumenical in principle, in practice it was fissiparous in the extreme. Having invoked the dangers of pan-Orthodoxy, Fortescue derided the 'extreme quarrelsomeness' that constituted the 'dominant note' within the Orthodox community.[38] The appeal to religion as a marker of nationality was encouraged, another writer observed, by 'the fact that Eastern Christianity tends to encourage national churches and has education in its hands'. Education on a religious basis would be 'a serious problem for the new state of Yugoslavia'.[39]

Numerous observers remarked upon the seeming indifference of Serbs in particular to religion in its spiritual rather than purely patriotic manifestations. The Yugoslavs in general, wrote Neville Forbes, were 'not naturally an intensely religious people', while the Eastern was 'the most conservative and the most passive of the Churches'.[40] The Encyclopaedia Britannica saw in the pitiful membership of Serbia's famous monasteries evidence of a lack of sincere religiosity in a nation whose priests had always been more active in the struggle for independence than in the care of souls.[41] Serbian church services, Sir Charles Eliot agreed, were 'little frequented'. For Seton-Watson the Balkans had really no religious life at all in a Western sense, the Orthodox Churches 'mere formalist machines which exist for political propaganda'.[42] And Brailsford was blunter still: the clergy's lack of education and preoccupation with secular nationalism revealed the 'essential barbarism of the [Orthodox] Church'.[43]

And yet a different tradition also existed in Britain. Anglican churchmen and theologians, hostile to the anational despotism of Rome, warmed to Orthodoxy's perceived national and democratic character, its vernacular language and resistance to centralised Patriarchal control. This line of thought strongly influenced Gladstone and those Liberal circles averse to Disraeli's pro-Turkish response to the 'Eastern Question'.[44] It remained evident during the war when Serbian requests to send ecclesiastical students to Britain were welcomed by the Anglican establishment and by Whitehall. It was a plea, W.H. Carnegie noted on behalf of the Archbishops of Canterbury, York and Dublin, Lord Salisbury, the Speaker of the House of Commons and other eminent figures, which 'appeals strongly to our sympathies as Churchmen'.[45]

But for the lay majority Orthodoxy's appeal as a contrast to the off-putting aspects of Catholicism was blunted by serious reservations. Representatives of Eastern Christianity and Anglicanism might feel strong 'mutual affinities' but there were also, to the western mind, fundamental differences. The image of Orthodoxy as more conducive to national development than Catholicism was thought misleading. Religious doctrine and observance were believed to shape the basic patterns of thought which constituted the national 'soul' or 'character'. But Eastern Christianity, for all its subtle theological speculation, seemed not to have engendered the philosophical, moral and political enquiry of Western scholastics. On the contrary, Orthodoxy's mysticism and asceticism had apparently militated against that individual initiative and intellectual freedom considered central to the rise of Western democratic nationalism.

'The religion of their laity', observed one writer, 'has been a very wonderful, unquestioning belief in the spiritual and the unseen'. But there had been 'far too little [instruction] to meet the needs of the inquiring mind and the critical spirit'.[46] It was this, married to a belief in salvation by faith rather than works, which, many British observers assumed, underpinned the seeming impassivity and stagnation of the Orthodox world. Nationalism might be a western export, another argued, but without the ethical and economic components provided by western Christianity and capitalism, genuine civilisation was impossible. An 'unholy alliance between Orthodox obscurantism and Asiatic autocracy' had failed to provide the 'moral civilising force' exerted by the Papacy:

> We ourselves, products of western civilization established by the Catholic Church – whose national renascence was engendered by the Protestant Reformation – [...] can scarcely realise the disadvantage to the growth of a community whose progressive forces get no inspiration from Protestantism and whose conservative forces are not firmly founded in Catholicity.[47]

The Orthodox God, the 'characterless natural force of Eastern Fatalism', had failed to foster that individualistic spirit considered the mark of 'European' civilisation.[48] This sociological analysis of Orthodoxy sat comfortably with less sophisticated popular conceptions of the 'fatalistic tendency' of Slavs in general, and of the 'unchanging East'.[49]

Insofar as it related simply and directly to the Serbian sense of nationality, however, British observers were impressed by the Church's unifying and affirming role. 'A Church should be the soul of a nation', declared one early 20th century writer, 'and is so most emphatically in Serbia'.[50] Emphasis was given to its role as 'the nursing mother of national independence' – preserving 'the spirit of nationality through the centuries of Turkish oppression' – before an autonomous state provided a new focus for national feeling.[51] Here again we may notice writers who purported to treat the South Slavs as one unitary 'nationality' also applying this label to a branch distinguished by their *religious* identity. In the early years of the century, before the shift of opinion produced by the war, this association of Orthodoxy with a Serb 'nation' was predominant in Britain. In 1908, the Encyclopaedia Britannica noted, many Serbs still aspired to the 'so-called "Great Serbian Idea"': the union of Serbia, Bosnia, Montenegro and 'Old Serbia', countries largely or near-exclusively Orthodox Serb.[52] In 1909 the British minister in Belgrade wrote of the 'religious element which underlies Serbian aspirations'.[53] We have seen before that some British analysts testified to an underlying, racial Serb-ness, distinct from confessional allegiance, which allowed Catholic and Muslim Slavs of Bosnia to be deemed Serb in a narrow sense (rather than simply as a synonym for South Slav). But there was no doubt in British minds that to be South Slav and to be Orthodox was to be a Serb. Specialists like Seton-Watson ridiculed the 'absurd theory' of Croatian extremists that Serbs living in Croatia might be Orthodox Croats.[54]

Though there were exceptions to the rule that Orthodox South Slavs considered themselves Serbs, in general, in the wake of 19th century nationalist 'awakening', the assumption was a fair one.[55] British observers inclined, nevertheless, to overstate the uniform nature of this identity. We will look in the next chapter at Yugoslav regionalism, which rendered over-simple the picture of a population in which the only significant divisions were religious. But even in the religious sphere it was overlooked that, before the creation of Yugoslavia, the Serbian Church was not a single entity but five autocephalous churches: the Metropolitanates of the Kingdom of Serbia, of the Kingdom of Montenegro, of Karlovci (Hungary, Croatia-Slavonia) and of Bukovina-Dalmatia (in the Austrian half of the Monarchy), and the Ecumenical Patriarchate of Constantinople (Bosnia, Sandžak, Kosovo-Metohia, Macedonia). Only in 1920 was the Church unified canonically under a restored Patriarchate.[56]

It is pertinent to consider this in relation to the one subset of this group which could plausibly claim a distinct heritage and identity: the Montenegrins. As the Britannica did recognise, not only was the Montenegrin Church an autocephalous branch of the Eastern Orthodox communion rather than an ecclesiastical subsidiary of Serbia, but the historical tradition of *vladikas* (prince-bishops) meant religious and secular authority were combined. Though temporal and spiritual powers were re-divided in 1851, the practice had served 'to unite the patriotic and the religious instincts of the people' – a statement which implies, in the past at least, a strong regional Montenegrin identity.[57] But very few in Britain noticed the independence of Montenegro's Church. It was simply assumed that since the inhabitants were Orthodox and South Slav, they must be of identical nationality to the Serbians. Certainly few in wartime Whitehall troubled to study the Montenegrin question closely. It was 'inevitable', Harold Nicolson minuted, 'that so small a country should tend to be fused in general statements regarding Serbia and the Southern Slavs'.[58]

The Catholic Church

It is scarcely necessary to elaborate here on the suspicion and hostility with which the Catholic Church had for centuries been eyed in Britain. But by the turn of the 20th century there was no longer the fear of Catholicism itself as militant or expansionist in the way that Orthodoxy seemed in its association with the Russian state. Conflicts of interest with Catholic powers such as France were rarely interpreted in a religious context. And Austria-Hungary seemed a threat more by its weakness and instability than by any residual imperialist momentum (for all that its annexation of Bosnia-Hercegovina in 1908 had extended its direct rule in Europe).

Croat identity was of course associated in Britain with Catholicism. A Croat, as we have seen, was often misleadingly identified as a 'Catholic Serb'. But a closer analysis suggests that the equations Croat-Catholic and Serb-Orthodox were not symmetrical. Unfounded fears of pan-Orthodox amalgamation coexisted with but did not undermine the association of Orthodoxy with *national* units and identities. Catholicism, however, seemed in name and principle to transcend national allegiances. While commentators could discuss the Serbian Church's relationship with a particular 'Serbian' identity, they could not tie Croat identity to religion in the same direct way. Here religion seemed a distinguishing mark of a negative nature – necessary but insufficient. The inclusion of Slovenes among the South Slavs meant that even within this group one could assume a Croat was a Catholic but not that a Catholic was a Croat.

And whereas the Serbian Church had defined itself in opposition to the religion of the imperial power against which Serb identity was itself long primarily affirmed, religion could not define Croat consciousness in an empire whose German and Magyar hegemons largely shared the same faith. It is true that even before the war British officials recognised in the 'Rightist' Frankist-Starčevist movements a strand of Croatian opinion more hostile to Orthodox Serbs than to Catholic Hungarians.[59] But as we will see, the importance of this element in Croatian culture which did bind Catholicism into a Croat national identity was consistently understated in Britain.[60] It is therefore not surprising that for as long as Budapest seemed the primary opposition to Croatian aspiration, British observers did not much stress Catholicism as defining Croat identity, though the standard modern interpretation holds that already in 19th century Croatia 'religion and nationalism were in effect synonymous'.[61]

Nor was it simply that Catholicism was a factor of unity rather than division between rival Croat and Hungarian 'nations'. Identification of the Roman Church as a pillar of the Habsburg realm ensured that, while Orthodoxy became associated with the rise of 'nationality' in East-Central Europe, Catholicism seemed not merely neutral but associated with the anational or anti-national *ancien régime* against which the new nations defined themselves, helping to nurture the wartime view of religion as outmoded in an age of ethno-linguistic nationalism. Seton-Watson's memorandum on Austria-Hungary listed the Church as one of those key political factors 'which hold power not in theory and law but in real fact'.[62] It was as a potent force for reaction within the Monarchy that Catholicism was perceived in Britain. 'The Emperor and Court have no real national feeling', another report noted, 'but they are strongly clerical, and are inclined to settle national questions along Catholic lines'.[63]

We will look shortly at the ways in which, during the war, British observers reconciled Croatian Catholicism (and Serb Orthodoxy) with a new-found faith in a single Yugoslav nation. We should briefly look first, however, at how they analysed the Catholicism of the monarchy's little-noticed Slovene population. The analysis itself was somewhat in contrast to that of Croatian religious allegiance, but the implication of that analysis only reaffirms the sense that to pre-war Britons Catholicism seemed rather at odds with national consolidation than its catalyst.

Clerical influences were generally believed stronger in the Slovene territories than in Croatia, to the extent that religious identity among Slovenes was thought to precede any ethnic or 'national' identity based upon race or language. As a result, the Slovenes were regarded in Britain (when they were regarded at all) as loyal Habsburg subjects.[64] It may be true, as historians have pointed out, that political Catholicism among Slovenes – seen in Britain as an immemorial feature of Slovene life – had been a 'marked novelty' as recently as the 1880s.[65] It may also be true that the devotion to the Monarchy suggested by the early 20th century strength of the clericalist party (seemingly, like other Catholic parties, a 'pillar of Habsburg order') owed as much to political realism as to genuine popular emotion.[66] But the British perception that Slovenes were both strongly clerical and loyal to the Habsburg dynasty fortified their association of Catholicism with supranational dynasticism rather than with ethno-linguistic nationalism. To be an overtly Catholic South Slav seemed in Britain to be less a Slovene or a Croat than an Austrian – in the non-ethnic sense of a supporter of the dynasty. This contrasted with Orthodoxy's association with the national movement (in spite of it being, in the context of a 'Yugoslav' nation, rather divisive than unifying).

Islam

The Yugoslav region's significant Muslim populations impressed travellers and analysts with their flavour of oriental exoticism. They reminded British observers of the area's long association with the Ottoman Middle East (until 1878, in the case of Bosnia, 1912-13 in Macedonia).[67] While it had tolerated other faiths within its borders, the Ottoman had remained an overtly Islamic empire. As a result attitudes in Britain towards Turkish rule on the one hand, and towards Islam on the other, were interwoven and it is not easy to disentangle the threads. But it is important to understand the ways in which the legacies of Ottoman rule, and of Islam in general, were viewed in relation to these European Muslim populations.

The old assumption that ethnic allegiance in southeast Europe followed the contours of religious affiliation – that the Orthodox were all 'Greeks' and the Muslims 'Turks' – had given way to racial and linguistic classification. It was significantly slower to do so in the case of Muslim populations, however, than in the case of Orthodox peoples whose 'national' churches and mutual antipathies proclaimed a lack of unitary consciousness. As late as Gladstone's celebrated foray into the Balkans the British premier could still, as Edith Durham remarked, presume all the region's Muslims were 'Turks'.[68] While few later observers made quite the same mistake, the sense still thrived of the Islamic world as impervious to modern nationalism (a presumption in which Britons had an interest due to their dominion over a third of the world's Muslims). If religious identity in general seemed to count for more in Ottoman and ex-Ottoman lands than other, conflicting bonds of ethnicity, this seemed most significantly the case in regard to Islam. In 1898 the respected Balkanist William Miller thought that among Bosnian Muslims religious affinities with the Turks counted 'for far more than the community of blood'.[69]

An aspect of British perceptions that is striking, in this connection, concerns the social position of Bosnian Muslims. It was assumed, with reason, that one legacy of Ottoman rule in this religiously-divided and economically-stagnant region was an imbalance in the distribution of wealth, and particularly of land. Whereas Catholics and Orthodox constituted a substantial majority (the Orthodox the single largest group) most estates belonged to a Muslim aristocracy. Since 1878 Austrian administrators had felt obliged to adopt a conservative approach to land reform in return for this class's support in quelling peasant unrest.[70] And Britons were right also to note the social conservatism of this Muslim upper class which, despite its elite status, tended to be poorly educated by western standards. What was skewed, however, was the assumption that Bosnian Muslims in general were of this privileged class. Typical was Sir Charles Eliot's view of the province's population as consisting of 'Mohammedan Beys, being Serbians who adopted Islam to acquire or preserve a privileged position, and a Christian peasantry'.[71] Diplomats and others likewise treated the Muslims simply as a privileged conservative class, exploiting a Christian majority. The dominant feature of the situation in Bosnia, the Foreign Office Historical Department's post-war report noted, was the juxtaposition of a strong, conservative, land-holding Muslim aristocracy and 'an oppressed Christian peasantry'.

The reality, however, was that this Bosnian upper stratum was small, consisting, according to the 1910 census, of only 2% of the Muslim population. While it is true that Catholic and (especially) Orthodox Slavs made up the great majority of the class known as *kmets*, customarily if loosely rendered in English as 'serfs', of the 'free' peasants a large majority were Muslim.[72] The latter's standard of living 'closely approximated that of their Christian fellow peasants who were serfs'.[73]

This distorted view of the position of most Muslims in Bosnian society served to encourage the British stereotype of Muslims in general as unwilling or temperamentally unable to move with the modern world. British observers, particularly among middle-class, liberal and non-conformist circles, tended to regard Islam as inherently primitive, backward and monolithic. To a progressive thinker like Arnold Toynbee it seemed a 'simplified version of Christianity lagging half a millennium behind its prototype'. It was, he argued in a government research paper, 'still in the stage of Christianity in the Middle Ages, when it was the strongest bond of union between those who professed it'.[74]

Such pejorative assumptions about Islam in general led observers into facile verdicts of religious 'fanaticism' among Balkan Muslims, a tendency encouraged by the fact that Muslims had been slower than Bosnian Orthodox or Catholics to give up traditional forms of dress after 1878.[75] The picture of Bosnia as a centre of Islamic opinion 'in its most reactionary and fanatical form', as Seton-Watson put it, seems not to have been thought inconsistent with the common view of the South Slavs as lacking, in their racial make-up, any innate religiosity.[76] It certainly gelled with the belief in an Islamic consciousness unified by what Toynbee characterised as a pronounced hostility towards the culture and values of the European middle class. That any such hostility was fully reciprocated is indicated by his subsequent judgement that European opinion considered Turkish rule over Christians a 'curious anachronism' in the modern age, and even an 'unnatural domination'.[77] Commenting on this report in the Foreign Office, T.W. Arnold warmly concurred with Toynbee's view that the Muslim (or 'Oriental') was inherently incapable of modern administration. 'The Muhammedans should recognise', he averred, 'that the days of the political independence of Islam are at an end'.[78]

But as Maria Todorova has shown, British attitudes towards the Ottoman Muslims had never flowed entirely in one channel. A tendency

existed concurrently in aristocratic circles to view the Turkish ruling class
less as Muslims than as heirs to a proud imperial tradition, upholding a
code of honour and values much more appealing to the British elite than
the unruly pretensions of subject nationalities.[79] More importantly (for our
purposes), a growing tendency in the late 19th and early 20th centuries,
enhanced by the 1908 revolution of the 'Young Turks', perceived the label
'Turk' rather in an ethno-linguistic than a religious sense. The natural
corollary of this development was that the Empire's Muslims were no
longer automatically bracketed as 'Turks', in the sense of being identified
with the imperial hierarchy or sympathetic to its ambitions. Where Miller
had assumed, as we have seen, a loyalty among Bosnian Muslims towards
Constantinople, ten years later Sir Charles Eliot denied this. The Muslims
of Bosnia, he insisted, 'do not regret Turkey'. They embraced Islam 'out of
policy', and their ideas were 'not essentially different from those of other
Serbians'. Islam could not override those more profound, racial affinities
and antipathies which distinguished the modern (European) world. All
South Slavs shared an aversion to Ottoman rule, and to the general
'Asiatic' indifference to good government. 'It is in vain', he wrote, 'that
you offer the Asiatic liberty, security, and good government', and in this
there was 'a great gulf fixed between Europeans and Asiatics'.[80]

It is noticeable in this connection that the many writers who
criticised the legacy and present reality of Turkish government (and any
vein of aristocratic respect for an empire of increasingly obvious
decrepitude was certainly much diminished by the early 20th century) were
much less likely than their mid-19th century predecessors to implicate
Islam directly. The 'Muslim yoke' had invariably become the 'Turkish
yoke', the phrases no longer treated as synonymous. Increasingly unusual,
too, was the sort of direct Christian identification with 'our oppressed
brethren in the East' which had marked earlier British works.[81] Lloyd
George himself, in the post-war debate about Turkish possession of
'Constantinople', denounced what he considered 'something of the old
feeling of Christendom against the Crescent' in the anti-Turkish
movement in Britain, an attitude he considered unbecoming of an Empire
with a substantial Muslim population. While hostility to this Muslim
presence in Europe remained, particularly among Lloyd George's fellow
non-conformists, most of the British press and political world took the
side of the Prime Minister.[82]

How, then, did British observers interpret the conscious identity of
Bosnian Muslims *within* the complex of South Slav 'nationality'? We have
seen before that, despite the identification of Serbdom with Orthodoxy, it
was often assumed that Muslims were in a profound racial sense 'really'
Serbs. Influenced by the more audible claims of Serbian (as opposed to
Croatian) nationalism, Bosnia was accepted unquestioningly as being 'by
blood, by language and by historical connection [...] purely Serbian'.[83] 'The

traditions even of the Muslim Serbs of Bosnia-Hercegovina', A.H.E. Taylor noted, 'were purely Serb and told of the glories of the ancient Serb Empire'.[84] Nor were the terms 'Serb' and 'Serbian' being used broadly here to mean 'Yugoslav'. Even in the context of intra-Yugoslav identities writers made it clear that *racially* the Muslims (and sometimes the Catholics too) were Serbs. A War Office report on Yugoslav unification broke the population down by province into Serb, Croat and Slovene groups. In the case of Bosnia 'Muslim Serbs' were, as the label indicates, included unquestioningly in the first camp.[85]

But if it was generally agreed that Bosnian Muslims *were* Serbs, racially and linguistically, harder was to know how this confessional group perceived themselves. Unlike the Orthodox Serbs, and to a lesser extent the Catholic Croats, the Yugoslav Muslims had no international voice. Before the emergence of the JMO (the Yugoslav Muslim Organisation) in the first decade of the 20th century, they had no political organisation at all.[86] While some British observers considered (or assumed) that Muslim loyalties followed their alleged racial affinity with the Serbs of Serbia, most detected no clear allegiance to Serbs or Croats. Their strong religious faith – or 'fanaticism' – seemed rather to suggest a lack of 'national' identity. The Bosnian Muslims might tend towards the Croat side, Seton-Watson wrote, but they had really 'no strong national consciousness'.[87] Though 'purely Serb in origin and in language', Forbes agreed, 'neither the Orthodox Serbs nor the Roman Catholic Croatians have as yet been able to enlist their political sympathies'.[88] The paradoxical situation was that this element of the Yugoslav population was both clearly 'Serbo-Croat' and at the same time, in its conscious 'political' identity at least, neither 'Serb' nor 'Croat'. Indeed, the self-identification of prominent Bosnian Muslims as Croatian Muslim or Serb Muslim was understood by British observers, as it has been by subsequent historians, as pragmatic political manoeuvring and no more than a superficial indication of ethnic identity.[89]

One prominent theme of recent historical treatments was, however, distinctly lacking from British analysis. No credence was given to the notion that there existed, aside from 'Serb' and 'Croat' identities, a genuine 'Bosnian' consciousness in which Muslims in particular took refuge.[90] Though the term 'Bosnian' was often used by pre-war British writers, it was intended, as we have seen, merely to entail residence in Bosnia rather than an 'ethnic' identity. Any who presumed from such usage the existence of Bosnian 'nationality' were disabused. Moreover, as a result of Austrian attempts to foster just such a phenomenon as a counterweight to Serbian or Yugoslav nationalism, they were dismissed as the dupes of Habsburg imperialism.

Nationality theorists did not, as today, consider that 'ethnic' identity could be multi-layered – that an individual could feel genuinely English and British, Catalan and Spanish, Croat *and* Yugoslav.[91] It was recognised that a person's sense of belonging was complex and rooted in a variety of potential milieus (family, locality, class, religion, trade, gender, nationality), but it was generally accepted that in the modern world this last had become qualitatively different and had acquired an ultimate status. 'National' identity seemed unique in being grounded not only in subjective consciousness, or in transient contingencies, but in the objective realities of race and (its seeming relation) language. The modern view that such 'objectivity' is no less illusory – or 'constructed' – than other levels of identity was largely absent from theoretical works.

And yet, examining the case of the Yugoslav Muslims, we do find pragmatic assumptions which in some ways anticipate the trends of modern theory. It was assumed that they were Serbs by race, that they lacked a distinct language, state tradition or any other such qualification for 'national' identity. But there appears nevertheless, in British writing, a sense that this group must for practical purposes be considered distinct, for no other or better reason than that they thought of themselves as such. For the time being at least Muslims clearly did possess something of the shared identity and common aspirations which characterised the Orthodox Serb and Catholic Croat populations. Wartime reports, dealing only in *de facto* realities, found it natural to refer to a deputation from Bosnia as consisting of 'a Serb, a Croat and a Mahommedan'.[92] As awareness grew after the war that Bosnian Muslims were not simply a landlord *class* but were a socially diverse community, this pragmatic assumption increased of a 'Muslim' identity, distinct from 'Serb' and 'Croat', conveying an ethnic as well as confessional allegiance.

The Impact of the War

We have seen that pre-war British commentators were accustomed to attach significance to religious affiliation as a determinant of identity within the South Slav group. (Though Catholicism might not have defined a Croat in opposition to a Hungarian or a Slovene, it clearly did so in opposition to a Serb). It was not the case that only the travails of a unitary Yugoslavia after 1918 established the paradigm of an 'ancient' rivalry between Catholic Croat and Orthodox Serb. We have also touched, however, on the increasing emphasis given to race and language as the ultimate arbiters of nationality in the period immediately before and during the war, and the concomitant sense that religion was outmoded as a primary category of personal identification. Nowhere can the effects of this transition have been more evident than in the case of British attitudes towards the religious divisions among the South Slavs.

In general this was a shift of which British analysts were conscious, and which they justified by pointing to a change in attitudes in the

Yugoslav territories. Indigenous publicists, like the influential Serbian Archbishop Nikolai Velimirović (who wrote and lectured widely in Britain during the war), talked fervently of a trend towards national unity within the Orthodox and Catholic Churches, and of an end to the sectarian divide.[93] Chedo Mijatovich insisted that religion had 'ceased to be the discordant and disuniting element in the life of the [Yugoslav] nations'.[94] This message was embraced in Britain. Robert Seton-Watson eulogised, in a preface to one of Velimirović's books, the 'new spirit' awakening in the Serbian Church, and praised the 'great work' of the Orthodox and Catholic clergy in 'kindling the flame of national feeling among the Southern Slavs'.[95] In his own propagandistic writings he was equally unequivocal. 'The old dividing-line of religion' had, he insisted, been 'well-nigh effaced'. Only 'here and there' were the 'last lingering traces of religious fanaticism' to be found. While as recently as 1909 the 'ultra-Clerical Croat fanatics' had demonstrated violently in Zagreb, 'four years later some of these very men were volunteers in the Serbian army'.[96]

Another writer agreed that the Serb-Croat religious division 'no longer operates as it has done'. Orthodox and Catholic priests had 'enlisted under the same national banner' and 'suffered in the same cause as good Southern Slavs'. Under the strains of war a new-found unity had been forged, ensuring that difficulties resulting from differing religious traditions within a Yugoslav state would be 'less than would formerly have been the case'.[97] And many writers marked the generational nature of this transition. The war, it seemed, had heralded the ascendancy in the South Slav lands of a younger age-group who, reared in a sectarian world, would 'have none of such ideas'. 'The old bitter Catholic Croat anti-Serb feeling', observed Crawfurd Price, was now 'dead except among a few politicians and their followers of the older generation'.[98]

In government and civil service the view was largely the same. A conference report on South-East Europe admitted that the religious divide, once fundamental, was still 'not altogether to be disregarded', but concluded that the 'idea of racial unity' had now 'to a very large extent swamped it'. It noted the role of Roman Catholic clergy, especially among the Slovenes, as the 'foremost protagonists of Yugoslav union'.[99] A War Office report agreed with Count Burian that, over the Southern Slav question, the war had acted as 'a hot house for forcing plants'. Political conditions in Croatia had 'only been assimilated with those of the Slovenes and Serbo-Croats of Bosnia and Dalmatia by the gradual realisation that all Yugo-Slavs are threatened by Austro-German domination'.[100] Austrian Serbs, Croats and Slovenes, reports reaching Whitehall in the summer of 1918 observed, had 'never been so united before': 'From the Catholic Priest to the Progressist the only cry is "Away with Austria"'.[101] Indeed it was among the Slovenes, who had been considered least responsive to the call of their South Slavonic blood, that

British observers noted the most remarkable shift. A memorandum on the prospects of revolution in Austria argued that, while the Yugoslav movement had begun later in Slovenia, it had 'gained ground even more rapidly than in Croatia itself', with the result that the hitherto conservative and loyalist Slovene Catholic clergy now appeared 'completely infected with Serbophilism'.[102]

Among Croatian clerical circles, it was later admitted, the picture was a little more equivocal: the clergy had not in fact been foremost in the Yugoslav movement before or during the war. They were, Charles Oman noted in a memorandum on the 'past history and present aspirations' of the Yugoslavs, among those unwilling to accept the 'new orientation' in Croatia towards amalgamation with Serbia.[103] Similarly, Temperley counted the Croatian clergy among those 'undercurrents of opposition' to a united Yugoslav state at the end of the war. Though 'national', he noted, they took no leading part in the Yugoslav movement.[104] But as far as the general Croat population was concerned, a different line was taken. In his influential report on the Yugoslav problem of June 1918 Temperley argued that Croats were nationalists first and Catholics only second. By 'nationalists', crucially, he meant not Croat but *Yugoslav* nationalists: an identification, in other words, which eschewed religious community as the primary mark of ethnicity in Yugoslavia.[105] Pre-war reservations in Croatia about Yugoslav union were attributed rather to pragmatic concerns – the desire to retain advantages; doubts about the pan-Orthodox intentions of Tsarist Russia – than to any strong, distinct 'national' identity.

And Whitehall officials referred routinely to the 'ethnographic principle' which was assumed to bind all South Slavs in a single, indivisible unit.[106] ('Ethnological Notes' drawn up on Dalmatia did not distinguish Serbs and Croats, but only Serbo-Croats and Italians).[107] While, as we have seen, Temperley's important reports did allude to differences of creed, script and so on, they also tended to assume that the guarantees of religious freedom in the Corfu Agreement (the 'Yugoslav Magna Carta') should allay fears of confessional strife, and that the Croats were, as the Hungarian press reported, 'saturated in national [ie Yugoslav] ideas'.[108] In his highly-regarded history of Serbia he was bolder. 'The spiritual unity of the Yugo-Slav race', he argued, 'has already been achieved'.[109]

As observers became increasingly impressed by a spirit of religious reconciliation and unity, their portrayal of past history shifted. 'Religious antagonism' in Serb and Croat history, the Foreign Office Historical Department's report on the Yugoslav movement noted, appeared 'on the whole to have been conspicuous by its absence'; the tie of blood and language had 'counted for more than religious differences'.[110] Added emphasis was given to those currents within both communities which seemed, with hindsight, to presage contemporary ecumenism.

On the Croatian side, this meant over-emphasising the 'progressive' tendency in Croat Catholicism – the broad-minded tradition associated with Archbishop Strossmayer which stressed the racial-linguistic unity of Yugoslavs over religious differences. In fact, as Pedro Ramet has noted, late 19th and early 20th century Croatian politics were deeply divided between this 'Illyrianism' – the 'integrating, embracing strand in Croatian national ideology' – and an alternative, historicist project aiming to restore Croatia's medieval independence. Ultimately it was the latter tendency which 'became more closely identified with the Catholic church' and which, led by ex-seminarist Ante Starčević, 'was in essence a Catholic movement working for the political independence of a Catholic Croatia'. (So consonant were the aims of the Church's Croatian Social Party and the Starčevist Party of Right that the two organisations merged in 1910).[111] But British observers, particularly in the crucial late-war years, tended to treat Starčević rather as an isolated extremist than as the representative of an important and enduring element in Croatian politics.[112]

On the Serbian side it meant finding in a Church long portrayed in Britain as absorbed in the struggles of secular *Serb* nationalism, an opposite vein of broad-minded tolerance. One writer applauded the Catholic clergy's adoption of a 'national point of view' for which 'the Orthodox Church has always stood'.[113] Given that the word 'national' is used here to connote 'Yugoslav', this is a remarkable (and misguided) transition. Crawfurd Price thought it in keeping with Serbian democracy and political liberalism that religious tolerance had developed 'to a marked extent'.[114] Laffan found it remarkable that a people so recently emerged from Turkish misrule should be 'so tolerant and open-minded and so progressive'.[115] An article published shortly after the war hailed a 'spirit of toleration' in the Serbian Church which had 'considerably facilitated the recent union of the Croat and Slovene Catholics, and, indeed, the Bosnian Mussulmans, with their Serbian brethren of Orthodox faith'.[116]

Inseparable from the shift in British assumptions about South Slav religion, and the Yugoslav cause in general, was the change in attitudes towards the Austro-Hungarian regime wrought by the war, which it is worth pausing to consider.

As historians have pointed out, Austria had long been favourably regarded in Britain. On a continent in which Russia and Germany had seemed the most likely threats to British interests, this 'ramshackle empire' seemed rather a benign presence.[117] A strong Austrophile tradition pervades British writings relating to the Yugoslav lands during the pre-war decades. Even those, like Seton-Watson and Steed, who would come to advocate full freedom for the Empire's submerged nationalities, staunchly supported the Habsburg realm (while advocating its internal reform).

Particularly pertinent to our focus on South Slav religion is the portrayal by British observers of Austrian administration in Bosnia (a region which in its confessional diversity seemed a microcosm of the Yugoslav region). Pre-war travellers and analysts who described Austrian rule after 1878 were markedly well-disposed to a colonial mission which seemed vastly preferable to the Ottoman rule which it replaced. Typical in his enthusiasm, William Miller eulogised this 'model Balkan state'. The region was administered, he wrote, with an 'utmost thoroughness, which forms an immense contrast with the slovenly government of the Turks'. In a country fractured by religious confession, the Austrian regime had handled delicate questions 'with great tact'. Only its 'impartial rule' had kept 'the various confessions of the country at peace'.[118]

Other travellers painted a similar picture. With the arrival of competent European administration the province had been 'rescued from Turkish rule'.[119] 'We in England', another writer observed, 'can form no conception of the marvellous transformation effected here by Austria [...], nor even faintly realise the almost magical rapidity with which the recently barbaric provinces of Herzegovina and Bosnia have been converted into growing centres of commerce and civilisation'.[120] Only a tiny minority disputed this orthodoxy. 'All the English and most of the European press', one such writer complained, 'take its inspirations from Vienna, the correspondents in the Balkans being all Austrians or Austrophil':

> Our view of Austrian rule in Bosnia is therefore almost exclusively through what may be called the Kállaydoscope; we read nothing but eulogies of Herr von Kállay and the wonderful way in which he has developed a barbarous district into a civilised and prosperous province.[121]

While it is true that British diplomats had opposed the 1908 annexation of the province, in general such exceptions to the standard view of the nature of Austrian administration were few.[122] Murray Beaven was stating a simple fact when he observed in 1914 that the British consensus that Austria had effectively carried out the task entrusted to her in Bosnia was 'not now disputed': the region had been 'effectively 'pacified'', with 'western civilisation [...] substituted for oriental anarchy'.[123] Sir Harry Johnston warmly approved Austria's ambitions in the direction of Salonika and looked forward to her bright future as a Slav power.[124]

Even during the war there was never the animosity towards Austria that there was towards Germany. But there *was* a significant shift in opinion, which affected perceptions not only of Austria's wartime policy but also of her past administration of peoples now regarded as allies of the Entente. In the face of vocal claims of national unity by leading Serbs, Croats and Slovenes, it became accepted in Britain, quite contrary to previous assumptions, that the disunity long noticed among the South Slavs had been deliberately and cynically fostered by Vienna. And as the war dragged on, and Austria's internal cohesion increasingly seemed a target for Allied propaganda, British publicists enthused by ethno-linguistic nationalism found ideology and self-interest in alignment. The more the Yugoslavs were portrayed as a homogeneous national group, bound by a powerful racial kinship, the more it seemed fair to assume that in the past outside influences had perpetuated an unnatural disunity. Turks and Austrians were found guilty of a deliberate policy of 'divide and rule'.

From 1914, therefore, British accounts became much more reserved about Habsburg policies in Bosnia and other South Slav lands. The Magyars in particular, it was often noted, had inflamed religious differences as a matter of policy.[125] The strategy of the Hungarian Ban of Croatia, Count Károlyi Khuen-Héderváry, had been, Seton-Watson insisted, one of 'playing off Croat and Serb against each other, [...] inflaming the petty passions and religious bigotry of Catholic and Orthodox'.[126] But while Magyar rule in Croatia had been criticised by a minority of pre-war writers, a widespread sense now emerged that this direction had emanated from Vienna as much as from Budapest. 'To keep Catholic Croatians and Orthodox Serbians in antagonism with each other and with the Muslims', Herbert Gibbons argued, '[...] has been the Austro-Hungarian programme'; Vienna had used the Catholic Church to '[divide] the Orthodox Serbians in Bosnia from their Croatian brothers of the Catholic rite'.[127] The governments of Vienna and Budapest, Forbes agreed, had in their South Slav territories encouraged the 'rivalry and discord between Roman Catholic Croat and Orthodox Serb'. In Dalmatia and Serbia as well as Bosnia their legacy had been one of severe persecution of the Orthodox faith.[128] Marriott even implied that Austrian rule in Bosnia had largely *created* the bitter confessional division. It was bringing the Habsburgs 'into the heart of Balkan affairs', he argued, which had 'made a tremendous breach in the solidarity of the Yugo-Slav race'.[129]

It was natural for British commentators to connect the apparent wartime surge of Yugoslav sentiment with the weakening of Habsburg authority in South Slav territories (though such sentiment, as historians have noted, was not marked in Bosnia as it was, for instance, in Dalmatia or the Slovene lands).[130] Observers surmised that such feeling had existed all along, in suppressed form. The war had shown, F.S. Copeland observed, that the political division by ecclesiastical demarcation was the result of 'mere external influences'. It had only taken time, he wrote, with the teleological sense that infused so many accounts of nationality, for the deeper bonds of 'language, blood and temperament' to overcome the ties of foreign allegiance. With 'the relaxation of alien force', in the context of war, 'the various branches of the nation drew together again'.[131] Another writer alluded to previous favourable perceptions of Austrian rule, before undermining them with similar arguments:

> To the casual traveller in Bosnia-Hercegovina it often appears as if Austria-Hungary had accomplished a fine work of civilisation there. She has established good roads, good hotels, and many other things [...]. Anyone, however, who saw behind the scenes and really came into contact with the people of Bosnia-Hercegovina found a condition of seething discontent [...]. One of the results of the war has been union between the various subject nationalities of Austria-Hungary such as, thanks to Austrian *divide et impera* policy, never existed before [...].[132]

The Foreign Secretary, Arthur Balfour, expressed the same view in a speech to the Serbian (Yugo-Slav) National War Aims Committee, attended by numerous British luminaries in July 1918. Historically it was 'the Turk', he argued, 'that really prevented the union of the Yugo-Slav people'. And 'what the Turk began Austrian bureaucracy has contrived to complete'.[133] His implication was clear: Serbs, Croats and Slovenes belonged together by the laws of race and language, and would have been so long ago but for the machinations of neighbouring empires. Only a few sceptics, like Edith Durham, protested that it was divisions among the South Slavs that had left them open to repeated conquest in the first place.

Most British observers, indeed, went further and blamed the prior appreciation of Habsburg rule on deliberate misrepresentation. In expressing contempt for the 'barbarous, turbulent and unprogressive Serbs', Laffan observed, Western nations had been 'largely misled by the exaggerations and misrepresentations of the Austrian press'.[134] Events since 1912, Seton-Watson agreed, had exploded 'the false and superficial estimation of Serbia with which the news service of Vienna and Budapest had so skilfully inoculated our press'.[135] It was with the assistance of 'the organs of the Jewish press both within and without the Monarchy', A.H.E. Taylor argued, ('for the Jews have for occult reasons been constantly opposed to Serb expansion') that Austria-Hungary had 'filled Europe with tales of Serb disorders, of Serb corruption and barbarism, and thus strove to prepare the way for acquiescence in a further move forward on her part'.[136] Of course this was in part simply wartime propaganda. But it had a real impact on the way Yugoslav nationalism was perceived in Britain. Traditional patterns of denigration, based on assumptions of religious bigotry and aggressive nationalism, were portrayed as – and increasingly believed to be – the fruit of cynical Viennese misrepresentation.

It is not perhaps surprising, given intelligence reports of the growth in Yugoslav feeling, that British observers should have reached the conclusions they did. In the wake of the Pact of Corfu in July 1917, and events in Russia of that year (which calmed Catholic fears of a Russian-imposed pan-Orthodoxy), the evidence for a dramatic spread of Yugoslav feeling increased.[137] But we do not need to question all of this evidence, as few historians have sought to do, to wonder at the uncritical attitude in Britain towards a phenomenon which had apparently developed with such speed, and in the face of such obstacles.

Little allowance was made for the fact that many Yugoslav spokesmen hailed from Dalmatia, a province unusually advanced in terms of Yugoslav sentiment, rather than from the more conservative, Catholic Croatia.[138] Evidence of such sentiment was enthusiastically greeted by British officials with little consideration of the differences of local circumstance which rendered it greatly more potent, and socially dispersed, in Dalmatia and the Slovene lands than in Hungarian Croatia-Slavonia.[139] Perhaps more importantly, there was a complete lack of appreciation during the war for the fact that Yugoslav feeling, and the easing of inter-confessional tension in particular, had developed in highly unusual circumstances, and might prove impermanent once peace was restored. A few well-informed commentators like Seton-Watson did express anxiety, in their non-populist writings at least, about a Serbian hegemonic strain personified by Pašić. But even these cautionary voices portrayed this as the minority voice of a fading generation, rather than a widespread tendency among educated Yugoslavs.[140]

It is interesting to contrast this complacency in Britain towards Yugoslav 'nationality' with attitudes towards certain comparable situations. Perhaps the most obvious parallel for British observers was the fraught Irish question – a parallel so superficially close (a territory united by race and language but sharply divided by religious identity) that it is surprising how rarely it was invoked by students of the Yugoslav question during the crucial late-war period. Here was a case, as Lloyd George himself stated in July 1919, in which language and race had failed to forge an integrated nationality: 'in religion, in temperament, in tradition [...], in everything that constitutes the fundamental essentials of a nation, unfortunately they differ'.[141] In December 1918 Bonar Law was asked in Parliament whether a definition of the term 'nation' had been reached, and, if so, whether it was to be taken 'that the Yugo-Slavs are a nation and the Irish and Scottish peoples are not a nation'. Since the answer to the first part was in the negative, came the reply, 'the latter parts do not, therefore, arise'.[142]

And while it is true that Protestant and Catholic Irish had not of late shown that desire to live in a unified state apparently manifest among Yugoslavs, nevertheless the unreliability of such impressions of mass opinion during wartime was scarcely allowed for. Another comparison is afforded by the following 1918 verdict on the Scandinavian question:

There can be no doubt that it is the stress of circumstances due to belligerent pressure which has led to the strong development of the Scandinavian co-operative movement. When the war is over it is more than likely that the old jealousies and antipathies will come to the fore and seriously handicap, if not frustrate, the efforts of those Scandinavians who believe that the closest cooperation in every field is essential to the future welfare of the Northern countries.[143]

One need not insist on a perfect parallel between the two situations to consider pertinent the contrast between this analysis and the British reading of the South Slav situation.

4

Tradition: British Attitudes to the Secular History, Tradition and Mythology of the South Slavs

For all the significance attributed to race and language as related determinants of nationality, clearly they were not decisive in all cases. The English language had not excluded a sense of American nationality, and 'race' could not be considered cohesive in such a diverse immigrant community. In Alsace a population apparently Germanic in race and language considered themselves French. Modern Columbians or Peruvians did not feel themselves Spanish; nor the Brazilians Portuguese. (And South America, like the North, was racially mixed).

Sometimes organised religion could explain divergent national identities within a language group: the two 'nations' of Ireland, or the Belgians and Dutch. And Croats and Serbs, of course, seemed a text-book instance of a race divided by religious allegiance. But in the South American states, Catholic like their former colonists, or the US, with its diverse Christian traditions, religion was no more a marker of nationality than language. Separate identities were explained with reference to broader historical tradition, borne of long cohabitation in a well-defined territory.

In fact it was clear to theorists that no national consciousness could exist without such accumulated tradition. 'A nation', wrote Sidney Herbert, 'must have a history'.[1] And of course only artificially did theorists separate religion or language from this secular tradition. All combined to form what another writer called that 'common civilisation which gives [men] a sense of unity [...] quite apart from the bond of the state'.[2] (In fact modern writers have argued that the symbols and rituals of national mythology assume the overtones and emotional resonance of worship, becoming in effect a 'civil religion').[3]

We have seen that race and language were attributed an objective solidity since superseded by the idea of the nation as an 'imagined community'.[4] The dominant metaphor was not, as now, the 'construction' of history in the service of national cohesion, but rather a nation's 'awakening' to its latent inheritance.[5] But despite lacking a sophisticated theory of constructed identities, many British theorists – more inclined than Americans to raise the voluntary element of 'will' over purely 'objective' criteria – rhapsodised the formative power of history and tradition. Invoking the revered authority of Mazzini, Mill and Renan, they emphasised origin traditions, past glories and sufferings, and the general accumulation of habit and experience: the 'possession in common of a rich legacy of memories'.[6] This 'voice of the anterior humanity' (Mazzini's phrase) remained, for one British disciple, 'the strongest of all forces that mould men into nations'.[7] Another, Ramsay Muir, concurred, in language whose romantic exuberance was typical (particularly during the war):

> Historical achievements, agonies heroically endured, these are the sublime food by which the spirit of nationhood is nourished. From these are born the sacred and memorable traditions that make the soul of nations [...].[8]

Of course none could deny the importance of a nation's history and culture any more than that of its language. But for that influential school which stressed the formative role of race, and saw in language the expression of this genetic make-up, historical tradition was treated similarly. Political institutions, literary culture, religious persuasion, military aptitude: all flowed ineluctably from the innate *racial* character. Traditions, as a later writer observed, seemed to express the true soul of a people.[9] The 'persisting and pervasive individuality of race', wrote E.G. Murphy, 'is the ground and basis of [a man's] essential culture'.[10]

This was an argument as hard to disprove as to prove. While British theorists reacted against the premise of this racialist argument – the notion of a racial purity which could meaningfully be measured or analysed – unthinking assumptions based upon it remained widespread.[11] Even for those who were sceptical of racial analysis, belief in a 'national character' produced by environment and history remained strong. In a circular argument, national tradition was seen as both the passive expression of this character and as its decisive formative influence.[12]

Within the broad category of national tradition, theorists highlighted elements of recurrent importance. One such was the sense of homeland borne of long occupation of a defined space (or at least the *idea* of such a territory).[13] Another was the sustained existence of institutions regarded (however anachronistically) as national: a tradition of state administration, whether ongoing or the object of revivalist aspiration. Of course Britain herself showed that unified administration need not forge a unified nationality. But political sovereignty, aligned with the ethno-linguistic raw materials, could foster national identity among a wider population – by education, improved communications, external conflict, and so on. The memory, furthermore, of an historical state associated with a particular nationality was a powerful spur to modern national ideology which could romanticise that past, mourn its demise and invoke its resurrection.

As with belief in racial unity, some noted that the veracity of traditions mattered less than their mythic potency: their enshrinement in a nation's legends, songs and literature, and in the rituals and paraphernalia (flags, anthems and other iconography) of its 'civil religion'.[14] A constructed past, however illusory, could legitimate a state's existence, or fuel a yearning for the territory and prestige of a former age. The 'soul and conscience of a nation', wrote Zimmern, lay not in space and population but in 'a sense of great things experienced in the past, and greater lying ahead in the future'.[15]

All of which is particularly pertinent in the case of the South Slavs because of their obvious *lack* of shared tradition. 'History', R.G.D. Laffan later admitted, 'gave no hint of Yugoslav nationality'.[16] This was illustrated at the moment of unification by the varieties of administration and infrastructure requiring amalgamation: according to estimates, three banking systems, four currencies, five incompatible railway networks, six customs areas and seven governmental regions (each with distinct laws, taxation and forms of representation).[17] Most strikingly, for over half a millennium the Yugoslav region had been divided between the two great empires of south-east Europe, Habsburg and Ottoman, with their divergent political and cultural traditions – and both in themselves diverse, as was evident within their respective South Slav territories.

A British wartime memorandum talked of settling boundaries by 'historically established lines of allegiance and nationality' as if this was a single criterion.[18] No contradiction, seemingly, was expected between nationality as defined by recorded history and ethno-linguistic evidence. The Paris Conference would find, of course, that such correspondence could not be assumed. And historians have come to see the South Slavs as a case in point: their 'distinctly separate histories' meaning the very term 'Yugoslav' was a 'subterfuge'.[19] 'In 1918', accepted wisdom runs, 'the Yugoslav peoples shared no common political philosophy and experience out of which they could construct a new political community'.[20]

And yet (as we have seen) a strong and widespread sense developed in Britain, especially during the latter half of the war, that 'Yugoslavia' was being forged by an irresistible historical necessity.[21] To understand this teleological view, we must look at how the various South Slav histories and cultures were represented in Britain in the early 20th century. How did it affect belief in a Yugoslav 'nationality' in 1918 that the sub-groups owned such divergent histories? In what ways did the cultural factors which united them seem to render the prospective state a viable proposition? And how far was British understanding of the multifarious strands of Yugoslav history and culture either reliably informed or unduly influenced by events shaping the region in the present?

It is perhaps not surprising to find a picture emerge similar to that relating to religious differences: a shift in emphasis during the war from cultural diversity to elements of a shared heritage; a change, too, in the interpretation of South Slav history – answering the needs of wartime propaganda but pervading also the work of influential British scholars.

A National Territory: the Geography of the South Slav lands

For many British theorists geography had played a crucial role in shaping patterns of national allegiance. Not only was a sense of homeland central to national consciousness, but this homeland's features had shaped the nation's history and thus moulded its consciousness in the first place. Cases were cited in which geography had caused the bifurcation of closely-related peoples: the mountains dividing Portugal and Spain or the impenetrable forest between Finland and Russia; and conversely, in which it had promoted, or facilitated, the sympathy underpinning nationality.[22]

It was widely argued furthermore, following Montesquieu, that environment more profoundly shaped a nation's character and culture. On such factors as climate and rainfall, Sidney Herbert noted, depend a people's 'forms of government, their family life, their intellectual culture, even their religion and morality'; it was obvious 'how powerful an influence making for consciousness of kind is common submission to a particular geographical environment'.[23] Even within a broadly unified region, local environments created differences of outlook and identity. The Balkans seemed a case in point: there, J.A.R. Marriott observed, 'nature points imperiously to a congeries of relatively small states'.[24]

In the narrower South Slav region British writers presented a similar picture, with geography accounting for the lack of shared political history. Lines of penetration, noted Marion Newbigin, led through the region rather than to its separate parts, with few cross-connections.[25] The difficult nature of the country, Neville Forbes argued, had militated against fusion. Mountains had had an 'immense influence' on the region's history, as had river courses which failed to connect the Adriatic coast with its interior. The effect of geography on early Serb and Croat history was, he observed, 'to emphasise the ethnographical difference between the two peoples, which originally was infinitesimal'.[26] The character of the country, A.H.E. Taylor agreed, 'mountainous and split up into a number of comparatively small valleys, and mountain-surrounded basins' prohibited national unity and 'fostered a sturdy love of independence and a vigorous local life'.[27] Indeed the historical independence of Yugoslav regions was often attributed to geography: that of Montenegro, for instance, its mountains a haven against the Turks; or of Dalmatia, its mountain backdrop and Mediterranean climate distancing it politically and culturally from its hinterland, a watershed sending the rivers of Bosnia north and east, towards the Danube and the Black Sea.[28]

This divisive impact of topography was much stressed by wartime advocates of unification, who found in it a neutral explanation for the historical absence of that political unity they now espoused: one which circumvented the argument that South Slavs, or Slavs in general, were innately fissiparous and incapable of large-scale organisation.[29] Geography, Robert Seton-Watson suggested, had 'acted on [Serbs and Croats] as a centrifugal force and shaped their fate into varying channels'.[30]

Too great an emphasis on this theme, however, risked undermining their case, a problem confronted in three ways. The first was to stress that the Yugoslav lands comprised a single, contiguous mass: 'a solid block of [...] territory', a 'compact geographical [...] unit' (which, though true, was no more proof of unity than in the case of Spain and Portugal).[31] The second, even less persuasive, was simple contradiction. Having cited geography as a centrifugal force in the South Slav lands, Seton-Watson wrote elsewhere that these lands formed a 'natural geographical unit', split into 'purely artificial fragments'.[32] Leon Dominian argued both that geographical diversity had hampered national unity, and that geography, like ethnography, pointed 'irrefutably to Yugoslav national unity'.[33] In such cases geographical arguments seem rather to have served a preconceived position than to have informed it.

Thirdly, and most plausibly, it was argued that technological progress had brought down the barriers of the past: that in the South Slav region geography had lost its formative power. Before man could tunnel through mountains, dry up marshes and render rivers navigable, Harold Temperley observed, 'the unity of the Yugo-Slav race was an impracticable dream'. The map showed, he argued, that 'the geographical unity of these lands has only become possible within recent years'.[34] Only in the last thirty years, Neville Forbes concurred, with improved communications and education, had all Serbs 'become fully conscious of their essential identity and racial unity'.[35] This claim applied more convincingly, however, to the potential for the future than to the meagre existing infrastructure.[36]

While, then, geography was often cited to explain the Yugoslavs' divided history, it rarely seemed an obstacle in itself to enthusiasts for the unification project. Insofar as it had fostered past political divisions, however, it had clearly encouraged the development of distinct historical and cultural identities existing within the Yugoslav region. It is these we must now consider.

In his *History of Serbia* Temperley admitted that, despite talk of a common future, to write a unified history of the South Slavs would be 'like threading a labyrinth'. The only course, he suggested, was to focus on one sub-group and to treat other sub-groups as they entered this frame. Significantly, he chose Serbia and Montenegro, judging this 'the most important' element in the South Slav story. 'These lands', he argued, 'are the core of that rugged stock which has preserved or achieved freedom, [...] a hope and a beacon to the Slavs enslaved under other rulers or imprisoned in other lands'.[37] Serbs of Serbia and Montenegro, he implied, had forged their own *Slavic* history, more relevant to Yugoslavia than that of kindred peoples obliged to live under foreign rule.

It seems obvious now that to consider the Habsburg Yugoslavs only as they impacted upon Serbian history, as lost sheep rejoining the national fold, is no adequate methodology for treating the South Slavs as a whole. We need to consider separately British attitudes towards the history and culture of each of the significant sub-groups, before assessing their impact on the broader picture of Yugoslav nationality in Britain at the time of unification. Given that Temperley's focus was predominant in Britain, however, we can turn first to the history of the Serbs.

'Guardian of the Gate': Serbian history and culture in British eyes

The Medieval Serbian State

Theorists have often emphasised the importance to a strong national identity of myths of a 'golden age': a period of perceived greatness for a state regarded (however anachronistically) as *national* in the modern ethno-linguistic sense. For the Serbs this halcyon epoch began with Stefan Nemanja, whose state emerged in the late 12th century from within the Byzantine Empire, and reached its apogee under his descendant Dušan seventy years later. 'Tsar Dušan' exploited a Byzantine civil war to conquer widely to the south and east, and at Skopje in 1346 was crowned 'Emperor of the Serbs and Greeks'.[38] The state's collapse after Dušan's death in 1355, followed by the destruction of Serbian independence during the century after the battle of Kosovo in 1389, rendered more poignant in retrospect the short-lived glories of this great Serbian Empire, ensuring its veneration by subsequent nationalist mythology.

Early 20th century British writers were struck by the immediacy for the Serbs of what seemed a distant medieval past. One of 'their most remarkable characteristics' seemed 'the reality of even the most ancient Serbian history to the minds of the people'.[39] 'Every true Serb', the *Encyclopaedia Britannica* noted, 'lives as much in the past as in the present', memories of past greatness fuelling the desire 'for a reunion of the whole race, in another Serbian Empire, like that overthrown by the Turks in 1389'.[40] Such 'grand ideas', William Miller observed, 'every Serb imbibes with his mother's milk and cherishes dearly'.[41] The 'glorious epoch' of Dušan was 'more than a historical memory: it is a political programme'; his conquests were 'the title-deeds of their race to lands that had long since ceased to be theirs [...]'.[42]

This obsession with a bygone epoch in the service of modern nationalism seemed to many in Britain a peculiarly (and pejoratively) 'Balkan' characteristic, and a source of the region's notorious instability. (Little attention was given, as we have seen, to the recent origins of rivalries which were represented as age-old and irremediable). 'There is no quarter of the world', A.H.E. Taylor suggested, 'where contending parties hark back to "rights" derived from so long distant a past, which not infrequently represent a possession quite ephemeral in character'.[43]

In pre-war Britain there was little sympathy for this fixation with medieval greatness. Miller was contemptuous of Belgrade's 'chauvinist politicians' captivated by the 'barren and impracticable glories of the great Serbian idea'.[44] And attitudes towards the culture and politics of this 'brief-lived empire' were condescending if not overtly negative. H.N. Brailsford was dismissive: the Empire's literary culture, he argued, was purely imitative, amounting largely to translations from Greek ecclesiastics, while its architecture was either derivative of Byzantium or built by imported Italian artists. 'Their civilisation', he concluded, 'was second-hand'.[45] As for Dušan himself, the great king-emperor of Serbian history was commonly referred to in Britain as 'the strangler' (an incorrect derivation of his name from the Serbian verb 'to smother').[46]

As we have seen, however, Serbia's image in Britain improved markedly during the war in response to her spirited resistance, and views of Serbian history and culture shifted accordingly. What had seemed a backward fixation with ancient history looked instead like an independent people's defence of national traditions against overwhelming odds. The Austrian assault on Serbia evoked parallels with the Ottoman advance five centuries previously. Dušan's state, like King Peter's, became a haven of democracy and egalitarianism confronting the might of a militaristic autocracy. Modern Serb history, Temperley argued, was unintelligible without reference to her 'splendid and tragic past': her laws and institutions showing great promise, her culture perhaps too freedom-loving and democratic for her own good.[47] Medieval Serbs, wrote Taylor, were no savages or copyists, and Dušan himself was no semi-barbarous monarch, his famous legal code superior even to western equivalents:

> The general position of the mass of the people was certainly superior to that occupied by the similar classes in central and

> western Europe [...]. There was no feudal oppression, nor
> feudal justice, or rather injustice [...] and the French peasant of
> the eighteenth century would probably have very willingly
> changed places with his Serb brother of the fourteenth.[48]

Dušan's Serbia, W.E.D. Allen agreed, was as advanced as the France of St.
Louis.[49] Dušan himself was now hailed as an enlightened lawgiver and
statesman.[50] The rise and prosperity of medieval Serbia, F.S. Copeland
proclaimed, was 'the fairest page of Southern Slav history'. The Serbs,
R.G.D. Laffan recalled, 'were a great people six hundred years ago' and
deserved again to 'take their place among the mighty nations of the
earth'.[51] 'Dušan's empire', hymned another, 'may yet be built up again and
unite all the Southern Slavs [...] under one sceptre'.[52]

What is surprising is that, for all the obvious imperatives of wartime
propaganda, British observers widely accepted the Serb picture of Dušan's
state as *national* in the modern sense. Stretching southeast of modern
Serbia and incorporating regions of Bulgaria, Macedonia, Greece and
Albania, it certainly had not united all the Southern Slavs. As Dušan's
adopted title made clear, he intended neither that it should do so, nor that
it should exclude ethnic varieties. Rather, in his deliberate use of Byzantine
ritual he sought to maintain the imperial tradition.[53] It was anachronistic,
therefore, for Neville Forbes to regret that Dušan's boundaries were 'from
the point of view of nationality [...] far from ideal'.[54] But few pointed out
that this was an imperial not a national state, or indeed that its duration
was short-lived even by the unsettled standards of the medieval Balkans.[55]

The Battle of Kosovo

Similar tendencies emerge in British presentation of the seminal event of
Serbian mythology, the 1389 battle on Kosovo Polje – the Field of
Blackbirds – at which the Serbian Prince Lazar Hrebeljanović fell. We
have noted the role of myths as bonding agents of modern nationality,
their potency unaffected (or enhanced) by the historical distortions
involved. If 'golden age' myths were often cited, and clearly applied to the
Serbian case, more strongly emphasised were those relating to great
national suffering or disaster. (They reinforced each other, of course: the
antediluvian years acquiring a roseate glow in the light of subsequent
misfortune). The memory of suffering and martyrdom, Bernard Joseph
noted, proved often more poignant than that of great achievement.[56]

And Serbia, of course, was much cited as a nation reinforced by
memories of defeat and adversity. Presaging her similar predicament
during World War I, Serbian accounts of Kosovo and the subsequent
Turkish occupation were accepted uncritically in Britain. A view was

willingly propagated of the battle as a climactic confrontation between the Ottoman Empire and an independent Serb race, causing the suppression of a great Serbian state and the subjection of its people to centuries of arid tyranny; a confrontation, moreover, not only between Serb and Turk but also (a century after the final crusade) between Christendom and the 'infidel': the final attempt to exclude Islam from the Balkans.

Thus, while Temperley rightly noted that Serbs had fought in the Sultan's army as well as Lazar's, helping to deal 'the final blow to the Serbian Empire', most in Britain eschewed such nitpicking in favour of the manichaean nationalist vision.[57] At Kosovo, wrote Forbes, 'Serbian armies from all the Serb lands [...] joined together in defence of their country for the last time'.[58] The Serbs, then as later, had stood bravely as 'guardians of the gate' between Constantinople and the Christian West.[59] In the eyes of the South Slavs, claimed Nikolai Velimirović (the Serbian bishop revered by Seton-Watson and others), Orthodoxy and Catholicism were always fellow Christian confessions, united against Islam.[60]

But as historians have noted, to present this medieval battle as a struggle between Serb and Turk, or a confessional clash between Christian and Muslim, was wholly anachronistic. Such accounts conceived the Serbs in a way in which they could not have understood themselves, and skewed the sociology of a period in which such confrontations occurred between 'alliances of feudal aristocrats of no clear ethnic or religious loyalty' employing mixed contingents of mercenaries and vassals.[61] Claims for the Serbs as defenders of Christendom were sheer romanticism (as later alliances with Turks against Hungarians made clear).[62]

Equally accepted was the Serbian view of the battle as a cataclysmic defeat, ending at a stroke a period of political and cultural greatness. Kosovo was 'the great disaster'.[63] It wrought 'the utter destruction of [Serbian] national existence'.[64] In 1916, with Serbia again conquered, publicists seized upon Kosovo Day as a symbol of resilience in defeat and of the irrepressible national 'soul' which would rise again.[65] The desperate Serbian retreat through Albania in the winter of 1915-16 chimed with the legends' theme of honourable death (the 'heavenly kingdom') preferred to earthly slavery.[66] Such myths of suffering endured and final redemption appealed to Christian writers, by their obvious parallels with Christian doctrine. G.K. Chesterton hailed a nation with 'that particular spirit which remembers a defeat rather than a victory' and insisted that 'Kosovo of the Serbians towers in history as the most tragic of such instances of memory':

It was under the sign by which Constantine conquered that Lazar fell in a failure that has been as fruitful as a martyrdom [...]. There is but one religion which can only decorate even its triumphs with an emblem of defeat. There is only one army which carries the image of its own captain, not enthroned or riding, but captured and impaled.[67]

Commemoration of Kosovo Day 1916 fired fresh enthusiasm for Serbia in Britain, France and America.[68] In Britain a rush of publications, by Serbian and British authors, recorded Kosovo traditions and songs. The historical reality – that the battle was one of a series (and not the most important) by which the Ottomans conquered the Balkans, that it was in the short term not a decisive defeat, and that Dušan's Serbian Empire had disintegrated three decades earlier – rarely intruded.[69]

Romanticism had entrenched the idea that in a nation's folk literature and music lay its 'soul'. Karadžić's publication of Serb popular epics had impressed Europe's *literati*, who vaguely imagined the Slav to be as innately poetical as he was politically incapable. While all the races of European Turkey liked ballads, Sir Charles Eliot noted, only the Serbs had elevated them into a national epic: 'the emotional and poetic, if somewhat undisciplined, character of the Slav finds adequate expression in the less formal styles of composition'.[70] And during the war this restrained enthusiasm swelled, seizing even otherwise judicious authors. 'So long as the songs of Kosovo are sung', Temperley hymned, 'and a Serbian exists in any land to sing them, so long there will always be a Serbia'.[71] (Bizarrely, one writer even suggested Serbia's borders could be defined by the spread of the epic ballad).[72] If the Orthodox Church had helped preserve national bonds, it was these songs – the 'National Muse' – which had 'kept alive the spirit of nationality during those centuries of living death under the Crescent'.[73] For centuries after the defeat at Kosovo, the *Balkan Review* enthused, while Serbia groaned under the heel of Turkish tyranny, 'only these heroic songs kept alive the soul of the country whose child was that Tsar Lazar who chose a heavenly rather than an earthly kingdom'.[74]

One significant side-effect of this romanticisation of Serb history was that British writers were happy, as a rule, to consider the Kosovo region a Serbian heartland, though it had been reclaimed by Serbia as recently as 1912 and was populated largely by Albanians.[75] Since Kosovo was accepted as Serbian sacred ground – one of the great 'shrines of nationality' – it was assumed to be rightfully Serbian.[76] For Arnold Toynbee it was 'Serbian irredenta'; for L.F. Waring it lay 'in the heart of Serbia'; and for H.N. Brailsford it had been 'real Serbian country'. Though Brailsford was surprised to discover a Muslim majority in the area, he attributed this emotively to 'emigration, massacre and forced conversion'. Serbian soil, he implied, had been unjustly encroached upon:

Year by year the Albanian hillmen encroach upon the plain, and year by year the Serbian peasants disappear before them.

Hunger, want, and disease are the natural accompaniments of this daily oppression.[77]

The Ottoman Occupation

Russian expansion made 19th century British policy firmly Turcophile and Slavophobe. The assumption that all the South Slavs were inferior and semi-barbarous was, as Maria Todorova has argued, 'a stumbling block for any solution of the problem of Turkey and her European provinces'. British upper classes more easily identified with Muslim governors than with their Christian subjects.[78] By World War I, however, the controversies over Turkish rule in Bulgaria, along with the diplomatic revolution of the alliance with Russia, had wrought a dramatic reversal. While British sympathy for Constantinople returned briefly with the Young Turks in 1908, and while Balkan politicians and writers continued to detect ingrained Turcophilia as it suited them, such an attitude is hard to find in early 20th century British writing on Ottoman rule in Europe.[79]

Western scholars, Bernard Lewis has noted, have tended to be 'influenced by the national historiographical legends of the liberated former subject peoples of the [Ottoman] Empire', to generalise 'the admitted failings of Ottoman government in its last phases into an indictment of Ottoman civilisation as a whole', and so to ascribe the shortcomings of the successor states to imperial misrule.[80] Nowhere is this analysis more clearly true than in the case of British attitudes to Serbian history. As sympathy for the Serbs burgeoned during the war, the Ottoman period was characterised as one of oppression and stagnation: 'dreary centuries'; 'hideous tyranny'; 'five hundred years of misery, bloodshed and decay'. Europe as a whole must atone, urged J. Holland Rose, for the 'immeasurable wrongs committed since the Ottoman hordes overwhelmed Serbia at Kosovo in 1389'. Overrun by 'Mohammedan hordes', wrote Laffan, the Serbs sank for four hundred years into a deep sleep: 'the gross darkness of Turkish rule covered the land'; the Turk had been 'a parasite living on the industry of Slav or Greek peasants'.[81] This latter image was a recurring one. The root of Balkan instability, Marriott argued, was 'the presence, embedded in the living flesh of Europe, of an alien substance [...] the Ottoman Turk'. Though dominion in Europe rarely aligned with ethnicity during the Ottoman period, 'the Turk' was portrayed as an intruder in a manner quite distinct from, say, Austrian rule in Poland or Ukraine, or Dušan's rule over his Balkan Empire (which, for all its Byzantine ritualism, had depended ultimately on conquest).[82] W.E.D. Allen's account was typical:

> For five hundred years an army of occupation has held South-Eastern Europe [...]. A few years, even a few months, of enemy occupation has a disastrous effect. Yet for five hundred years the South-East of Europe has suffered this. When the 'Turkish Night' overshadowed the Balkan lands, all trade, all art, all literature, all education, all social progress ceased.[83]

And it was this allegedly obliterative effect of the Ottoman occupation which explained and justified, for many British observers, the Serb obsession with medieval history. 'Under the Turk', noted one writer, 'there was no history'; Kosovo, therefore, 'does not seem to the Serbs as though it were a distant day'.[84] Serbs and other Balkan races, Miller agreed, had 'stepped straight out of the middle ages, after the long night of Turkish rule, into the full blaze of modern civilisation'.[85]

Only rarely was this simplistic picture moderated by the sense that Ottoman rule had once represented 'not only military might, but also wealth, status and civility'.[86] Temperley was one of very few to question the Serb nationalist caricature. Until at least the late 16th century, he suggested, Turkish rule seemed less oppressive than that of a Latin conqueror might have been; the lot of Serbian peasants under Hungarian rule was probably improved by Turkish conquest in 1526. 'As a race', he argued, the Ottomans had been 'superior in morality to those whom they conquered', Sultans and peasants alike 'men of simple faith, earnest ideals, and heroic bravery'.[87] Even he, however, made concessions to the stereotype, bemoaning 'the terrible effect which Kosovo produced on the Serbs', and stating baldly, in contradiction to his subsequent analysis, that the Ottomans 'were alien barbarians, with a lesser civilisation'.[88]

Independent Serbia 1812-1914

Leopold von Ranke wrote in his history of Serbia that the character of Kara Djordje, leader of the first Serbian revolt against Ottoman rule, recalled the heroes of the Serbian national songs.[89] But British observers were unimpressed by the parallel, not inspired by modern Serbia's early independence as they were by the medieval legends: 'so remote', Forbes remarked, 'that it cannot thrill us'.[90] (Equally, perhaps, not remote enough to permit the romanticisation embraced in the case of the Kosovo myths). Certainly the Serb cause never provoked in Britain the emotional response that the Greek struggle famously did.[91]

In fact little in 19th century Serbian history enthused pre-war Britons, who portrayed the independent Serbs as a typically turbulent 'Balkan' people. While increased contempt for Turkish rule did elicit sympathy for their difficult history, long confinement in an oppressive and stultified culture seemed to have moulded their own society and government. They were not to blame, but they had 'been brought up in a bad school'.[92] National consciousness, one writer observed, constituted 'the only basis of European culture' in the Balkans, centuries of subjection to 'Asiatic Byzantinism' having stunted the ethical and economic elements of civilisation.[93] Serbia had seemed 'the most volcanic of the Balkan lands', 'the least scrupulous and the least civilised' of the 1913 Balkan allies, 'not exactly a credit to civilisation'.[94] 'One cannot say', Brailsford observed, 'that her political extinction would be a serious loss to Europe'.[95] Only a 'benevolent autocracy', Miller thought, was suited 'to an Oriental people, lately emancipated from centuries of Turkish misrule'.[96]

The same pejorative assumptions dominate Robert Seton-Watson's pre-war writing. He cautioned strongly against the pan-Serb solution advocated by 'the Chauvinists of the Serbian Kingdom'. No one who had visited Belgrade and Zagreb, he suggested, could suppose such a course attractive to Croats or educated Serbs in Austria-Hungary: 'the corruption of public life in Serbia, the stagnation caused by embittered party factions [...] and the interests of European peace combine to render such a solution highly undesirable'. The pan-Serb idea would mean 'the triumph of Eastern over Western culture, and would be a fatal blow to progress and modern development throughout the Balkans'.[97]

These aspersions now seem a little undeserved. Though portrayed as backward in comparison with the Habsburg lands, Serbia possessed a more democratic parliamentary system than Dalmatia or Croatia-Slavonia, where the franchise remained highly restricted.[98] Since the early 1880s Serbia could claim a period of genuine parliamentary politics, with established representative institutions, and parties defined by socio-economic ideology rather than (as in Croatia or Slovenia) a nationalistic stance.[99] The constitution of 1888-9 had expanded the power of the Skupština, abolished appointed members, assured secret ballots and broadened civic freedoms.[100]

While pre-war British works often alluded to Serbian 'democracy', and to the egalitarian social structure resulting from Ottoman displacement of the indigenous ruling class, one must be sensitive to the tone of these remarks. It is easy now to miss the semantic ambivalence in terms such as 'democratic' and 'egalitarian' at a time before Britain had adopted a universal franchise, and when most Britons accepted without question the role of class differentiation in a stable modern society. 'Democracy' seemed a threat to Britain's 'cherished hierarchies of class'.[101] Phrases like 'peasant democracy' highlighted the perceived primitivism of Balkan societies lacking a refined class system. 'Progress', a ubiquitous buzz-word, was equated less with democracy or constitutional rights than with economic and administrative advancement. Miller's condemnation of the 'folly' of bestowing full representative government 'upon an Eastern nation before it has had any chance of obtaining a training in public affairs' was typical. The 'unlimited' or 'absolute' democracy of the Balkans was a phenomenon to be deplored not applauded.[102]

In Britain such attitudes were vindicated and reinforced by the event which did most to define assumptions about Serbia in the early 20th century. The murder in 1903 of King Alexander Obrenović and his wife sent 'a thrill of horror throughout Europe'.[103] The British representative was withdrawn in protest for three years.[104] Rather than an isolated crime, it seemed 'symptomatic of the depravity of the governing classes'.[105] 'Christianity and humanity', wrote one (not unsympathetic) observer, 'are at a shockingly low ebb in a country where such horrible deeds of savagery can not only be perpetuated by the few, but also be praised and glorified by the many'.[106] For most Britons this was the only known event of recent Serbian history and it naturally fortified preconceptions about the Balkans.[107] ('There is little to choose in bloody-mindedness', Brailsford lamented, 'between any of the Balkan races – they are all what centuries of Asiatic rule have made them').[108] As one British soldier recalled:

> When the war began most of us thought of the Serbs only as Balkan barbarians [...]. That horrible murder of Alexander [...] and his Queen, Draga, was practically all we knew of Serbian history, and it stuck in our gizzards [...].[109]

But while pre-war writing took a firmly hostile line on this 'deplorable event', the war years again saw a significant shift.[110] The incident, it was now widely claimed, had been misinterpreted. 'To an outside world ignorant of Serbia's great past', wrote J.A.R. Marriott, 'the impression was inevitably conveyed that Serbia of the present consisted of half-civilised swineherds'. 'How false that impression was', he concluded, 'it has required a political martyrdom to prove to the world'.[111]

In unison wartime writers presented the regicide as a regrettable but necessary evil. The full facts, it was claimed, went far to palliate a crime whose gory details had been 'much exaggerated'.[112] A tendency to mourn the rule of the last Obrenović was displaced by a view of Alexander and Draga as symbols of the indolence and corruption which had hampered progress in Serbia.[113] Alexander's pro-Austrian leaning, little resented in Britain before 1914, became much condemned as Austro-Serbian relations were caricatured as 'a prolonged struggle between the forces of autocracy and democracy, oppression and freedom'.[114] The 'steady, enlightened rule of King Peter, and the wise statesmanship of M.Pašić' with hindsight mitigated the sanguinary end to Alexander's 'troubled, autocratic, irresponsible reign'.[115] Noel and Charles Buxton's assessment was typical:

Though the manner of that regicide cannot be excused, yet it is idle to ignore the fact that the extirpation of the dynasty was but the symbol of a great national revolt against the policy of subjection to Austria for which that dynasty stood [...]. The regicide policy was brutal, but it was a desperate struggle for life, and the nation breathed freely when it was done.[116]

The great change in British attitudes towards the Serbs was remarked by the American writer H.A. Gibbons. 'What a miracle', he exclaimed in 1914, 'has been wrought in the decade since "an immoral race of blackguards, with no sense of national honour", has become "that brave and noble little race, spirited defenders of the liberties of Europe"'.[117]

And as the general outlook towards the Serbs shifted, so did pejorative attitudes towards Serbian society. In its primitive peasant culture were discovered rare virtues. 'The Serbs in their broken forest country', wrote one author, 'have retained in their character many more of the mystic qualities of an earlier civilisation'; a population of pig-dealers were also 'nearly all poets'.[118] That 'democracy' which had seemed a mixed blessing at best was heralded by wartime propaganda as a contrast to the autocratic regimentation of Austro-German culture. Such despotism was 'not to the taste of the democratic Serbs', who, as before in their history, were bravely 'holding the gate of freedom of life, of freedom of thought, against the sinister forces of moral enslavement'.[119] Left-leaning writers like George Trevelyan, opposed to the iniquities, as they saw them, of the British class system, found in the egalitarianism of Serbian society something to admire rather than patronise. In Serbia, he observed in 1915, 'there is none of that division of class from class, such as you find in western countries, nor any of that unwillingness to cooperate that is found among the farmers of other countries'.[120] The Serbians, agreed W.F. Bailey, 'are, and have ever struggled to be, a free people [who] desire not the peace brought by the drill sergeant of "civilisation" – that tramples on all individualism and national freedom – that grinds the souls of the people and destroys their liberties in the name of progress'.[121] They were:

> the most democratic of nations [...]. The cult of democracy has penetrated every phase of national life. These descendants of the men who led the Balkan races in the struggle for freedom enjoy perfect social, political and legal equality. Their constitution is of the most liberal, and religious tolerance has developed to a marked extent.[122]

If this constitution related to the pre-war Serbian *state*, furthermore, one can also detect a shift in British conceptions of the Serbian *nation*. Observers had long recognised the aspiration to include all Serbs in a

'Greater Serbia' (and scorned this as primitive chauvinism). The project was assumed to embrace the lands to the south-east secured during the Balkan Wars, along with Bosnia-Hercegovina, southern Dalmatia and Vojvodina. It was rightly viewed, in other words, as a *Serb* rather than a Yugoslav project.[123] But in wartime works little distinction was made between this Great Serbian idea which had dominated 19th century Serb thought and the Yugoslav one which had a heritage in the west but lacked deep roots in Serbia. Not only was Yugoslavism presented as a natural extrapolation of Serbianism, but the former was superimposed upon the latter, rendering 19th century Serbian ideology Yugoslav in intent, and removing any historical distinction between the two. 'Of the Southern-Slav movement', Marriott wrote in 1917, 'Serbia was, throughout the nineteenth century, the most conspicuous and powerful champion', preparing herself 'for the great part which she believed herself to be destined to play as the liberator of the Southern Slavs, who were still under the heel of Habsburg and Turk, and as the centre of that Greater Serbia, the Yugo-Slav Empire, which is still in the future'.[124]

Serbia during World War I

The cause of these changing attitudes was a war in which, during the winter of 1914-15, Serbia fought with more courage and success than many Britons had anticipated. But the precipitating crisis, of course, had done little for Serbia's stock, the shot that began the conflict fired by a Serb nationalist amid allegations of Belgrade's complicity. Sarajevo initially seemed another blot on the reputation of Serbia and the Balkans: 'to hell with Serbia' a typical expression.[125] And in Government circles sympathy for Serbia played little part in the desire to avoid a large-scale conflagration: on the contrary, there was strong sympathy for Austria over the assassination.[126] 'If [Austria] could make war on Serbia and at the same time satisfy Russia', Sir Edward Grey told the Austrian ambassador, 'well and good; but, if not, the consequences would be incalculable'.[127]

A hostile witness like Edith Durham could not forget South Slav responsibility for the war.[128] But for most Britons Austria's full-scale invasion, and her failure to crush Serbia by the first winter, caused an upsurge of enthusiasm which effaced prior hostility. There was no evidence, it was stressed, to prove Serbian complicity in Franz Ferdinand's murder.[129] Any such assertion was 'unworthy of consideration'.[130] The 'splendid pluck' with which Serbia faced the 'Austrian Goliath' evoked romanticised memories of resistance to the medieval Ottomans.[131] The Serbian stand, wrote W.F. Bailey in 1916, 'had in it all the features of the ancient wars of Freedom'.[132] The idea soon took hold, furthermore, that the root cause of the war was Germany's imperialist ambition in south-east Europe and beyond. Sarajevo, in other words, was a mere pretext (perhaps even deliberately engineered) for a long-planned assault on Serbia, whose suppression constituted 'a corner-stone of the foundation of German domination'.[133] For Seton-Watson, the reason why Serbia was attacked was 'not far to seek':

> Just as in earlier centuries Serbia lay on the route of the Turkish conquerors moving westward, so today she blocks the route of the German conquerors moving eastward. She is the holder of the gate that leads to Constantinople and Salonica, the last obstacle towards the achievement of that programme which Germany has so long considered secretly, and is now openly and boastingly proclaiming [...] – the programme of Berlin to Bagdad [...]. The events of 1912, 1913, and above all of the past fifteen months have for ever exploded the false and superficial estimation of Serbia with which the news service of Vienna and Budapest had so skilfully inoculated our press [...].[134]

Serbia was now implausibly 'the shining tower of the East, anxious only to dwell in peace', who had been 'used as a stalking-horse for vast ambitions bent on war'.[135] A 'martial inclination' forced upon her by centuries 'pressed between Turk and Teuton' had 'never shown itself in aggressive action'.[136] And in this context her success first in resisting the Austrian invasion, and later in the re-invasion through Macedonia, wholly reversed old pejorative attitudes. The Serbian soldier, recently dismissed as 'a slouching, ill-favoured lout', now had 'no superior in Europe'.[137] He combined 'the heart of a child with the strength and technical skill of a man'.[138] 'He loathes fighting', wrote one representative observer, 'but loves – with the enthusiasm of a poetic nature – his family, his home, his bit of land, and his country'.[139] This unruly Balkan country had become 'our brave ally, gallant Serbia', producing 'prodigies of valour' equal to anything in the war.[140]

Nor was it only successes which were turned to propaganda advantage in Britain. As we have seen, Serbia's fall in the winter of 1915-16, and the surviving army's dreadful winter march through the mountains of Montenegro and Albania to avoid surrender, seemed a modern-day expression of the Kosovo spirit.[141] British soldiers and relief-workers serving alongside the embattled and disease-wracked Serb troops wrote popular accounts acclaiming their stoicism and bravery. The second Serbian campaign had been, one soldier affirmed, 'tragically glorious for the armies of King Peter'.[142] The Serbs were a great people six hundred years ago, Laffan enthused, but 'never have they been more glorious than in their present humiliation, exile and disruption'.[143]

Many of these writers, impressed by the Serbs' martial qualities, proceeded to elaborate upon the wider qualities of the Serbian nation. 'Nothing in all history is more wonderful', wrote Mabel St. Clair Stobart, 'than the way in which the Serbian people have, during centuries, struggled, then suffered passively [...], then struggled again for [...] the ideal of race freedom'. In religious imagery recurrent in the writings of relief workers, many of whom served with Christian organisations, she hailed that ideal of freedom which had been Serbia's 'pillar of cloud by day, and of fire by night, pointing to the Promised Land'.[144] In similarly ecstatic language, Alice and Claude Askew compared the tears of Serbia to 'the bloody sweat that fell at Gethsemane'. This little nation had:

> never been more glorious than in her moment of earthly defeat. In the sight of the unwise she seemed to die; but she has laid hold of life immortal, for the spirit of Serbia is unconquerable, the soul of Serbia is uncowed.[145]

A leader in the *Daily Mirror* declared:

> Serbia is ruined. Serbia, as at Kossovo, is defeated. But that omen is now as then it proved to be – favourable, eternal, as the omen of recurrent Spring after bleak Winter. Serbia will rise again as she once rose from her magnificent dust.[146]

The Habsburg South Slav lands: one 'culture-nation'?

The Croatian State Tradition

Croats, in contrast to Slovaks or Ukrainians, were considered one of the Habsburg realm's 'historic' nationalities: they could claim a distinctively *national* political history, while their ruling classes maintained, locally at least, a position of authority.[147] Unlike the Serbs under Ottoman rule, they had retained a layered social structure, presided over by an aristocracy which conceptualised its privileges in terms of ancient constitutional right. The medieval Croatian state had not, it was argued, been conquered as Serbia was by the Ottomans; rather, in 1102, it had accepted dynastic ties with Hungary while remaining politically distinct, Hungarian rulers being separately crowned king of 'Croatia and Dalmatia'. Croat identity was held to have survived not just in the cultural field (like the Serb), but in an unbroken political tradition from the days of King Zvonimir.[148]

British attitudes to this Croatian political heritage are harder to analyse than attitudes to Serbia since the Croats received markedly less attention than the Serbs in Britain (as also in France) before 1918.[149] Inevitably, an independent state secured more coverage than an Austro-Hungarian minority. And Croat national traditions lacked propaganda potential for wartime British writers. As a result reactions tended to be more complex and ambivalent.

On the one hand Croatia's hierarchical society meant that, despite its majority peasant base, it avoided the negative connotations attached to Serbian 'peasant democracy'. Zagreb, with its long history and variegated social fabric, had a culture which seemed 'greatly superior to that of Belgrade'.[150] Centuries of association with Central Europe was assumed to have left a lasting imprint: ('latin and teutonic influences', Temperley observed, 'penetrated deep into [Croatia's] fibres'), a view which generally conveyed positive implications of culture and stability.[151] The condescension of educated Croats towards a primitive and 'oriental' Serbian society was viewed sympathetically before the war. And many post-war analysts would likewise identify with Croat attachment to regional traditions and institutions in the face of a centralising Belgrade.[152]

Inevitably, however, the war which so changed British attitudes towards Austria had an impact also on attitudes towards the Croats, whose assumed teutonic influences and (many still argued) loyalties had grave negative implications. While early supporters of the Yugoslav Committee enthusiastically accepted Croat allegiance to the Allied cause, and to the kindred Serbs, a strain of opinion in Britain remained suspicious of Slovenes and Croats as reactionary loyalists to Catholic Vienna. During the 19th and early 20th centuries, furthermore, a strain of admiration for the Magyar aristocracy as representatives of a tradition of constitutional liberalism (uncritically identified as the analogue of British Gladstonianism) caused Croats to be cast as lackeys of absolutism for their role in suppressing the Hungarian revolution of 1848-49, and in Austrian attempts to frustrate Italian independence. (Mazzini, like Kossuth, was a revered figurehead for British liberals). 'It was the Croats', Lloyd George later recalled, 'who had been used by the Habsburgs to crush and keep down Italian liberty'.[153] The enthusiasm with which Croats waged Vienna's war against their southern enemy after 1914 confirmed to some in Britain that their dynastic allegiance remained pre-eminent.[154]

But while the Croats never fully shared in the prestige acquired by the Serbs for their martial endeavours and stoicism during the war, and (retrospectively) for their long liberation struggle against Ottoman rule, by 1918 the propaganda campaign of *The Serbian Society* and its affiliates had succeeded in establishing the idea of Croat attachment to the Yugoslav cause. For obvious reasons, however, the narrower traditions of the Croat nation were less widely propagated in wartime Britain, according neither with the pro-Italian view of the Croats as Habsburg loyalists, nor the Yugoslavist conviction of a unified South Slav culture. Nevertheless, among the few who contemplated it, the idea propagated by Croat nationalists of the 'triune' state of Croatia-Slavonia-Dalmatia had an appeal which might be thought surprising given both its tenuous historical basis, and its incompatibility with the Yugoslav idea.[155] (Medieval Croatia was never, like the medieval Serbian Empire, anachronistically elided with the cause of modern Yugoslavia).

In October 1914 Seton-Watson proposed that the monarch of a united Yugoslavia 'be crowned not only as King of Serbia, but with the Crown of Zvonimir, as King of the Triune Kingdom of Croatia-Slavonia-Dalmatia, thus reviving the historic traditions dating from the tenth century and never abandoned or forgotten'.[156] The following year Toynbee noted that, in any move towards South Slav unity, the first impulse of Croats would be restoration of this 11th century triune kingdom, and that entrance into a wider Yugoslavia would depend upon large autonomy for this entity within a federative structure.[157] Steed and Seton-Watson's manifesto for the Yugoslav Committee described this triune kingdom as a genuine constitutional reality.[158]

On the other hand suspicion did exist of the historicist constitutionalism which dominated Croatian political theory. Before the war, while a few independent observers like Seton-Watson backed the 'trialist' programme espoused by Frankists and Starčevists (by which a revived triune Croatia would be elevated to equal status with Austria and Hungary), officials tended to consider this aspiration unrealistic and inflammatory.[159] As Robin Okey has noted, 'a proud empire like 19th century Britain was more likely to sympathise with the Dualist establishment than with a Russian-tinged Slav nationalism'. British reportage generally accepted those stereotypes imposed by the Hungarian authorities, with the Croatian Party of Right represented as the Croatian 'Jacobins' and Starčević himself the 'Croatian Parnell'.[160] No Magyar could be expected to tolerate a scheme which 'would [...] deprive Hungary of the dependent kingdoms of Slavonia and Croatia, which have been hers for 800 years'.[161] Frankists and Starčevists seemed simply 'chauvinist and anti-Hungarian'.[162]

These groups were in fact little studied before the war, partly because Britain had no representative in Zagreb and the Budapest consulate provided only a sketch of Croatian politics, and partly because they were represented as extremists out of tune with mainstream opinion. Their intolerance towards the Croatian Serbs, considered by Seton-Watson chief among the 'grave faults' which vitiated the Frankist-Starčevist position, was also cited by officials.[163] (If the 'Pure Right' party hated the Hungarians, Esmé Howard noted, it seemed 'to hate the Serbs still more').[164] Ante Starčević himself, like Vuk Karadžić or Juraj Strossmayer, was one of the few individuals associated with the 19th century growth of South Slavic national consciousness with whom British commentators were familiar. But while Karadžić was hailed for his linguistic scholarship, and Strossmayer for his urbane and progressive Yugoslavism, Starčević was known (reasonably enough) for a vehement *Croat* nationalism and a fixation with Croat state tradition which seemed outmoded. With the rise of the Serbo-Croat Coalition suggesting a significant new atmosphere in Yugoslav politics, this trait marked Starčevists and Frankists as reactionaries, in spite of their radical aims for the Monarchy. 'They represent', Howard noted, 'the old Croatian as opposed to the new Pan-Serbian idea', associated with both a conservative social agenda and a strong support for the Catholic Church.[165]

And during the war Britons increasingly enthusiastic about Yugoslav unity became less sympathetic towards those whose zeal for Croatian state tradition was accompanied by hostility to union with Serbia and inflexibility over the rights of Croatian Serbs. To those keen to redraw boundaries on an empirical, ethno-linguistic basis, talk of ancient hereditary right and constitutional tradition seemed backward and 'short-sighted'.[166] Seton-Watson scorned those whose 'juggling with high-sounding constitutional phrases' masked a chauvinistic pan-Croat agenda.[167] And at a time when Serbs, Croats and Slovenes seemed only branches of a Yugoslav nation, this emphasis on Croatia, however framed, was not nationalism but narrow provincialism. The fact that an ideology which emphasised constitutionalism and legitimism tended to uphold the sovereignty of the Habsburg Emperor, furthermore, made it distasteful to British observers during the war in a way it had not been previously. A Croatian nobility which had seemed to represent history, culture and societal sophistication came to seem not only selfish and reactionary but even traitorous to their national cause and that of the Entente.[168]

Provincial Identities within the Habsburg Monarchy

i. Dalmatia, Croatia-Slavonia and the Austro-Hungarian Divide

It had often been emphasised that the western and eastern halves of the new state were heirs to divergent cultural legacies. One effect of this was to homogenise the Austro-Hungarian South Slavs in British eyes, differences seeming inconsequential beside the fundamental Habsburg-Ottoman divide. It is true that British use of provincial labels like Dalmatian or Slavonian seemed acknowledgement of distinct identities. This practice was widespread before the war and remained common up until 1918. But this was largely due to ignorance of Austria's ethnic composition. Little thought was given to regional variations of history and outlook, particularly in the context of Yugoslav union.

The most obvious regional division affecting Habsburg South Slavs in 1918 was that which since 1867 had demarcated Austrian and Hungarian spheres.[169] Historians have considered significant the different experiences of, say, Croats of Croatia and Croats of Dalmatia.[170] In Dalmatia distinct patterns of landholding, combined with the mercantile culture which supported an urban middle-class, produced differences in social structure most noticeable at the level where national ideology originated and exerted most influence.[171] Budapest's inclination to forge a unified Magyar state by undermining internal autonomies – while Vienna was more decentralist – is significant: it was Croatian Croats, used to equating their interests with legalistic obstruction of central government, who were the least enthusiastic Yugoslavs and the most hostile to Serbian centralism.[172] The culture which developed in early 20th century Dalmatia, by contrast, was characterised by a strong civic identity and an ethno-linguistic Yugoslav nationalism rather than 'state right' historicism.[173]

To a limited extent British writers did note provincial differences. There were, it was conceded, 'latin influences' in Dalmatia. Dalmatian Croats, Seton-Watson observed vaguely, were 'more complex': 'in them the subtleness and aloofness of the Italian mind is grafted onto nature that is at once childish and reckless, full of poetry and the sea [...]'.[174] The mode of life of the Dalmatian Slavs, another writer noted, was 'entirely different from that of the Slavs of the interior'.[175] And anti-Austrian feeling was strong in Dalmatia, Forbes observed, in a way that (by implication) it was not in Croatia, due to Vienna's neglect of the former's economic interests.[176] But little of significance to the Yugoslav movement was attributed to such differences (that anti-Austrian feeling in Dalmatia might, for instance, have fostered Yugoslav sentiment of untypical fervour). The division of South Slavs between Austrian and Hungarian spheres seemed simply an example of that machination which had sought, in vain, to undermine their unity.[177] It was suggested that this created problems for Vienna and Budapest, but not that it did so for the Yugoslavs themselves.[178] Even the Slovenes, with their distinct heritage, were bracketed culturally and temperamentally with the Croats, though the Austrian-ruled duchies of Carniola, Styria and Carinthia were markedly different environments to semi-autonomous, Budapest-ruled Croatia.[179]

In over-stressing the unifying features of South Slavic experience British students reacted against the ignorance in pre-war Britain of the genuine bonds and geographical spread of 'Yugoslav' culture. Regarding Dalmatia, for instance, they confronted a popular misconception that the familiar Italian toponymy (Spalato and Fiume rather than Split and Rijeka) indicated a population of Italianate origin and culture. The controversy over the 1915 Treaty of London also produced an over-emphasis on the Slavic heritage of Adriatic towns like Dubrovnik which *had* absorbed significant Italian influence.[180]

That doubt centred more on the Yugoslav feeling of the Dalmatians than the Croats in fact assisted the case for unification. Seton-Watson's response to an inaccurate intelligence report suggesting 'Croats' had little in common with 'Dalmatians' is revealing. On the contrary, he wrote: 'it is notorious that the most ardent advocates of South Slav unity are just the Croats of Dalmatia'.[181] The fact that Dalmatian Croats were more enthusiastic Yugoslavs than Croatians was presented, in other words, not as a point of difference but as a confirmation of unity. Nor was significance drawn, as a result, from the over-representation of Dalmatians on that Yugoslav Committee which so influenced western opinion, and whose claim to represent all Habsburg South Slavs was readily accepted.

ii. The 'Prečani' Serbs

If Croats and Slovenes were often elided in British analysis, this was primarily in opposition to the Serbs, whose eastern culture was contrasted with that of Austria. ('The Croats and Slovenes have a Western, and the Serbs an Eastern mentality', Miller observed: 'the result of their respective histories').[182] But in this formula many Serbs, who had for generations been under Habsburg rule, were misrepresented. For while the assumption was that Croats and Slovenes were Habsburg in background while Serbs were Ottoman, in reality the Serbs were divided between the empires.[183]

Despite this common simplification, British students were aware, of course, of the many Orthodox Serbs in Austria-Hungary. The Ottoman invasion, Taylor noted, had split Serb history into two streams: that of independent Serbia, now emerged from its long occupation, and that of those who had fled the Turkish advance into Hungary.[184] Others marked the intellectual role played by more advanced Serbs in Vojvodina. 'It is no exaggeration', wrote Temperley, 'to say that the Serbians of Serbia were saved from despair by the Serbians of Montenegro and from ignorance by the Serbs of South Hungary'.[185]

But in assessments of Serb attitudes, observers accorded little significance to differences of background among the various groups. In their national ideology, and their attitudes towards unification, they were taken to be homogeneous. The mindset of Habsburg Serbs was, it was assumed, conditioned by the same national mythology which had shaped the historical sense and present outlook of their brethren in Serbia. The Serbs had emerged from occupation, one anonymous diplomat observed:

> [...] the most Slav of Slavs, and all the more Slavonic for having been a Turk, an Austrian or a Hungarian, according to the vicissitudes of the time. It would seem as though the deeper the submergence and the more sweeping the inundation the

more does anything atrophied or alien get purged out of the national character, leaving only the […] essential elements.[186]

Education in the Monarchy, Laffan noted, was organised on a church basis, allowing Serb traditions to survive outside Serbia (as they had in Ottoman Serbia) through the Orthodox Church and the folk culture which transmitted an idealised Serb history.[187] Constant intercourse between Hungarian and Ottoman Serbs had, Temperley argued, reinforced the idea of a single Serb nation.[188] And this *nation*, it was sometimes observed, was prioritised by nationalists over the interests of the pre-war state.[189] In fact, then, the British stereotype of Serbs as 'eastern' was not simply a careless generalisation, but argued a shared culture which transcended the Habsburg-Ottoman frontier. Nevertheless, by comparison with modern convention, British analysis undersold regional differentiation among the pre-war Serb population which, despite allegiance to Serbia and an almost universal Orthodox faith, was characterised by marked variations of outlook:

> The descendants of the soldier settlers of Austria's Military Border differed from the middle-class Serbs of Zagreb, the landowning and professional Serbs of Voivodina and the educated Serbs of Dalmatian towns; the Serbian bourgeoisie of Bosnia from the tied peasants of the Muslim-owned estates; the Montenegrins from the Ottoman Serbs of Macedonia and the long-suffering Serbian minority in Kosovo; and all of these from the Serbs of the kingdom of Serbia […].[190]

The suspicion with which Serbians regarded a seemingly alien central European civilisation extended, it has been observed, to the Serbs of the Monarchy, who were pejoratively labelled 'Swabians' (though it had been the influence of European ideas, channelled by Hungarian Serbs, which sparked Serbia's national revival from the late 18th century).[191]

And significant for the early post-war period were the contrasting attitudes among Serbs towards the structure of the unified state. The distinct outlook of prečani Serbs, John Allcock has argued, was reflected in the opposition between Radicals and Democrats: the latter (dominated by Svetozar Pribićević, a Serb from the old Croatian military frontier) espousing a doctrinaire centralism which reflected the fear of Serbs detached from the national body of isolation in an autonomous Croatia.[192]

iii. The Slovenes

We have noted before that the Slovenes, least numerous of the Yugoslav peoples, were little noticed by pre-war British writers, and when they were, were dismissed as a genuine nationality or as part of a putative South Slavic unit. Given the plausible Slovene claim to a distinct linguistic tradition, often considered a hallmark of nationality (albeit the claim was not always credited), this may seem surprising. The theme of history and tradition, however, is here particularly important. The crucial point, Seton-Watson observed in 1911 (justifying excluding the Slovenes from the 'southern slav question') was that they had 'no distinct history'.[193]

Slovene publicists in wartime Britain tried to shift this negative perception. They traced modern Slovene consciousness not only to a distinct linguistic culture but also to a medieval polity (the early 7th century Carantanian principality) portrayed as a prototype Slovene 'nation-state':

> The Slovenes were the first among the Yugoslavs to create an independent State system. The heart of the Slovene state was Carinthia, and to this day the oldest Slovene traditions are preserved in this province.[194]

They recounted a long Slovene history of resistance to Germanic expansionism (a theme of obvious propaganda potential at the time). 'The history of the Slovenes', wrote Ivan Žolger, 'is from beginning to end one continuous struggle against the Germanic element'; 'for over a thousand years the Slovenes have arrested German expansion towards the South'.[195]

At the same time, the Slovenes were portrayed as the final outpost of the west, frontiersmen of European culture on the border with an uncivilised east (a self-image shared, of course, by Croats, Serbs and other Christian peoples of south-east Europe). Slovenes more than any Slav nationality except the Czechs, Vošnjak argued, were imbued with western civilisation. Among Yugoslavs they alone could act as bridge between west and east (another recurrent metaphor). Their inclusion in 'Yugoslavia' was thus not just desirable but essential if it was to 'enter completely into the world of Western culture and [...] discard the last remnants of Oriental manner and Byzantine traditions'.[196]

But while the mythology of Serb resistance struck a chord in Britain, this similar caricature of Slovene history failed to stick. Not only had the Slovenes barely entered British consciousness, but they had not played the wartime role which in the Serb case vividly coloured their national traditions. British writers, far from regarding Slovenes as a 'bulwark against Germany', considered them to have been for centuries – right up to 1914 – decidedly Germanophil in their inclinations. They had, Toynbee wrote, 'been well treated by their German masters' and had 'no independent tradition or civilisation of their own'. Ljubljana had 'a thoroughly German character', and the wider province of Carniola would likely choose to remain with the Germans 'with whom politics have knit the district for five centuries'.[197]

It was perhaps significant, given the elision of 'Great Serbia' and 'Yugoslavia' in British discourse, that the Slovene lands – unlike other Habsburg South Slav regions – were unclaimed even by extreme Serb nationalists.[198] But with increasing British enthusiasm for a Yugoslav state during the war, a more positive attitude did develop towards the inclusion of Slovene populations. They seemed, Toynbee admitted, to have been 'roused to active consciousness' by that 'wave of national enthusiasm' triggered by Serbia's victories over Turkey and Bulgaria; they might now conceivably, for the first time, 'take an initiative of [their] own'.[199] Known for their loyalty to the Emperor, Taylor wrote, Slovenes had come only now to value their kinship with Serbs and Croats and to proclaim a Yugoslav 'solidarity and unity'.[200] Yugoslav sentiment in Slovenia before 1914 had been 'present but not conspicuous', Laffan wrote, but had since developed rapidly.[201] Before the war, Whitehall agreed, clerical influences and dynastic loyalty had prevailed, the Slovenes 'quite satisfied to remain Austrian subjects'. But having realised Austria was a German tool, they were now 'firm in their demand for independence' and as committed to Slavonic unity as their neighbours.[202] (For all that Slovenes might claim an advanced 'European' culture, however, they were considered a 'long-conquered and rather backward race').[203]

If anything historians have tended to be more sceptical of Slovene national consciousness. Natural barriers, and administrative fragmentation under Austrian rule, had fostered a 'mosaic-type pattern of small entities'.[204] The geological variety of Slovene lands, from mountains to karst, prevented a consistent identification with landscape as happened in Montenegro.[205] Though economic development had begun to extend horizons, the familiarity of region remained attractive, as the 1920 Carinthian plebiscite showed. (Integration in 'Slovenia', of course, was scarcely less an unknown than 'Yugoslavia'). Even for educated Slovenes, higher education was in German until 1919, and key centres of Slovene cultural life – Trieste, Vienna – would be severed by Yugoslav borders.[206]

And though Britons often lumped Croats and Slovenes together as South Slavs of Central European heritage, historians have little credited the publicists' vision of two peoples living as brothers 'from time immemorial'.[207] The fact that Slovenes lived in Austria rather than Hungary had created a barrier to political cooperation.[208] And even when this came down, Slovenes resented a Croat tendency to treat them as protégés not equals.[209] As we shall see, furthermore, British observers certainly overestimated the social penetration of the Yugoslav ideal.

Varieties of the Yugoslav ex-Ottoman lands

i. The Montenegrins

If the Slovenes had an ethnic identity but no history, the Montenegrin case seemed the opposite. Racially and linguistically they were assumed to be pure Serbs. But their separate existence since the 15th century had wrought a strong regional identity. If Serbian history, moreover, told of brave resistance but ultimate subjection, Montenegro claimed a tradition of unbroken independence earning it honorary precedence in the Greater Serb and Yugoslav movements. 'No South Slavonic community', wrote Toynbee, 'cherishes so glorious a tradition as she'.[210]

In Britain, one pre-war writer observed, Montenegro had been practically unknown before the Russo-Turkish war of 1877-8.[211] Ignorance remained widespread. ('I suppose', Forbes was asked, 'the natives are black?').[212] But since that time the Montenegrin heritage had appealed to liberals who railed at Ottoman obsolescence, an enthusiasm disseminated in the speeches and writings of figures like Gladstone and Tennyson. Numerous British writers cited Tennyson's poetic tribute to those:

[...] Warriors beating back the swarm
Of Turkish Islam for five hundred years,
Great Tsernagora! Never since thine own
Black ridges drew the cloud and broke the storm,
Has breathed a race of mightier mountaineers.[213]

In this 'primitive race [...] little affected by modern civilisation' were discovered those primary virtues of courage, stoicism and honour often romantically attributed to such peoples.[214] Harry de Windt had never met a better fellow than the Montenegrin: 'he has been called the "Afghan of Europe", and if the latter be as brave as a lion, generous in his dealings, and the soul of honour, the simile is correct'.[215] The Montenegrin claim, widely accepted in Britain, to descent from Serbian nobles who had escaped from the Turks, added to their romantic appeal.

And in the person of King Nicholas was found an exotic and appealing figurehead for a country unsullied by modern life – a personal ruler in the medieval fashion, who had ruled 'wisely and well for over fifty years', and had led his troops into battle.[216] 'Amid the prosaic dullness of the modern world', Laffan enthused, 'King Nicholas has been a striking figure of romance'.[217] His image in pre-war Britain was very positive. Since 1880, noted the 1911 *Encyclopaedia Britannica*, the country had advanced in prosperity under his 'autocratic but enlightened rule', the progress of education in particular 'very remarkable'.[218] This, as we will see, was in striking contrast to the contempt he aroused among officials after 1915.[219]

It is true that primitive virtues seemed offset by concomitant defects (indolence, vanity, male chauvinism). The blood-feud, associated with Dinaric highland culture, seemed to illustrate the primitivism and endemic turbulence of Balkan society (though sociologists now stress its stabilising function in regions of weak state power).[220] But during the war the Montenegrin's martial reputation ensured a good British press even as officials privately bemoaned his Government's equivocal conduct. The tradition of unbroken resistance to the Turks fed hopes of a similar stand against Austro-German expansion. 'Perched on inhospitable crags of mountains round Cetinje and ruled by their bishops', wrote Laffan, 'a remnant of the people hurled defiance at the Muslim'.[221] From the walls of the Black Mountain, wrote Temperley, 'wave after wave of Turkish onslaught rolled sullenly back'.[222] Britons recalled that Montenegro had 'for centuries alone upheld the banner of Christianity in the Balkan peninsula' against 'the unspeakable Turk'.[223] Only the British official in Cetinje anticipated historians in suggesting that Montenegrin independence under its prince-bishops was somewhat mythical.[224]

In fact the Foreign Office, in spite of popular romanticisation, assumed before the war that Montenegro was not a viable entity, and that amalgamation with Serbia was a matter of time.[225] Before the success of Yugoslav propaganda after 1914 Serbian nationalism was, with reason, viewed as a pan-Orthodox ideology targeting Serb irredenta in Montenegro, Bosnia and Macedonia. The 'acid character' of relations between the courts of Petrović and Karadjordjević (each contemplating Greater Serbia under its own aegis) was not considered to reflect popular feeling.[226] For all their proud independence Montenegrins, officials persuaded themselves, did recognise advantage in a wider union.[227]

But before 1913, of course, the two Serb states had not shared a frontier. And Austria-Hungary's rigid opposition to union looked set to continue frustrating Greater Serb aspiration.[228] Only after the unexpected victories of 1912 had yielded a common boundary did a brisk if staggered union seem possible in spite of Austrian antipathy. Little store was put by Nicholas' desire to make his state viable by expansion into Albanian-populated territory. His country, it was noted, could barely administer the territories it had recently acquired. Reports of anarchy and mass emigration seemed 'not encouraging as to the future of Montenegro'.[229]

ii. Bosnia-Hercegovina

The complex history and traditions of the contiguous provinces of Bosnia and Hercegovina defied any such black-and-white mythology as was accepted in Britain in the cases of Serbia and Montenegro. Parts of the region had belonged, at different times, to medieval Croatian and Serbian states, while it boasted significant periods as an independent kingdom (if under varying degrees of Hungarian suzerainty).[230] From 1580, with sections of neighbouring provinces, it existed as a distinct Ottoman *eyalet* (province), and maintained this status for the rest of the Ottoman period.[231] For early 20th century observers, however, its position in relation to the Habsburg-Ottoman division was ambiguous, since from 1878 it was under Austrian rule (before being annexed in 1908). While the largest part of its population was Orthodox and so assumed to be Serb, furthermore, this group lived alongside substantial Catholic and Muslim communities, while the land belonged overwhelmingly to the Muslim element.

Sometimes medieval Bosnia's distinctive church, with its allegedly 'Bogomil' theology, was held to indicate a tendency towards regional independence, as was the autonomy enjoyed to varying degrees by the district's Ottoman governors.[232] But the notion of a genuine Bosnian identity was dismissed in Britain, particularly during the war, as Austrian propaganda.[233] Typically, as we have seen, the region was associated with Serbia, whose claims were most audible, and its population was considered purely Serb in spite of its confessional variegation.

Nor was this simply a question of race. Muslim historical traditions, it was claimed, were 'purely Serb and told of the glories of the ancient Serb Empire'.[234] Even for those few pre-war observers who still linked the identity of Muslims rather with Turkey than their Christian neighbours, their 'Serb' race and language meant they could be expected, with Turkey's retreat, to develop a Serbian consciousness. And in general the Muslim presence served to fortify British visitors' impression that the region was, in terms of tradition, on the eastern (Serbian) side of that fundamental boundary separating Europe from the Orient which was assumed to have shaped both customs and psychology.

This left the Catholics who looked to Zagreb, and who supported the Emperor, a distinct minority. There was no sympathy for the Croat aspiration to include Bosnia in a revived triune kingdom, 'a scheme of aggrandisement going beyond their constitutional claims'.[235] And in fact even the Croats in Bosnia were assumed to bear the Ottoman stamp. 'In Bosnia', Seton-Watson noted, 'Turkish influence has introduced among Serb and Croat alike something of the fatalist element'. [236] The region, an official report argued, was 'by blood, by language *and by historical connection* […] purely Serbian'.[237]

Insofar as Austrian rule of the province was concerned, it will be recalled that the war promoted a significant shift in attitude: fulsome praise for the progress achieved in a backward and divided province was displaced by the view that divisions had been consciously instigated.[238] Before 1914 Bosnian Serbs and Croats were assumed to be profoundly divided, not only by religion but also by the national traditions of the matrix-states with which they felt aligned. Bosnian Serbs in particular were observed to feel a strong cultural affinity with Serbians and Montenegrins. Back in 1875 (before Austria had had any chance to foster division) Arthur Evans had noted that Serb national songs:

> [make] the Bosnian Serb [...] forget the narrower traditions of his half alien kingdom in these more glorious legends, which override the cant of geographers and diplomatists, and make him see a brother in the Serb of the Black Mountain or Old Serbia, or the free Principality.[239]

Later pre-war writers, well disposed to Austrian rule, lamented these 'feelings of kindred nationality' among Bosnia's Orthodox ('stimulated by Serbian and Montenegrin journals'), and the internecine strife which seemed sure to follow a Habsburg withdrawal.[240] Diplomats assumed a bitter communal rivalry. A combined protest by Sarajevan Serbs and Croats against Hungary's autocratic rule in Croatia had only emphasised, the British consul noted in 1912, their divergent ambitions for Bosnia's future, and shown 'how effervescent [the Southern Slavs] are and how hopelessly divided by their religions'. (The United Muslim League, he added, were guided by an 'instinctive antagonism to the Serbs').[241]

During the war, however, assumptions of hostility between the communities in Bosnia dwindled as the Yugoslav propaganda campaign caught on. What was emphasised instead, in relation to the Yugoslavs as a whole rather than just Bosnia-Hercegovina, was the attachment of all groups to a shared culture. 'In their songs, dances, folk-lore and customs', noted one typical British wartime account, '[...] the [Serbs and Croats] show their race unity'.[242] The claim of publicists like Bogumil Vošnjak that in their 'racial, intellectual and mental life' the three Yugoslav peoples were fundamentally one made a remarkably quick impact. 'Within a very short time', Vošnjak himself noted in 1917, 'the idea that Serbs, Croats and Slovenes form one "culture-nation" has gained general acceptance'.[243]

We have noted before the impact made, for instance, by the sculptor Meštrović, whose interest in Serb mythology seemed proof that Croats and Slovenes shared Serb oral culture, and a veneration for the old Serbian Empire.[244] ('Meštrović the Dalmatian shepherd boy', Seton-Watson wrote to Herbert Fisher, 'is the living proof that Kosovo means as much to the Croat peasants as to the Serbs of Central Serbia').[245] Enthusiasm for Yugoslav unitarism was greater, as we have seen, in the sculptor's native Dalmatia than in Croatia-Slavonia. But it happened that his work made a profound impression upon Western Europe, and was interpreted as – what it purported to be – the expression of a broader cultural unity than had hitherto been appreciated.[246]

In his War Office report Temperley remarked that Zagreb's displays of Serbian colours, singing of Serbian songs and cheers for King Peter seemed a 'sure indication of the pace and direction travelled by Croats and Slovenes since the war began'.[247] A little later he noted, more sweepingly, the 'great importance' of the fact that 'the peasants of Croatia have the same songs, feelings, manners and customs as the Serbs'.[248] It was not considered that such manifestations might, as in the past, have expressed hostility towards Vienna or Budapest as much as empathy with Belgrade.

iii. Macedonia and Kosovo

We have noted the complexities of Macedonian race and language which left British observers flummoxed by rival claims. In general, while Macedonians often seemed an intermediary group, there was greater support for the Bulgarian case, particularly when securing Bulgaria became an Allied interest. Though both had a claim to this 'Naboth's Vineyard', Miller suggested before the war, Serbia's case was weaker 'historically'.[249] Some wartime publicists, enthused by Serbia's medieval traditions, were impressed by her *historical* case. 'If historical arguments count for anything', wrote Laffan, 'Serbia has the better claim'.[250] Had not Dušan's realm encompassed the whole of Macedonia, its capital at Skopje? Was not Prilep home to the legendary Serb hero Prince Marko?[251] But to many Serbian cession of Macedonia seemed the only hope for Balkan peace, and her refusal the work of a reactionary minority. Seton-Watson and his allies, for instance, blamed the Serbian Minister in London, whom they considered a narrow chauvinist.[252] They underestimated the sacred nature of the 1913 gains in Macedonia to a wider political class.[253]

Foreign Office records of 1913-14 show awareness of the substantial non-Serb population in Serbia's new territories, and of the problems it posed for Belgrade and the wider region. A campaign undertaken to liberate co-nationals, Paget observed, had become one of territorial aggrandisement. As the Serbian army moved into Kosovo and the Sanjak, 'a spirit of wholly uncompromising chauvinism swept through the army and the country'.[254] But Belgrade's argument that the 'various nationalities' could in time be 'firmly welded together' seemed plausible. While it prompted one official to sneer that the new Serbia would be 'a jolly place to live in', Sir Eyre Crowe was less judgemental: 'theoretically', he minuted, 'the Serbian position is not only sound, but corresponds with what every other State has done in similar circumstances'.[255] It was, Crackanthorpe wrote two months later, too early to say that Serbia would be unable in time 'to assimilate her new population and raise the standard of civilisation in Macedonia'. A contented population in Serbia proper showed she could govern well under normal conditions.[256]

In fact British analysis of Serbian administration in Macedonia was surprisingly divided. On the one hand, consular officials in Skopje and Monastir repeatedly denounced the corruption, incompetence and heavy-handedness of Serbian officials towards both the Muslim population, many of whom had been rendered refugees, and that Orthodox peasantry considered to be Bulgarian rather than Serb. An earlier prediction, wrote Walter Peckham, that Bulgar peasants would be amenable to Government 'Serbizing' had assumed an administration superior to that of the Turks. 'Unfortunately', he added, 'Serbian administration is infinitely worse'; after experience of Serbia 'even the Macedonian Serbs would prefer autonomy to the certain evils of the present administration'.[257]

Discussing the Kosovo Albanians his colleague in Monastir, meanwhile, found it 'abundantly clear' that Muslims under Serbian rule could expect only 'periodical massacre, certain exploitation, and final ruin [...]'.[258] Belgrade's intention, he reported, seemed to be to compel Muslims to abandon their villages, to expropriate their land, and to settle it on Serbians returning from the USA. 'The assignment of the whole of the Metoya [Metohia] to Albania', he wrote, 'is the only policy which will avoid infinite trouble in the future'.[259] And nor was this 'dread of subjection' limited to Albanians:

> In Serbian Macedonia it is shared by the Muslim, Bulgar, Grecoman, Vlach and Jewish subjects of a penniless State, which, indifferent to the present and future sufferings of a new colony and bent on satisfying its own immediate needs by a barren system of calculated administrative robbery, is paralysing agriculture, commerce, and education, and draining every community of its means of existence to an extent unknown in the blackest days of the Turkish regime.[260]

Accepting these reports at face value, some officials were shocked by this 'gloomy picture of Serbian misrule'. 'The conduct of the Serbians in their new territories', minuted one, 'is really disgraceful'; only 'the plainest speaking at Belgrade' could 'save the Muslim population from being wiped out'.[261]

But senior officials were unruffled, and doubted the atrocity claims. 'Natives of these countries', Crowe warned, 'are notoriously unreliable witnesses'.[262] The Serbians, he noted, had administered their country fairly well hitherto; and these territories had a chequered history: 'Macedonia has been the theatre of every kind of outrage committed by every nationality there'. The same applied in Kosovo. 'These frontier regions', he argued, 'have been unsettled and the scene of tribal feuds from time immemorial'.[263] Trouble was inevitable, Arthur Nicolson concurred: 'the liquidation of the Turkish heritage, with the greedy claimants to it, cannot be carried through smoothly, rapidly or peacefully'.[264] Officials on the spot, Crowe agreed with Crackanthorpe, had become 'carried away by [their] feelings'; 'the atmosphere of the Balkans', he wrote loftily, 'tends to exaggeration even in the case of British vice-consuls'.[265] A proposal to condemn Serbian misgovernment publicly was firmly quashed.[266]

Of particular interest here is Whitehall's attitude towards the national identity of Muslim refugees. The only 'satisfactory and lasting solution', Crackanthorpe advised, was 'the emigration of these destitutes to their own country'.[267] Britain, Crowe insisted, was not the guardian of Serbia's Muslim subjects: 'it is really for the Turkish government and not for HMG to take up the matter of [these] oppressive measures'.[268] Unlike the Muslims of Bosnia, in other words, whose Yugoslav identity was recognised in Britain (even if their ultimate allegiance was at times in doubt), Muslims in Macedonia continued to be seen essentially as Turks, for whose decent treatment in Serbia Constantinople should look out.

During the war discussion in Britain focused on a Yugoslav state, and little was said about non-Serb minorities in Macedonia or Kosovo. Amid the controversial union of Serbia with Montenegro, and of Serbia with the Habsburg provinces, (and with Croats and Slovenes reluctant to raise an issue unimportant to them), the fate of a recognised Serbian region barely arose, and was certainly not treated as a 'national problem' in its own right.[269] (As Sir James Headlam Morley later noted, the minorities treaties drawn up after the war did not apply to old Serbian territory: in Macedonia '[the Serbs] would be allowed to do what they liked').[270]

The Existence of Yugoslav Consciousness

We have noted the emphasis many British theorists of nationality, for all their concern with 'objective' attributes such as race or language, placed upon 'will'. After all, if the latter could scarcely exist without the former, peoples with similar racial and cultural characteristics had often lacked a conscious shared identity. This was what Ramsay Muir meant when he wrote that a nation must prove its right to existence 'by a show of unshakeable will'.[271] And, crucially, it is this criterion by which the notion of a single Yugoslav nation in 1918 has failed to convince many modern historians. In the Yugoslav lands at the time of unification, Ivo Lederer has suggested, 'no such state of mind obtained'.[272]

In this respect, as in others, the years of the world war (and, to some extent, the preceding Balkan Wars) saw a dramatic shift in British attitudes towards South Slav unity. Even an enthusiast for Yugoslav amalgamation like Seton-Watson had been reserved before the war about a union embracing the independent states of Serbia and Montenegro. He (and others like Steed) had emphasised not only the Habsburg Empire's geopolitical importance but also the real differences of psychology and experience dividing the western Yugoslav population from their brethren in the ex-Ottoman East.

Pre-war diplomats stressed divisions between Serb and Croat, Orthodox, Catholic and Muslim, above any shared racial and cultural inheritance. 'Old jealousies between Serbs and Croats and Muslims', reported the consul in Sarajevo, were liable to 'break out on the least provocation'.[273] To Esmé Howard in Budapest (his words reflecting a Hungarian viewpoint) the 'danger' of pan-Slav co-operation in Croatia remained a 'bogey'; despite much talk of 'national aspirations' and the 'South Slav idea' there seemed 'little or no probability of the South Slavs making a united effort in any one given direction'.[274] And even the Dalmatian Slavs recognised, the vice-consul in Dubrovnik reported, 'that their past hopes [of an independent Slav kingdom] are futile'. 'Their aspirations are nebulous', one official in London concluded.[275]

From early 1912 Yugoslav feeling did seem to be increasing. The suspension of the Croatian constitution, Paget reported from Belgrade, had excited fresh animosity against Austria and 'revivified the idea of Southern Slav Union and Solidarity'. 'This South Slav movement', Arthur Nicolson minuted, 'is not one that can be disregarded'.[276] Among Habsburg Yugoslavs Serbia's victories in the Balkan Wars aroused obvious enthusiasm. An Austrian, one official recalled, had insisted that Serbs and Croats of the Monarchy hated each other too much to combine, let alone with the Serbians. 'He was wrong', he observed, 'for though they were opposed for many years they have joined together and just at the time when the success of independent Serbia has rendered her a far more important nation than she was two years ago'.[277] Seton-Watson recalled the 'indescribable wave of enthusiasm' he had witnessed in Dalmatia at the news of Serbia's victories.[278]

Pre-war officials remained cautious, however. Serbs, de Salis reported, had been 'deeply stirred' by the successes of their race. But while these had at first enthused all elements of the Serbo-Croat Coalition, he wrote, 'the intolerance of the Orthodox in victory tended to alienate the sympathies of the strong clerical element among the Catholic Croats, inspired rather by anger against Austria or Hungary than by any real affection for the Serbs on either side of the frontier'.[279] It was impossible, Cartwright agreed, to gauge disloyal sentiment among Austrian Slavs during the first Balkan War:

> It was undoubtedly greater than was admitted by official circles, but was probably also exaggerated by Slav enthusiasts. The difference of religion must always be a bar between the Slavs of Austria and those of the Balkans [...].[280]

During the war (and particularly 1917-18), however, officials accepted propagandist claims about the rapid growth of Yugoslav sentiment both in Serbia and Austria-Hungary. Temperley noted 'the pace and direction travelled by Croats and Slovenes since the war began'. While pre-war Yugoslav feeling had been 'largely sentimental' except in Dalmatia, Bosnia and Serbia, circumstances had now 'led Croatia and the Slovenes to forget their particularist interests and to fling in their lot with the other Yugo-Slavs'.[281] The feeling was that, as a leader in *Le Temps* put it, sufferings endured in common had set the seal on Yugoslav unity.[282]

And the same was even more true of independent writers in Britain, for whom pan-Slav propaganda revealed 'the intense national consciousness of the South Slavonic race'.[283] Its very recent emergence did not seem, during the war at least, to cast any doubt upon its deep roots or enduring nature. The fact that Czechs and Slovaks had 'never shared a common tradition' was significant, Toynbee observed, given that they gave 'few indications at present of a common national consciousness'; but the possibility of amalgamation remained: 'the relation of the Croats to the Serbs remained precisely parallel till as recently as 1912'.[284] The seeming contradiction (and wishful thinking) in the analysis of George MacAdam was representative, if extreme. Having noted that a united Yugoslavia would be 'one of the most striking examples of the creation of a nation founded upon racial kinship, whose boundaries are fixed by ethnic limitation', he went on to remark that there was in fact 'no such thing as a "Jugo-Slav"', it being 'simply a handy term of inclusion' for peoples who would identify themselves first as Serbs, Croats or Slovenes. Nevertheless, he continued, the forces seen during the war – as at the conference at Corfu – were 'apparently making for the welding of the Jugo-Slavs into a compact, strong nation'.[285]

Insofar as differences of culture and temperament did continue to be noticed, moreover, they were seen as complementary rather than problematic. Supilo's argument that Yugoslavia could be the 'harmonious product of all our national strengths' was echoed in British writing.[286] 'If Serbia is the steel which struck thought into flame', Temperley argued (in a bizarrely tangled metaphor), 'Croatia is the flint enclosing the spiritual fire'.[287] More prosaically, General Plunkett, the military attaché in Belgrade, foresaw a fruitful division of labour: 'the Serbians will provide higher military training and organisation while the standard of living in Serbia should be raised to the greater culture and learning of the Croats and Slovenes [...]'.[288] Seton-Watson, his sons have argued, did not believe in 'a single, artificially stitched together "Yugoslav nation"', but in 'one state with three nations', which 'must live together as equals as the English and Scots lived together as equals in Great Britain'.[289]

Of course evidence of intellectual opinion available to British observers *did* suggest enthusiasm for the Yugoslav ideal (though the four official centres of Yugoslav activity commonly differed in their approach to it, and it is now becoming clear that Yugoslav sentiment – before as well as during the war – often coexisted with, rather than effacing, older mindsets of Habsburg dynastic allegiance or Croatian 'State right').[290] What is surprising, however, is how rarely its social permeation was analysed, given that historians have seriously questioned the degree to which the population at large identified with a broader Yugoslav nation. 'Yugoslavism', Dimitrije Djordjević has noted, had originated as a rational intellectual creation rather than an inborn or emotional national feeling.[291] The notion of 'Jugoslaventsvo', Ivo Lederer agrees, 'was by no means comparable to the emotional poignancy of *Italianitá* or *Deutschtum*', however effective the symbolisation of Serbia as the Piedmont of the Southern Slavs.[292] While the Yugoslav political ideal made strong progress in Dalmatia and the Slovene lands during the war, Mark Cornwall has similarly argued, the same sort of mass mobilisation did not occur in Croatia: 'Croatia [...] was taken into the Yugoslav state by its intelligentsia, but they had failed to carry the masses with them'.[293]

Contemporary British accounts made little distinction between elite and mass opinion, or between that of zealous exiles and the populations they claimed to represent. One war office report did caution that 'large sections of the masses are not educated enough to achieve national aspirations or to produce social revolution', describing such ignorance as 'the firmest sheet-anchor of the existing regime'.[294] But in official and unofficial writing such caveats were few.[295] It seems to have been assumed that, as education improved, mass opinion would move towards that of the elite. Politics, it was still presumed, *was* an elite preoccupation. Little allowance was made for the fact that national movements were by definition democratic (in their appeal to a wide constituency which broadened the social basis of politics, if not in their solicitude for individual rights); nor that, needing to appeal to a mass electorate, elite opinion was as likely to be shaped by peasant allegiances as to shape them. In a new era of mass suffrage the British assumption that nation-states emerged in accordance with an inner historical necessity was an unhelpful model for a Yugoslavia whose creation was, as John Allcock has noted, negotiated pragmatically by cliques with little reference to popular opinion, but which would be strongly influenced by this popular opinion in its future constitutional direction.[296]

During the final months of the war, and the period which immediately followed, the tensions first between the Serbian Government and the Yugoslav Committee, then between the central Yugoslav Government and the non-Serb provinces, forced a shift in British perceptions. Fears of Serbian hegemonism produced a revived emphasis on differing traditions, histories and identities in the various South Slav regions (and a correspondingly reduced emphasis on shared race and language as sufficient national characteristics). This period, however, we will consider in a subsequent chapter.

Part II

The New State of Yugoslavia in British Foreign Policy, 1914-1921

Introduction

Having attempted a thematic study of the elements of Yugoslav nationality as they were interpreted in Britain before and during World War I, we must turn to the development of the Yugoslav question during and immediately after the war. Since we will be dealing less with background attitudes and preconceptions, and more with specific responses to political and military events, it will be best to shift from a thematic approach to one more carefully chronological. Since, furthermore, the great majority of detailed information available in Britain about the fluid and unstable Yugoslav situation between 1914 and 1921 took the form of confidential government reports, the focus must now narrow. Thus, the ensuing chapters will constitute less an analysis of British attitudes in general than a more conventional study of the formulation and evolution of official British foreign policy.

The purpose of the preceding chapters, however, was to explore such underlying presumptions as existed in Britain regarding Yugoslav nationality questions – in Whitehall as much as among the general population. It is important therefore that their conclusions are borne in mind as we explore British policy development. It may naturally be difficult, without direct evidence, to prove that the responses of a particular official, or of a department in general, were shaped by the common preconceptions we have explored. But assumptions which are widespread and taken for granted are quite liable to remain unspoken – or unwritten. This need not mean that they were not influential.

Crucially, moreover, the latter period of the war saw an important shift in the relationship between foreign policy and public opinion in Britain, which makes it more than mere presumption to think that many of those attitudes we have analysed in preceding chapters *did* exert an increasingly telling influence in policy-making circles.

Before 1914 there had been, as we have seen, little consistent interest among even the more educated strata of society in matters of international politics, particularly regarding regions such as the Balkans in which Britain appeared to have little directly at stake. Senior officials – who themselves paid little concerted attention to the internal affairs of small Eastern European states, or to the national struggles of their kindred populations within the multinational Empires – certainly had little reason to heed the opinions of unofficial British observers. Minimal use was made of independent academics, journalists or travellers who might have provided insights into the history or politics of little-known peoples and regions. There was, as Zara Steiner has observed, a clear distinction between the professional diplomat and the amateur, the former considering himself part of 'a separate and privileged class entitled to conduct their own affairs without outside interference'.[1]

By late 1915, however, there was much public disquiet at the 'general lassitude of Asquith's administration', its perceived mismanagement of the war (and culpability for its outbreak).[2] There was disquiet too at the 'remoteness and aloofness' – and deliberate secrecy – with which the Foreign Office had conducted pre-war diplomacy.[3] At the same time, the British Government itself faced an increasingly urgent need for expertise concerning the internal condition of the Habsburg Monarchy and other regions of East-Central Europe, and was forced to look beyond the cloistered confines of the diplomatic service. Suddenly, during 1917 and 1918, numerous individuals emerged, many of them academic historians, who wrote in the public sphere – in books and articles in the press – and who could at the same time influence directly the development of British diplomacy. It was, as the MP and *New Europe* contributor A.F. Whyte observed in Parliament in July 1918, a 'remarkable circumstance' (and one that said much about the pre-war FO) that when the Foreign Secretary sought to strengthen his Intelligence Department, he 'found his most useful assistance not in the ranks of the official professional Diplomatic Service, but almost altogether in outside circles'.[4] These developments will be considered in the appropriate place. But it is worth briefly discussing here some of the key individuals who illustrate this transition.

When in August 1914 Robert Seton-Watson, the leading British expert on the minority Habsburg nationalities, offered his services to Whitehall unsalaried for the duration of the war, he was declined.[5] Though he was close to certain officials – George Clerk in particular – in general his relationship with the Foreign Office was distant, and in the aftermath of the Treaty of London it declined into acrimony. During 1917, however, this began to change. While his employment by the Intelligence Bureau of the Department of Information (set up against Foreign Office wishes) did not immediately dissipate the distrust he provoked in some quarters, it did bring him within the ambit of Government. And while he declined to work for the Foreign Office's new Political Intelligence Department in the spring of 1918, fearing (unduly as it turned out) that Sir William Tyrrell would exert a stifling influence, his work under Northcliffe at the EPD, and his continued writing and lobbying, secured him unsurpassed sway within the former organisation. Arnold Toynbee, Lewis Namier, George Trevelyan, Harold Nicolson, Alfred Zimmern, and Rex and Allen Leeper were just some of the key members of PID openly indebted to Seton-Watson for their ideas about the peace settlement in general, and about the South Slavs in particular. (And like Seton-Watson, of course, many of them – not government officials by training or inclination – were active in commentating on international affairs in public as well as in private).

As Austria-Hungary collapsed in the autumn of 1918, and at the peace conference which followed the war, Whitehall turned directly to Seton-Watson for insight into the present turmoil and future realignment of this fragmented empire and of the wider Balkan region.[6] As Robert Evans has noted, in the immediate post-war period, with both Germany and Russia prostrate, the 'lands inbetween' acquired an unprecedented importance in their own right; it is therefore not surprising that 1919-20 marked the 'moment of peak intensity' for cooperation between the Foreign Office and the growing band of freelance experts in the field.[7] Seton-Watson's own belief that he and his close allies had managed to exert a decisive influence on government thinking was no mere hubris.[8]

Nor was Seton-Watson the only writer who both produced influential publications for the general reader and helped shape foreign policy behind the scenes. Another such was the historian Harold Temperley, a long-term friend of Seton-Watson's, who shared the latter's views on national self-determination and his enthusiasm for the South Slavs in particular. Temperley's knowledge of Serbia (recorded in his respected *History*) saw him employed in June 1917 as head of MI2(e), a new research organisation created by the Directorate of Military Intelligence, and subsequently as a member of the British conference delegation. In Serbia between mid-October 1918 and April 1919, Temperley produced reports and minutes on the Yugoslav situation which significantly shaped official attitudes, within and without the Foreign Office.[9] Meanwhile a fellow member of MI2(e), R.G.D. Laffan, was another who influenced both popular and official attitudes to the Yugoslavs. His populist work *The Guardians of the Gate* had, as we have seen, a significant impact on British assumptions about Serbian history and national mythology.[10] And there were others too – men like Wickham Steed, or Sir Arthur Evans – who, while not employed by the Government in an official capacity, were nevertheless sufficiently well-connected with those who were, to exert significant influence on official attitudes towards the approaching peace settlement.[11]

In part, then, events themselves obliged the Foreign Office to become more responsive to public opinion. High levels of dissatisfaction with the manner in which the administration of Asquith and Grey had managed the war effort prompted Lloyd George's National Government to pay more heed to the views of public campaigners and influential sections of the media. But this process was not simply a response to external pressures. Increasingly, towards the end of the war, it was driven from within, as an urgent need for expertise which could not be met by Foreign Office resources caused Whitehall to open its doors to independent academics and writers prone to a more ideological, less pragmatic outlook on diplomacy, and inclined both to respond to and to attempt to shape public opinion in a manner disdained by more conventional government hands.

This was not a transition wholly without tension or disquiet. The PID was not, as E.H. Carr observed, unanimously welcomed by older Foreign Office hands, for whom it contained too many eccentric individuals unschooled in the subtle arts of diplomacy.[12] Only slowly did it earn the respect of traditional elements.[13] And a division remained between the career diplomats (a remarkable two-thirds of whom had been to Eton), and the more heterogeneous and cosmopolitan group of academics and journalists who dominated the new intelligence organisations.[14] A significant part of the motivation for the Foreign Office to open its doors to such influential opinion-formers, and to bring the think-tank bodies to which they contributed within its compass, was a concern to arrest its increasing marginalisation under Lloyd George, and 'to reassert its central position in foreign policy'.[15] In this it was at least temporarily and partially successful: in the period of its existence the Political Intelligence Department of the Foreign Office came to constitute 'the hub of the peace-planning machinery', and on the settlement in Eastern Europe in particular – an area of less immediate concern for the Prime Minister and his entourage – many of those intellectuals associated directly or indirectly with Seton-Watson's *New Europe* group exerted a strong influence on government thinking and policy.[16]

In the three remaining chapters we will follow in detail the evolution of this British foreign policy thinking with regard to the wartime Yugoslav question and the embryonic Yugoslav state up to 1921. There will be times when the influence on official thinking of such common British preconceptions about South Slav history and culture as we have hitherto encountered will be suggested overtly by the written records. In such cases it will be discussed directly. But there will be others in which it will be no more than hinted; or perhaps merely a matter of conjecture. In general, therefore, it is hoped that the discussions of preceding chapters will be borne in mind and that – given what we know about the increased sensitivity of official diplomacy to broader, informed opinion in Britain as the war proceeded – they will enhance the detailed analysis that follows.

Let us now turn first, before we consider the evolution of British attitudes to the Yugoslav question as a whole, to the thorny problem posed by the fate of the independent state of Montenegro: a problem whose particular difficulties cast light upon the manner in which the present and future of all the Yugoslav peoples were understood in Britain.

6

'Montenegro – finis!': Britain and the Submergence of Independent Montenegro, 1914-1921

On 6 November 1918, as their empire collapsed, Austrian troops withdrew from Cetinje after nearly three years. Irregular Serbian bands quickly appeared. And within days an assembly was convoked on the authority of three men, the single Montenegrin among whom had not, Count de Salis reported, held 'any position [...] which would entitle him to take the lead in such circumstances'.[1] Events, as an American intelligence officer observed, were 'railroaded through'.[2] On 19 November, five days after they were decreed, elections were held by an unfamiliar system. Five days after that the elected candidates assembled, not in the traditional Skupština hall in Cetinje but in a store-house of the Italian tobacco régie at Podgorica. Isolated communities were unaware an election had occurred until after the results were announced.[3]

During the elections there had been much enthusiastic talk of Yugoslavia. But few of the delegates, it was later claimed, had anticipated incorporation into Serbia, as opposed to entry as a unit into a broad federation. Nevertheless, on 26 November a resolution was passed deposing the Petrović dynasty and declaring the union of Montenegro with Serbia under Peter Karadjordjević. A five-man committee was deputed to govern the region pending a permanent administration.[4] By 1 December 1918, therefore, when a delegation of the Serb-Croat-Slovene National Council arrived in Belgrade to authorise union between the Austrian South Slav territories and Serbia, Montenegro had disappeared as a sovereign state. Prince-Regent Alexander proclaimed 'the unification of Serbia with the lands of the independent State of Slovenes, Croats and Serbs in a single Kingdom of the Serbs, Croats and Slovenes', making no reference to the formerly independent kingdom of Montenegro.[5]

None of this was yet recognised by the Powers, who faced a barrage of protest from members and partisans of the exiled Montenegrin

Government. But the Serbian regime insisted the amalgamation was the will of the Montenegrin people and irreversible. British officials resented this attempt to force their hand. 'It is impossible', Oliphant complained, 'for His Majesty's Government to admit the principle of the *fait accompli*'.[6] But ultimately, while disapproval was expressed of the means, few saw British interest in seeking to reverse the end.

The Paris delegates faced many issues as intractable and many of greater moment. And within a few years Montenegro had largely disappeared as an international issue. But for the few years that the problem simmered on unresolved, it raised a disproportionate clamour in Britain. Arguably, moreover, no problem of the post-war settlement better illustrates the conflict of loyalties affecting British policy-makers, as – to paraphrase Carlyle – formula and reality wrestled it out. The demise of an independent state which had fought, however ineffectively, on the Allied side presented awkward dilemmas. 'Few of the smaller problems', Harold Nicolson later recalled, 'caused us such heart-searching and left us with so durable a sense of dissatisfaction'.[7] At times officials could not mask their frustration at the interminable complications and correspondence produced by 'this ridiculous question'.[8] At others, in moments of conscientious reflection, some confessed themselves 'not at all at ease' with their Government's public position.[9]

Since no scholarly study of British attitudes to the demise of Montenegro exists, it will pay to trace in detail the development of the problem through British eyes. And while it may seem unbalanced to focus on one of the smaller of those territorial units which merged in the Yugoslav amalgam, and not to accord similar focus to the Slovenes, for instance, the rationale is two-fold.

On the one hand, the case of Montenegro – a kingdom and sovereign state – was unique. Not only had the Slovenes lacked autonomy or administrative unity in Austria, but their individual identity was acknowledged in the nomenclature of the new state. Any Montenegrin claim to an independent regional or cultural identity was unrecognised. For the two independent states absorbed in the new Yugoslavia fate could hardly have been more contrasting. Serbia provided the dynasty and the capital city, it dominated the military and the civil administration, while its name endured both in diplomatic parlance and in European political consciousness, which often regarded Yugoslavia as the 'Great Serbia' of Belgrade's imagination. Montenegro shared the fate of its monarch: a period at the centre of a minor international controversy followed by a lonely death, mourned only by its inhabitants and a few diehard enthusiasts, unremembered even by Yugoslavia's internal boundaries.

On the other hand, paradoxically, we can justify a focus on Montenegro because of the similarities it *did* have with other Yugoslav regions. The complications of this question from the perspective of international law – a sovereign Montenegrin monarch and government, recognised by the Allies, who refused to approve the Serb-orchestrated unification – meant it received considerable attention in Allied capitals, while Belgrade's relations with other regions were overlooked as internal matters. While British attitudes to other questions are sometimes unclear from the diplomatic record, the fact that Montenegro's position after the war was, in Sir Eyre Crowe's words, 'very similar to that of almost any of the outlying Yugo-Slav lands', means we can hope from this problem to inform our understanding of broader British attitudes to the new state.[10]

We have discussed British perceptions of Montenegro in the pre-war period and need not revisit that curious amalgam of ignorance, romanticisation and disdain. It is worth recalling, however, the official assumption that union with Serbia was inevitable and desirable. On the eve of war this process seemed underway. The minister to Serbia suspected frontier talks in late 1913 had also produced agreement on a customs union and common army, and rumours mounted of a plan for full unification.[11] It seemed, the British representative in Cetinje later noted, that Montenegrin absorption by Serbia 'might be an early result of South Slav aspirations towards political unity'. A common frontier, combined with the fact that Montenegro '[owed] to Serbia almost all her territorial gains of the war' seemed, another noted, to make this 'inevitable'.[12] And outside Whitehall Seton-Watson, for one, assumed union had been 'nearing completion' at this time.[13]

The outbreak of war, of course, changed everything. On the one hand, projects in the pipeline were put on hold. On the other, it became plausible to contemplate radical changes in the Balkans that were previously the province of dreamers. A pre-war trend towards Serb-Montenegrin unification had become, as de Salis noted, 'merged into the wider questions which depend on the issue of the present war'.[14]

On 27 July Nicholas telegraphed to Alexander of Serbia an assurance of full support, and the following day a general mobilisation was ordered.[15] Save a 'desultory' exchange between the Austrian fort in Kotor and Montenegrin batteries on Mount Lovćen, however, no operations were undertaken until mid-August, when a Serbian military mission organised a combined defence. Montenegrin forces occupied the Serbian army's left flank as it struck into Bosnia to within twenty kilometres of Sarajevo. But in mid-October the Montenegrins suffered severe losses and retired hastily, exposing the Serbians and forcing them also to retreat. Nicholas had to travel to Nikšić personally to placate his mutinous troops.

Despite Montenegrin involvement in Bosnia, Allied commanders were dissatisfied from the outset. Appeals for information on the movement of ships off Kotor were 'systematically evaded'. French officers on Lovćen reported an equivocal attitude among the Montenegrin military.[16] Early in the war there was 'hesitation to take any decided action against Austria'. Nor were further operations attempted after what later seemed a 'half-hearted' advance. In May 1915 de Salis complained that almost nothing had been done on the Bosnian frontier for six months, while the Court openly absorbed itself in designs on Albanian territory.[17] In fact, as early as August 1914 the Allies warned Cetinje not to jeopardise the war against Austria by causing trouble in Albania. (Though, as officials were aware, their high horse was diminished by the nugatory assistance Britain had afforded her Balkan allies early in the war).[18]

During June 1915 Montenegrin troops crossed the Albanian frontier on the pretext of securing supply routes, then descended into Scutari, removing Albanian flags and declaring the population Montenegrin subjects. Incredulous Allied representatives were told that the town's inhabitants had requested the occupation.[19] The Powers warned against further encroachment and on 29 July refused to recognise the annexation (though it was only the stubborn resistance of Albanian tribesmen that forced a truce).[20] Anger at this flagrant pursuit of state interest was compounded by intelligence reaching London of repeated contacts between Montenegrin Headquarters at Budva and the Austrians at Scutari. Over the subsequent months evidence mounted of a clandestine understanding. It was inconceivable, de Salis argued, that action against Albania would have occurred had fear existed of an Austrian offensive.[21]

During November and December Serbian and Montenegrin armies fell back towards the old Montenegrin frontier, and early in January the stronghold of Lovćen was surrendered. French officers reported Austrians ascending the fortress without deploying in attack formation. By the end of January Nicholas and his Court had left for Rome en route to the French town of Neuilly, remaining nominally at war with Austria. The new Montenegrin Prime Minister urged the Allies that endemic disorder, caused by famine and disease, had compelled an honourable peace.[22]

The stock of the Petrović regime, however, had long since fallen in the Allied capitals – none more so than London. Already by mid-1915 Nicholas' self-interested equivocation had hardened attitudes. After a series of warnings and broken promises the occupation of Scutari seemed an intolerable betrayal. Montenegrin statements, de Salis complained, had been 'an unbroken series of falsehoods'.[23] His report seemed in Whitehall a 'severe indictment of Montenegrin honesty'.[24] Given her recent behaviour, wrote one official, Britain should 'give her services up' and 'regard her no longer as an ally'.[25]

Britain's failure to provide military assistance gave her little clout. She could revoke unilaterally only the transportation of reserves or deliveries of food and medical supplies, as well as threatening to veto any loan. But despite the public relations issues in cutting relief to a beleaguered ally (especially one admired in Britain for a history of embattled resistance), these were measures Whitehall thought would become 'imperative'.[26] 'We have to bring Montenegro to her senses', George Clerk argued, 'and to do so must, "inter alia", cut off supplies, which increase want and sickness [...]'.[27]

When Britain suggested this to her allies, however, all – to her surprise – deprecated the proposal, forcing a reluctant retreat. But officials remained determined to squeeze Montenegro as tightly as possible. Grey set the tone: 'we should', he minuted, 'do as little as possible for Montenegro'.[28] It was agreed with France and Russia that the 'greatest caution' be exercised in advancing money.[29] 'Personally', noted Sir Arthur Nicolson, 'I am not inclined to show any generosity to Montenegro'.[30]

But events – and the attitude of her Allies – again forced Britain's hand. As the Austro-German offensive in the late autumn pressed towards southern Serbia and Montenegro, a last-ditch bid to shore up these states seemed the only means of maintaining a foothold on the peninsula. 'If we are to continue to try to maintain some focus of resistance to the Central Powers in the Balkans', Lord Eustace Percy suggested, 'we shall have to adopt a much more forthcoming attitude towards Montenegro'.[31] Its Government might be hopeless, but the people were 'still with us'. So while de Salis continued to discourage a loan (and to stress that the French Legation's primary aim was to supplant Italian influence), officials in London no longer felt able to demur.[32]

Guilt at the inadequacy of Western assistance at this critical time did also soften Britain's stance. Officials expressed exasperation with military leaders blind to the political cost of neglecting an alliance. 'Our military authorities', Percy noted with disgust, 'consider Montenegro an entirely negligible factor in the war and do not think it worth while moving a finger to help her'.[33] A Montenegrin statement justifying Cetinje's attitude, and bitterly protesting inadequate Allied supplies, caused officials briefly to descend from the moral high-ground and to admit 'the force of much that [Radović] says'. De Salis was told to express understanding of Montenegro's position and to explain that, along with transport problems, there had been a need to husband resources for more active theatres. There was 'no thought', he was untruthfully to insist, 'of stinting Montenegro of what she needs'.[34]

Though military sources continued to report little serious fighting between Montenegrins and Austrians, officials bowed to their Allies' view that the population should not be punished for government misdemeanours.[35] It was suspected, in any case, that cession of all supplies would make a Montenegrin peace with Austria 'almost certain'.[36] Despite uncertainty of Montenegro's attitude, the department concluded, continued supplies were 'the only means of strengthening the hands of

Serbian staff at Cetinje to resist [the] King's desire to make peace'.[37] From 'the political point of view', furthermore, it seemed 'advisable [...] to keep in the field any Ally of His Majesty's Government, however weak'.[38] But as we have seen, any dim hope proved short-lived and by 11 January Lovćen, fabled bastion against the Turkish horde, had fallen without a struggle. As news of this final conquest reached Whitehall, Lord Eustace Percy's summation was succinct: 'Montenegro – finis!'.[39]

Whitehall gave only limited consideration before 1918 to the post-war configuration of the Balkans. Officials were reluctant to assume even hypothetically the total victory which would allow a dictated peace, and preferred, where possible, to keep options open. As a result one cannot, with certainty, pinpoint British thinking at the moment Nicholas left his homeland for the final time. But it is tempting, nevertheless, in the light of the available evidence and subsequent events, to read in Percy's brief final minute an acknowledgement not only of a military defeat but also of a dissolution which even an Allied victory would not reverse.

It is true that in July 1915 Grey had promised that in the event of victory Serbia, Montenegro and Croatia would have 'for division between themselves' the territory west and south of the Drave-Danube line, implying the three would be separate entities (though leaving the division of territory tactfully unexplored).[40] His further suggestion, however, that with Croatian approval Britain would 'guarantee to facilitate the union of Serbia and Croatia' may be taken to suggest – what was widely believed though not publicly stated – that Montenegro was not viable outside such a grouping. Her distinct traditions seemed unlikely to prevent a demand for modernisation, which was to say broader amalgamation, among an impoverished people. By undermining respect for a regime whose rights were the primary obstacle to integration, the events of 1914-15 consolidated this official British view.[41] And the personal nature of Montenegrin government meant feeling against the king as an individual affected attitudes towards his realm. In his influential report on the events of 1915 de Salis posed the question directly: was it desirable for Montenegro (or anyone) that Nicholas should reclaim his throne? 'No sound policy', he concluded, 'could involve reliance on him'. The Montenegrin people:

> [...] with their own history and traditions, might seem to merit better than to become a distant province of an enlarged Serbia. Yet their fate as such might be preferable to remaining a separate State incapable of establishing a solvent administration, under a dynasty dependent for its existence on doles from foreign Governments and ever for sale to them.[42]

The memorandum drawn up with an eye to a future peace by Paget and Tyrell in the autumn of 1916 strongly endorsed this view. Should Montenegro be revived as an independent State or be absorbed into Serbia? For his treacherous conduct since the outbreak of war Nicholas, the authors observed, deserved 'no consideration' from the Allies; indeed his restoration 'should be so far as possible opposed'. Montenegro's resurrection under another king, it was half-heartedly admitted, should 'presumably depend on the wishes of the Montenegrins themselves'. But:

> It should be borne in mind that in any case such a State will serve no useful purpose; it will in the future as in the past not be self-supporting, and be dependent on the charity of the Powers. Its absorption by Serbia is therefore on the whole much to be desired.[43]

In general, this memorandum was in advance of what might be considered a British policy position. Before late 1917 the priority remained to keep options open. But in this regard what is telling, concerning British thinking in 1915-16, is what was *not* said. In a parliamentary debate in March 1916 the Government was asked whether Montenegro was included in the promise made to Belgium and Serbia that their restored sovereign independence was a specific Allied war aim. Lloyd George parried with a genial fudge. 'The interests of Montenegro', he replied, 'will not be lost sight of by the Allies in the final settlement'. But in private officials were more forthright. 'Montenegro certainly does not', one wrote, 'deserve the same promises as have been made to Belgium and Serbia'.[44]

The implication of such reticence was confirmed privately a year later. To a tabled inquiry whether Britain would allow Montenegro to settle its own destiny, Harold Nicolson drafted an affirmative response, but was overruled by Robert Cecil. Discussion of Montenegro's future, he argued, could not serve 'any useful purpose at the present time'. 'We may', he added, 'want to hand her over to Serbia'.[45]

It would be too much to say that, for most of the war, this was a settled policy; but it certainly seemed a possible, and also a desirable outcome. And as such care was taken not, by careless promises, to obstruct it. Reports suggesting Nicholas' wartime equivocation had undermined his domestic position were seized upon since they enabled hostility to his regime to be portrayed as consonant with (or, better still, motivated by) Montenegrin opinion. A letter from Edith Durham in June 1916 claiming 'Old Nikola' was 'extremely unpopular' in his homeland only restated, Nicolson observed, 'what we have already heard – namely that the present Royal Family will never again be allowed to rule in Montenegro'.[46] And if his phraseology here suggested simply a passive recognition of public feeling, different was his emphasis eight months later when intelligence suggested Nicholas was still intriguing with Austria. 'To counter this', he declared, 'we should put all our money on the Crown Prince of Serbia. In other words the Montenegrin dynasty must go – in spite of Italy'.[47]

Officials were aware, however, that the Montenegrin court, and perhaps also the general population, would resent being bumped into a Greater Serbia on Belgrade's terms. (One mid-1916 report of ill feeling between Serbs and Montenegrins seemed, it was noted, to '[augur] very ill for a future fusion between these two states').[48] They knew too that the question would be awkward in terms of the presentation of British policy and of its underlying principles. This may be why, for much of the war, the matter was not confronted. By the autumn of 1917, however, with evasion increasingly difficult, a clearer line was needed. In September Nicolson minuted the department, expressing British policy assumptions as they stood, and urging the need for greater clarity. The British Government, he argued, should:

> agree with their allies (or rather with France and Russia) as to what policy should in future be adopted towards Montenegro. There is a general idea that the Montenegrin Govt have behaved badly, that the King and his family merit no sympathy, and that the great majority of the Montenegrin people desire union with Serbia. This end is clearly desirable for many reasons [...], but it is a policy which may awake criticism in this country.[49]

This, then, was Britain's vague position on the eve of the final year of the war: the need for a more detailed, robust policy had been recognised, but not met. 1918 would be the first of several difficult years for officials assigned to the Montenegrin question.

Things were not helped by the publication in January of a high-profile document from which it was found impossible to exclude reference to Montenegro's rights as an ally: a reply to President Wilson's 'peace note' of 22 December which, in its scrupulous vacillation, intimated the difficulty ahead. In paragraph VII it promised at once 'the restoration of Belgium, Serbia and Montenegro, with the compensations due to them', and the 'reorganisation of Europe [...] based at once on respect for nationalities and on the right to full security and liberty of economic development [...]'.[50] Here, in a few carefully-worded lines, was an uneasy dual commitment both to the codes of the 'old diplomacy', with its obligations to established Allied governments and treaties, and to a brave new world of territorial rationalisation, with boundaries redrawn according to ethnic allegiance, economic infrastructure, and the strategic prerogatives of continental topography. A document so subtly balanced provided, over the subsequent months, succour to rival groups, each finding in it what suited them. Only thus could a statement reaffirming obligations to Allied Governments, specifying the restoration of Serbia and Montenegro as independent states (and repeatedly cited as such by Nicholas' partisans) be acclaimed in a *New Europe* editorial as a clarion call for 'Southern Slav unity' and 'nothing less than a landmark in the history of the world'.[51]

Up until Montenegro's liberation early in November official attitudes tended only to harden towards the exiled dynasty and its entourage. Sir George Grahame, the sympathetic British representative with Nicholas' court, did highlight a Serbian campaign – with French connivance – to undermine Montenegro's status and promote her absorption into Serbia.[52] But in London this tough and possibly underhand treatment of the Montenegrin Government did not seem unmerited. The French, Sir William Tyrrell argued, had 'every reason to mistrust the Montenegrins', the Serbians 'still more reason to do so'; de Salis had clearly described Montenegro's 'record of treachery'.[53] Whatever qualms might exist about French support for Belgrade, Nicolson concurred, Nicholas could 'scarcely believe' that Britain 'would move a finger to preserve his dynasty'.[54] He was, it was agreed, an 'old ruffian', 'a reactionary, selfish and disreputable old man', who deserved (and received) little sympathy.[55]

And while Grahame protested that the pro-Serbian Montenegrin Committee for National Unification was an organ of Belgrade-inspired propaganda, it was given much credence.[56] It represented, Leeper argued, 'the views of all Montenegrins except King Nicholas' immediate entourage'.[57] Since mid-1917, in fact, the Intelligence Bureau of the new Department of Information, in which Leeper and Seton-Watson worked under John Buchan, had reported a sharp divide in Montenegrin opinion between the Court and a 'tiny clique' of 'reactionary' politicians on the one hand, and the majority of younger men on the other. The views of Radović's Committee, it claimed, would 'find a ready welcome among most progressive Montenegrins, who see Montenegro's political and economic future indissolubly bound up with the union of all the Yugoslav lands'.[58] Recent events showed beyond question, Leeper wrote in July 1917, that 'practically the whole of intelligent and independent feeling in Montenegro is solid for Yugoslav union, and that the King will be unable to secure any real support among his subjects in defence of the particularist interests which his dynasty represents'.[59]

Though there were occasional doubts, in general this view prevailed in Whitehall during late 1917 and 1918. [60] Harold Nicolson, an ally of Leeper's who later confessed his intoxication with the Yugoslav idea, influenced his senior colleagues. In August 1917 he hailed a declaration by Radović as 'important and authoritative'.[61] Contrary to Grahame's view, he later minuted, the King and his Government 'do <u>not</u> represent Montenegro'.[62] Most Montenegrins, he wrote (in a draft letter to Lord Derby in Paris), desired a union with Serbia which 'would be in strict accord with the principle of nationality'.[63] The despatched reply was more cagily phrased. 'Some sympathy', it disingenuously began, 'must naturally be felt for an aged monarch reduced to exile'; but it was doubtful whether the exiled Government was 'in any real sense representative of Montenegrin opinion or desirous of working in Montenegrin national interests'; Radović's committee should be examined 'not only in the light of previous history *but with some prescience of inevitable future developments*':

> As Your Lordship is aware, the whole tendency of the future of Serbia is towards national union and it is our hope and endeavour to secure the liberation from Austrian domination of the Yugo-Slav races of Bosnia, Herzegovina and Croatia. A glance at the map will show that if this union is eventually secured the State of Montenegro will become little more than an enclave within Serbian territory, and this fact, taken in conjunction with the very real movement which exists in Montenegro for complete fusion with Serbia renders it possible that a separate Montenegrin Dynasty may not survive the settlement at the Peace Conference.[64]

Clearly the inclination of British policy was to pre-empt the verdict of Montenegrin democracy by backing that broader union which seemed an 'inevitable future development'. A sympathetic telegram sent to Nicholas by President Wilson, promising that the 'integrity and rights of Montenegro' would be 'secured and recognised', caused concern among officials who feared the phrase might be exploited 'in an anti-Yugoslav sense'.[65] The following month, in a bid to prevent Nicholas sending a consul to the US, Nicolson argued that Petrovićist propaganda was 'anti-national, anti-Yugo-Slav, and to that extent anti-entente'.[66] Why, it was asked, should a position hostile to Allied policy, certain to complicate the peace negotiations, be popularised with Allied funds?

It is not hard to understand Whitehall's motives over Montenegro in 1917-18: the appeal of a large Yugoslavia governed by the sort of progressive, pro-British politician who represented the Yugoslav Committee in Britain; the lack of sympathy for the feudal ruler of an insolvent and expansionist minor Balkan state. But one detects in the files, nevertheless, a semi-conscious suppression of that moral ambiguity which would surface over the ensuing months. There was, for example, an obvious flaw in the oft-repeated claim that most educated, progressive opinion in Montenegro backed union with Serbia. The country's population, as officials well knew, was among the least educationally or politically sophisticated in Europe.[67] The majority of 'educated' opinion could scarcely be said to equate with a democratic majority. It is indicative of a wilful over-estimation of the spread of 'progressive' (liberal nationalist) opinion at this stage that this obvious objection was overlooked.[68]

Occasionally, it is true, uncertainty did emerge. The Montenegrin question, Nicolson admitted in May 1918, would be one of the most difficult of the Peace Conference. Little progress would be made without a plebiscite which, in practice, would be 'difficult, if not impossible, to realise'.[69] But for the most part officials like Leeper, less susceptible to doubt, saw in the Corfu Agreement the dawn of a South Slav union and the welcome demise of parochial factions like the Petrović court. The protests flooding in from Neuilly were simply 'very much out-of-date'.[70]

From early November 1918, however, the rapid sequence of events following the Austrian evacuation compelled recognition of the question's complexity. For weeks Whitehall struggled to follow the situation: in mid-December officials were still asking the War Office to send someone who might 'find out exactly what is happening in Montenegro'.[71] Accusations and counter-accusations pouring in from Neuilly, or from Radović and Belgrade, were clearly partisan (though the fact that Radović *was* increasingly viewed as such suggested a shift in attitude). Under such a barrage officials tended to fall back on settled preconceptions; and in the case of mutual recrimination among Balkan politicians – pots bawling at kettles – credence was the order of the day. ('I have no doubt', Cecil had declared, 'that everything said by the Serbian about the Montenegrin and vice versa is perfectly true').[72]

Nevertheless, such was the contempt in which Nicholas' Court was now held, and such the credibility Radović had gained thereby, that officials initially doubted reports of intimidation in Montenegro. It was possible, one noted, that the Serbians had killed some of Nicholas' officials who had colluded with the Austrians, but it was 'difficult to see why the Serbians should massacre the Montenegrins, whom they wish to attract into the Yugo-Slav State'.[73] 'I have no doubt', another wrote a few weeks later, 'that some of the complaints of King Nikita against the Serbians are true but [the general tone was unchanged] I regard all his complaints with some suspicion and he deserves little sympathy'.[74]

Early reports reaching London of the Podgorica assembly did not question its conduct or validity; the measures passed chimed with the accepted picture of Montenegrin opinion. Nicholas' return, intelligence continued to indicate, would be 'very much against the wishes of the people'.[75] A War Office report in mid-December considered the matter closed. Even 'allowing for the King's disadvantage in being virtually interned in France', it seemed 'that the National Committee does represent Montenegrin feeling and that the separate existence of Montenegro has come to an end'.[76]

For months 'all evidence' had shown popular support for a Yugoslav state, but little distinction was yet made in terms of how Montenegro entered it.[77] Nicholas' claim that Montenegrins must choose between a confederation (in which he would retain his throne and regional autonomy) on the one hand, and a centralist pan-Serbia on the other was, Leeper complained, a 'deliberate falsehood'. What most Montenegrins (as other Yugoslavs) wished was neither of these but union according to the Pact of Corfu.[78] Since Podgorica confirmed this, claims that the assembly had been rigged could be dismissed; the émigrés, he scoffed, 'had better persuade the Montenegrin people of this!'[79]

Despite the assurance of Yugoslav enthusiasts like Leeper, however, towards the end of 1918 a sense of unease did gradually develop about Montenegro. Recurring reports of Serbian heavy-handedness, from a variety of sources albeit questionable, suggested an element of truth. Grahame accepted that the Podgorica assembly had been convened 'under pressure of [Serbian] bayonets', and he in turn convinced some senior officials.[80] Lord Robert Cecil urged that an official complaint be lodged with Belgrade. It was a question, he argued, not of whether Montenegro be absorbed by Serbia but of the way the action had been effected; Serbian conduct had been 'thoroughly lawless and should not be passed over'.[81] On 31 December the head of the British Military Mission in Albania telegraphed that while reports from Montenegro remained 'too unreliable to form any just conclusion', there was 'no doubt that many people are swinging back towards their ancient Monarchy under the pressure of Serbian occupation'.[82] A report for the Peace Conference cautioned that the Serbians seemed 'to have exercised considerable pressure in order to obtain support for the declaration of union with Serbia'.[83]

With little reliable information from Montenegro itself, external developments had an impact on British perception of the issue. Since late 1917 officials dealing with the Yugoslav question had become increasingly uneasy about the tendencies of Serbian policy, and those of Pašić in particular. The optimism prompted by Corfu – that he would, while rejecting extreme federalism, accommodate decentralist desires – had given way to a fear that his public assurances masked a centralistic and chauvinistic agenda.[84] Officials responded by emphasising the attachment of Southern Slavs to their historical provinces. Claims for Montenegro's independent traditions and regional pride (especially when combined with professed Yugoslav feeling) began to receive a more sympathetic hearing. Persistent rumours of intimidation in Montenegro late in 1918, therefore, were lent credence by doubts already developing about Pašić's integrity.

For the first time officials began to ask not just whether Montenegro would join the projected union, but also how, and on what terms.

Meanwhile the conduct of Britain's European allies was also muddying the waters. On the one hand Italy was busy, from positions in Albania, promoting Montenegrin independence in a bid to undermine a Yugoslav state. And on the other, growing evidence of collusion between Belgrade and Paris suggested France was sponsoring a Greater Serbia for her own ends (a suspicion wholly confirmed by recent French scholarship).[85] French refusal to warn Belgrade off Montenegro was, Grahame argued, 'one more proof' that the French Foreign Ministry and the Serbian Government were 'absolutely hand-in-glove'.[86] 'Asking the Quai d'Orsay about anything to do with Montenegro', he complained, 'is just as if one asked Belgrade'.[87] In a minute applauded by Lord Derby and circulated to London, he explored the implications of French policy:

> Probably the whole French influence will be used to make the Yugo-Slavs [...] come right in under Serbian rule with as little federative regime as possible. People tell me that large financial and banking interests and concessions are already involved, and the French intend firstly, that Serbia shall be as big as possible, and secondly, that she shall be under their aegis. This will mean that they will favour the elimination of Montenegro in the Serbian interest, and come up against Italy. France is going to be the dominant power on the Continent with a 'pléiade' of these new States in formation looking to her. [...] The French may do lip-service to the idea of a League of Nations and the like, but they intend to profit to the utmost by the extraordinarily favourable situation in which they now find themselves in Europe.[88]

Whitehall recognised 'very great truth' in this view. 'It bears out', noted Laurence Collier, 'what we have heard from other sources about French policy'.[89] But if it raised doubts, it did not yet bring a decisive shift, if only because cynicism existed on both sides: if French motives for backing Belgrade were sordid, Collier observed, those of Italy in supporting Nicholas were 'if possible, even more sordid'.[90] The case should be viewed solely on its merits (which included, of course, an estimate of 'our interests' in the matter).

That such questions should have emerged to test the foundations of British policy at this time was inevitable given the unpredicted speed with which the Central Powers had collapsed. Suddenly Britain faced demands not only that Nicholas be allowed to return to his homeland, but also that

Montenegro be admitted as an ally to the peace conference. Both presented awkward dilemmas.

Officials felt they could hardly prevent Nicholas returning now the armistice had removed the pretext of 'war conditions'. 'It is impossible', Oliphant exclaimed, 'to keep him practically a prisoner!'. 'Why should we bother?', asked Balfour: 'it is the French who are keeping the old ruffian from his country – let him fight it out with them'.[91] Indeed (though officials admitted it only obliquely) the King's return to confront a Serbian occupation had at least the advantage of forcing a resolution; and intelligence suggested it would be in the sense desired.[92] But the French refused to take the risk.

The question of Montenegro at the conference was more intractable. In mid-November Derby told Nicholas' Prime Minister that Montenegro had not 'made out any case for [...] being considered as a belligerent Ally'.[93] Whitehall agreed it had met none of the obligations attached to such status. But its claim to a seat remained hard to deny; entry was granted to many non-combatant states as well as to some, like Romania, with a record as equivocal.[94] By rights, Collier conceded, Montenegro should be admitted to sessions discussing her affairs. But as 'Montenegro' meant Nicholas, there was 'sure to be trouble if she is admitted'.[95] But in fact the question remained unresolved precisely because it could not be decided whether Montenegro *did* mean Nicholas. Radović claimed that it was his democratic provisional Government which should participate in the conference. Evidently this question could not be resolved until the Allies had decided how to respond to events on the ground.[96]

A memorandum drafted for the peace delegation provides, in its measured tone and considered judgements, the clearest picture of British thinking on Montenegro at the end of 1918. The premise was clear and unchanged: it was in the 'obvious political and economic interest of Montenegro' to be incorporated in any Yugoslav union. There seemed 'little doubt' this would be welcome to Montenegrins, and would thus accord with 'the doctrines of self-determination and nationality' (those hallowed principles too readily assumed to operate in unison). But opposition from Nicholas' camp was inevitable. On the one hand he merited little from his 'former' Allies, his wartime conduct open to the 'gravest suspicion'. (London still lacked firm evidence of duplicity). On the other hand it seemed 'scarcely equitable' to suppress his dynasty without a hearing. It would be advisable, therefore, to set up an impartial commission to gauge Montenegrin wishes. 'Presumably' this would 'decide overwhelmingly in favour of the union of Montenegro with the new Serbian State'; but Nicholas would be left with a 'justifiable grievance' if he was prevented from making his case.[97]

This memorandum is noteworthy in several respects. Firstly, Montenegrin independence still seemed politically and economically unviable, and against the interests both of Montenegrins and of all with a stake in the region's stability. Secondly, despite reports that Serbian rule might be reviving Nicholas' popularity, Whitehall remained convinced that few desired his return. A commission was mooted not because its verdict seemed in doubt but because its evidence would undermine the ex-King's campaign. Thirdly, there remained a tendency in London to regard Nicholas' exile as condign punishment for his wartime conduct, by which he seemed to have brought his misfortunes upon himself.

More significant, perhaps, is what the document did not contain: any analysis of the manner in which Montenegro should amalgamate with the other Yugoslav lands. Concerns that Pašić's Great Serb vision was incompatible with the Corfu Pact were dismissed: 'the Greater Serbian idea and Serbian local prejudices have in some cases died hard', it was noted, 'but for practical purposes we may regard them as dead'. Only a unitary state, rather than a federation, could serve the Yugoslav race. The Montenegrin problem, in other words, was still analysed in terms of two possibilities: complete absorption in a united Yugoslavia or (improbably) continued independence under the Petrović dynasty.[98]

It is not surprising that no thought was yet given to Yugoslavia's internal constitutional structure. But it is striking that none was given to the manner of Montenegro's amalgamation as a Serbian province.[99] The rhetoric from Belgrade and from Radović's regime implied Montenegrins brought no distinct identity to Yugoslav union, but were simply Serbs restored to their heartland. And yet Whitehall countered Petrovićist anger by citing Montenegrin enthusiasm for a *federation*, repeating that it was 'to our interests, and to those of the Montenegrins themselves, to encourage union *with Yugoslavia*'.[100]

If seeds of doubt had been sown, then, on the surface little had changed. We should leave the Montenegrin appeal alone, Oliphant advised: 'I doubt […] whether this moment is opportune for starting any fresh line of policy as regards Montenegro'. 'I agree', wrote Tyrrell.[101]

For British officials the first two months of 1919 were the most difficult of the controversy's duration – a period of painful awakening both to the problem's true complexity and to their inability to resolve it. And if it was upsetting for those directly involved, it also resonated more widely, the first major blow to the facile trust, pervading Whitehall as much of the press, in the mantra of self-determination and national unification. Looking back late in February Nicolson thought December 1918 the critical moment of disillusion, with the 'extremely painful' realisation that Podgorica had not been the free popular expression it had purported to be.[102] It was then, as we have seen, that doubts began to take root. But Nicolson predates the crucial moment. Not before the new year did their accumulated pressure split fissuring cracks in Britain's hitherto complacent policy towards Montenegro.

In the first days of January the situation reached its most alarming stage. Opponents of unification stirred autonomist tribes to rebel and besieged Cetinje and other towns, prompting brief but bloody confrontations with the Serbian Army and Radovićist militias.[103] Whitehall now began to receive, for the first time, intelligence derived from British sources. On 1 January a report that Serbian terrorism was provoking a 'revolution' had been treated with scepticism. ('All our information', Collier minuted, 'is to the contrary effect').[104] But on 3 January, after a week-long mission of enquiry, Temperley reported major unrest in the Njeguš region above Kotor (Nicholas' heartland) as well as among the Muslims of Podgorica, and even in more pro-Serbian Nikšić.[105] Six days later the Commodore of the British Adriatic Force talked of 'revolution' against the Radović party (though he rightly reported that serious insurgency was now limited to the outskirts of Cetinje).[106] And General Phillips, head of the British mission to Albania – who sent a member of his mission, Captain Brodie, to investigate – reported on 11 January that his man had 'walked straight into a revolution in Montenegro', and that while the rising seemed to have failed, participation had been widespread and sporadic fighting continued. 'I do not think', he warned, 'the trouble is in any way over'.[107] Trying to make sense of the 'obscure' situation in Montenegro, officials talked of 'civil war [...] raging' between the pro- and anti-Radović camps.[108]

Initially Whitehall clung to short-term, remediable (and plausible) causes: economic deprivation, Serbian insensitivity and foreign machination. The British Commodore had blamed the rising on Italian provocation (his source here Radović), and to 'acute hunger and hatred of Serbian troops'.[109] Temperley too referred to Montenegrins' 'distress', and to their 'fear and dislike of the Serbian soldiers'.[110] 'Lack of food and possibly Italian intrigues', wrote one official, 'are doubtless responsible for the present state of affairs'; supplies would be a priority for the Inter-Allied Committee in Paris.[111]

The heavy-handed conduct of Serbian troops (no longer in doubt) might be alleviated, it was still hoped, by a joint protest to Belgrade. But Paris remained reluctant, claiming 'every reason to believe that Montenegrins are desirous of unity, and that this desire takes the character of a fusion with Serbia'. Whitehall felt bound to accept their diluted text which was despatched to Belgrade (Grahame lamenting London's failure to 'break loose from French leadership in these matters').[112] But little hope was held out for its impact. 'However severe a protest was made', Derby complained, 'the Serbs would know that the French at any rate do not mean them to take it too seriously'.[113] It would serve at least, officials reasoned, to show before the conference that Britain (and France too, for all that her actions suggested otherwise) did not accept Belgrade's *'fait accompli'* over Montenegro.[114]

London's reluctance to be bullied into accepting Serbia's absorption of Montenegro increased during January as it became clear that the upheaval was about more than Italian intrigue, scarcity of resources or Serbian misrule. There must, Temperley had stressed, be more to it:

> Something must be allowed for the intense conservatism of the people [...]. The Montenegrin always fears for his freedom and too great dependence on the Serbs may endanger this. All Montenegrins say they are for Yugoslavia, but some seem to be afraid of accepting the Kara George dynasty and are therefore Republicans or pro-Nicholas [...].[115]

Here, almost for the first time, the assumption was challenged that union with Serbia under Radović and entry into a broader Yugoslavia amounted to the same thing. 'Montenegro, on the whole, wanted to join <u>as a country</u> a Federal Yugo-Slav State', Phillips wrote to Graham, 'but not to be absorbed into Serbia'.[116] And though he referred to a 'Royalist' uprising, most witnesses denied it was primarily any such thing. On the contrary, the British naval commander reported: the rebels were strongly hostile to Nicholas.[117] They wished, Captain Brodie agreed, 'to preserve their independence and become federated with the Yugoslavs'; they demanded a referendum; but there was 'no movement on foot to bring back the King'.[118] When from Rome de Salis (no friend of Nicholas) assessed the evidence, he concluded that 'opposition to annexation by Serbia' was too widespread to be attributed 'solely to King Nicholas and his clique'. 'The resistance', he wrote, 'is of a more serious character and the possibility of a union with a Yugoslav state is likely to strengthen it'.[119]

Initially officials focused, with relief, on the apparent lack of support for the king, and on favourable Montenegrin attitudes to the Yugoslav project. Feeling against the return of the Petrović dynasty, Major-General Thwaites observed, seemed universal, 'if the desire for complete union with Serbia is not perhaps so apparent'.[120] This latter phraseology is indicative, however, of the rather head-in-sand attitude still existing in Whitehall towards Serbia's absorption of Montenegro. A strong protest was unnecessary, Graham implied, since there was 'little doubt but that, ultimately, Montenegro will be joined to Serbia in the new State'.[121]

As the weeks passed, however – ironically as open rebellion petered out – officials accepted that Montenegrins felt betrayed by the Podgorica proceedings: that, despite enthusiasm for Yugoslavia, many wanted an elected government to negotiate entry on their own terms. While the insurrection was not monarchical, the DMI noted on 22 January, it was 'a movement in favour of federation of Yugoslavs but not absorption in a greater Serbia'.[122] The November elections, it became accepted, had not constituted a free expression. While Temperley had gently suggested that a non-unanimous vote would have had more force, Brodie was more forthright. The rebels considered the elections a farce, he reported; they desired union with Yugoslavia but 'objected to Serbian support of a Government they considered illegally constituted'.[123] Officials still felt that most might settle down as part of Serbia. ('We do not yet know what the Montenegrins really want', Nicolson minuted in late February).[124] But they rejected the French claim that Radović was opposed only by a small *ancien régime* party. British sources, George Warner minuted, suggested there were three parties in Montenegro: one supporting complete absorption in Serbia, one favouring federation in Yugoslavia, and one faithful to the old regime. The two latter seemed 'stronger than the first and united by this common dislike of the Serbians'.[125]

And if doubt remained about the parties' relative strength, Montenegrins, officials now felt sure, had been denied fair democratic expression. It was desirable, wrote Sir Robert Graham, that Montenegro should enter 'the new Yugo-Slav State or Confederation of States'; but 'the people ought to have a fair chance to express their wishes [...]'.[126] From Belgrade General Plunkett argued that since the 'real interests of Montenegro' (and of Britain) lay in its amalgamation, 'details' of electoral injustice were 'unimportant'. But in London his reports now seemed unduly Serbian-influenced. The issue, wrote one official, was 'not so much what is good for Montenegro as what she wants'.[127] An American intelligence officer's report that most Montenegrins wished to enter a Yugoslav state while maintaining 'their separate entity and their state autonomy' was greeted as supporting 'our point of view'.[128]

For the past year and a half, Sir George Grahame lamented on 3 February, Europe had been treated to the 'extraordinary spectacle [...] of one allied State being allowed to treat another smaller one as a boa constrictor treats a guinea pig found in its cage'; and while the French had 'actively connived at this carnivorous proceeding', Britain had 'looked on passively'.[129] But for officials who – if they did not go quite so far – had come to sympathise with Grahame's impassioned view, the question, of course, was what could be done? In theory the answer was obvious: a small-scale Allied occupation, to replace Serbians and Italians with troops from Britain, America or (less ideally) France, able to organise a fair referendum. But in practice difficulties abounded. As early as 1 January Collier had noted that an international occupation without Italy was 'no doubt the best theoretical solution of the problem', though Britain could not carry the scheme against French and Serbian opposition.[130] And in general, during the first half of January, Whitehall accepted France's view that no occupation was necessary.[131]

The matter was complicated by the fact that two distinct issues were involved. First was the imperative of ensuring public order, preventing the region relapsing into anarchy or civil war. Second was the perceived duty to allow Montenegrins to shape their own future. While it was unrest which had prompted British unease about Podgorica, the two were not necessarily related: order might indicate repression rather than contentment, as Whitehall in fact believed to be the case. (The fact that Montenegro was now calm, General Bridges reported, was 'thanks to the 14th century methods adopted during the late elections').[132] On this point Britain and France were at cross-purposes. Paris would contemplate an occupation to secure order, but refused to undermine a stable situation by pushing for a plebiscite. British officials came to feel that, whether or not Serbia had secured control, long-term stability depended on the just settlement only an occupation could secure. The Montenegrins should have the chance to express their wishes freely, Graham observed, and 'the only hope of their getting it seems to be an American or British-American occupation of the country'.[133]

Under pressure from Wilson (who sympathised with the Montenegrins) France agreed to send General Franchet D'Esperey to investigate and to back an intervention should he recommend one.[134] But while this proposal was welcomed in Whitehall ('so surprisingly good', Graham enthused, 'that one instinctively considers whether it does not contain some pitfall') it should have been clear that for Paris the litmus test was disorder, *not* the validity of Podgorica. Since his report suggested the situation was more stable, Paris rejected an occupation, while in London enthusiasm only increased. It seemed now 'specially necessary', Hardinge noted, that Montenegro be occupied by Allied (not Italian or Serbian) forces.[135] It was clear, Warner agreed, 'how urgent an impartial allied occupation of Montenegro is'. But no doubt the French, he etched sarcastically, would claim 'that "all is for the best in the best of worlds" in Montenegro'.[136] With no agreement frustration mounted. Could an occupation not be expedited, Hardinge asked: 'while we wait the pitch is being queered apparently with French connivance'.[137]

But the obstacles proved considerable. Despite Wilson's sympathy, American feeling was increasingly hostile to European commitments.[138] The US reply forwarded by Derby declared an occupation 'not at present desirable'. Perhaps, it suggested, all forces occupying Montenegro could be withdrawn, 'leaving to the people of that country determination of their own future'.[139] But this was transparent fantasy. The idea, Warner wrote, was 'most unfortunate':

> It will be absolutely impossible to counteract undue pressure by Serbian agents if there is no impartial Allied force in the country to watch the situation. Even though the Serbian troops

were withdrawn Serbian comitadjis would be able to continue the work of terrorisation.

The decision, Graham wrote, 'simply means handing over Montenegro to the Serbians'; without an allied occupation Montenegrins could never express their real views. Lord Curzon agreed. Washington should be pressed to reconsider. And if that failed, 'a British and French occupation or even one with the Italians would be better than nothing': better at least than leaving Montenegro 'at the mercy of Serbian comitadjis'. Let us, Curzon affirmed, 'have the best allied occupation we can get'.[140]

But without US involvement any occupation was beyond British power to implement. France remained obstructive. Italy, Paris pointed out, would demand to join any Allied venture; Serbia would then refuse to withdraw; and, as Britain knew, it was 'the Serbians whom it is vital to exclude'. The nationality of a non-American occupation, Warner conceded, 'bristles with difficulties'.[141] With 'so much friction in the Near East between British and French officers', Grahame cautioned, a Franco-British occupation might be 'the occasion of fresh trouble'.[142] And while a purely British presence might have been pressed on all parties, it seemed doubtful her army could contribute to a joint operation, let alone tackle the job single-handed. (On 12 February officials learnt that due to commitments in Italy and elsewhere the Chief of the Imperial General Staff opposed sending any British troops to Montenegro).[143] The only, unpromising course, it seemed, was to press America to reconsider. If they refused, there seemed 'little hope for the Montenegrins'. A French occupation would be pro-Serbian; a Franco-Italian one impossibly fractious. By the end of February any occupation seemed unlikely. If so, Britain could only try to persuade Serbian troops to leave. But, Warner lamented, 'very few, if any, will go'.[144]

Under pressure in press and Parliament, the Foreign Office sought an alternative resolution.[145] The suggestion had previously been made of a commission to investigate Montenegrin opinion and report to the Conference. De Salis had seemed an excellent candidate. He might go to Montenegro, Grahame had suggested, 'with a mandate [...] to establish tranquillity so that elections may be held'.[146] But such a mission plainly required substantial military back-up, and once this was ruled out, the appealing notion of an Allied Commissioner acting as temporary governor had also to be dismissed.

In ruling out military commitment, however, Wilson had hinted he might support an Anglo-American 'Commission of Investigation'. For officials confronting the need 'to eat our words' and accept the US proposal for a general evacuation, this was a straw to be clutched. A simple withdrawal, Graham still insisted, would leave Montenegrins to be 'coerced by Serbian comitadjis'. But perhaps, he mused unconvincingly,

General Phillips' dismissal of a commission without troops had been too pessimistic. It would at least beat abandoning Montenegro to 'conditions of Serbian coercion or civil war which must render any real self-determination impossible'.[147] With occupation ruled out this seemed 'the only hope for Montenegro'.[148] Wilson approved the plan and a young colonel, Sherman Miles, was appointed to accompany de Salis. The pair met in Scutari and on 3 May arrived together in Cetinje.

Meanwhile, Allied commanders had ordered all forces to withdraw from Montenegro. On 6 April General Bridges reported, to no one's surprise, that the order had been ignored.[149] The Serbians, considering Montenegro 'national territory solemnly reunited to Serbia', alleged that 'grave internal troubles' would follow their withdrawal. Among officials long adamant that a full Serbian and Italian withdrawal was vital for Montenegrin self-determination, however, the prospect of de Salis' mission – an active measure after months of wrangling – had wrought a sudden change of attitude. Weary cynicism was replaced by sanguine expectation. Though this refusal would not help de Salis' task, Warner minuted, 'in view of the approaching commission the question is less important than it was'.[150]

But disillusion soon returned. De Salis' primary mission was to gauge Montenegrin opinion: to ascertain the circumstances of the November election and the Podgorica decision to unite with Serbia, and to estimate 'the true wishes of the population as regards the future status of Montenegro'. Did they wish: '1) absorption in the new Yugo-Slav State, 2) union on a federal basis, 3) complete and separate independence'. In the case of 2) or 3), did they desire the return of the King?[151] Before reaching Cetinje, however, de Salis complained to London that Miles' remit was at odds with his own. Miles was to inquire into alleged atrocities in the Gusinje region (during conflicts with local Albanians), but had 'no instructions whatever' to investigate the elections or the true wishes of the people.[152] And the situation, he added, made it in any case hard to fulfill what was asked. The Provisional Government had been disbanded, its powers passed to a Serbian delegate, while Montenegrin provincial prefects had also been replaced by Serbians. Bar Italian and Montenegrin troops at Antivari and Vir, the country was under a military occupation which had 'got a tight hold on it'. Its opponents were in prison:

> In these circumstances Colonel Miles considers it would be very difficult to make enquiries from people with regard to their wishes especially as we cannot guarantee support to those who oppose the present regime. I agree with him.[153]

For Whitehall this was dispiriting. For Miles to be told only to investigate atrocities, Howard-Smith lamented, was 'useless', and de Salis' doubts about assessing public opinion 'a pity'; they should try to overcome these obstacles. Balfour sent reassurance. It was never his intention, he wrote, that enquiry should be limited to atrocities: they had been sent to ascertain majority Montenegrin wishes 'in regard to union with Yugo-Slavia'. The impression remained, he observed, that 'Montenegrins as a whole do desire such union', and that the separatist movement was engineered by Nicholas' circle. He made clear what he wanted to hear: 'you will of course realise that in general British interests it will be to our advantage if Montenegro enters the Yugo-Slavia Federation in some form or other'.[154]

For all the clamour from Neuilly, however, this 'some form or other' was precisely the issue. On 9 May Britain had followed the US (and Norway, Switzerland and Greece) by recognising the Serb-Croat-Slovene State. While the Quai d'Orsay claimed America had thereby recognised Montenegro's union *with Serbia*, Whitehall denied this.[155] Though it was assumed that the new state must encompass Montenegro, it no longer seemed as it had after Podgorica, 'quite natural that Montenegro should be represented in the same way as other Yugo-Slav States – ie, by the Serbian representatives'. Though de Salis was not expected to report widespread separatism, he was to indicate the *nature* of the union desired: information which, Harmsworth told the Commons, the Conference could act upon.[156]

Other than as a salve to British conscience, however, the mission was of little interest to a Conference preoccupied with external frontiers. (At the Conference, one American delegate had remarked in April, 'slowly but irrevocably' the Montenegrin problem had 'faded from the picture').[157] In the satisfaction resulting from belated action, an awkward question was suppressed: how, if de Salis reported strong opposition to the Serbian annexation, could the Powers respond? The opinion much rehearsed in January and February – that only an occupation could rectify Serbian abuses – seems to have been temporarily quashed. Only occasionally did this feeling of impotence resurface. ('The fact is', Graham lamented, 'that the commission comes too late, as the Serbians have effectively laid hands on the country').[158]

Before much feedback from de Salis, Whitehall received the report of Colonel Miles, ordered to wrap up his enquiry quickly. Though no Balkan specialist Miles said much to confirm British suspicions: the November election had likely been influenced ('as politics have always been in Montenegro') by military power; since then Belgrade had executed a 'quiet coup d'état', substituting Serbian for Montenegrin officials and securing real power for the Serbian Army. As a result it was quiet, only a few Royalists opposing the regime 'in a feeble manner'. But concerning Whitehall's declared priority – Montenegrin public opinion – Miles' verdict was unwelcome:

It would be absolutely impossible to ascertain the real wishes of the Montenegrins, except under a British or American occupation of the country. Even then a plebiscite would have to be taken under conditions which would permit the people to understand very clearly what they might expect from union with Serbia, union with Yugoslavia, or from independence, and under what guarantees. [...].[159]

To restore Montenegro to independence would certainly be a mistake, Miles argued. The country was geographically unsuited and Nicholas' Government (to which no alternative existed) was discredited. Since an Allied-imposed referendum was 'practically inadmissible', Montenegro's inclusion in Yugoslavia should be recognised under guarantees of local autonomy. Her political rights should be 'equal to those of the Serbs, Croats, and Slovenes'. Even then it was 'practically certain' that the Serbians would use repression for political control in Montenegro (though ultimately such tactics would backfire against this 'warlike, mountainous people'). Nevertheless, to abandon Montenegro wholly to Serbian control, 'would be a political crime'.

Pending his final report, de Salis sent similar impressions. He found (as expected) that most Montenegrins supported a Yugoslav union; but to direct incorporation into Serbia, apparently by force, there was 'a good deal of opposition'. The leaders of this, however, were 'imprisoned or in flight'. And since Serbian and Italian troops showed no sign of leaving, 'free expression of opinion cannot [...] be expected'.[160] A month later de Salis amplified these judgements. Opposition leaders were 'categorically in favour' of Yugoslavia, but desired to enter it 'as free Montenegrins in accordance with [the] desires of their country and not as subjects of Belgrade'. Their claim that this was the majority wish, he observed, '[might] well be the case'. But a genuinely representative Montenegrin Government could 'only be secured through a freely elected assembly', impossible while the country was controlled by 'Serbian officials from Belgrade, supported by Serbian troops', and while 'Montenegrin leaders who oppose this regime are kept in prison as rebels'.[161]

As an acknowledged expert on Montenegro (and one clearly not partial towards Nicholas) de Salis wielded strong influence in Whitehall, especially since his views were corroborated by other sources. General Phillips, for instance, thought Montenegrins now resented the Serbian occupation more than they did Nicholas. The tendency, he reported, was for Royalists to ally with supporters of a federal Yugoslavia. In the unlikely event that Serbian troops obeyed orders and left a ballot might back the King if this meant freedom from 'the Serbian Yoke'. But if Montenegrins thought they could remain a country under its own name and Government, without the King, as an integral part of Yugoslavia, 'there would be a large majority for Federation'. Serbian methods of carrot and stick – large-scale bribery and arrest – had ensured, however, that there were 'no leaders of any consequence' to direct and coordinate the people. In effect, he lamented, Montenegro 'may be described as part of Serbia'.[162]

Although Young did report from Belgrade that the SCS Government was investing substantial aid in Montenegro (information seized on by Leeper), most in Whitehall accepted the verdict of their men on the spot. Faced with this criticism of Serbian conduct, optimism that Yugoslav union heralded a progressive dawn in South-East Europe leached steadily away. The Serbs, Howard-Smith complained, were being 'typically "Balkan"' in their treatment of Montenegro'.[163] Britain, officials insisted, could not accept Belgrade's assertion that the union of Montenegro with Serbia '*and thereby* its incorporation in the Kingdom of the Serbs, Croats and Slovenes' was a 'fait accompli'. The 'cardinal point', Howard-Smith observed, was that Serbs and Italians 'must both be cleared out'.[164] But such musings were now invested with little real hope.

In September de Salis' formal report confirmed his previous judgements. The Serbians, he wrote, had 'a tight hold on the country and intended to maintain it'. The Government, 'purely one of military force', was ruling by 'a regular system of terrorism'.[165] Both elections and assembly had been conducted 'under the bayonet of the Serbian forces', behind whom lay 'bands of lawless komitadjis'. Discontent remained obvious. There was 'good ground for thinking' that the whole country between Nikšić and Cetinje, the heart of 'Old Montenegro', backed the rebels. The area was not in contact with Italian troops so could 'scarcely be affected by Italian influence'. One could not be sure: in a country becoming 'a second Macedonia', free expression was impossible. But the Powers had recognised the exiled Government since 1916 and could not in good faith now ignore it. Certainly the Podgorica decisions – 'illegal and irregular' – furnished no basis for doing so. Only a free election could show which Government, if either, represented most Montenegrins.

Exploring the attitudes underlying Serbian policy, de Salis noted that Radović, endorsed by Belgrade, had denied that Nicholas' personal failings justified the union. Even had he been beyond reproach, it was claimed, the Serb people would have required it.[166] For Belgrade the amalgamation was simply a *reunion*, the end of an artificial Montenegrin independence caused by the Turkish conquest of medieval Serbia. There was no place in this programme for Montenegrin federation with Croats or Slovenes, 'only for incorporation into a revival of the ancient Serb Empire' which had yet to regulate its relations with the other South Slavs.

This picture of Belgrade's attitude had been put to Whitehall by Petrovićist publicists but not by a trusted official. Its ramifications, as de Salis stressed, extended beyond the fate of Montenegro. The 'Greatest Serbia' policy might prove 'a fatal obstacle' to that free Yugoslav state for which there was support in Montenegro and elsewhere. While the Powers might consider unification based on Serbian force the easiest means of averting trouble in the short-term, in the long-term this was dangerous. The 'declared or sullen opposition' of annexed populations might 'render such a settlement far from durable and open the door to the very intrigues from outside which it is thought so desirable to eliminate'.

Officials in London were already convinced of the injustices committed by Radović's regime. (There seemed little doubt, one had noted in August, that the Serbs were 'behaving badly to the Montenegrins', and that this would have a 'most unfortunate' effect on British public opinion).[167] De Salis' report confirmed this view. It represented 'a damning case' – 'a severe but doubtless fully deserved indictment of the Serbs'.[168] The difficult question, however, remained unanswered: how were Britain and her Allies to respond to this 'deplorable situation' in Montenegro?[169]

Decision-making was hampered during 1919 by the fact that senior officials and Government ministers were in Paris for long periods. Those left behind to read reports from trouble-spots could telegraph advice, but felt detached from debates thrashed out (or left to stagnate) in the corridors and ante-rooms of the French capital. In the case of Montenegro the perspectives from London and from Paris clearly diverged during the summer.

For one thing, officials in London were influenced by greater proximity to press and parliamentary opinion. Since Serbia's occupation of Montenegro a small but vociferous lobby had denounced Belgrade and lamented the predicament of King Nicholas.[170] In the Commons the Government was harried for not safeguarding the right of Montenegrins 'to determine for themselves whether or not they shall be included in [the SCS] Kingdom', and for not being open about its policy.[171]

Particular difficulty was created by the de Salis report, eagerly anticipated by unofficial lobbyists as by the Government. With questions long parried on the grounds of insufficient or unreliable information, this was expected at last to produce a clearly articulated policy. Its arrival, Howard-Smith commented, heralded 'many awkward questions' in Parliament, and the Government had 'practically promised' to publish it. A letter to Crowe in Paris pressed for prompt action on Montenegro:

> I anticipate that highly inconvenient questions will be asked when Parliament reassembles after the Recess, and it will be very difficult to reply satisfactorily to those questions unless some settlement of this vexed question is in sight. There is apparently considerable feeling in this country at the delay in settling this matter.[172]

Crowe should know, Hardinge commented, that it would be 'almost impossible' to prevent publication of the report, and that questions were inevitable; he should be asked whether Montenegro was soon to be addressed by the Supreme Council. Publication would provoke 'a fierce controversy', Curzon warned, but the report was 'able and impartial' and this course seemed 'very desirable'.[173]

Crowe's responses, however, indicate the disagreement between Whitehall and the Peace Delegation over both the de Salis report and Britain's whole approach to Montenegro. While officials in London, pressured by lobbyists and with time to reflect, viewed the problem as *sui generis* and requiring immediate, separate attention, Crowe (a great influence on Balfour and the delegation) denied any distinction. The Council, he noted, while yet to reach a formal decision, had always assumed the question would be 'impossible to separate from that of the rest of Yugo-Slavia'. The present regime *was* 'irregular and unsatisfactory'; but in this respect, he argued, Montenegro was 'no isolated phenomenon in South-Eastern Europe'. Many regions were suffering during 'the prolonged state of belligerency and unrest' pending a final settlement. The Montenegrin situation, moreover, was 'an integral part and natural consequence of the present state of the Yugo-Slav question'. Ethnically, geographically and economically tied in with Yugoslavia, it was embroiled in the 'great and prolonged political controversy which at last, during the past month, has come to a head throughout the Yugo-Slav Kingdom'. Its position resembled 'that of almost any of the outlying Yugo-Slav lands'.[174]

Resolution of Yugoslavia's difficulties depended, Crowe argued, on the defeat by the 'more honest and intelligent' Yugoslavs, working for a constitution based on the ideals of the Pact of Corfu, of that 'reactionary current' embodied by Pašić and Protić. It was imperative that elections be held soon for an assembly to define the state's structure. There was no doubt, he stressed, that this would secure for Montenegrins, and others who desired it, 'a very large measure of provincial autonomy'. But (and for Conference delegates this was the nub) such elections must await the finalisation of the state's borders. Resolution of the Montenegrin question, in other words, like that of the Yugoslav constitution, required a resolution of the Adriatic dispute. After this there was 'no doubt' that political pressure would 'sweep away the obstructions artificially made by the Old Guard of Serbian politicians'.[175]

In London, as in Paris, Crowe commanded respect. His concerns about publishing de Salis' report at a delicate stage of the Adriatic talks were reluctantly heeded.[176] 'The Montenegrin question', Hardinge minuted gloomily, 'must still continue to hang fire'.[177] But with the failure to release the report meeting the anticipated hostile response, Whitehall's patience could not last. Was it denied, Ronald McNeill demanded in Parliament, that this report gave a 'most appalling description of the proceedings of the Serbians in oppressing the Montenegrins?'. In the face of transparent evasion by official spokesmen, even the former Under-Secretary of State Robert Cecil was moved to demand a résumé of the facts. 'It is really becoming little more than a scandal', he asserted, 'the lack of information we have on foreign affairs'.[178]

At the same time the complicating issue of financial assistance to the Petrović court re-emerged. Since France, at the beginning of 1919, had again terminated its share of the subsidy, the Treasury had been paying it alone. In November it decided that, due to financial constraints and Montenegro's abolition, the subsidy should be ceased, a decision bitterly resented by Nicholas' Government, and censored by Sir George Grahame:

> It is not in any way the fault of this unhappy Government that their principal Allies delay a consideration of what is to be done with regard to their country. None of the Allies have recognised the validity of the seizure of the country by Serbia, and Monsieur Plamenatz's Govt is therefore still the legal Government of Montenegro [...]. In these circumstances the Allies are morally bound to assist the Montenegro Government financially until a settlement is arrived at, and while they are kept here as powerless exiles owing to the forcible occupation of the country by Serbia.[179]

Officials in London sympathised. 'I agree entirely [...]', Frederick Adam (of the Southern Department) noted, 'and share his feeling of shame at the treatment which the Treasury have forced us to accord to the legal Government of Montenegro'.[180] (A long way, this, from the general contempt for Nicholas twelve months previously). To stop payments before a settlement would give the impression Britain had 'prejudged the Montenegrin case in favour of Serbia'.[181] Officials pressed in vain for a reconsideration.[182] 'It is a deplorable decision', wrote Adam in January, but 'nothing can be done'.[183]

Increasingly uncomfortable, Whitehall no longer accepted Crowe's call to await the outcome of the Adriatic question. Curzon telegraphed Crowe to urge again that Montenegro be placed on the Supreme Council agenda at the 'earliest convenience'.[184] *Pace* Crowe, Howard-Smith argued, 'the Montenegrin question must be treated separately'; the Allies must 'stand up to the Serbs as they have done to the Romanians'.[185] Nicholas' suggestion of an assembly organised by Anglo-American occupation, whose outcome he would accept, seemed 'eminently just' and 'the right way to reach a settlement'. But since occupation was impossible and the Serbians obstinate, all hope lay with the Supreme Council; it was 'high time', wrote Hardinge, that the latter took action.[186] While the pro-

Montenegrin lobbyists in Britain were not many, Adam noted, their case was 'exceptionally strong'. Britain was 'committed to not letting the Montenegrin nation lose its chance of free and peaceful development'. Lord Curzon accepted, he wrote, that the question was part of the Adriatic settlement, but thought Britain obliged to ensure Montenegrins entered Yugoslavia 'only on an equality with the Serbs, Slovenes and Croats'. The Council must promptly ensure that they 'not be absorbed as a province of the Serbian Kingdom'.[187]

But what were the Council to do? Adam's attempt to answer this revealed the misapprehensions prevalent in Whitehall in late 1919. It was surely not too late, he argued, for the Powers to secure Montenegro recognition as a separate unit in a Yugoslav Federation. Failure to acknowledge Montenegrin nationalism might mean 'that a martyr has been made of such poor stuff as King Nicholas'. Crowe should secure the same status for Montenegro as accorded to Croatia and Slovenia.[188]

Officials, however, were misled by the ideals of Corfu and the state's tripartite nomenclature. As Crowe quickly pointed out, the difficulty lay 'precisely in the fact that no such status is at present definitely accorded to any portion' of the SCS kingdom. In any case, he added, the Supreme Council had no authority to impose such a decision, and nor could the Yugoslavs themselves while their frontiers were uncertain. But he remained strikingly sanguine. 'There is not', he wrote, 'the slightest danger that, in such an assembly, the wishes of Montenegro would be disregarded or not be fully respected'. Curzon's view that Montenegro desired to join Yugoslavia as a discrete unit was shared, he felt, 'by the great majority of responsible Yugo-Slav politicians and public men'. Apart from 'a small reactionary clique of politicians', he wrote, 'I doubt if any Yugo-Slav would deny this necessity'.[189]

Officials in London continued to waver, but were swayed by Crowe's arguments, and by his assurance that France and America agreed. 'It is impossible to know what to think', Howard-Smith lamented; but the US position did seem to be that Montenegro join Yugoslavia.[190] Parliamentary questions over British policy towards Serbia's 'fait accompli' continued to be ducked. 'The future of Montenegro', Bonar Law told the Commons on 28 April 1920, 'can only be settled on its merits by agreement between the Allies'.[191] Only once the Adriatic dispute had been resolved, he said, could steps be taken 'for determining the status of Montenegro as part of the Serb-Croat-Slovene Kingdom'.[192] A memorandum for Curzon now assimilated Crowe's view completely:

> The exact status of Montenegro within the Serbo-Croat-Slovene State can only be determined by a Constituent Assembly in which Montenegro as well as all the other Yugo-Slav territories will be represented. The Constituent Assembly

cannot be elected until it is decided what territories are to be included in the Serbo-Croat-Slovene State. This depends on the general Adriatic settlement, which is still under negotiation.[193]

This was the position officials had been obliged to accept. But unease remained. For while it was not admitted, Crowe's argument was specious. Since most Montenegrins favoured a broader union, he reasoned, their inclusion in the SCS State could be assumed, and that union's constitutional structure was an internal matter not one for the Powers. But this ignored the fact that Montenegro, whatever its people's wishes, had not by any process recognised by Britain or the US dissolved itself in a Yugoslav State. Serbia had united with the ex-Habsburg territories to form an entity which had been internationally recognised. But Montenegro's inclusion hung on its previous incorporation as a province of Serbia. Since Britain had refused to recognise this process, it must still consider Montenegro an independent State, and the exiles at Neuilly its legitimate representatives. As Nicolson admitted, Montenegro was in the SCS State *de facto*, but 'not yet legally'.[194]

It was Nicolson, in fact, who most clearly expressed the discomfort palpable in the Foreign Office records. 'We are', he exclaimed, faced with drafting another parliamentary reply, 'in a quite impossible position as regards these questions on Montenegro'. With no official representative in the country, with news derived either from Belgrade or Alex Devine (both sources biased 'to say the least'), 'we are perfectly unable to answer these questions either honestly or accurately'.[195] A week later he confessed himself 'not at all at ease about all this Montenegrin business'. 'We are', he lamented, 'being manoeuvred onto weak ground owing to the fact that we do not, and perhaps cannot, say what we think'.[196] Though the issue here was alleged Serbian brutality, one senses a deeper unease about British policy (a supposition amply confirmed by his memoir of the period).[197] In a long minute in mid-August he set out the assumptions, and the wilful blindness to legal nicety, which had characterised the British position, before hinting euphemistically at its unstable foundations:

> Hitherto we have only been able to proceed by deduction on the following principles: a) the whole history of the present generation in Montenegro, not excluding King Nicolas himself, has been the story of a constant struggle to secure union with Serbia […]; b) now that the Yugo-Slav ideal has been realised it appears a priori impossible that any thinking Montenegrin could contemplate remaining outside the union. Economic considerations alone would seem to render this union inevitable.

From this we deduced, and all the 'authorities' share in this deduction, that the great mass of the Montenegrin people desired union with Yugo-Slavia, and that the only problem was that of the <u>form</u> which this union should take. This problem, however, was not for us but for the Montenegrin people themselves, acting through a Constituent Assembly to decide.

Since the armistice, however, three elements have arisen to confuse the logic of this deduction, namely 1) the intrigue of King Nicolas who wished to keep his throne, 2) the activities of Italy who desired at all costs to prevent the union, and 3) the futile behaviour of the Serb-Croat-Slovene Govt, who endeavoured by every means to make Montenegro a mere off-shoot of the Belgrade administration.[198]

The absorption of Montenegro by Serbia was admitted, therefore, not by a recognised legal process (none, it was accepted, had taken place) but by deduction on the grounds of historical and economic inevitability. Given clear evidence that Montenegrins wished to enter the Yugoslav union, Curzon wrote, 'I wish to do nothing which may complicate or defer such union'. The form would be decided by Constituent Assembly and it was beholden to Britain simply to verify the fairness of the elections and to ensure that, when the assembly met, Montenegrin opinion was adequately represented.[199]

But even this limited prescription was not universally accepted. On one side the conscientious Nicolson embraced a solution to the ethical impasse. Belgrade must know, he wrote, that Montenegro's union with Yugoslavia would be recognised only if the elections were seen to represent the popular will.[200] Britain must then ensure the views of Montenegrin representatives were not 'summarily quashed in [the] assembly'.[201] Her guarantees, and Parliamentary interest, meant Britain could not disinterest herself. But in Belgrade Sir Alban Young demurred. Was it wise, he asked, to do anything which might disturb the status quo? The Serbians were more sensitive about Montenegro than any other question (as angry reactions to Britain's refusal to recognise the union showed).[202] Did the Allies really intend, he asked, to shadow Montenegrins in the assembly and to attempt to enforce their desires? Stability was the priority, and Britain 'should abstain from enquiring too closely into the extent to which the democratic principles of free elections and self-determination are applied in practice'.[203] To interfere would be to meddle 'in a kettle of very lively fish', the danger that Montenegro (with Albania) would form 'fresh ingredients in the witches' cauldron of seething European politics'.[204]

Senior officials sympathised. Basing everything on these elections, Hardinge minuted, could produce 'stormy possibilities'. Supposing Montenegrins did want the King back? Better, he wrote, 'to let well alone and turn a blind eye to the elections which in oriental countries are carried on in a way quite unknown in the West, by official, police and military pressure coupled with corruption of the most flagrant kind'.[205] Crowe agreed, declaring himself 'much impressed' by Young's arguments.[206] Unfortunately, Curzon pointed out, parliamentary declarations meant Britain could not disinterest herself: 'we have promised to get fair play for Montenegro; and if she is stamped out by unfair elections we should be held guilty of a breach of faith'.[207] But the observer, Young was assured, would gauge the election 'not on Western standards but on standards usually current in Balkan countries'. The Government must be able to defend its handling of the question in Parliament without jeopardising Montenegro's inclusion in Yugoslavia. Britain was bound, Curzon noted cynically, to secure 'at least the appearance even if not the reality of legality and free choice'.[208]

On 10 November, therefore, Parliament was told that Britain's attitude would depend on the electoral result, and on satisfaction that it reflected popular wishes.[209] Thus, in essence, Whitehall had accepted Belgrade's position that Montenegrins must define their relationship with their fellow Yugoslavs not by negotiating entry as a state unit (a position of obvious strength), but by participating in an internal consultation process in which, as a small minority, they could have little leverage. What may seem legalistic quibbles, in other words, were of marked significance.

Crowe's argument, however, should be considered from a broader ethical as well as legal perspective. It was the case, for instance, that the Slovenes – a population with an identity arguably stronger than the Montenegrins – might be in the same position: a minority in an assembly unable, other than by fortuitous political bartering, to dictate the terms of their participation in the union. The fact that the Slovenes had owned no independent state was of juridical significance, but surely did not affect their position from the point of view of the principles of nationality and self-determination?

Even on this ground, however, the British position was not credible. It was true, as Crowe observed, that no people was guaranteed autonomy in the new state. But whereas the separate sub-national identities of Serbs, Croats and Slovenes had been repeatedly acknowledged, recognised (against the wishes of unitarists) in the nomenclature of the state, for Montenegrins there was no such assurance. On the contrary, Serbia had repeatedly claimed them as Serbs, dismissed their identity as a superficial provincial allegiance, and treated the union of Serbia and Montenegro as an internal matter in which Croats and Slovenes had no right to interfere.[210]

In Britain it was of course accepted that Montenegrins *were*, by linguistic, religious and even voluntarist criteria, essentially Serbs. But it was also accepted, partly due to the post-war resistance, that they had developed a distinct heritage and psychology, entitling them to separate and equal status among the Yugoslav peoples. As would become clear, Crowe's assurance that this would be granted was entirely baseless.

Two further reports were compiled by British officials who visited Montenegro: the first by Harold Temperley, after a visit in the late autumn of 1920, the second by Roland Bryce who (after Temperley withdrew in ill-health) fulfilled Britain's promise to monitor the elections of 28 November. On the basis of these Britain felt able at last, with relief, formally to accept Montenegro's absorption into Yugoslavia.

In basic content Temperley's report differed little from that of de Salis.[211] He distinguished the same three categories of opinion: Petrović loyalists, pro-Serbs and pro-Yugoslav autonomists. He confirmed, as expected, that the first was the weakest: even heartland regions were tranquil, with much less evident support for Nicholas than earlier in the year. International relief and credits from the SCS Government had apparently convinced this 'primitive people' they needed the Yugoslav state. Regarding the second two categories, Temperley (like previous observers) was unsure. The pro-Serbs – supporters of direct incorporation into Serbia – were strong, he thought, particularly among the intelligentsia, but their precise strength was hard to gauge.[212] 'Autonomists', meanwhile, was a generic term for a range of dissidents. Some wanted a republic, some a federal solution, some a limited form of regional autonomy. But all, Temperley stressed, agreed on the 'main point': inclusion in the Yugoslav State.

But as this summary suggests, while the evidence Temperley presented largely echoed de Salis, his emphasis, and his tone, were different. While for de Salis the 'main point' was resentment of the Serbian occupation, for Temperley it was pro-Yugoslavism (which, given that Whitehall already assumed this tendency, was hardly the point requiring investigation). While de Salis had denounced the Belgrade-imposed administration, Temperley was more sympathetic. It had spent, he noted, substantial resources to win Montenegrins round, and faced 'very great' difficulties. Furthermore, local discontent was inevitable whatever government was established. Montenegrins had no understanding or experience of efficient government, their traditions 'bound up with those of lawless and untrained valour'. It was difficult to accommodate them to 'the idea of discipline and control'.

Added (by implication, exaggerated) importance had been lent to the autonomist opposition, he suggested, by the country's martial tradition: 'opinion in Montenegro has always been armed before it was articulate'.

Reversing the concerns of de Salis and most previous British observers that Serbian troops and irregulars were suppressing legitimate opposition, Temperley feared that in some districts armed autonomists might intimidate other factions.

While the report soothed Whitehall's conscience over the manner of Montenegro's integration with Serbia, in terms of the presentation of British policy it resolved nothing. Since recognition had been stated to depend on the conduct and outcome of the Constituent Assembly elections, only a study of this process could provide closure. But the feeling that a resolution was now within reach was heightened by the development upon which the elections themselves, and progress over Montenegro, had long seemed to depend: the November 1920 Rapallo treaty resolving the Adriatic dispute. Particularly promising was the fact that, in return for what seemed in Britain an unduly favourable deal in Dalmatia, Italy agreed to cease support for Montenegrin separatism.[213]

All now depended on the elections. Within two days of the poll Bryce sent preliminary impressions. 'The actual voting', he wrote, 'was perfectly free and secret and there was an entire absence of gendarmes or any visible pressure'. Bar one incident the poll had been peaceful.[214] (In Britain this was seized upon, and Parliamentary statements lauded this enlightened conduct).[215] The result soon filtered through: four of ten Montenegrin seats won by Communists, two by Republicans, one by the Democrats, one by the Radicals and one each by two small local parties. But what mattered for British purposes was the *interpretation* of this result. In the absence of a separatist list, what was the meaning of Communist success in a region with no urban bourgeoisie? How important were the abstention rates? To decode from the voting Montenegrin attitudes to the union would, Bryce cabled, take time.

Meanwhile officials speculated. 'Communists', Temperley noted, probably meant republicans or left-wing autonomists rather than bolsheviks. At any rate they were unlikely to be pro-Nicholas.[216] But Young was less sure. Nicholas' partisans, he suggested, doubtless had voted for the Communists who were thought to have rallied the discontented of all hues.[217] While the result had not alarmed Belgrade (where it seemed 'the humorous feature of the elections') the possibility that Communist voters desired an independent Montenegro, possibly in the shape of a Soviet republic, seemed 'a dangerous speculation'.[218] Whitehall inclined also to view the vote as anti-Serbian if not pro-Nicholas. Communists had 'rallied in many districts those elements which are dissatisfied with Serbian administrative methods'.[219] But a final verdict, all agreed, must await Bryce's report.

On 16 December Bryce submitted his analysis. His approval of the electoral conduct remained unreserved. In an area with high illiteracy, the secrecy and voting method (coloured balls) seemed 'unimpeachable'.

Police and military were withdrawn and there was 'no evidence of interference or pressure' by any Government authority. Given communication difficulties and political lethargy in mountainous regions abstentions were 'satisfactorily low'.[220] (67.31% of registered voters – themselves 17% of the population – had voted, he reported).[221] Concerning the party lists, and patterns of voting, Bryce's analysis gave Whitehall exactly what it hoped to hear, his desire to please evident in conclusions questionable or over-emphatic even on the basis of his own testimony.

Chief among the difficulties of interpretation from a British perspective was that, as Bryce reported, the question of union with Serbia 'was not specifically raised as an election issue'. With moderate and extremist opponents failing to unite, none of the seven Montenegrin lists had opposed the union. But in any case the moderates, Bryce claimed, were the great majority. While unhappy about Montenegro's 'unfair and unnecessarily harsh treatment' in the past two years, they were willing to work for a Yugoslav Constitution granting Montenegrin equality. Within the 'numerically insignificant' ranks of the 'extremists', meanwhile, Bryce distinguished four groups: Nicholas' circle, those who had suffered persecution under Radović, those who blamed the regime for their present ills, and those who rued the loss of an accessible sovereign for one distant and impersonal. The opinions of the first two, he argued, were 'largely vitiated by the invariable intrusion of the personal element' (his implication, bizarrely, being that oppression was invalid grounds for opposition). The latter two groups included 'only the older generation of less enlightened peasants'.

For most Montenegrins, Bryce concluded, there was one question: communist or bourgeois? Over a third of voters – 37.99% – gave the first answer, comfortably more than for any other party (the Democrats came next with 27.8%), and the highest communist vote in Yugoslavia. Bryce ascribed this success to intense Communist propaganda, an emphasis on historic Montenegrin ties with Russia, the popularity of the leader Tomašević, and inadequate understanding of communist ideology. But partially plausible as these explanations were, his dismissive conclusion that the Communist vote was proportionately 'very little higher than in Serbia proper and in Macedonia' was quite wrong.[222]

The possibility Bryce seemed anxious to avoid was that, in Montenegro as in Macedonia, voting for a violently anti-establishment party represented an inarticulate protest against Belgrade. It is true, as he noted, that the KPJ was centralist and rejected 'bourgeois' historical identities, an unlikely vector – to an educated observer – for Montenegrin autonomist sentiment. But among a politically unsophisticated electorate the party targeted a general sense of deprivation and exploitation. Most subsequent historians have related Communist success in Montenegro directly to feelings of national disaffection. Without national political movements, Aleksa Djilas has noted, Montenegrins and Macedonians saw Communists as their defenders, in spite of their centralism and unitarism, because they opposed hegemonic Serbian nationalism and advocated fundamental change:

> [...] from the beginning the party was perceived, in matters relating to the national question, as the defender of the oppressed. As a radical opponent of the status quo, it was for many a 'protest party' for all kinds of dissatisfactions, including national discontents.[223]

The paradoxical but readily comprehensible idea that support for a centralist party could represent a regional protest against Serbian hegemonism was also absent from Bryce's brief analysis of the Radical and Democrat parties. Rightly he generalised that while Radicals espoused limited administrative decentralisation to protect historic identities, Democrats urged rigid centralisation to eradicate them. The fact, therefore, that the latter had fared much better in Montenegro (27.8% to 13.41%) seemed to Bryce a rejection of federalism or local autonomy, and helped justify the amalgamation of 1918.

This was a misleading impression, however. We will discuss the major parties later, but, contrary to Bryce's implication, the Radicals' proclaimed respect for historical and cultural differences entailed no recognition of separate Montenegrin identity; and the unitaristic centralism of the Democrats was, like that of the Communists, in part a reaction against Great Serbianism. (Democrat success in Macedonia, Kosovo and Sandžak similarly indicated wariness in the southern borderlands towards this ideology).[224]

This lack of sophistication in Bryce's analysis (for which, as a non-specialist, he can scarcely be blamed) manifested itself in his conclusions, which were wholly sanguine and reassuring. The elections, he declared, had been 'very satisfactory':

> No trace can be found of party or body of opinion in Montenegro which is against the abstract idea of union with Serbia in Yugo-Slavia. On the subject of the *de facto* union existent, opinion is unequally divided into – (a) a very small minority, who, basing their opinion on their experience of the past two years, assume that the projected Constitution will not give them equal rights with their brother Serbs [...] (b) a very large majority who support the *de facto* union with varying degrees of enthusiasm.

Provided, he affirmed, that the Constitution turned out to be a general one for all Yugoslavs, the minority's case would disappear and 'the last obstacle to the co-operation of the whole Montenegrin people in support of the union of their country with Serbia in Yugo-Slavia would thus be removed'. In London the report was, of course, warmly welcomed:

> It definitely establishes [Adam enthused] the fact that the great majority of the Montenegrins desire to join a Yugo-Slav state and have freely expressed their desire in a fair and well-conducted election [...]. HM Government have therefore secured the first object of their policy, as declared in both Houses of Parliament, viz. that the Montenegrin people should achieve the form of government that they desire by a free vote in the elections for the Yugo-Slav Constituent Assembly.

No one, Nicolson agreed, could read the report without conviction of its sincerity and truth, and 'some slight irritation' that Devine's propaganda had rendered Bryce's mission necessary.[225] (A few months previously he had declared the evidence of oppression in Montenegro 'overwhelming' and had been foremost in demanding such a mission).[226] 'The result', Curzon minuted with satisfaction, 'is a complete justification of our policy in insisting on having a representative in Montenegro during the elections' which ought to silence (though it probably wouldn't) the government's domestic critics.[227]

By the time the Constituent Assembly finally got down to drafting a constitutional document in late January 1921 the publication in Britain of the Temperley and Bryce reports, emphasising Montenegrins' pro-Yugoslav inclinations, had significantly cooled the controversy.[228] British attention, both in and out of Whitehall, had tailed away rapidly. While Devine continued to denounce Serbian hegemonism and British connivance, he struggled to find an outlet in the mainstream press.

Previously, of course, officials had argued that justice for Montenegro would depend on monitoring not only the election but also the subsequent fate of Montenegrin deputies. This second element, however, was quickly and quietly discarded. Faced with persistent pressure from (Serbian) Yugoslav diplomats to recognise Montenegro's absorption, Whitehall initially stalled, resolving to await the outcome of the Assembly, but soon wearied. If Montenegrin deputies had taken the oath to King and State, Nicolson asked in February, could Britain not follow France and America, withdraw exequaturs from the exiled Montenegrin Government, and end this 'tiresome question'?[229] The oath, Temperley agreed, proved the 'desire for union in the Yugoslav state'; Britain need only cancel the consular appointments.[230] This it promptly did, ending its involvement in the controversy. Only Italy declined to follow suit.

That this was not, however, the principled closure that Whitehall claimed, but rather a somewhat shifty retreat, is suggested by a continued misrepresentation of the Assembly's function. In Parliament the Government was asked whether an invitation to send delegates to an assembly in another country marked the fulfillment of British pledges to secure Montenegrin self-determination. This, Nicolson reacted, confused the issue 'in a foolish and [...] unscrupulous manner'. In the Commons Harmsworth responded that the assembly would indicate 'whether the dispersed elements of the Yugo-Slav race desire union, and, if so, on what terms they wish this union to be secured'.[231] It should now, Nicolson argued, be left to the Montenegrin delegates to demand independence if they desired it.[232]

Whitehall felt sure they did not desire independence. But it assumed Montenegro expected (and was right to expect) significant autonomy. Since it also assumed most deputies would wish to satisfy this desire, the question of how ten among over four hundred could secure their claim need not arise.[233] Officials continued, with seemingly wilful complacency, to portray Montenegrin delegates in Belgrade as negotiating terms of entry to the union. (Britain had no doubt, Crowe assured the French, that the assembly would work out a federal scheme *under which Montenegro would become part of the new State*).[234] They continued, in justifying British policy, to distinguish only between full independence and entry into a *federal* union. Britain had not changed its attitude, Lloyd George told Parliament; it was a question of Montenegrin wishes: 'if they are really desirous of entering into a great Slavonic Confederation, there is no reason why we should force independence upon them'.[235]

To regard this misconception as culpably complacent, if not as a deliberate misrepresentation, is only to amplify the view of Sir Alban Young, who had often stressed that Montenegro's union with Serbia, and so with Yugoslavia, was deemed to have occurred at the end of 1918 and to be entirely non-negotiable. The Constituent Assembly, he repeatedly pointed out, was not an instrument for the negotiation of conditions of entry. Reading with shock Harmsworth's parliamentary statement, he wrote:

> I do not know what M. Vesnić and his colleagues will think of His Majesty's Representative in Belgrade, from whom they will presume this information was obtained when they read this answer. I thought I had been untiring in my efforts to explain in my reports that, in the eyes of the Government, the conveners of the Assembly, the latter had neither of the attributes assigned to it by Mr Harmsworth. The union was

decided on by the pact of Corfu and confirmed by the
declaration of the 1st December 1918, and the preceding
resolutions of the Croatian National Assembly.[236]

But even such warnings from their minister in Yugoslavia did little to
undermine Whitehall's assurance. His comments, Adam suggested, need
not 'be taken too seriously'. The Assembly should secure 'the successful
negotiation of a federal Constitution'.[237]

Within months it had become obvious that a federal constitution was not,
after all, a likely outcome. On 1 April Temperley noted that Belgrade had
carried its scheme of dividing the State on non-historic lines (deliberately
breaking up units with a distinct historical identity).[238] Nicolson,
commenting later in the year on the law dividing the country into districts,
noted that Montenegro had been split into two, and that its very name,
'Crna-gora', was being suppressed. 'This can only', he lamented, 'lead to
trouble in the future'.[239] As reports of disorder in parts of Montenegro
continued to reach London during 1921 officials relapsed into gloomy
resignation. 'It is all hopeless', Nicolson minuted.[240]

And yet the sympathy once strong in Whitehall for the plight of
Montenegrin nationalism had by now largely dissipated. The 1920 election
had demonstrated Yugoslav sentiment in Montenegro, and the bitterness
left by the prior, forced union with Serbia was ignored. Ongoing
disturbances (unlike those in Croatia) were willingly dismissed as what
Belgrade claimed them to be: the acts of brigands and desperadoes,
showing that 'the Serbs have some justification for the strong hand in
Montenegro'.[241]

During late 1921 and into 1922, amid mounting reports of Serbian
arrogance over the Croatian question, Whitehall's limited information
about Montenegro was supplied almost wholly by Belgrade.[242] One
military official (for whom Montenegro remained 'somewhat uncivilised')
happily credited his Serbian source: 'any feeling that exists today in
Montenegro against the Serb regime is, I was told, confined to former
adherents of the late King Nicholas' regime and is in a distinct minority
[which] in a few years [...] would die away'.[243] Officials explained
disturbances as a spread from Croatia of Radićist discontent, forgetting
that anti-Serbian unrest in Montenegro had arisen at least as early as in
Croatia, and that sufficient cause existed without external intrigue.[244]

As other questions arose, and as officials familiar with the original
dispute moved on, memories grew hazy. With unrest worsening during the
economic hardships of 1922, and the dispute over the Yugoslav-Albanian
border ongoing (Italy still refusing to recognise Montenegro's inclusion in
Yugoslavia), an international crisis again threatened. One official
requested, for reference, an account of Montenegro's absorption by

Serbia: 'I know', he wrote vaguely, 'there was a popular vote by the Montenegrins to that effect'.[245] When a parliamentary question was tabled in November asking whether the Government approved the 'continued occupation of Montenegro by Serbian troops', private minutes were similarly hazy about both the question and previous British policy. Montenegrin sovereignty, Troutbeck asserted, was not abrogated by any treaty or convention but by the Montenegrins themselves at the 1918 Podgorica assembly: 'we on our part recognised the fact when the SCS Kingdom and not Serbia signed the Treaty of Versailles' – a complete misrepresentation of the British position between 1919 and 1921.[246] The act of Podgorica had anyway been, Crowe noted, 'fully condoned' by the free elections held for the Constituent Assembly, a statement arguable regarding Nicholas' deposition, but not regarding Montenegro's absorption by Serbia.[247]

The British view, in short, was that since the Constituent Assembly would shape Yugoslavia's constitution, it could be overlooked that Podgorica had merged Montenegro directly into Serbia rather than only into a broader union. To a degree, this is understandable. But attitudes on this narrow issue were symptomatic of that general failure to appreciate the depth of Serbian nationalist feeling towards Montenegro (as also towards Bosnia, Macedonia, and parts of Croatia-Slavonia) which explains the misreading of the Assembly. The wider question of the constitution will occupy us in the next chapter. In the meantime, it has been hinted that there was an element of wilfulness in British inconsistencies over Montenegro. If so, what underlay any reluctance to confront the issue?

We have noted before the assumption that an independent, insolvent Montenegro would be an unsustainable and destabilising element in Balkan politics and that she must, therefore, enter the Yugoslav union in whatever form it took. We have commented, likewise, on the practical impossibility for British policy-makers, denied support from major allies or their own War Office, of securing the military intervention which alone might have enabled a free plebiscite. But fundamentally, it must be emphasised, officials recognised an interest in good relations with a Yugoslav state they conceived as a pro-British bulwark against German imperialism. In the immediate post-war years, as the Adriatic controversy ground on and tilted (despite British sympathy for the Yugoslavs) towards Italy, Whitehall feared Belgrade might turn against its western patrons. With reports of rising anti-Western feeling in Yugoslavia, there was a reluctance to antagonise Belgrade unnecessarily.[248] 'We are always nagging the SCS Government for one cause or another', Nicolson commented, 'and have never really helped them when they were in the right as in the Adriatic Question'.[249]

While it was claimed, therefore, that attitudes towards Montenegro were 'entirely unconnected' with considerations concerning Italian policy, this is questionable.[250] In fact, while Yugoslavs complained that the Allies' anti-Yugoslav attitude over Dalmatia reflected an imperialist conspiracy which underpinned a similarly anti-Yugoslav attitude over Montenegro, the reverse was true. Guilt over the former, in which the Yugoslavs seemed the innocent party, tempered the expression of indignation over the latter issue in which they – the Serbians at least – seemed culpable. Concerning Nicholas' 'eminently just' last-ditch proposal one official wrote: 'I doubt whether the Serbs will accept and we cannot say anything to them'.[251]

The discomfort which resulted from being pushed, for clear pragmatic reasons, into a public stance which felt morally ambivalent, particularly with hindsight, was expressed most overtly by Harold Nicolson:

> The story of the submergence, or as Lord Cushendun would say, the suppression, of Montenegro, is not a very pleasant story [...]. [It] raised in my own mind a very serious conflict of motives. I disliked and distrusted King Nikita, yet I felt he was almost in the right. I had a passion for the Yugoslav State, and yet I felt they had behaved badly about all those bayonets and that Podgorica Assembly. I knew that it would be better in the long run, for economic and political reasons, were Montenegro in fact to be absorbed by Serbia, or, as we then preferred to phrase it, 'admitted into close union with the Serb, Croat and Slovene State'. Yet I felt extremely uncertain whether such a solution was in fact that desired by the Montenegrin population themselves. Here was a case in which dynastic interests on the one hand, were balanced against the union of a fine and liberated people. It was awkward to reflect that the balance of right inclined towards the dynasty, and the balance of wrong towards the Serbian liberators. It was in connection with this problem of Montenegro that my early faith in Self-Determination as the remedy for all human ills became clouded with doubts and reservations.[252]

Britain and the Idea of Yugoslav Unity, 1914-1918

Before discussing British analysis of the constitutional settlement in Yugoslavia between 1918 and 1921, we must examine the process by which the very notion of an independent South Slav state came to be embraced by British policy-makers. In terms of European geopolitics this was a revolutionary idea. Pre-war diplomats had noted closer political relationships among the South Slavs. But these trends were of such recent origin (at least in their latest manifestation), and faced such a monumental obstacle in the Dual Monarchy, that the idea of 'Yugoslavia' seemed hopelessly far-fetched. Before August 1914, Lord Eustace Percy observed during the war, it had 'entered into the minds of none but a dozen students'.[1] And yet in a short time it acquired – for an obscure foreign question – considerable popular appeal, was sponsored by a coterie of influential figures, and was ultimately welcomed (if largely after the fact) by the British Government.

Britain and the Yugoslav idea 1914-1918

The war which broke out in August 1914 concerned, in its genesis, Serbia's future as an independent state. If it did not seem obvious to many on the day Austrian armies crossed into Serbia, as it did to Seton-Watson, that a Great Serbian state had at that moment become 'inevitable', it is not surprising that the future of Serbia and her Habsburg kinsmen soon became the subject of debate.[2] Within four months Whitehall was having its attention drawn, by both the embryonic Yugoslav Committee and the Serbian Government, to aspirations towards South Slavic national amalgamation.[3] A memorandum submitted by Supilo to the British Government in January 1915 stressed that Serb, Croat and Slovene were 'three designations for a single ethnic unit', and that the 'palliative' of Slav autonomy under Habsburg rule could prove no lasting remedy.[4] The Serbian Government, Sir Charles des Graz reported from Belgrade in April, harboured similar aspirations, and had sent emissaries to the Allied capitals to propagate its view.[5] In May a Yugoslav Committee manifesto (co-authored by Seton-Watson) was delivered to Parliament and published in the press. It stressed the unity and indivisibility of the Yugoslav nation, 'alike by identity of language, by the unanswerable laws of geography and by national consciousness', and that nation's determination to unite its territories in a single independent state.[6]

Those who lobbied the British Government to approve the principle of a united Yugoslav state, furthermore, were never so unrealistic as to bank on the idealistic appeal of national liberation and unification. Repeatedly they emphasised the role a large state might play in obstructing Germany's route to the Near East. 'Serbia is not fighting only for Serbia', proclaimed Bishop Velimirović, 'but at the same time for India and Egypt'; the South Slavs were Britain's 'unique friend between Hamburg and Baghdad'.[7] To fail to create a South Slav state with its fullest ethnic borders, Seton-Watson urged Whitehall early in 1915, was to 'renounce the creation of a really effective barrier to German expansion in the Balkans and the *Drang nach Osten*'.[8] Independent Serb or Croat states would inevitably be sucked into the German orbit.[9]

Officials were certainly susceptible to such arguments. When one referred in August 1915 to the 'really large Serbia, which I am convinced it is our interest to encourage', he implied at least a significant encroachment on Austrian territory.[10] Prior to the war the Monarchy, for all its weaknesses, had seemed a strategic necessity. ('Great Britain has everything to gain from a strong Austria-Hungary', Eyre Crowe had written in 1909, 'on condition that [she] is not dominated by Germany and does not oppress Italy').[11] But the war had cast German aspirations in a more voracious light and gravely undermined faith in Habsburg independence of Berlin. Ideally, many still felt, a strong Austria would act both as a barrier to German ambition and as a counterpoise to Russia.[12] A federal Monarchy might, it was hoped, fulfil the role of bulwark between Teuton and Slav. But some officials certainly agreed with Namier that Austria must always be 'the backbone of German imperialism in Europe', her continued existence 'a definite victory for Germany'.[13]

Regarding a full, independent South Slav union, however, there was no question of commitments at this stage. British representatives were happy to make positive noises. Supilo recalled that both Grey and Asquith had promised to back a settlement 'according to the principle of Nationality'.[14] In July Lord Crewe, accepting an amended Yugoslav Committee manifesto, promised the English people's warm sympathy for the principle of nationality and 'goodwill' towards Yugoslav aims 'after the victorious conclusion of the war'.[15] But in private George Clerk (sympathetic to the Yugoslav cause and Seton-Watson's closest Foreign Office ally) cautioned that 'the time is not yet come for a detailed consideration of these questions – we have still to beat Germany'.[16]

This caution proved misguided, however, as Whitehall was plunged immediately into just such detailed consideration, not by ideological sympathy for the Yugoslav cause or long-term strategic analysis, but by the more pressing exigencies of the war. Already in early 1915 the question of an expanded South Slav state was raised by the military imperative to secure new allies in southern Europe. By that summer, with the war going badly, this need was increasingly critical. The two countries of most interest – Italy and Bulgaria – lay at opposite ends of Yugoslav territory, and it was in both cases with parts of this territory that diplomats hoped to induce allegiance to the Allied cause. The extent to which any principle of ethnic integrity was subservient at this stage to military necessity is shown by the fact that, while 'nationality' was disingenuously invoked in one case, in the other it was consciously violated.

British attempts to tie Bulgaria into the anti-German alliance, or at least to secure her neutrality, were ill-fated.[17] But for some time it seemed she might be tempted by Macedonian territories allotted to Serbia in 1913. The national identity of the population concerned had, as we have seen, been thought inchoate. Once it suited Britain to propose a transfer to Bulgaria, however, the justice of the Bulgarian claim seemed more apparent. A sententious memorandum by Lord Eustace Percy considered Serbian concessions necessary to the reconstitution of a Balkan bloc, the 'only worthy object of Balkan statesmanship'. And while hitherto the Government had, with 'patience and forbearance', refrained from pressing the point, a public newly alive to the cause of nationality expected no less:

> The unanimous opinion of students in this country [...] is one favourable to the occupation of Macedonia by Bulgaria on the ground of the national principle itself. There is in this country no doubt whatever that the principle of nationalities assigns these regions to Bulgaria, and that, without the cession of these territories, no peace in the Balkans can be assured.[18]

Fortunately, the difficulty of asking an ally fighting for survival to cede territory to a rival who had remained on the fence seemed softened by the scope for compensation in the west. The fact that certain Habsburg lands were claimed as rightful Serbian territory, and that there was sympathy in Britain for the claim, meant this too could be ascribed to principle rather than *realpolitik*. To British strategists, whose calculations underestimated Serb passions over the recently-acquired territories in Macedonia, this was an admirably holistic solution, promising long-term Balkan rapprochement and a united front against the Central Powers in South-East Europe.[19] The British public believed, a Foreign Office memorandum argued, 'that a certain injustice was done to Bulgaria in the settlement of the Macedonian question in 1913', that Britain was partly culpable, that this failure should be redressed, and that in return Serbia should receive 'all, and far more than all, that she dreamt of in 1912 on the Adriatic and in the Slav lands of Austria-Hungary'. The satisfaction of Serbia in the west and of Bulgaria in Macedonia formed 'interdependent parts of one policy'.[20]

But despite the lofty justifications, this was plainly wartime diplomacy as usual. The nub of the matter, as Grey expressed it, was that for Bulgaria to be secured without alienating Serbia, Pašić must be given 'a definite guarantee of the territories which Serbia will receive as the result of a victorious war'.[21] Here, Clerk observed, lay both 'Serbia's real avenue to progress and the justification for the cession to Bulgaria which can alone secure us united Balkan support'.[22] Allied victory, Grey promised in May 1915, would 'secure for Serbia at least the liberation of the whole of Bosnia and Hercegovina and their union with Serbia, and wide access to the Adriatic in Dalmatia'.[23] The enlarged state envisaged by British policy at this stage was not, therefore, 'Yugoslavia' – the political union of all South Slavs – but simply an expanded Serbia. Bosnia, Hercegovina and southern Dalmatia (a strip stretching north to the Neretva delta and therefore incorporating Dubrovnik) were reckoned, as we have seen, Serb territories. No form of popular consultation was suggested.

With regard to Croatia proper, Whitehall was more circumspect. Officials were not opposed to the broader Yugoslav idea, and they were anxious to persuade Serbia to make concessions in Macedonia. But they were also acutely sensitive to the views of their allies. And while France was rightly presumed to favour Serbian aggrandisement, it seemed uncertain how Russia, or subsequently Italy, might react. The tendency in pre-war Russia, particularly in ecclesiastical circles, to oppose an association of their Orthodox brethren with the Catholic Croats, meant that in London the Russian attitude seemed 'all important'.[24] In fact, though, as the Russian position deteriorated during the summer of 1915, St. Petersburg became desperate to secure Bulgarian assistance and was happy to promise Croatia in return for Serbian sacrifices. But by then Italy had entered the war and strongly opposed a Serbo-Croat union.[25]

When in August Pašić sought clarification of the territories offered, discussions were held to agree an Allied response. As a result Serbia was assured Bosnia, Srem, Baćska, part of southern Dalmatia (to be split with Montenegro), and Slavonia if it was in Allied hands, while the fate of Croatia was reserved. Essentially this was a British-brokered compromise between the Italian desire to restrict Serbian aggrandisement (and to forge a bond with Hungary), and the Russian position.[26] British officials certainly did not view Croatia as rightful Serbian territory like Bosnia or southern Dalmatia. If justice was to be done to its distinct religious and historical identity, some form of consultation would be required. Union between Croatia and an enlarged Serbia would, Grey informed Niš in May, 'naturally be a matter to be decided by the Croats themselves' (though subject to their approval, he later wrote, Britain could 'guarantee to facilitate the union').[27] Nevertheless, British solicitude for Croat self-determination owed as much to Italian feelings as to those of Croats.[28]

That sympathy for South Slav nationalism was firmly subordinate to military priorities was made amply clear by the terms of the Treaty of London in April 1915. British strategists convinced their superiors that Italian involvement would decisively affect the war. (It would be, Grey affirmed, 'the turning point' which would 'very greatly hasten a successful conclusion').[29] On this basis the Cabinet agreed to promise Italy the territory she demanded in Istria and Dalmatia, with its 1.3 million Yugoslavs, and to press Russia to concur.[30]

It was inevitable, of course, that military imperatives seemed paramount. (One should indeed avoid importing 'the ethical standards of tranquillity into the emotional atmosphere of danger').[31] At the same time it is not clear that Whitehall's discomfort at the Italian terms was as acute as some officials subsequently liked to suggest.[32] While the territory in question was known to be ethnologically more Slavic than Italian, and while it was regretted (for pragmatic reasons) that the Serbs should be further antagonised, few yet regarded 'nationality' as a presiding geopolitical principle. Clerk may in private have commented that Allied ministers would deserve 'to be hanged' unless Italy decisively tilted the balance of the war, but at his desk in Whitehall he brushed protests aside.[33] 'We cannot', he asserted, 'strain the principle of nationalities to the point of risking success in the war'.[34] 'We wish the war to be ended as far as possible on the basis of nationalities', he minuted, '[...] but we did not set out on a Nationality Crusade'. 'What we are doing', wrote Grey, 'is to take the best means to ensure that the Slavs get all but a fraction of their claims', since without Italian cooperation 'the Slavs might get less than nothing'.[35] Any national boundary would have its 'ragged fringes'.[36]

Territories offered to Serbia were still conceived, in other words, as reward for services to the Allied cause or as compensation for sacrifices elsewhere, rather than as rightfully hers on ethnic grounds. Pašić should appreciate, it was noted, that Serbian aspirations were now heeded to an extent 'far beyond anything that seemed possible a few months ago';[37] he should recall the distance the British Government had travelled towards acceptance of aspirations hardly considered before outside Serbia itself.[38] A Yugoslav Committee memorandum seemed to Clerk 'almost menacing in its insistence on the Allied Powers creating a vast Yugo-Slav State'.[39] Such a demand seemed not natural and principled but presumptuous and unrealistic. A draft message to Serbia was couched in language wholly conventional in its pragmatism: 'the following territories are reserved for Serbia in the event of a successful war [...]'.[40] And it was pointless, officials noted, to pretend otherwise. Would the Allies, the elder Nicolson asked rhetorically, continue fighting simply to uphold promises to Serbia?[41] 'We all know perfectly well', wrote Lord Eustace Percy, 'that we cannot and will not continue the war until Yugo-Slavia is constituted'.[42] Whatever the vague encouragement given to pro-Yugoslav campaigners, this, in essence, remained Britain's position until the eve of the armistice.

1916 saw Yugoslavia largely disappear as an issue for official Britain, just as it burgeoned in the popular consciousness. With Serbia conquered and its government in exile, Bulgaria allied with the Central Powers, and Italy making no impression on the southern front, the future disposition of the South Slav territories seemed uncertain.[43] When the subject was raised, as when Alexander Karadjordjević visited London in April, the principal concern was to avoid commitment. 'It will be desirable', warned Sir Arthur Nicolson, 'to be very cautious as to what is said to the Crown Prince in respect to a Serbo-Croatian union'.[44] (Of the various hints and assurances made during the frantic diplomacy of 1915 none, as things had turned out, was considered binding).[45] There was scant official enthusiasm for the propaganda campaign launched to mark Kosovo Day in 1916, and unease at Lord Cromer's appointment as President of the newly-formed Serbian Society (for fear that apparent government sponsorship might upset Italy). While Seton-Watson remained close to certain officials, his relations with the Foreign Office were increasingly strained.[46] The British Ambassador in Italy criticised 'certain people in England' who saw themselves as 'heaven-born interpreters to other nations of what they ought to think'.[47]

Nevertheless, the failure of the 1916 offensive did foster for the first time the possibility of a negotiated peace, and memoranda began to be drawn up considering the key principles of a European settlement. The most important of these, drawn up by Sir Ralph Paget and Sir William Tyrell, assumed a total Allied victory, and advocated the destruction of Austria-Hungary and South Slav unification. 'We consider', they wrote, 'that Great Britain should in every way encourage and promote the union of Serbia, Montenegro, and the Southern Slavs into one strong federation of States with the view to its forming a barrier to any German advance towards the East'.[48] Such ideas, if they were the logical conclusion of previous statements, were nevertheless much starker than most official thinking at this stage. (For one thing, prior to Russia's collapse the break-up of Austria seemed likely only to enhance the former's already uncomfortable influence in Eastern Europe and the Near East).[49]

Early 1917 saw critical developments both for the conduct of the war and for its political aftermath. On 10 January the Allied reply to President Wilson's conservative 'peace note' was published. While the latter had been condemned in *The New Europe* for overlooking the modern movement of nationality, this reply was greeted rapturously as a 'charter of emancipation', a landmark in world affairs.[50] Despite calling for the restoration of Serbia and Montenegro to their pre-war independence (a fact not lost, as we saw, on the exiled Petrović court), the call for 'the liberation of the Italians, as also of the Slavs, Roumanians and Czecho-Slovaks from foreign domination' was hailed as a commitment to Yugoslav unity and independence. Three months later the Russian revolution, combined with the prospect of US engagement, seemed to favour a campaign based explicitly upon the principle of 'self-determination' proclaimed by the Russian socialists. The implosion of one imperial regime had shown, some argued, that an open commitment to the oppressed nationalities of Austria-Hungary could destabilise that state from within. The employment in May of Seton-Watson, alongside like-minded colleagues like Lewis Namier and Rex and Allen Leeper, by the Department of Information's new 'Intelligence Bureau' (with a remit to study internal conditions in foreign, particularly enemy, states) seemed to promise a shift towards direct allegiance to the principle of nationality.[51]

But in fact the impact of these developments on British policy towards the Yugoslav question was less significant in the short term than Seton-Watson and others were led to hope, their optimism on this score largely, as Victor Rothwell has observed, 'wishful thinking'.[52] The reply to Wilson had been primarily a propaganda gesture directed at American opinion; it was certainly not intended as a commitment to dismember Austria-Hungary. In fact clandestine attempts had already begun – and would continue for another fifteen months – to detach Austria-Hungary from Germany by a separate peace, thus assuring the former's survival. While Seton-Watson considered that Allied commitments led 'logically and inevitably' to the break-up of Austria-Hungary, officials thought Britain bound only to ensure a measure of federal autonomy for the subject nationalities.[53] In July 1917 the War Cabinet decided that discussion of specific war aims be postponed as long as possible.[54] Most of its senior members remained opposed to Habsburg dismemberment even during the final months of the war.[55]

And while in retrospect none can doubt the impact of the Russian Revolution on the geopolitical outcome of the war, its immediate effect was not obviously favourable to the Yugoslav cause. For one thing, it gave currency in Britain, particularly on the left, to the idea of an armistice without annexations or recriminations and a return to the *status quo ante*, a tendency which appalled those campaigning for an end to imperial subjection in Europe.[56] Their attempt to reclaim the moral high-ground by hailing the principles of self-determination and democratic choice had not, by the early summer of 1917, made a significant impact. Nor did Seton-Watson believe that events in Russia would be repeated. While political conditions in the Monarchy were increasingly tense, with the 'leaven' of the Russian Revolution working among all classes and races, it would be, he argued, 'a grave mistake to suppose that there is any analogy between the situation of Petrograd last March and that of Vienna or Budapest today'. In Austria-Hungary there was 'no real basis for a revolution'.[57]

Nor does it seem with hindsight that the employment by the Intelligence Bureau of Seton-Watson and other *New Europe* contributors marked an important policy shift. The Department of Information, of which the Bureau was a subsidiary, had poor relations with senior Foreign Office officials, who mistrusted its intentions, resented its direct access to the Prime Minister, and feared the disruption these zealous individuals might cause. Confidential information was deliberately withheld, not least about the peace negotiations in progress with Austria-Hungary.[58] Its members, the Foreign Office insisted, should 'confine themselves to facts and refrain from recommendations and advice'.[59]

But while they might not have directly altered British policy towards Austria, the events of early 1917 and the Russian Revolution in particular did induce developments among the South Slavs – most notably the July Corfu Agreement between the Serbian Government and the Yugoslav Committee – which influenced British attitudes to the Yugoslav project.[60]

In accordance with their desire to keep options open regarding Austria-Hungary, initial British reaction to the Corfu Declaration was muted. (Indeed at the time the gathering had aroused suspicion: 'what are they conferring about?', Cecil asked: 'it sounds to me rather ominous').[61] An Intelligence Bureau memo written by Seton-Watson in mid-September eulogised a pact which represented 'the unanimous and considered view of every serious party in Serbian politics'.[62] But not until 28 November, over four months after it was announced, was there any official reaction. His Majesty's Government had received the text of the Declaration, Lord Robert Cecil announced blandly in Parliament, 'with great interest and sympathy'. It was not, he responded to questions, desirable to say more.[63]

There certainly *was* sympathy in many quarters for the ideals expressed at Corfu. Memoranda prepared by the Political Intelligence Department (which succeeded the disbanded Intelligence Bureau in March 1918) backed a redrawing of European boundaries with reference to ethnicity. This was not, it was argued, a departure from traditional notions of diplomacy (as was imagined both by romantic enthusiasts and their conservative opponents); on the contrary, the 'balance of power' would remain fundamental. But states based on conscious common nationality would 'be more durable, and afford a firmer support against aggression than the older form of State, which was often a merely accidental congeries of territories without any internal cohesion, necessary economic unity, or clearly defined geographical frontiers'. In this respect, it was argued, 'our interests entirely coincide with the principle of nationality and the doctrine of self-determination, though there must be very great difficulties in applying it'.[64] The Yugoslavs specifically had 'incontestably' shown 'almost unanimous determination to construct a united independent Yugoslavia'; if difficulties were presented by their diverse traditions, they were 'indisputably one race'.[65] While the doctrine of self-determination could not be applied universally, there was no problem in this case; the Habsburg Yugoslavs wanted simply to join an existing state with which they shared a racial and cultural affinity: 'here [...] there is no question of anarchy, but simply of transference of authority'.[66]

As we have seen, however, this sympathy (always strongest among Whitehall's younger elements) did not preclude attempts to reach a peace with Austria quite incompatible with the goals of Corfu. It was one such effort which finally induced the Government to produce a statement of war aims, delivered by Lloyd-George to a trade union audience on 5 January 1918. While this referred to Polish independence, it talked for the other Habsburg nationalities only of 'genuine self-government on true democratic principles'.[67] Three days later Wilson's Fourteen Points referred likewise only to 'the freest possible opportunity of autonomous development' for the peoples of Austria-Hungary. An agitated Serbian enquiry as to whether Britain supported a Yugoslav State was ducked. Speaking personally, Cecil proffered, given a complete Allied victory he would favour a Yugoslav State; but 'how far any such object would be attainable depended on the fortune of the war'.[68] In private Lord Hardinge rejected complete Yugoslav independence as, under present conditions, 'an unrealisable programme'.[69] Though ignorant of the negotiations taking place, South Slav activists were acutely alive to Britain's reluctance to commit to their cause, and lamented her 'lingering liking for Austria'. Despite 'much sympathy for the Yugoslav cause among Allied circles', wrote one campaigner, 'that cursed Austria still enjoys the sympathy of the official classes here [...]'.[70]

On Steed's advice Lord Northcliffe, heading the new Department of Propaganda in Enemy Countries (EPD), urged clarification of Britain's attitude to Austria-Hungary. The Government was, he argued, perched between two contradictory policies: seeking a separate peace which would preserve the Monarchy, while simultaneously encouraging subject nationalities in their quest for independence. On 5 March, with hope declining for the first policy, the War Cabinet tentatively approved the second. But no careless promises should be made, it cautioned: 'we must not promise them complete independence if the best we could get was autonomy'.[71] Later that month a final approach to Austria failed, and on 12 April the publication of the Sixtus letter ended all hopes of a separate peace. When in May Lord Derby asked which horse Britain was riding, Cecil replied that the policy of detaching Austria must finally be abandoned and all support given to the oppressed nationalities.[72]

In private this was the moment at which the British Government endorsed an independent Yugoslav State. A clear public statement, however, was obstructed by Italy. On 3 June a declaration by the Allied Supreme War Council calling explicitly for 'a united and independent Polish State' expressed only an 'earnest sympathy for the nationalistic aspirations towards freedom of the Czechoslovak and Yugoslav peoples'.[73] In Britain, a PID memo argued, there was 'no idea of making any difference of principle or of treatment between the Poles on the one hand, and Czechs and Yugo-Slavs on the other'; the latter's aspirations were 'in full accord with the fundamental principles for which the *Entente* is fighting'.[74] Nevertheless, while Balfour now privately admitted the break-up of the Monarchy was the 'best solution in the general interest', Britain never publicly matched the US statement on 28 June that all branches of the Slav race should be completely freed from German and Magyar rule.[75]

By August it seemed certain, in any case, that internal pressures would cause Austria-Hungary's collapse.[76] In the event, therefore, as the PID admitted, Austria's demise and the creation of a Yugoslav union came upon the Entente before any conclusive decision had been made.[77] Despite widespread sympathy for the Yugoslav project, Britain had ultimately felt unable to commit: rather, as Seton-Watson expressed it, 'like a bather who undresses but remains standing on the brink'.[78] For all that officials talked as if South-East Europe was theirs to shape, delegates assembling for the Peace Conference were faced in the ex-Habsburg lands with a *fait accompli* they were powerless to alter.[79]

The problem which quickly emerged for British officials was in what manner to recognise those groups claiming authority over the Empire's South Slav lands. While in the case of the Czechoslovaks one unchallenged body – the Czechoslovak National Council – claimed to act as a provisional government, a bitter dispute had developed between the Serbian Government and the Yugoslav Committee. While the former asserted a right to represent all Yugoslavs, the latter held out firmly for separate recognition. Already, therefore, by the time a Yugoslav state was declared at the beginning of December 1918, Britain had to respond to an internal crisis with serious ramifications for its future structure and stability. But let us first retrace our steps, and look at the assumptions already made in Britain about the constitutional shape of a Yugoslav state.

Expanded Serbia or new 'Yugoslavia'? – The Shape of a United South Slav State in British Thinking 1914-1918

We have noted the increasing tendency in wartime Britain to view the Yugoslav groups as a single nation, to relegate religious and historical differences beneath a fundamental racial-linguistic unity and apparent

Yugoslav consciousness. And we have seen that, while not official government policy, the concept of a united Yugoslav State – distinct from an enlarged Serbia – acquired late in the war a wide currency in Britain. But to what extent, before December 1918, did British observers contemplate the constitutional structure best adapted to a state with such disparate provinces and traditions?

The Government considered an enlarged Serbia during 1915-16 predominantly in the context of compensations for Macedonia. Bosnia, Southern Dalmatia and Slavonia were to be integrated in the pre-war Serbian state. The Croats, however, were to approve any union with their Serb brethren, a recognition of distinct identity which manifested itself also in vague assumptions that the resulting union would be federal. Whether a 'Federation of Croatia' followed the enlargement of Serbia, Grey wrote to des Graz in May 1915, would be a matter for the Croats themselves.[80] His proposal that Serbia, Croatia and Montenegro should have most of the intervening territory 'for division among themselves' implies a hazily-imagined tripartite federal or confederal arrangement (though the awkward matter of internal frontiers was not broached).[81] The Paget-Tyrrell memo of autumn 1916, which boldly advocated the dissolution of the Habsburg Monarchy, talked of a 'future confederation of Southern Slav States'.[82]

From early in the war Supilo highlighted the pitfalls awaiting a unification process. Already in January 1915 he stressed that the Austro-Hungarian South Slavs must see the war as one 'not [...] of conquest but of redemption and liberation'. Serbia, he stated, must expect to come to provinces like Bosnia or Dalmatia 'not as a conqueror of new territories but as a liberator of her own people' who would immediately participate in the country's administration.[83] In August he complained that the Allied promise of Bosnia, Slavonia and half of Dalmatia (all with Croat populations) directly to Serbia, while Croatia was left free to choose, might jeopardise a stable union by creating Croat irredentism in Serbia, Serb irredentism in Croatia, and a temptation for Catholic Croats to separate from the Orthodox Serbs. Either all Croats should be assigned to Serbia or all should have the option.[84] Yugoslav national unity, he urged Pašić, 'should not be divided and offered in pieces to Serbia as a basis for compensations' but should be viewed as a single 'ethnic entity'.[85] In October Supilo again warned British officials that unless Serbia reformed, 'instead of liberation, union and fusion of the Croats and Slovenes with the Serbs, it would [...] be a simple case of conquest and domination inspired by Serb-Orthodox exclusivism'. In this case the Habsburg Yugoslav regions might prefer a separate union around Croatia.[86]

A few in Britain were strongly influenced by Supilo. Seton-Watson in particular agreed that unless the Yugoslav region was treated as one, an amalgamation might prove divisive rather than unifying. Immediately he urged that the problem be treated 'on truly Southern Slav (as opposed to merely Serbian) lines'; transferring Bosnia alone from Habsburg to Serbian hands would settle nothing – Bosnia, Dalmatia, Croatia-Slavonia and the Slovene lands were too entwined by geography and sentiment.[87] Union must come voluntarily from within, not by conquest from without. It must preserve for the Habsburg South Slavs 'their existing political institutions and culture as a worthy contribution to the common South Slav fund'. The natural solution would be a federal union, with a Croatian Parliament in Zagreb parallel with that in Belgrade, and a central federal Parliament, either based centrally in Sarajevo or rotating between the various provincial centres.[88] Like Supilo he stressed that no satisfactory boundary could be drawn between a separate Croatia and an enlarged Serbia; the two sisters, he warned Prince Regent Alexander, would be enemies, each plagued by irredentism among their respective minorities.[89]

But as we have seen, the claim that South Slav union must be complete if it was not to prove divisive was little heeded by officials unwilling to commit to securing Yugoslavia, and in this context des Graz's assumption at the end of 1915 that the Serbian Constitution would simply be extended to new territories may have been widely shared.[90] Certainly, beyond vague talk of a Croat-Serb 'federation', little thought was given to the problems of forging a single state from the disparate Yugoslav groups. Though he impressed officials he met, Supilo's submissions went unminuted. And while Grey did tentatively agree that, with Pašić's approval, Bosnia, Southern Dalmatia and Slavonia might – like Croatia – choose their own fate, Pašić's refusal caused little concern. The Balkan discussions, wrote Sir Arthur Nicolson, were tangled enough; Supilo's scheme would make matters worse.[91] Although by the autumn of 1915 Seton-Watson felt, rather optimistically, that an impact had been made upon British thinking, Clerk reminded him that 'the S[outhern] S[lav] question is quite a new one, which has only just begun to force itself upon the attention of public men'.[92]

In fact Whitehall largely ignored Supilo's concerns until they were forced on its attention prior to the peace conference. As we have seen, between the defeat of Serbia and the first Russian Revolution, the Yugoslav question, while increasingly prominent in the British media, largely passed from official consideration. From his position in the Intelligence Bureau Seton-Watson tried to return it to the agenda. In May 1917 he hailed the Russian Socialist principle of 'self-determination' as 'the method of deciding the future of the Yugoslav race (including the Slovenes)'.[93] His report on the Corfu agreement hailed its prescription for Yugoslav unity. While Pašić had deprecated any extreme form of federalism, he noted, he and others had 'accepted as an axiom the need for considerable local autonomies to meet the varying requirements of the various provinces'. And if all agreed on the need for a strong central parliament, the Serbians were clear that 'if [...] Croatia or other sections of the Yugo-Slavs insisted on a federal solution they would be prepared to accept this'. There was 'to be a settlement by amicable agreement and Serbia repudiated any idea of forcing her will upon the others'.[94]

But not before the foundation of the Political Intelligence Department in March 1918 was there any official inclination to deliberate the internal shape of a Yugoslav state, or that state's position in a general peace. As we have seen, Seton-Watson and others had supported Supilo's insistence on a federal (or at least decentralised) constitution which would respect the region's diverse traditions. Interestingly, however, the memorandum on South-East Europe drawn up by Nicolson, Leeper and Paget which discussed the issue of 'incompletely conciliated rivalries' based on geographical and historical factors took a different view. The Pact of Corfu had represented, it argued, a consensus that to overcome the 'artificially created' divisions of the past there should be emphasis on 'the complete union of the race, not in any federal system, which would allow the old rivalries to continue, but in one united State wherein all three branches of the race should enjoy absolute equality'. The Greater Serbian idea had 'in some cases died hard', but might now 'for practical purposes' be considered dead. It was 'indisputable' that a unitary state was 'the only possible solution'. On such a basis there was 'no reason why [...] the new Yugoslav State should not work well'.[95]

Until at least October 1918 most British officials were insensitive to Croat and Slovene concerns about their position in the embryonic state, and to the tendencies in Serbian political circles which underlay these concerns. One who was not, Horace Rumbold, reported from Berne in May 1918 that Austrian Yugoslavs distrusted the Corfu Agreement as 'a mere trick of Pašić'. 'All the opposition parties', he wrote, 'are utterly opposed to Pašić's centralising and imperialistic tendencies, which would turn Yugoslavia into a second Macedonia'; they were 'determined that even the smallest provinces should have full autonomy, and be able to develop freely'.[96] Though in some respects confused, Rumbold saw accurately the deep mistrust between the Serbian Government and the Austrian Yugoslavs. His information, however, was dismissed in Whitehall. The agreement, Allen Leeper insisted, had been 'universally welcomed among the Yugoslavs' with only very insignificant exceptions.[97]

When in June Harold Temperley wrote an intelligence report on the Yugoslav problem he recorded that the Pact of Corfu had 'proclaimed the Yugoslav programme beneath the aegis of Serbia', a wording highly insensitive to the insecurity of Habsburg South Slavs. Initially, he argued, Croat and Serb interests were not quite the same: 'the Serb conception of Yugo-Slavia tended to be that of a greater Serbia and the Croat conception was federalistic'.[98] But during the war 'national feeling' (a phrase used always at this stage to indicate *Yugoslav* feeling) had spread markedly. The

Pact of Corfu and the demise of the 'Russian-Orthodox bogey' had given the Croats and Slovenes a feeling of security. If the terms of the pact were not ideal from their point of view (there being no mention of federation), the securities given had substantially allayed the earlier suspicion of Serbian intentions. This report significantly influenced official British opinion. (In December it was reprinted and circulated with minor amendments).[99] Though it did, unlike the previous PID report, acknowledge a Croatian desire for federalism, it attributed this to concerns originating *before* the early summer of 1917, implying that a subsequent growth of Yugoslav sentiment had removed the need for a federal arrangement. A slogan published by Croatian and Slovene officers in Russia ('No Great Serbia, no Great Croatia, no Great Slovenia. Federated Yugo-Slavia was and is our ideal') Temperley described as 'extreme'.[100]

The western Yugoslavs, Harold Nicolson minuted with similar insensitivity, were in a different position to the Czechs and Poles since they 'will not form a distinct State, but will be assimilated to Serbia'. He dismissed the Yugoslav Committee's request for a distinct army formed from Austrian Yugoslavs imprisoned in Italy, considering it – as Pašić did – 'only natural' that these join the Serbian Army.[101] Since 'nationalist' (Yugoslav) feeling was presumed to dominate in Croatia by this stage, there was scant sympathy for the Committee's wish to be recognised as a provisional authority, with its own armed force, distinct from Belgrade.[102] (In part, of course, the Committee had itself to blame for overstating to the Allies in the past its common ground with the Serbian Government). When Seton-Watson pointed out the changed attitude of Serbs from Bosnia and Croatia towards Pašić ('till lately [his] most ardent supporters [...] now entirely disillusioned'), few were interested. It was, Lord Hardinge observed dully, 'difficult to follow the intricacies of Serbian party politics'.[103] Des Graz, meanwhile, presented the 'growing opposition to the personal ascendancy of Pašić' simply as a split within Serbian politics ('the causes of which lie far back'), without relating it to the broader Yugoslav picture.[104]

With the Yugoslav project still far from secured, even Seton-Watson continued to stress, particularly in public, that Serbia's problems were ones of personality and party politics rather than fundamental disagreement over national unification.[105] Though he warned against any attempt by the 'old guard' to revert to a narrowly Serbian rather than Yugoslav ethos, he did not suggest this process was actually underway. On the contrary, he wrote, this 'wretched party feud' had happily not infected Serbian enthusiasm for Yugoslav unity; the Declaration of Corfu still represented 'the unanimous voice of every section of the Serbian nation'. 'The unhappy misunderstandings of the last year must not', he argued, 'be taken as a sign of any slackening or uncertainty in the national ideal'.[106]

By early October, however, with the Empire collapsing and the Yugoslavs dictating their destiny on the ground, it was no longer necessary to exaggerate a unity of purpose. For the first time the antagonisms which had been boiling under the surface became unavoidably apparent to British officials. Ante Trumbić delivered to Whitehall a memorandum expressly highlighting the divergence of views between the Committee and Pašić's Government. While careful to deny that this was a conflict with Serbia as a whole, he attacked Pašić bitterly for refusing to back separate recognition for the ex-Habsburg Yugoslavs as an Allied nation. He was, Trumbić complained, animated by a spirit not of liberation but of conquest; he assigned to Serbia a position of 'Prussian primacy' and would hold the western Yugoslavs 'in a position of subjection and humiliation'. He failed to appreciate that provinces 'in matters of civilisation and public administration more advanced than Serbia' would 'not be willing to be subjected to a Government which is not on the same plane'.[107]

At the same time Seton-Watson submitted a paper entitled 'The Policy of Mr Pašić and the Yugoslav Problem'.[108] The Government must realise, he urged, the motives behind Pašić's policy and the extent to which he had alienated not only Habsburg Yugoslavs but also political circles in Serbia. Abandoning his insistence that Corfu had unanimous support, he argued that Pašić had been forced into it by external events – the Russian Revolution and growing American influence – and that, despite paying lip-service to its principles, had never intended to honour them.[109] The 'whole basis' upon which Corfu rested, he insisted, was that the Serbian Government and the Yugoslav Committee were 'absolutely equal contracting parties'. In opposing recognition for the Committee and claiming Serbia alone represented the Yugoslav people, the Serbian Government was 'violating the whole spirit of the Agreement'. And this was no mere question of form. 'The issues at stake are fundamental', he insisted: 'it is a struggle between the Pan-Serb solution, as represented by Pašić and Protić and [the] Yugoslav idea, as accepted by the great body of Serbian and Yugoslav intellectuals'.

In Whitehall these blunt memoranda evoked mixed feelings. It did seem, Leeper observed, that Pašić had 'practically disregarded all Parliamentary methods' in confronting his Serbian opponents. (Des Graz had often said so from Corfu). But having been persuaded by Yugoslavs and their British allies of the unity of feeling existing between Serbians and their western brethren, there was a tendency – certainly a desire – to regard these claims as overstated and alarmist. Pašić might at times have behaved arbitrarily, Leeper admitted, but:

> [...] the bogey that Trumbić raises of a Serbian annexation of the Yugo-Slav countries of Austria-Hungary is purely fantastic. Serbia is far too small and exhausted to carry through such an

annexation against the wishes of the population even in the
unimaginable eventuality of the Great Powers permitting such a
flagrant violation of the rights of peoples. There is no real
evidence that Mr Pašić contemplates any such absurd policy
[...][110]

While for Seton-Watson recognition for the Committee as the
representative of a distinct Allied nation was simply the fulfillment of the
Corfu Agreement for which Britain had, albeit vaguely, vouched its
support, Whitehall was unsure. There was certainly sympathy for the
Yugoslav demand for 'a fair share of the direction of the whole question'.
But Italian reservations could not be ignored. And if there was doubt over
Pašić's democratic mandate and his support among the Serbian political
class, he was right to claim both a stronger mandate than Trumbić and
vastly greater governmental and diplomatic experience.[111] The Committee,
Leeper agreed, had 'at most only a theoretical, certainly not an actual
mandate from their fellow-countrymen'. Recognition might be accorded
only 'to the point of view represented by the Committee collectively
[rather] than to the Committee in its personal aspect'.[112]

Concern for democratic legitimacy, however, was not the main
concern.[113] More important was the feeling that, if 'Yugoslavia' was to be a
united state, its representatives must speak with 'one voice not two'.[114]
Pašić, Cecil noted, considered himself the real head of the Yugo-Slav
movement.[115] And while Seton-Watson urged that Serbian Government
and Yugoslav Committee be recognised as equal contracting parties, many
officials assumed that the former should occupy a position of precedence:
it was, Leeper observed, the 'natural nucleus' of a Yugoslav state. To allay
suspicions Pašić, he suggested, should form a national Government
incorporating members of the Serbian opposition and at least two
members of the Yugoslav Committee. On 9 October this proposal was
urged by Balfour upon both Trumbić and Pašić.[116] But while a gesture
towards inclusiveness, this was scarcely the coming together of equals
which the Yugoslavs desired; and it suggested that, whatever sympathy
existed for the latter, officials did regard a national Government as
fundamentally a continuation of the Serbian.

Soon, however, Whitehall was compelled to rethink. As events on
the ground gathered pace (the Habsburg Yugoslavs, Leeper noted on 15
October, had 'practically declared themselves an independent State') it
became essential to secure inter-Yugoslav cooperation and progress
towards amalgamation.[117] Officials began to lose patience with Pašić's
claim that Serbia's wartime sacrifices entitled her to represent all
Yugoslavs, and became sympathetic to Trumbić's concerns. 'The relatively
advanced Slavs of Croatia etc', Robert Cecil declared, 'will never consent
to be "bossed" by the bands of dishonest and murderous intriguers which

constitute the backbone of the Serbian Government'.[118] Lord Acton's report of Serbian opposition to Pašić seemed to confirm Seton-Watson's view that the Prime Minister headed a narrow 'clique' out of tune with opinion in Serbia as in western Yugoslavia.[119] Pašić's claim that Britain should consider the Austrian Yugoslavs her allies simply because Serbia was an ally was absurd, Leeper minuted:

> Our reason for recognising [the Austrian Yugoslavs] as friends and extending to them privileges as such is the evidence we have from them direct, both by their formation of volunteer forces to fight on the side of the Allies and by their ever-increasing antagonistic attitude to the Austro-Hungarian Govt. What Mr Pašić is aiming at, but has discreetly involved in several pages of verbiage is that the Yugoslavs of Austria should have no contact with us nor any claim on our consideration except through the mediation and in reward for the gallant behaviour of Serbia. This is, of course, a perfectly impossible position.[120]

Initially support remained for Pašić's vision of a unitary, centralised state. The Corfu Pact was accepted as the basis for Yugoslav union, and while a few, like Seton-Watson, emphasised that agreement's implication of equal status for Serbian Government and Yugoslav Committee, officials noticed first its commitment to the creation of a unitary kingdom under the Karadjordjević dynasty. Crewe House's suggestion in mid-October that Britain grant separate recognition was dangerous, Leeper argued. Not only would this be 'inacceptable [sic] to Mr Pašić', but, more importantly, it risked 'reopening [...] the whole question, settled by the Declaration of Corfu, of the necessity of one united Yugoslav State'.[121]

By the end of October, however, with no sign of a broad-based Government, attitudes towards recognition of the Austrian Yugoslavs began to shift. Though Balfour remained anxious to unite the parties before any formal recognition was granted, hope was diminishing. 'I am afraid', Sir Robert Graham lamented, 'that it is not possible to bring M. Pašić to reason and that we shall finally have to recognise the Committee'.[122] When, three days later, Nicolson also urged that Britain recognise the Committee 'without further delay', Graham proposed that action be taken directly Balfour returned from Paris.[123]

There were signs too of a shift in attitude towards the structure of the Yugoslav state. Lord Acton quoted the Serbian Minister in Switzerland as stating that all question of federalisation had been dropped since a federal system would be too cumbrous and would provoke friction between the component states. This was precisely the argument of Nicolson, Leeper and Paget's PID memo, which had dismissed federalism as likely to incubate old rivalries. Amid the recriminations of October 1918, however, the statement struck Nicolson as an example of that 'extreme chauvinism' which it was to be feared might permeate the Serbian Government.[124]

A shared Franco-Italian interest in limiting the influence of the Habsburg Yugoslavs made it very unlikely Britain would persuade her European allies to join her in recognising the Committee.[125] And in the event no move towards recognition was made before an apparent breakthrough persuaded the British Government (again) to await developments. On 3 November came a message from the Serb-Croat-Slovene National Council that it was 'prepared to form a common State with Serbia and Montenegro' ('the first formal declaration to the world', it was later noted, 'of adhesion to that union which the Pact of Corfu had proclaimed').[126] Then a South Slav conference in Geneva offered fresh hope of 'some definite Slav organism' uniting Serbian Government and Yugoslav Committee which Britain might recognise. When, despite reports of Pašić's obstinacy, an agreement was announced on 9 November for a Cabinet with equal Serbian and Austrian Yugoslav representation, all prayers seemed answered. In the meantime Serbia agreed to recognise the Zagreb National Council as legitimate representative of the western Yugoslavs. All economic frontiers were to be dissolved. 'The new State exists', it was proclaimed.[127] The new Government, Sir Arthur Evans reported, would control all foreign affairs, internal security and infrastructure, so that 'as far as the outside world is concerned it [...] represents the complete fusion of Serbia and all the Yugo-Slav lands'.[128]

Again Britain faced pressure to respond. 'The formation of this supreme joint council', Allen Leeper noted, 'together with the construction of a Serbian Coalition government, marks a most desirable advance towards complete unity of action [which] raises in a still more cogent form the question of recognition by the Powers'.[129] But while a united Yugoslavia was, as Seton-Watson affirmed, 'an accomplished fact, with which the *Entente* must reckon', the agreed joint administration was not, and uncertainty remained over a response.[130] Some argued for positive action. Since the National Council's request for independent recognition had now been publicly supported by the Serbian Government, Leeper wrote, there seemed 'no further reason against this recognition being accorded, save, possibly, the attitude of the Italian Government'.[131]

But still Balfour was unwilling to commit. On the one hand the question remained complicated both by the hostility of the Italians (whose occupation of territories promised by the Treaty of London raised fears of armed conflict with the South Slavs) and by disorder in the Yugoslav lands which cast doubt on the National Council as an effective temporary administration after the collapse of Austrian authority. On the other hand, Pašić's sincerity at Geneva already seemed questionable. He had, Sir Ralph

Paget reported on 21 November, raised doubts about the joint council appointments, and it looked as though he 'did not intend to run quite straight'.[132] (In fact, ten days earlier, on a hint from Pašić, Protić had resigned from the coalition cabinet on behalf of his Radical colleagues, rejecting this 'expression of mistrust in Serbia').[133] A few days later Sir Arthur Evans informed Derby that Pašić had 'intrigued against [the Geneva agreement] by every means in his power'. In his 'oriental evasions', he noted with disgust, 'he is just like a Pasha'.[134]

Nothing, consequently, was done before on 1 December 1918 a delegation sent by the National Council to Belgrade declared loyalty to Alexander, and received in turn the proclamation of a single unitary kingdom. Pending a constitution for a common Government, Alexander (representing his incapacitated father) had provisionally assumed executive power, Evans reported on 4 December, 'throughout what is now one united Kingdom of Serbia and Yugoslavia'.[135] This, wrote Laurence Collier, profoundly altered the situation. Recognition of the National Council of Zagreb had been withheld, but 'to recognise this new State would be a different matter [...], and indeed, it is difficult to see how we can avoid recognising it, as we recognise Serbia, which it has absorbed [...]'.[136] Nevertheless, ongoing political instability dissuaded Britain even now from formal acknowledgement. (At Alexander's behest Pašić resigned as head of the first joint Ministry on 16 December and was replaced by Protić).[137] The Foreign Secretary, Graham minuted on Christmas Day, wished to defer action until it was known what lay behind this resignation and whether a durable united government was really in existence.

When, some three weeks later, uncertainty remained, it was decided to dress procrastination up as policy. The Allied Governments had studied the notification of the union of all Serbs, Croats and Slovenes, the Foreign Office instructed their representative in Belgrade, but 'cannot recognise a political transformation accomplished on the eve of the Peace Conference, which alone can pronounce on the definite disposal of territory and on the constitution of the new States, due regard being paid to the general situation and the wishes of the populations concerned'.[138] And indeed, despite all evidence to the contrary, it was sometimes still implied that this Conference, not the Yugoslavs themselves, would actuate South Slav union. The Conference, Balfour wrote in late November, 'will surely desire to bring into being a single and united Yugo-Slav State'.[139]

Before turning to the post-war period, we should look further at British expectations of a Yugoslav State at the moment of its creation. Since, as a PID memo admitted, the Austrian collapse had occurred 'before any decision had been made upon the Yugo-Slav question', little thought had been given to the political difficulties and constitutional choices facing a united Yugoslavia.[140] But by December 1918, if not before, it seemed obvious to Whitehall that Britain's principal European Allies were fostering opposite tendencies among the South Slavs. While Italy, hostile to a Yugoslav state, sought to foment separatism among Croats and Montenegrins, the French – regarding such a state as a potential ally in southern Europe – pressed on Belgrade a firmly centralist agenda, arguing that federalism would divide the country and weaken it internationally.[141] Both, in other words, centrally-governed themselves, equated federalism with weakness and centralism with stability and strength.

Unlike Italy or France, Britain, her officials maintained, viewed southern Europe's future impartially. Lacking territorial ambitions or strong commercial interests she sought only the stability which would avert another major war, hoping for the region's new or enlarged states simply that their foundation on the principles of nationality and self-determination would ensure 'a firmer support against aggression than the older form of state'.[142] Of course such 'honest broker' pretensions were not wholly ingenuous. The settlement would provide, it was also suggested, 'an unprecedented opportunity for the legitimate extension of British influence'. And the fact that the balance of power remained 'fundamental' to British diplomacy in Europe meant London could not stand aloof from this jostling for position. Foreign Office files on southern Europe reveal a marked suspicion of French intentions in the Balkans, observers vaguely surmising 'some sinister territorial, strategic or economic motivation'.[143] ('We do not want the Balkans to come entirely under French influence', Lord Derby minuted in January 1919, 'and the French are leaving no stone unturned to increase their influence throughout the peninsula').[144] Nevertheless, British self-interest *was* enlightened in the sense that its primary aim – a Yugoslav state politically stable, strategically significant and independent of excessive great power influence (given that any such was unlikely to be British) – accorded with that of the South Slavs themselves.

In terms of how this aim was best achieved, the winter of 1918-19 was a crucial transitional period in British attitudes. Despite the oft-expressed concerns of Yugoslavs like Supilo, Trumbić and Hinković, some British officials still conceived Yugoslavia as Great Serbia and, as Pašić had hoped, saw Serbia as its natural administrative centre. Recognition seemed unavoidable, Collier wrote on 21 December, since the new state was 'only an extension of Serbia, in the same way as the newly-formed united Romanian State of Romania, Transylvania etc, is an extension of the old kingdom of Romania'.[145] Perhaps inevitably, Serbia's decades of independence bequeathed it a certain precedence. But it required a blindness to the sensitivity of Austrian Yugoslavs to declare that the National Council wished 'to be embodied in one State under the rule of Serbia';[146] likewise to report that the entire Yugoslav population was 'anxious […] to work efficiently and willingly under Serbian direction and command'.[147] Nor did Whitehall continue referring simply to the 'Serbian Government' only while recognition for the Serb-Croat-Slovene State was impending. Throughout 1919, months after recognition, 'Serbia' and 'Serbian' were used as short-hand for the cumbersome new nomenclature.[148]

Nevertheless, by the time Yugoslavia became a reality, concerns were already developing in Britain over the Serbian regime's intentions towards the other South Slav territories. Increasing credence was given to complaints by western Yugoslavs and their British allies that Pašić was a chauvinist seeking to substitute the overlordship of Belgrade for that of Vienna. Having long seemed in Britain Serbia's unchallengeably pre-eminent statesman, he began to seem out-of-touch with progressive opinion both among Austrian Yugoslavs and in Serbia itself. Following the likes of Steed and Seton-Watson (now exerting strong influence in government circles), officials portrayed Pašić, Protić and their 'reactionary connections' as a minority clique, shoring up their position by unconstitutional machination.

When, in late November, an assembly in Novi Sad declared unilaterally for direct union with Serbia (one of numerous such declarations by Serb groups in Bosnia, southern Dalmatia, Srem and elsewhere), Whitehall's reaction was noteworthy. The word 'annexation', Leeper noted, was 'strongly to be deprecated':

No Austrian Yugo-Slav will permit himself to be annexed to Serbia; that is the root of the whole trouble between Pašić and a few 'Greater-Serbians' on the one hand and the rest of the Yugo-Slav race on the other.[149]

Two aspects of this analysis are worth highlighting for what they show about British thinking at this stage. Firstly, there is the assumption we have noted that most Yugoslavs, whether Serbian or Austrian in background, opposed Pašić's policy of securing a dominant position for Serbia. This stemmed from a repeated emphasis by Seton-Watson and others that the Yugoslav Committee worked with and shared the aims of Pašić's Serbian opposition, and it profoundly influenced assessments of Yugoslav politics between 1918 and 1921.[150] Crucially, however, it was fundamentally mistaken, and skewed, as a consequence, all analysis which took it as a premise. Serious divisions *had* developed among Serbian politicians in Corfu; Pašić's autocratic and at times unconstitutional rule riled both his political opponents and those 'progressive' Serbian intellectuals with whom Britons like Seton-Watson tended to correspond.[151] The anti-Radical opposition *did* cooperate with the Yugoslav Committee while it tried to negotiate a favourable coalition cabinet after the Salonica trials.[152] But it was mistaken to infer that the two groups opposed Pašić on similar grounds, or shared a vision for the State. On the contrary: as Ivo Banac points out, while Serbian Opposition leaders were happy to exploit the Committee's clash with Pašić, they 'in no sense objected to Pašić's idea of unification'.[153]

Secondly, it is noteworthy that Leeper characterised the primary division among the Yugoslavs as one between the 'Serbian' (or at least an older generation of 'Greater Serbians') on the one hand and the 'Austrian Yugo-Slav' on the other. No suggestion was made of 'national' divisions within the Austrian Yugoslav region, between Croats, Slovenes and Serbs. In this respect Leeper's analysis was representative of British assumptions at the time, which emphasised the cultural fault-line between west and east, Habsburg and Ottoman. The dishonest intriguers of the Serbian Government, Cecil had noted, were opposed by 'the relatively advanced *Slavs* of Croatia etc'.[154] Seton-Watson, the most influential expert on the Yugoslav question, was at pains to stress not only that the Pašić Government had little support inside Serbia, but also that it was unanimously rejected by the Serbs of Austria-Hungary. None on the Yugoslav Committee were more opposed to Serbian disrespect for the spirit of the Corfu Declaration, he noted, than the Serb members from Bosnia and Slavonia; the ex-Habsburg districts were unanimous in their refusal to be treated as annexed territory.[155]

To a degree, this was not surprising. The dominant political conflict was between Serbian Government on the one hand, and Yugoslav Committee on the other. The latter's membership, as befitted an organ representing the South Slavs of Austria-Hungary, included representatives from all three groups, as did the 'Yugo-Slav' delegation which met the Serbians at Geneva. Having for so long argued the unity of the South Slav 'nation', and the kinship of Serbs and Croats in particular, the Committee could scarcely present their differences with the Serbian Government as being in any sense the conflicting aspirations of distinct Serb and Croat nations. Instead Trumbić, for instance, emphasised the civilisational division, which justified the concerns of those wary of Serbian domination without questioning the essential, long-term unity of the Yugoslav race. The western districts were, he urged, 'in matters of civilisation and public administration more advanced than Serbia and would not be willing to be subjected to a Government which is not on the same plane'.[156] To the 'Serbians of Old Serbia', Balfour noted, the (Austro-Hungarian) Yugoslavs considered themselves 'superior [...] in education and culture'.[157]

We have discussed the sense of cultural and political superiority which characterised the attitude of western Yugoslavs towards their counterparts in Serbia, Montenegro and Macedonia. This was a genuine phenomenon, not reducible simply to an opposition between Serb and Croat (though it certainly flavoured that opposition). But to present the jealousies of late 1918 simply, as Balfour did, as between Serbians on the one hand, and their 'kindred over the frontier' on the other, was to provide a misleading picture which hindered British understanding of the situation developing in Yugoslavia.[158] It was to listen to Trumbić's claims of Habsburg cultural superiority, but to ignore Pašić's contrary argument: that the Serbian Government's right to speak for all Yugoslavs rested not only on Serbia's wartime sacrifices but also on the 'unanimous wishes' of the Serb inhabitants of 'Yugo-Slavonia'.[159]

The insistence of Trumbić and others that they spoke for all Austro-Hungarian Yugoslavs blinded British observers to contrary evidence. In the chaos which afflicted the collapsing Monarchy in the late autumn of 1918, the newly-established 'National Council', without significant forces of its own, found its authority confined to the towns. In Serb regions there was strong support for Pašić's vision, with local councils urging the establishment of a 'monarchist, united, and centralist' state, refusing to recognise the Council's authority, and proclaiming unilateral unifications with Serbia.[160] While reports of these events did reach Whitehall, their implication of tension and disunity between prečani Serbs and their Croat and Muslim neighbours was, as Leeper's response indicates, overlooked.

Nor, crucially, was there an adequate understanding of the balance of forces on the Council itself. In Britain its outlook tended to be equated with that of the Yugoslav Committee (which, it had been agreed, would represent it abroad). The Slovene President of the Council, Anton Korošec, had, after all, publicly supported both the Committee's position and the Geneva agreement. (Any obstruction directed against the Joint Ministry formed at Geneva would, he assured Seton-Watson, be seen in Zagreb 'as an affront for the Southern Slav idea').[161] But Korošec did not represent the majority view of his Council. And Protić's rejection of the Geneva deal seems in fact to have been prompted by awareness of the growing division between Council and Committee.

The Council had only with difficulty won the allegiance of the Serbo-Croat Coalition, the leading political group among the Austrian Yugoslavs during the decade prior to 1918. But, having entered the Council, the Coalition quickly dominated it. Its leader, Svetozar Pribićević, was nominated a vice-president and quickly became the Council's leading figure: effectively, as Ivo Banac puts it, 'the power arbiter in Zagreb'.[162] An Orthodox Serb from the old Croatian Military Frontier, he favoured a centralistic unification.[163] During the last quarter of 1918 he liaised covertly with Belgrade, and it was he who, having rejected the Geneva agreement, 'forced the pace of liquidating the sovereignty of the National Council'.[164] But his crucial role in the unification, the rigid centralism which inspired him, and his general influence at this stage, were missed by British observers.

Perhaps more understandable was the lack of consideration – or at least lack of respect – in Britain for those currents of opinion in ex-

Habsburg Yugoslavia hostile to the unconditional declaration of union, and to allegiance to the Karadjordjević dynasty in a unitary state.[165] In late 1918 these seemed insignificant, or at least were difficult to disentangle from such discontent as seemed inevitable in a collapsing empire after a long war. If Dalmatia (the heartland of Pribićević's HSK), and perhaps Bosnia too, were recognised as the vanguard of the movement for unity, it seemed only that they were 'even more for unity than Croatia', rather than that Croatians harboured significant doubts.[166] Those violent protests by Croat soldiers in Zagreb's Jelačić square on 5 December which resulted in thirteen fatalities, and which seem now a sign of serious discontent at the unconditional cession of sovereignty to Belgrade, were dismissed as the work of 'Bolsheviks and reactionaries'.[167]

No one, Temperley insisted, had dared seriously oppose the declaration of unity under the Serbian dynasty. Serb troops in Croatia had adopted a conciliatory attitude and seemed popular, and the National Council, while inefficient, had served its purpose and secured wide approval. If now the unstated exception to the first assertion – that of Stjepan Radić who, alone on the Council, refused to support an unconditional union – seems a noteworthy oversight, this is not to say there was fault in the omission.[168] As leader of the Croatian Peasant Party Radić's constituency remained, before 1920, almost wholly disenfranchised, and his hold over the Croat masses had yet to become manifest. His party, Temperley reported, was 'not now very important'; it did not 'at present appear to constitute any very serious danger to national unity'.[169] (Though a slight, almost subliminal foreboding might be detected in these qualifying phrases – 'not now', 'not at present' – and a War Office report did note that the party had *until recently* been 'anti-Serbian', in general the significance of any unrest was played well down).

Nor did the views of the other prominent personality on the Council – Pribićević's fellow vice-president Ante Pavelić – cause British observers concern. His Starčevist Party of Right (SSP) was included by Temperley among those strands constituting an 'undercurrent of opposition'. (Another prominent member of the SSP, Mate Drinković, was also on the Council's seven-man Executive Committee). And it was noticed that such 'considerable support' as it had enjoyed owed much to its being 'Croatian rather than Serbian in conception'.[170] Strangely, however, the movement's ideological basis was characterised simply as republican, and its previous anti-Karadjordjević rhetoric as deriving wholly from anti-dynastic principle. The fact, therefore, that Pavelić had headed the delegation offering the loyalty of Austrian South Slavs to Alexander, and that his party had made a declaration of support for the dynasty, seemed to assuage all concern.

But while Starčević himself had opposed the Habsburg Monarchy, the SSP, after it split from the Frankist movement in 1908, happily cooperated with the regime while it supported Croat interests.[171] The ideological basis of the SSP was less republicanism than simply a loyalty to Croat State tradition. (As the party slogan ran: 'neither with Austria nor against it, neither with Hungary nor against it, neither with Serbia nor against it, but only for Croatia').[172] Pavelić accepted the idea of a federal Yugoslavia in 1918, but not the principle of Yugoslav 'national oneness' or the unitarist implications of the address he himself delivered to Alexander after a debate within the National Council. It should have been inconceivable that he and his following would calmly acquiesce in the centralist state scheme which Pašić and Pribićević were known to favour.

There were signs during late 1918 that Whitehall was no longer assuming a Yugoslav state *should* be centralist in structure (though it remained convinced of 'the necessity of one united Yugoslav State' as opposed to a loose confederal arrangement), but its attitude was hard to pin down.[173] Officials called increasingly for a degree of federalism or local autonomy to satisfy feelings of cultural difference, but there was little thought about what these terms might mean in practice, or what they did mean to Yugoslav politicians.

At times officials seem to have vaguely envisaged a continuation of the bipolar Serbian/ Habsburg-Yugoslav division familiar from the wartime opposition of Serbian Government and Yugoslav Committee. Since British observers had often stressed the cultural division between ex-Habsburg and ex-Ottoman, it could seem that the former as a group required institutional protection in the new state. And such an arrangement had seemed foreshadowed at Geneva, when a joint Government was constituted consisting of three (subsequently nine) members each from Serbia and the Habsburg provinces, implying a recognised reality for the two distinct halves.[174] The memorandum on the unification drawn up in December 1918 suggested that, once Italian pressure was removed, the 'Yugo-Slavs of Austria-Hungary' might well demand autonomy; if they did so, and if Bulgaria joined, Yugoslavia 'would then enjoy a constitution not unlike that of the US but under the Serbian Royal House'.[175] As we have seen, however, the Yugoslav regions of Austria-Hungary, subject for centuries to different influences and administrations, hardly constituted an historic entity. And though in the past the possibility had been (implausibly) raised of a Yugoslav unit in a trialist monarchy, the fact that Bosnia, southern Dalmatia and Slavonia had previously been promised directly to Serbia was hard to reconcile with the notion of a distinct ex-Habsburg unit.

But more often British analysts thought in terms of the continued existence of, and limited autonomy for, the various historic provinces of Yugoslavia. Prior to unification Seton-Watson had urged that a principle be established of 'complete equality between the various Kingdoms and provinces', with a constituent assembly in each formally approving the wider union.[176] In an interview with Pašić in October Steed stressed that 'the Southern Slavs of Austria-Hungary were deeply attached to their historical provinces'.[177] Until the eve of the 1921 constitution it was, as we shall see, Whitehall's firm assumption that limited autonomy for the existing provinces would be the presiding principle.

It should already have been clear, however, that these were both implausible prescriptions for the Yugoslav state. Any notion of 'complete equality' which reduced Serbia to the status of one among multiple units was anathema to those for whom it was the core around which other provinces had gathered. As we have seen, the British distinction between Serbians and Austrian Yugoslavs was rejected not only by Pašić and his Radical allies, but by most educated Serbs, for whom the Yugoslav whole was most importantly divided into Serbs, Croats and Slovenes. The British failed to appreciate the relative unimportance of Yugoslav ideology in Serbian political culture during the pre-war decades, and certainly missed the extent to which it was the unification of all *Serbs* which remained during the war the Serbian Government's primary ambition. The preservation of historical provinces which divided the Serbs of Bosnia, Croatia-Slavonia and Dalmatia from each other and from Serbia (and left them at times a vulnerable minority in their region) was out of the question. Seton-Watson's satisfaction that at Corfu Pašić had approved 'considerable local autonomies to meet the various requirements of the various provinces' was thus misconceived. Pašić never contemplated, as Seton-Watson did, autonomies for the existing historical regions.[178]

Nor, in reporting Pašić's potential openness to a federal solution, did Seton-Watson appreciate the *caveats* which vitiated that offer. For one thing, the realisation of such a wish was made almost impossible by the rejection of Trumbić's request that the constitution be secured by a parliamentary majority 'qualified tribally' (to ensure Serbs, Croats and Slovenes an equal say rather than one weighted according to population), a crucial decision which was overlooked in London. For another thing, a 'federal' Yugoslavia, Pašić made clear, would mean not a preservation of historic boundaries but a three-way tribal division, in spite of the intermixing of populations which practically, as both he and Trumbić recognised, rendered such a scheme unviable. Furthermore, the criterion for identification would be linguistic, a sign-post of South Slav identity unknown to British observers, restricting the Croatian unit within borders no Croat could accept.[179]

Perhaps most importantly, British observers failed to appreciate the degree to which the unanimity proclaimed in December 1918 was the artificial product of a particular external threat, and that when this diminished a much more divided picture was likely to re-emerge. Lacking forces of its own, and struggling either to maintain order in its heartlands or to present a plausible deterrent to Italian adventurism, the National

Council had no option but to request the assistance of the Serbian Army.[180] The influential South Slavs of Dalmatia in particular, long at the forefront of the Yugoslav movement, demanded immediate union with Belgrade partly through fear for their independence. To be fair, British analysts did at times recognise that Italy had acted, unwittingly, as 'a political solidifier'.[181] But what was observed was too readily assumed to be a profound and permanent shift, rather than a superficial and pragmatic response to circumstances. The strained internal relationships within the National Council – which indicated that Austro-Hungarian South Slavs, and South Slavs in general, were not as unified in their objectives as they seemed – were overlooked, just as, as we saw earlier, the atypical circumstances of the war in general had been too little credited with the marked rise in Yugoslav feeling that was widely and enthusiastically noticed in Britain. The next chapter will show how British observers responded to (and exhibited) the disillusionment which inevitably followed during the first three years of peace, and how their assumptions about the constitutional future of Yugoslavia shifted as a consequence.

8

Britain and the First Yugoslav Constitution, 1918-1921

By the time delegates convened in Paris in January 1919 the Habsburg Empire had been effectively dead for two months, while its southern borderlands had declared their unification with Serbia and Montenegro in a single unitary state. Initially the Powers withheld formal recognition, citing the prerogative of the Conference in such matters, and it was as the representatives of Serbia that the combined Serb-Croat-Slovene delegation was officially received. Nevertheless, Yugoslavia's existence was acknowledged and favourably perceived by Britain, France and the US, and only Italian insistence that it remained a 'theoretical hypothesis' prevented a formal Allied acknowledgement (though Britain and France were happy to be able to assess the new grouping's stability before committing themselves).[1] Nevertheless, in February the US recognised Yugoslavia unilaterally, and over the next few months Britain, France and most other European states followed suit.[2]

Officials often talked as if the Conference would reshape the European map, but in south-east Europe its work was the fine-tuning of frontiers rather than their broad outline (along with minority-protection and other matters). And since Yugoslavia had disputes involving six of its seven national boundaries, delegates had plenty to occupy themselves.[3] Of all the new states, *New Europe* sympathised, 'none is confronted with so many delicate problems as Yugoslavia'.[4] Nor was any frontier dispute facing the Conference more intractable, or more potentially explosive, than that between Yugoslavia and Italy over the Adriatic coast and the port of Fiume.[5]

The frontier questions are well treated elsewhere. But it is important to recognise the impact which these had on the development of the embryonic state. For nearly two years the lack of established frontiers was 'a circumstance that affected adversely every facet of its national life'.[6] Italian hostility in the border regions, and attempts to subvert the Yugoslav union politically, significantly affected the process of that union.

The Zagreb National Council, needing Serbian military support, could not hold out for a conditional union with Belgrade. And uncertainty over the state's constitutional shape was prolonged since, as Whitehall accepted, Constituent Assembly elections were impossible until the extent of Yugoslav territory was known.

Nor can the Adriatic dispute's impact on British attitudes be ignored. Not only did it absorb much official time and patience, but it affected the way Yugoslavs were perceived. The fact that most contact with Yugoslav politicians occurred in the context of a dispute over which Serbs, Croats and Slovenes were broadly united gave an exaggerated impression of Yugoslav unity, masking internal divisions. And while at times this seemed merely another intractable squabble between chauvinistic southern European nations (confirming entrenched prejudices), in general Yugoslav conduct was favourably received. Whitehall felt guilty about the 'regrettable' Treaty of London, sympathised with the Yugoslav position, and was impressed by the forbearance of Yugoslav politicians who, Sir Eyre Crowe wrote in September 1919, had been 'most exemplary in their attitude'.[7]

Our focus here, however, is on those internal questions for which the international conference in Paris had little time and did not (except insofar as they affected conference representation) count within its remit. For two years, in the shadow of the conference, Yugoslav groups jostled for position. How, in the period leading up to the constitution of June 1921 did British observers perceive the political state of the country, relations between its various provinces and peoples, and its likely political structure?

The apparently unanimous declaration by the Serb-Croat-Slovene National Council of allegiance to a united South Slav state under the Karadjordjević dynasty had been welcomed by British officials happy to believe the exaggerated claims of Yugoslav consciousness made to them by exiled publicists. Concern had grown during 1918, however, at the obvious tension between the Serbian Government and the Yugoslav Committee over the manner in which unification was conceived. The obstinacy and subterfuge with which the Committee's hopes of recognition had been undermined, and the Geneva agreement reneged upon, had set Whitehall against the superannuated Pašić in particular as a relic from a chauvinistic past. And while at the time of his first Ministry in December 1918 Protić had seemed 'less obnoxious to the Yugoslavs', his hatred for Pribićević quickly earned him a reputation for equal if not greater intransigence.[8] Neither, it seemed, could promote the 'progressive' Yugoslav state which younger, idealistic officials hoped would encourage stability in the region.[9]

Thus the assumption common in Britain before the war of a fundamental cultural divide between the East/Orthodox and West/Catholic regions of South Slav population was replaced by the demonisation of a few individuals. Officials influenced by the testimony of wide popular commitment to the Yugoslav ideal largely ignored the pro-Yugoslav camp's obvious interest in masking internal differences before the union had been secured. The attitudes of Pašić's regime, rather than representing general tendencies in Serbian politics, were portrayed as those of an outmoded minority clinging to power. Even their underhand manoeuvring could not in the long run, Whitehall felt sure, secure the old Radicals against the tide of progressive Yugoslavism.

And in terms of the constitutional question – the political problem of integrating populations with diverse cultures and identities – the anticipated ascendancy of a 'progressive' generation strengthened Whitehall's early assumptions. Though little careful thought was given to this question early in the war, it was always vaguely assumed that the outcome would be a 'federation'.[10] Only thus, it seemed, could distinct Croat, Slovene and Montenegrin identities be incorporated in a genuinely Yugoslav union (as opposed to the expanded Serbia officials had initially envisaged). And while after Corfu some in Whitehall concluded that federalism might in fact 'allow old rivalries to continue', and that a centralist state would best integrate a diverse population, the final months of the war saw a strong reaction against a policy which in the hands of Pašić and his allies seemed tainted by Serbian chauvinism.

The dominant view in London, shaped by an exaggerated faith in Yugoslav Committee claims to represent the population at large, was that not only were the great majority united behind a genuinely Yugoslav as opposed to Great Serbian policy, but that there was also wide agreement about how such a policy was best pursued: by means of significant autonomies to protect the distinct pride and culture of historic regions. This was a view which, in the face of much conflicting evidence, proved curiously persistent in Whitehall during 1919 and 1920. In fact, studying British analysis of the debates which took place in an atmosphere of increasing rancour between 1918 and 1921, it is difficult to avoid the conclusion that it was unsystematic and complacent, particularly in the case of officials in London who seem at times barely to have read reports intended to correct cherished misunderstandings.

Attitudes towards the Radicals changed little in Britain during 1919 and 1920. If anything they became more hostile, as the party's leadership was blamed for the tensions undermining fraternal Yugoslav feeling. As head of the Yugoslav delegation, Pašić was in Paris for much of this period, but Protić seemed a conduit for his mentor's outmoded ideas. There was, Crowe observed in October 1919, 'a reactionary current […] impervious to any new ideas' trying 'to retain the same close militarist and bureaucratic control as they have in the past exercised to the detriment of Serbia'.[11] When Leeper urged in February 1920 that Yugoslavia discard the 'bad old party traditions' of Serbian politics, he had the Radicals in mind.[12] No Government with Pašić in it would do much good, Temperley insisted; it was essential 'to get rid of the "old gang"'.[13] Pašić represented, Nicolson agreed, 'all that is worst in the old Belgrade tradition'.[14] And though he was at times still fêted in the British popular press, and Lloyd George for one retained a great respect for him, officials now paid scant respect to the Radical tradition of constitutionalism and democracy in independent Serbia. Protić in particular was uncredited for a loyalty to these ideals certainly greater than that of prominent 'Democrats' (a party label often as incongruous as that of the 'Radicals').[15]

At the same time officials continued to take heart from the assumption that the Radical leadership was a small 'clique', without a strong constituency, and at odds with the attitudes of the younger generation. Certain political developments during 1919 consolidated this view. The formation in April of the Democratic bloc left the Radicals a 'decided minority' in the Provisional National Assembly.[16] Even in Protić's cabinet Radicals were significantly outnumbered: eleven of seventeen members were Democrats. And by August his Government had ceded to a purely Democratic ministry.

In other respects, however, cherished assumptions were challenged during the spring of 1919. Perhaps most important of these was the fond notion of a monolithic, anti-Radical progressive consensus. We have noted already the British tendency to accept Yugoslav Committee spokesmen as true representatives of Habsburg Yugoslav opinion, and, mistakenly, to equate the agenda of the Serb-Croat-Slovene National Council with that of the Committee. In the months following the unification, and the dissolution of the Committee, members of the latter most trusted and admired by Whitehall – Ante Trumbić in particular – found themselves without a strong party base and unable to exert the influence British officials had expected. Instead, significant political influence was wielded by groups whose attitudes diverged from that progressive 'Yugoslav' ethos which was assumed to prevail.

One important example during 1919 was Ante Pavelić's Starčevist Party of Right. At the end of 1918 officials had rationalised Pavelić's 'considerable support' in Croatia with reference to his stated allegiance to a united state under the Karadjordjević dynasty. Optimistically, they saw him as a convert to the moderate movement for a decentralised Yugoslavia. In April 1919 des Graz regretted that the Government now contained no member of the 'important' Starčevist party.[17] But, as we have seen, Whitehall had long considered the Starčevist agenda (like that of the Serbian Radicals) essentially chauvinist and reactionary, and they soon resumed this opinion.[18] The sense revived during 1919 that Starčevist and Frankist ideology – 'Croatian in conception', and therefore divorced from Yugoslav feeling – was regressive, extremist and rooted in ignorance. On a visit to Srem Bryce reported that the views of leading locals were of an 'extreme Croat complexion', putting Croatia first and advocating a Yugoslav federation embracing an autonomous Croatia linked with Slavonia and Srem. Underpinning this attitude, he observed, was an 'extreme ignorance about Belgrade and the old Kingdom of Serbia', which left Croats 'groping in semi-darkness for a solution of the best future', and 'open to the promptings of those, like Hungarian officials, with ulterior motives'.[19] In a memorandum in July, after talking with Pavelić and others, he condemned their agenda more forcefully, arguing that their policy was underpinned by 'an intense and deep-seated jealousy of the Serbians', and denying their fears of Serbian hegemony were shared by the average Croatian. Their views, he wrote:

> were in the main destructive rather than constructive, and [...] were to a great extent biased by party considerations and jealousy of their opponents, especially of M.Pribićević [...]. The average man in Croatia [...] appeared to have only one desire, namely to be generous in his attitude towards those in authority, and to assist them by every means in his power to carry out successfully the difficult problems which naturally confront a new State [...]. This desire seems to be entirely lacking in the counsels of the 'Starčevist' Party, whose main object would appear to be to harry the Government as much as possible and to subordinate the well-being of the State as a whole to purely local feelings and prejudices.[20]

The principle conclusion drawn from this report in London indicates a somewhat self-deluding attitude towards Yugoslav politics. At the time that Pavelić's declaration of loyalty had brought the Starčevists within the pale, so far as British officials were concerned, the breadth of his support in Croatia had been recognised. (His party's adhesion to the dynasty was clear proof, Temperley had observed, that the state had popular feeling on its side).[21] Once the party's anti-Serbianism was re-emphasised, however, it was consigned once more to the status of a hard-line minority. Bryce's report confirmed, PID minuted, 'that the separatist movement in Croatia is not very important' (a conclusion which illustrates too the hazy differentiation in Britain at this stage between 'autonomists' or 'federalists' and genuine separatists).[22] The fact that Temperley, in a slightly earlier report which highlighted the same Starčevist sins – ignorance of the Serbs, 'personal bitterness', lack of a constructive agenda – had presented their vague desire for federation as in tune with Croat opinion, was conveniently forgotten.[23]

But perhaps the most important development in Yugoslav politics during the spring of 1919 was the emergence of the Democrats. While the significance of this was plain to British officials, they again contrived to overlook or to underestimate respects in which it undermined key assumptions concerning the country's likely constitutional path.

When the DS first coalesced at Sarajevo in February 1919 it embraced only parties from the former Monarchy: the HSK (its leader Svetozar Pribićević the driving influence), the anticlerical Slovene liberals (themselves a fusion of Carniolan Progressive Party and Styrian People's Party), and a dozen smaller unitarist groups. Subsequently parties joined from Serbia and Montenegro: Serbian opponents of Pašić like Ljuba Davidović's Independent Radicals, and Montenegrin pro-Yugoslavs. But it is not surprising that British observers regarded the new party initially as a representative product of the ex-Habsburg provinces. This, by and large, is how it seemed in Belgrade.[24] And the lack of any permanent official in Croatia during 1919 left Britain reliant on its legation in the capital. (Des Graz admitted that what he saw came 'mainly from Serbians and may well have a Serbian tinge').[25] Both Starčevist and Democrat parties, Bryce reported in July, were now 'seeking support in various provinces of the SHS outside Croatia proper'. The latter, like the former, he implied, was Croatian if not Croat in origin.[26]

Officials soon noted, with enthusiasm, the party's success in broadening its horizons. It had become, des Graz wrote from Belgrade, the first genuinely nation-wide party, transcending the division between old Balkan states and ex-Habsburg regions. The participation of 'Young' Radicals and other Serbian groups as well as 'most if not all Montenegrin representatives' illustrated the 'important fact', he observed, that 'this is a new Democratic Party for the whole united kingdom and is not on a provincial or regional basis'.[27] Given the manner in which British analysts viewed the Radicals, the creation of a political grouping embracing parties from the breadth of the new state, from Slovenia to Montenegro, allayed fears that Yugoslavia might struggle to establish a unified political system. Parties seemed to be grouping themselves 'on political and not national […] lines'.[28] And the fact that the alliance's anticipated bloc of 140-150 seats in the Provisional Assembly gave it 'a clear majority and preponderating influence' – an 'unwelcome surprise to the Old Radical Party' – was entirely welcome to British observers who deplored the influence of Pašić and his associates.[29]

We have seen that the tendency in Whitehall during 1918 to regard one-nation centralism, combined with a modernising socio-economic agenda, as the progressive blueprint for the country's future had diminished as centralism became associated with the policies and outlook of the Old Radicals. But the emergence of the Democrats, with their vision of a centralised state working to overcome 'tribal' rivalries and the instability and corruption associated with Balkan politics, revived this sympathy somewhat. Agrarian reform, Temperley noted, constituted the Democrats' 'trump card': a 'direct and bold appeal to the peasant in Croatia, Slavonia and Bosnia' which would demonstrate the benefits of 'Serbian rule'. And this policy, he argued, involving the redistribution of feudal estates to create a small-holder class, 'only a centralised government could effect'.[30]

And if British observers sympathised with Democratic ideals, they also warmed to Pribićević, the party's driving influence. Little known to officials as leader of the HSK, as Interior Minister in Protić's Government he had become a manifestly important figure:

> He has the reputation [Young reported] of being very able, and is clearly a man of prompt action. His ability and personality produced a strongly-favourable impression from the moment of his arrival here before the proclamation of the union of the Yugo-Slavs with the kingdom of Serbia [...]. That impression has remained and has increased, and he may therefore become a very important factor in the internal politics of the united kingdom.[31]

Though some Croats were known to distrust him and his centralist ideology, his enemies were seen in Britain, particularly during 1919 and early 1920, as sectarian, parochial and unrepresentative. And just as the Democrats' standing in Britain grew by default from the censure attached to other Croatian parties seen to be clinging to vested interests, so it did from British hostility to the Radical leadership's narrow Serb nationalism. With Protić's reputation in Whitehall as a leader of the Serbian 'old gang', reports of vitriolic clashes between himself and Pribićević redounded distinctly to the latter's credit.

But perhaps the most important single issue disposing officials against the Serbian Radicals and, in consequence, in favour of the Democrats, was that which (along with the Adriatic dispute) dominated British interest in Yugoslavia during 1919: the fate of Montenegro. Though we have examined this question already, it is of interest here for the manner in which it affected broader assumptions about the course of Yugoslav politics, and for the confusions in British thinking which resulted.

Since the Democrats were not strongly linked with Serbia, their reputation in Britain was little tainted during 1919 by Belgrade's heavy-handed policy in Montenegro and the Austrian provinces. As the year drew on, and Montenegro came to seem less an exceptional case than an archetype of 'Old' Serbian intentions towards the 'new' provinces, Whitehall's regard for the Democrats became increasingly contradictory. While deploring the attempt to 'coerce' Croatia, Slovenia and Montenegro into a centralised state, and noting rightly that the Democrats considered any autonomist programme 'altogether inadmissible', it continued nevertheless to view Davidović's ministry as the best hope for positive development in Yugoslavia.[32] When it fell in February 1920 Leeper mourned a cabinet 'representative of the best younger elements'.[33]

As a result British assumptions were left in a state of (largely unacknowledged) confusion. While Radicals represented for British observers all that was regrettable and outmoded in Yugoslav politics, Democrats, with their agenda of land reform and the submersion of 'tribal' identities in a single nation, seemed progressive and broad-minded. That such rhetoric should have appealed to idealistic Whitehall officials is not hard to understand (and Democrats exploited this, lamenting to the British 'the old Balkan or Oriental traditions' with which Radical leaders were imbued, and insisting the latter were 'in no way representative of the Serbian people').[34] At the same time, awareness of the resentment towards Belgrade in some regions led to wide agreement in Britain that rigid centralism would ill serve a state comprising such disparate traditions and identities, while a federal constitution (or one granting substantial local autonomies) offered a path to harmonious national development.

But it was the 'progressive' Democrats who espoused a doctrinaire centralism, while some 'Old Radicals' – Protić in particular – *were* willing to recognise and uphold regional identities.[35] (Pašić, it is true, was on the party's more centralist wing and so was happier to collude with the Democrats in late 1920). And yet, until at least the spring of 1920, the Democratic Party's reputation in Britain was untainted, despite the fact that the Davidović ministry had centralised zealously: extending Serbian military law nation-wide, further undermining autonomy in Croatia, and establishing in Slovenia a regional government with no seat for the autonomist Slovene People's Party.[36] The fact that what seemed a reactionary policy in the context of the Yugoslav national question was advocated by many whose socio-economic agenda distanced them from the old Serbian past was too little appreciated in Britain, and as a result the likelihood of what seemed the progressive decentralist solution was seriously misjudged.

In general British analysis of the constitutional options facing Yugoslavia, and of political trends on the ground, was deficient. In part this was because attention was monopolised by the Montenegrin and Adriatic questions. In part also it was because certain officials – notably the British minister in Yugoslavia Sir Alban Young – saw stability as the overwhelming British priority in the region, and thought this better served by an imposed settlement than one which tried to address the concerns of every province and group. The Constituent Assembly, he wrote:

> seems to me to contain potentialities of violent discord, and, given the nature of the different peoples who will be represented in it, I should think that the only safe method of avoiding a lapse into anarchy will be for the responsible leaders to force through a practically agreed scheme. I must once again earnestly express my opinion that if we want peace in this corner of Europe we should abstain from enquiring too closely into the extent to which the democratic principles of free elections and self-determination are applied in practice.[37]

This attitude is evident in the unsystematic fashion in which officials analysed the constitutional options. So far as Yugoslav politicians were concerned, there were essentially four alternatives. First was the rigid centralism espoused by the Democrats, in which historic provincial boundaries would make way for much smaller French-style *departments*, and legislative and administrative power would be concentrated in the capital. Second, at the other extreme, was a federal system, by which was generally understood a tripartite 'racial' or 'tribal' federalism, with frontiers redrawn to create discrete Serb, Croat and Slovene units, each with substantial administrative and legislative independence. In between were two varieties of autonomism: regional autonomy for the historic provinces which had merged to create Yugoslavia – Croatia-Slavonia, Dalmatia, Bosnia, Montenegro etc; and local autonomy for new sub-regions of Yugoslavia, shaped according to economic and geographical criteria, with a view to eroding ingrained provincial or 'tribal' allegiances.

In Britain, however, with most analysis relating to the Montenegrin question, these alternatives and their ramifications were not methodically identified or studied. (It is remarkable that in December 1919, a year after Yugoslavia's formation, Crowe should have had to point out to officials who talked of granting Montenegrins the 'same status accorded to Croatia and Slovenia' that no such special status had been accorded).[38] There was, of course, awareness that autonomist sentiment in regions with a strong historical consciousness was increasingly at odds with a centralising Government. But rather than the above four options, British observers conceived only a simple dichotomy: centralism or decentralism. The words 'federative' and 'federal', loosely used, were not distinguished from the concepts of regional or local autonomy, nor was any significant difference between these latter phrases identified. When Pašić and others rejected 'federalism' – i.e. a tripartite 'tribal' division – on the grounds that no border could separate intermingled Serb and Croat populations, this was interpreted as the rejection by a narrow clique of the very idea of a decentralist constitution.[39] It was condemned despite respected Yugoslavs like Trumbić having similarly dismissed such a disruptive scheme, and though Whitehall had never contemplated the idea, equating decentralism with limited independence for the traditional provinces of Yugoslavia.[40]

And despite the increasing pessimism we noted in minutes relating to Montenegro, the assumption persisted that the Assembly would in due course approve a federative settlement on the latter basis. Thus in May 1919 Balfour reminded de Salis that it would be in the British interest for Montenegro to enter 'the Yugo-Slav Federation'.[41] And later in the year Crowe thought the Assembly would 'no doubt' secure 'a very large measure of provincial autonomy' for Montenegrins, Dalmatians, Bosnians, Slovenes and the people of Croatia-Slavonia. Pressure in the Yugoslav State would be strong enough, he argued, 'to sweep away the obstructions artificially made by the Old Guard of Serbian politicians'.[42]

But the British representation of Pašić and his allies as isolated reactionaries who had only by subterfuge retained a position of influence was misleading. Protić was able during 1919 to forge tactical alliances with both the Croat National Union (HZ) and the Slovene People's Party (SLS), who had more to fear in the short-term from the centralising zeal of Pribićević. As the 'Parliamentary Union' this bloc owned a majority in the Provisional Assembly, disrupted the Democrat Government, and by February 1920 – to Whitehall's surprise and disgust – was in power.[43]

Of course, Radical attitudes towards the 'historical rights' of Serbs, vis-à-vis Croats and Slovenes as well as non-Slav minorities, *were* extreme and uncompromising. (In fact, as we have seen, the extent of territory and population claimed by Serb ideologues was unappreciated by British observers, who ignored the linguistic element of Serb nationalism). But the vilification of old Radicals as a reactionary 'clique', instigated by the Yugoslav Committee and their British associates, blinded Whitehall to the prevalence of such attitudes. Demands like that of the Bosnian 'Serbian National Organisation' for a Greater Serbia incorporating Bosnia, Dalmatia, Lika, the Banat (and more) were treated as fringe extremism, but in fact represented a common aspiration of the Serb political class.[44]

During early 1920 political relations in Yugoslavia became increasingly tense and antagonistic as the question of Constituent Assembly elections, and that of the future constitution, loomed larger. Leading politicians talked of preparing a draft constitution in advance, for debate and ratification. In a fraught atmosphere in which strikes and unrest plagued the western provinces, in which 'riotous scenes' afflicted the provisional assembly and party newspapers attacked opponents with increasing vitriol, while the public became 'disgusted with the intensity of the party feeling' delaying electoral legislation, and in which the very adhesion of Croatia to Yugoslavia seemed to British observers 'daily less certain', Young confessed he would 'not be surprised' to see the military take power. The political situation was similar, he wrote, to that in Greece in 1908 when parties so ignored the interests of the country that the military stepped in: 'a development along the same lines is not excluded'. Nor did he seem averse to such a firm line. The military, he noted, was the most efficient branch of the government.[45] Officials whose perspective derived from residence in Belgrade little empathised with the impetuous behaviour and demands of the 'more excitable Yugo-Slavs of the west'.[46]

In the aftermath of Davidović's resignation, however, Young and others did begin to appreciate the share of blame attributable to the Democrats for the acute unrest. Whitehall officials still praised a Government 'sensible to the need for a united and progressive Yugoslav state' and keen to expunge Serbia's 'bad old party traditions'; and bemoaned the new coalition of Radicals and autonomists as unlikely to endure but capable of doing 'infinite harm in the interval'.[47] But on 2 March Young reported that the resignation of a party 'in favour of the centralisation of Government at Belgrade' had prompted demonstrations against the union in Croatia and Slovenia. At first unsure how to interpret these (still without a consul in Zagreb), he soon linked discontent to the policies of a party 'all for centralisation and unity of Yugo-Slavia'.[48]

And what fully convinced him that doctrinaire Democrat policy had been fomenting unrest (rather than simply old Radical prejudice) were that month's municipal elections. 'Throughout the new provinces', he reported, 'the Democrat Party was routed'.[49] Communists had made 'startling' gains. (In Zagreb 25 of 40 National Club representatives made way for 20 Communists, a trend repeated throughout Slovenia and Croatia-Slavonia). And while Belgrade insisted that non-Yugoslav minorities had voted Communist 'to show their hatred for the Serb', Whitehall accepted the Croat claim that the results expressed simply 'dissatisfaction with the present administration'. 'There is no doubt of the correctness of this view', Temperley minuted, 'and we need not look for the [Belgrade] press explanation of German and Magyar intrigues'.[50] Though it was Protić's coalition in power at the time of the elections, primary responsibility seemed to rest with those Democratic decrees passed without mandate from the assembly between August 1919 and February 1920.[51]

In the socio-economic sphere, no less than the political, Democratic zeal seemed culpable. The enforced break-up of large estates (without compensation for non-Yugoslav owners) had caused unrest and disruption. The likely 'serious shortage of harvest in Croatia', Temperley noted, was due directly to 'the mismanagement of the Government and the policy of Pribićević'.[52] Democrat policy had bequeathed 'an unpleasant legacy', Young admitted, while Protić's line had been more moderate: 'not averse to establishing small holdings like those which make old Serbia a peasant State' but 'more conservative as regards the vested rights of the proprietors'.[53]

In general, the Democrat Party, hailed in Britain hitherto as a pan-Yugoslav alliance of progressive elements, a break from the country's 'bad old party traditions', began to seem themselves a narrow-minded faction, putting doctrine and party interest before that of the state. Having been identified first with the Habsburg provinces in which the HSK had its roots, then with Yugoslavia as a whole, they came instead after the municipal election defeat to be associated with Serbia, and with a centralisation drive predicated on Serb hegemonism rather than a genuine belief in Yugoslav nationhood. They had become, in Young's political survey of the summer of 1920, simply one of the 'old Serbian parties'.[54]

Obvious too, by the winter of 1919-20, was a shift in British perceptions of the autonomist movements in Croatia, Slovenia and elsewhere. We have seen that, while there had long been sympathy for Montenegrin opposition to Belgrade rule, the Starčevist and Frankist movements most clearly committed to retaining Croatian autonomy (and to some extent also the autonomist Slovene People's Party) were regarded as reactionary and obstructionist, and were denied the respect accorded to individual opponents of Pašić like Trumbić or Smodlaka. During 1920, however, there was a marked rehabilitation of Croatian national feeling in Britain. This owed much simply to growing disillusionment with the centralists in Belgrade. But also important was the development of decentralist associations in the interim parliament.

First came a loose alliance known as the National Club comprising, as Ivo Banac notes, members from 'fairly distinct political traditions': Starčevists of the SSP – Pavelić, Drinković and others – who headed the Croat wing of Zagreb's National Council, Croat dissidents from the HSK, Starčevists from Istria, and independents (including former members of the Yugoslav Committee). Then in May 1919 Pavelić and others formulated a single programme before uniting, in July, in a new party: the Croat Union (HZ).[55] The tenor of its ideology during 1919-20 was moderate, rejecting centralism and defending the integrity of 'our ancient provinces', but embracing the 'one nation' idea and eschewing any notion of tribal federalism. Its membership was predominantly urban-intellectual, for which constituency they seemed 'the only respectable Croat party'.[56] While the logic of their autonomism and of their Croat identity (which did attract a more aggressive Frankist element) gradually undermined their loyalty to the one nation ideal, they were untainted in Britain by the reactionary reputation of their constituent 'Starčevist' faction. An unofficial association with Trumbić's National Club lent the HZ the respectability which adhered to a Yugoslav politician admired in Britain above all others.[57]

So while a fervent unitarist like Leeper remained suspicious of Croat 'particularists', in general a more positive attitude emerged towards those who would take 'wise and generous account of the desires of the different Yugo-Slav lands to retain their peculiar local institutions of self-government in the form of a regularised provincial autonomy'.[58] In mid-1920 administrative devolution and legislative unity, the HZ's official position, seemed to Temperley 'the proper ideals at present'.[59] Britain need not mind growing autonomism, Adam argued, provided it refrained from 'a definitely disruptive tendency'; its constitutional opposition would 'serve as a useful curb on the militarist tendencies of the Serbs of Serbia in the new Yugo-Slav State'.[60] The HZ was welcomed as autonomism's moderate face.

By the spring of 1920, furthermore, this movement attracted British observers in its opposition not only to the intransigence of Radicals and Democrats, but also to a 'Communist' threat which loomed substantially larger in the aftermath of the March municipal elections.

It is not easy now to recapture the vague sense of menace exerted in Britain (as also in France) by an ideology which had toppled one major government, threatened to spread like the Spanish influenza germ through central and eastern Europe, and yet was scarcely better understood. (Not only had 'soviets' been declared in Germany, but the Bolshevik Béla Kun had for a time taken control in Hungary on Yugoslavia's northern border).[61] Assuming that communist ideology was likely to make its strongest appeal to the industrial working-class, some officials – those in Belgrade in particular – associated this threat with the more developed Croat and Slovene provinces, and as a consequence regarded Serbia favourably as the country's stable core. The western countries might be more advanced, observed des Graz, but Serbia 'may be held to represent the more stable element and fixity of purpose':

> With such continuous mention of Bolshevism in certain other countries the subject has naturally come in to every one's thoughts but a purely agricultural land like Serbia, where each man has a holding or part of one, is ground particularly unsuitable for the propagation and adoption of Bolshevist ideas.[62]

The hazy understanding of this phenomenon is indicated by the fact that officials barely differentiated between two movements which were ideologically and institutionally quite distinct: the Communist Party of Yugoslavia (KPJ) and Stjepan Radić's Croatian Peasant Party (HPSS). Little attention was paid to the latter in Britain before 1920, nor significance attributed to it by officials inclined to emphasise both the shared culture of the Serb and Croat peasant and his lack of interest in politics. ('The general impression I have', wrote Temperley in March 1919, 'is that Radić [...] hardly constitutes a serious danger').[63] And since Radić's political ideology was little examined, his traditional peasant socialism tended to be labeled 'communist'. Des Graz referred to Radić as the leader of the 'Communist Agrarian Party', Temperley to the HPSS as 'parochial and local Bolshevik'.[64]

Thus although the 'startling' gains in the elections were predominantly for the KPJ, it was in the context of Radić's growing prominence that the results were interpreted. Municipal communism was new in Croatia, Temperley reported, but was 'bound to be connected with the old communist movement under Radić which was popular among the peasantry before the war'.[65] (Contact between the two groups was frequent on market days, he noted rather unconvincingly). Young's reports of Radić's release from prison after eleven months, and of the prompt resumption of his 'extremist campaign', were not unnaturally associated with word of increasing protests in Croatia and Slovenia 'hostile to the union with Yugoslavia', and of the Communist electoral successes.[66]

Officials confronted by the worsening unrest in the western provinces during the spring of 1920 were faced with one fundamental question, and it was one which had important ramifications for the state's constitutional settlement. To what extent was the turmoil a reaction to short-term economic dislocation which, after the upheaval of the war and its aftermath, could be considered inevitable (even if it was unnecessarily exacerbated), or rather a sign of real ethnic rivalries within the Yugoslav 'nation'?

This does seem to have been a turning point. As we have seen, the elections showed British officials both how alienated Croats and Slovenes had become from the policies of Democrats as well as Radicals and, in consequence, how 'Serbian' both principal parties seemed in outlook and motivation. For the first time, moreover, unrest *did* seem more than a symptom of transition. If communist success was merely an anti-Government protest it would die down quickly, Temperley observed; but 'I am [...] inclined to think myself that there is more to it than this, and that troublous times are ahead'.[67]

There still remained, however, a certain reluctance to view the disturbances as, at root, the expression of *national* hostility between Croats and Slovenes on the one hand, and Serbs on the other. Railway strikes in April, followed by a wider national strike in Croatia, seemed, Adam commented, a 'Bolshevik action' among Croats and Slovenes. His suggestion that this was also in part 'a political movement among Croats and Slovenes against Serbs' was crossed out.[68] In a subsequent minute he subtly shifted tack: the SCS authorities were faced, he observed, with 'a centrifugal political agitation among the Croats and Slovenes, combined with a formidable strike movement'.[69] He refrained, in other words, from directly linking the two phenomena – that is to say, from concluding that economic unrest was an expression of national animosity.[70]

When further more serious unrest broke out among the Croatian peasantry in the autumn of 1920, sparked by a requirement to register animals for military service, British analysis remained uncertain on this point. A strong link was made with Radić's party (as it has been by historians). In Belgrade, Young noted, the risings were widely attributed to the preaching of 'the peasant agitator Radić', and from Zagreb Maclean reported that the district suffering the most serious disturbances was a stronghold of the HPSS.[71] A few officials – Leeper in particular – continued to deny that this was a substantial movement against unitaristic Yugoslavism, stressing short-term economic dislocation, and crediting the claim that Radić had conspired with foreign agents. 'It is easy', he wrote, 'to rouse peasants' suspicions when their property is concerned and probably Hungarian agents (if not Italians) lose no chance'.[72]

But in general there was now an increased acceptance that economic problems both aggravated and were aggravated by widespread national tensions. The upheavals were to be deplored, wrote Gordon Maclean (the British consul in Zagreb), since they would 'add to the friction between Croat and Serb which certainly does not tend to diminish and which is the factor most antagonistic to the peaceful and prosperous development of the SHS kingdom'.[73] And Young too admitted that the unrest was a genuinely popular Croatian response to political and economic problems. Belgrade newspapers 'pretend', he noted, that it was engineered by the Italians.[74] But in Croatia, alone in the SCS State, there was clearly 'a body of peasantry at once republican and violently anti-Serb'. Most alarming of all: anti-Serb feeling in Croatia, he now pointed out, applied to all Serbs 'whether of Croatia or Serbia-proper'. The old British assumption that the primary cultural division was between 'western' Yugoslavs and 'eastern' Serbians was undermined as observers belatedly recognised a polarisation on national rather than regional grounds.[75]

From this realisation followed another, whose potential consequences were alarming. Now, very late in the day, it was recognised that the ideological distance between the two leading Serb parties might have been overstated. In the context of growing autonomist strength, socio-economic questions such as agricultural reform were, it was now recognised, of secondary importance beside a shared hostility to Croat, Slovene and Montenegrin nationalism.[76] The latter, Young suggested, might lead them to forge a coalition, 'thus ranging Croats and Montenegrins and Slovenes against Serbs'. This, Temperley warned, was a 'highly dangerous possibility'.[77] Not only did it raise the prospect that Yugoslav politics might remain violently polarised, but it threatened to overturn cherished British assumptions about the balance of forces in Yugoslavia, and so about the likely shape of the constitutional settlement.

Before looking at the Constituent Assembly elections, we should look more closely at the effect the unrest of 1920 had on these British expectations for the Yugoslav constitution. We have noted that analysis during 1919 was constrained by an over-simplistic centralist-federalist dichotomy. Amid the tensions of 1920 British officials in Yugoslavia did belatedly begin to move beyond this, and to convey (though still inconsistently) the more complex issues at stake in the framing of a Yugoslav constitution. In June Young drew attention to the debate not only over the autonomy provinces would enjoy, but also over these provinces' definition. A key question, he noted, likely to cause 'acute controversy', would be whether they should be defined 'to obliterate as far as practicable the traces of a former existence as separate entities of the different portions of the Kingdom, or whether the historical limits of the various provinces should be preserved'.[78] This was the first sign of awareness among British analysts that the 'large administrative autonomies' which even centralists like Pašić had happily promised foreign diplomats need not entail the survival of Yugoslavia's historic provinces.

At the same time Temperley clearly distinguished federalism and autonomism (while continuing to associate the former with devolution to historic provinces rather than 'racial' units). On the basis of early constitutional drafts, he noted, federalism seemed 'unlikely': no probable Government could 'admit such an extension of self-government to the component parts'. (Even the few proposals preserving Croatia and Slovenia marked, he noted with an eye to Whitehall's first interest, 'the end of any federal or devolutionary scheme for Montenegro').[79] Administrative devolution and legislative unity were 'the proper ideals'.[80] William Strang, meanwhile, also tried to temper officials' assumption that Yugoslavia would be federative, and their association of centralism with a narrow and reactionary clique. While the 'forward movement' in western countries was towards devolution, he pointed out, in Yugoslavia federalism was associated with a dislike of change – with the maintenance of strong Croat, Serb and Slovene identities, and thus with a reluctance to embrace the progressive 'Yugoslav' idea. [81]

When Temperley analysed the various proposals, he brought a rare experience of the political atmosphere in western as well as eastern Yugoslavia, and (not coincidentally) an appreciation uniquely nuanced among British officials. One could not, he noted, be 'wholly conclusive' as to the future form of the Yugoslav state. But all existing drafts (including those of Protić and Trumbić) agreed:

> [...] either in substituting geographic or economic units for
> historic ones, or in adopting measures which lead to the same
> result, ie the advantage of Serbia. Even M.Protić's draft does
> this, for Croatia and Slovenia, which are politically, at any rate,
> states nearly equal to Serbia proper, become two out of nine
> provinces, and will, as provinces, therefore carry little weight,
> even though they may obtain much administrative
> independence. This in one form or another is indispensable.
> You will never get an assembly at Belgrade interested in the
> fishermen of Dalmatia or the miners in Slovenia.[82]

Here, then, was a clear indication of the obstacles facing those who would
preserve the historic provinces, and a wake-up call to those in Whitehall
who assumed a settlement would be on this basis. It is also interesting to
note, in the analysis of one who had spent time in Croatia, a concern for
the upholding of Croat and Slovene interests against those of the
dominant Serbs, and a consequent subtle shift towards the view that
Yugoslavia's structure should reflect its tripartite national division by
according equality of political influence to Serbia, Croatia and Slovenia.
(Though there is no indication of how these 'states' might be defined if
old provincial boundaries, inadequate as ethnic boundaries, were
abolished; and the implication of administrative independence for
Dalmatia might suggest he had still in mind the historic region of Croatia-
Slavonia rather than a broader ethnic Croatia).

Later, on the eve of the elections, Young, Strang and Temperley
continued to stress that the situation was complex and hard to predict.
Certainly the autonomist movement had 'gained greatly of late', with
visible support in Slovenia and Bosnia as well as Croatia and Montenegro
(in Bosnia a US colleague, Young reported, considered autonomism 'very
marked').[83] 'Administrative autonomy in the provinces', they suggested,
seemed likely to be 'the real election cry' outside Serbia.[84] His implication
was that 'the provinces' might, if they had their way, be retained in historic
form. Having said that, of the two major parties, he and Young continued
to stress, one – the Democrats – favoured centralisation, while Radical
'decentralisation' involved the abolition of historical boundaries.

Overall what is clear, reading the reports sent to London during
1920, is that there was both an awareness of worsening intra-Yugoslav
relations, and a growing appreciation of the complexity of the
constitutional problem. While usage of terms like 'autonomy' and
'federalism' remained loose, due to an ongoing failure to pin down the
various alternatives, the inadequacy of the primitive dichotomy of
'centralism'/ 'decentralism' (or 'centralism'/ 'federalism') was recognised.

When we turn to the attitudes of Whitehall officials who read these
reports, however, the picture is different. So ingrained was the expectation

of a 'South Slav federation' that advice that a federal arrangement was in fact unlikely made astonishingly little impression. Instead, politicians and officials continued to refer unthinkingly to a Yugoslav 'Federation'. (No doubt the talk of increasing autonomist sentiment, and of Radical support for 'local autonomies', did not discourage this misapprehension). In September 1920 Leeper proclaimed it an axiom of the Balkan settlement that Montenegro would take its place in a 'Yugo-Slav federation'.[85] Similarly, again in relation to Montenegro, Crowe assured the French Ambassador that the British Government 'had no doubt that the [Constituent] Assembly would in due course work out a federal scheme'.[86] Six days later, as the first election results reached London, Adam noted that the forthcoming Bryce report would show whether Communist gains in Montenegro indicated a desire 'to be outside the Yugo-Slav Federation or not'.[87] The Prime Minister, meanwhile, talked in Parliament of Montenegro's decision to join this 'Great Slavonic Confederation'.[88]

It is not surprising, given the clear guidance he had provided to the contrary, that Young should have found this tendency exasperating. The use of the word 'federal', he warned regarding Crowe's comments to the French Ambassador, was ill-advised: 'if it were made public that His Majesty's Government thought that a federal construction of the Yugo-Slav State was to be expected, I should incur the reproaches of the Government here for having so misled you as to the tendencies of the Coalition Government or any of the Governments which have been in power since my arrival over a year ago'. There was, he impressed, 'nothing federal' about the draft constitution it was intended to force through the assembly: the Serbian element likely to have a majority which would 'effectually prevent the discussion of any federal scheme'.[89] A Serbian stranglehold on the Assembly – entailing the collaboration of Radical, Democrat and smaller groups – was not, it is true, a possibility much discussed until the eve of the election. (At the time Young was writing, moreover, the results were known, and the possibility that Radić's party might not participate increased the likelihood of Serb domination). But he was right to insist that strong opposition to a federal settlement had been reported by the embassy, and that London's almost wilful inattention placed him in an awkward position with Yugoslav politicians. Much good his protests did: three days later, again regarding Montenegro (where Serbian politicians had least intention of granting autonomy), Adam noted that the question of separate diplomatic representation would lapse 'if and when the assembly work out a federal scheme'.[90]

British observers had few complaints about the conduct of the elections of 28 November. In fact they had little to say on the subject. In his substantial report of 3 December Young restricted himself to noting that, aside from small incidents in Montenegro and Bosnia, they had taken place 'in perfect calm'.[91] His silence on the electoral system recalls his previous stated intention not to enquire too closely into the election's democratic credentials.[92] When he had forwarded the electoral law in late September, Nicolson had greeted it warmly. On paper, he wrote, the programme seemed 'perfectly just and reasonable' and the distribution of seats 'quite fair'.[93] Detailed analysis in Whitehall limited itself to two questions – Montenegro and the position of non-South Slav minorities – towards which Britain was felt to have an obligation. These seem to have been foremost in British minds and to have taken precedence over other, broader (and arguably more significant) questions of Yugoslav politics.[94]

The results did not, in any case, lead officials to suspect Serbian foul-play, seeming to demonstrate that shift of power previously noted towards the autonomists of the 'new provinces'. 'My despatches will have shown', Young wrote, 'that during the last few months there had been growing evidence that the people of Yugoslavia were not going to range themselves unthinkingly under the Old Serbian Party divisions as had been once expected'. The fact that in an assembly of 419 members Pašić's Radical Party would control only 95 seats, and Davidović's Democrats only 93, showed, he argued, 'that the old leaders will have lost their domination in Yugo-Slav politics'.[95] Young made clear, Temperley observed, the 'decisive defeat of the Democrats as a nation-wide party', and the emergence of other groups in their place.

The most noteworthy and surprising demonstration of this swing for British observers was the success of Radić's HRSS: 'the sensation of the election', Young called it.[96] Of 93 seats in Croatia-Slavonia (the only province in which it presented a list) the party won 50. Seemingly overnight Radić was transformed from minor irritant to significant player. He had, Young observed, 'suddenly acquired a political importance which may turn his head'. The moderate Croat Union, meanwhile, which had seemed the principal force in Croatia, slumped to a showing of only four seats – an illustration of 'the immense chasm between the intellectuals and the peasant masses'.[97] Furthermore, success for autonomist groups in other non-Serbian regions – in particular for the JMO in Bosnia – seemed to confirm this picture of Serbian centralists losing their grip on the political situation.[98]

In general, Young noted, it was 'the fashion' to consider the results 'satisfactory from the point of view of the unity of Yugo-Slavia'. But to a British official for whom such unity was the primary concern, this optimism was unconvincing. The only clearly defined political party from the new provinces, Young wrote, was Radić with his fifty Croatian peasant republicans. And despite British observers' sympathy for decentralism as the right way to amalgamate Yugoslavia's disparate regions, this 'demagogue' was still viewed with strong suspicion. While the prospect of ministerial office and significant influence might undermine his prior intention to remain in Zagreb, it remained uncertain whether he would prove 'an amenable opportunist or a fanatic adhering to his convictions'.[99]

More fundamentally, the evidence of Croatian feeling caused Young to question the strength of that Yugoslav solidarity accepted so uncritically in Britain in 1918. Noting the 'perhaps well-founded' anxiety in Belgrade at a possible return of the Habsburg dynasty, Young marked the 'undeveloped racial self-consciousness' of Croatian peasants: an open admission that 'Yugoslav' identity had yet to penetrate beneath the educated classes. ('More than one person casually met who knows the old Austrian provinces', he reported, 'says that a plebiscite among the peasants would give an overwhelming majority to the ex-Emperor Karl').

And similar uncertainty concerned the electoral success of the Communists, whose fifty-eight seats left them Yugoslavia's third largest party. Again, Young reported, Belgrade's reaction had been sanguine. In fact, given their recent municipal election successes, the dominant emotion had been relief that they had not won more. But his own reactions were mixed. On the one hand, so far as the union was concerned, it was assumed that whatever else the Communists might be they would be 'good Unionists and even centralists'.[100] On the other hand, it was doubted that those voting communist had genuine communistic convictions, or any real grasp of the KPJ's ideological platform, beyond an awareness of its anti-establishment stance. The party's success therefore seemed further testimony to a reaction against Serbian-style centralism, showing 'discontent with the Government and anti-Serbian feelings'.

In London, however, officials were more optimistic. The results were assumed to mark a further swing away from doctrinaire centralism, and to guarantee the decentralist constitution now unanimously backed in Whitehall. 'Local devolution of power in one form or another', Temperley minuted confidently, 'is inevitable'.[101] And the assumption remained that this would entail a federalism based upon Yugoslavia's historic provinces. Young warned that the Assembly was not, contrary to recurrent misconception, a chance for distinct provinces to discuss the terms of unification; this phase was 'already accomplished'. But such cautions need not, Adam minuted, be taken too seriously: 'the Constituent Assembly seems to be satisfactorily launched; and the attitude of M.Protić, representing the Radical party, should ensure the successful negotiation of a federal Constitution'.[102] Though the SCS Government were thought to have a constitution ready to submit to the assembly, they would probably be forced to modify it 'in the direction of establishing 5 or 6 provinces with executive autonomy in local affairs'.[103] Even concerning Radić there was little alarm. 'Probably [...]', Temperley wrote, 'his Communism, like that of Montenegro, will not be incompatible with Yugoslav unity' (the same highly misleading confounding of the ideologies of the KPJ and the HPSS which we noted earlier).

In the immediate aftermath of the election it was Radić who remained the centre of attention. A party meeting he called in Zagreb for the 8 December was the subject of concerned speculation. It was feared in Belgrade, Young reported, that he would declare an independent Croat peasant republic and (refusing to recognise any political proceedings since the original declaration of such a republic on 29 October 1918) claim its right to negotiate entry into a Yugoslav union on its own terms. Since Belgrade refused to countenance such a claim, any such Croat manifestation was likely, Young wrote, to be suppressed by force, and the situation overall seemed 'very grave'. Though the Radićists were not a large majority, he observed, the boast of a union of hearts would be vain if a constitution had to be forced upon them.[104] In fact, he noted, feeling was growing in Belgrade that if the Croats persisted in making trouble it would be better to revert to the idea of an Orthodox Greater Serbia, and to leave a (truncated) Croatia and Slovenia to fend for themselves.[105]

News that at this meeting Radić had indeed declared a republic (in the presence, Young reported, of some 20,000 people) alarmed Whitehall and in part undermined its complacency regarding the constitutional settlement.[106] On the one hand there was some sympathy, among officials wary of Serbian hegemonism, for Radić's demand (supported by the Croat Union) that the three 'nations' be equally represented in the Assembly rather than in proportion to their populations. This confirmed the view, Adam minuted, that 'only by a slow process of federation under the King of the Serbs, Croats and Slovenes can the Yugo-Slav races achieve unity'.[107] On the other hand, Radić's tactics and temperament were the subject of strong criticism. Trumbić had always hoped, Nicolson remarked, that the Croats might be the decisive factor in the Assembly, but Radić was 'scarcely the man to exercise any useful influence'.[108] He was a 'man of ill-balanced judgement', Adam agreed, a 'fire-brand' who was 'not likely to succeed in constructing any stable form of government in Croatia'.[109] Since early life he had shown, Maclean reported, that 'intransigentism which has characterised the whole of his political career':

> Although highly intellectual, he lacks stability of character to such a degree that many of those who know him well frankly describe him as mad [...]. His gift of flowery oratory and what might be called personal magnetism give him an enormous influence over his peasant followers, and renders him a grave potential danger to the young State.[110]

Radić's political agenda (as opposed to his personal character) had, Adam thought, three fundamental aspects: it was 'a) republican as against the king of the SCS State; b) peasant as against the artisans; and c) Croat as against the Serbs'. Of these, he suspected, 'only the last is permanent and genuine'. The republicanism was probably in fact 'another expression of the same tendency', and would, he implied, be appeased by 'some form of autonomy to a diet or Council for Croatia'. This common view that Croatian republicanism was rooted less in a philosophical ideal than in the perception of this monarchy as a specifically Serbian institution was justified: Radić had, after all, supported the Habsburgs until 1918.[111] (We may recall Temperley's earlier conclusion that a republic's attraction for Croats was precisely that it was 'Croatian rather than Serbian in conception').[112]

On the general question of republicanism versus monarchy Whitehall did not exhibit strong views. Its priority was for the system which would be supported and would therefore promote stability. No doubt, however, there was an unstated assumption that constitutional monarchy was most conducive to such stability. Certainly the Corfu agreement that Yugoslavia be unified under the Karadjordjević dynasty was welcomed. And once this unification had taken place, with apparent majority approval, there was no sympathy for ideologues who would depose the dynasty and declare a republic. The Prince Regent was widely admired in Britain and, at least until early 1921, applauded for a Yugoslav sentiment which distanced him from Serbian chauvinism. When, late in 1920, Young reported the Assembly's early problems over the oath of allegiance for incumbent candidates, officials were little interested. Britain, Adam observed, could 'regard these early difficulties of the SCS Government [...] with equanimity', a view scarcely suggestive of sympathy for republican aspiration in Yugoslavia.[113]

Radić's own brand of republicanism was, however, characteristically idiosyncratic. He claimed not to oppose Alexander as King of Serbia, but only his sovereignty (consecrated by no formal process he recognised) over all the Yugoslavs. His 8 December declaration was of a narrow Croatian republic, which he seems to have imagined joining a broader Yugoslav federation on its own terms. Interpreted literally, this quixotic agenda inspired little sympathy in Britain. For one thing, the parallel with Britain's own increasingly inflammatory Irish national question was becoming too close to ignore. (Radić wanted, Young reported, to negotiate the union of Croatia with Yugoslavia 'on the basis of equality, just as Mr de Valera appears to desire in the case of Ireland and her relations with the British Empire';[114] his party, Adam remarked, combined 'much of the spirit of the earlier Sinn Fein movement with a taste for "oaths" and "covenants" that Ulster might envy').[115] In this context, Whitehall had no intention of promoting interference in such 'internal' matters, whether by independent powers or by the embryonic League of Nations. The SCS Government, Adam observed, 'cannot admit a republic in Croatia any more than we can in Ireland'; 'HMG should keep out of this controversy with the SCS Government, which like the Irish controversy, is an internal question'.[116]

In general Radić's vision of a peasant republic within a broader federation seemed so impractical and unlikely that British analysts hesitated to take it seriously. 'If he can successfully entwine a Croatian Peasant Republic into a united Yugoslav Monarchy', Young remarked, 'he will accomplish a feat which we should no doubt like to emulate at home'.[117] For all his inconsistency and impulsiveness there was, Temperley suggested, little reason to suppose Radić's party genuinely wished to separate from Yugoslavia: 'the "Republic" is very probably a "beau geste" to insure definite autonomy on a federal basis'.[118] For Radić, an admirer of the American model, the same writer argued the following spring, 'a monarch stands for unity and a republic for federalism'.[119]

In their sanguine moments, some officials continued to regard the stand-off between Radić and the centralists merely as a temporary obstacle before the necessity for a decentralist constitution was recognised. 'When Radić has proved futile and Vesnić tried repression', wrote Adam, 'wiser and more moderate counsels' would obtain a hearing; then it was to be hoped that the country would turn to Trumbić.[120] In general, however, British analysis became increasingly pessimistic during December 1920 and January 1921. Importantly, it was recognised that Radić's republicans were by no means the only group opposed to Belgrade's vision. (Just as Whitehall was preoccupied with Montenegrin autonomists before the election, so in its immediate aftermath Radić tended to monopolise British analysis of the anti-centralist opposition). If Radić might prove as formidable an obstacle to union as the Petrović dynasty, Adam commented, the Slovenes could 'hardly be counted on as enthusiastic supporters of Serbian policy'.[121] By the end of the month Young was reporting strikes in Bosnia and Slovenia, as well as a general strike in Croatia.[122] Two weeks later he noted that some in Belgrade considered Korošec and his Slovene Clericals a greater danger to the state than Radić, while the Muslims of the JMO, who had effectively put themselves up for auction, seemed to be favouring 'the Croat and Slovene point of view'.[123] The rivalry between Orthodox Serbs and other communities in Bosnia, his consul in Sarajevo confirmed, was 'increasing in bitterness'.[124]

In this increasingly tense atmosphere, British observers began to fear not only long-term instability but even dangerous confrontations in the short-term. On New Year's Eve Young referred gloomily to the forecast by the Moscow Congress of Communists that civil war would break out in Yugoslavia by the end of the forthcoming year, and that this unstable conglomeration of races (a view of the supposed Yugoslav family now becoming general in British policy-making circles) was ripe for revolution.[125] The situation, Adam wrote, was serious: it was 'all-important' for the state to preserve internal order, but intelligence continued to suggest external intrigue intended to aggravate tensions – in Macedonia, where Communist strength seemed testimony to Bulgarian propaganda, as well as in Croatia by Habsburg and d'Annunzist agents.[126] In the circumstances, Young commented ruefully, 'the prospect of a stable Government being established which can accomplish peaceful work seems remote':

> I cannot foretell what will be evolved from all these conflicting elements; the Yugo-Slavs aligning themselves against the Old Serbs. Perhaps the latter by their strength of character, and in virtue of their strong right arm, will impose their will, but no one wishes to be dominated by the Serbs. Perhaps the younger Serbs will break away and find some solution which will combine centralisation with emancipation from the Serbia of Balkan traditions.[127]

Certainly the incumbent Government's response to this delicate situation seemed rashly provocative to British observers. 'The Serbians', Young lamented, 'seem to be convinced that difficulties are best overcome by forceful methods [...]'.[128] They had 'immense self-confidence in their ability to impose their point of view'.[129] It was 'curious', he wrote, that though Serbs as well as foreigners recognised the incapacity of the Serbian civilian administration, 'no Serb seems to think this a reason for approaching the question of the structure of the Union on any other basis than that of Serb predominance'.[130] Belgrade's plan of 'forcing [a ready-made constitution] down the throats of Croats, Slovenes and Montenegrins alike' (a basic strategy Young had previously commended in the interest of stability) now seemed ill-advised. 'Only by militarism', Adam argued, could such a policy be maintained.[131] And Young rued Pašić's refusal to consider the autonomist programmes of Korošec and the JMO. (If nothing was to change, Pašić asked, for what did Serbia fight? In any case, he claimed, the draft constitution provided regional autonomies to satisfy the interests and needs of all Yugoslavs).[132]

In Britain, however, officials were beginning to appreciate the gulf which separated Pašić's conception of 'regional autonomies' from that of the western Yugoslavs (and their own), as well as the implications of a settlement imposed by a Serb majority on other national groups. By early December it was known that the Council of Ministers composing the draft constitution had decreed that provincial divisions be independent of 'any historical or nationalist or even topographical distinction' (only Korošec on the committee had dissented, demanding Slovenia constitute a province).[133] The published constitution, Adam noted on 14 December, provided for 35 artificial prefectures on the French model:

By taking no account of racial differences it cuts at the root of any federal system, and is no doubt intended to do so by its Serbian authors. The Government apparently will not be willing, if they can maintain a majority in the Assembly, that any federal scheme should be discussed. If they maintain this attitude they will not only play into the hands of their Hungarian and Italian rivals for the favour of M.Radić, but will probably bring into opposition the whole body of Croats, Montenegrins and Slovenes.[134]

Nevertheless, as we have seen, even at the end of December officials in London still assumed federalist pressure would prevail, in spite of Young's warnings that such optimism was misplaced. And it is interesting to note here an ongoing confusion about the form of a 'federal' settlement. A federal system, Adam suggested, was one which *did* heed 'racial' differences, a criterion which – for all the wartime talk of a single Yugoslav race – was now clearly assumed to distinguish Serb, Croat and Slovene, and even Montenegrin (though the latter had always been regarded in Britain as of pure Serb stock).[135] But as Adam made clear in the same minute, the constitution he (like most British officials) envisaged was based upon historic provinces. Trumbić, he wrote, was 'probably well aware of the futility of parcelling out four or five ancient provinces, each strong in racial prejudice and racial pride, into arbitrary administrative divisions'. He was 'no longer a member of the Government which conceives this folly to be the surest means of cementing the Yugo-Slav union'. Yugoslavia, he insisted, would have 'to work out its constitution on a federal basis, reserving to the central government the general functions of legislature, while devolving on Croatia, Slovenia, Bosnia, Dalmatia, Old Serbia and Montenegro the duties of executive provincial administration'.[136]

We have discussed before this common British over-simplification which equated autonomy for the 'ancient provinces' with 'racial' federalism. To be fair, devolution to the historic provinces was, by and large, the demand of non-Serb autonomists, albeit in slightly varied forms. The Croat Union, for instance, suggested a six-way provincial division: Serbia with Old Serbia and Macedonia; Croatia with Slavonia, Dalmatia and Medjomurje; Bosnia; Montenegro; Slovenia; and Vojvodina. The Slovene Clerical scheme varied only in attaching Dalmatia to Bosnia rather than Croatia. The Muslim Club proposed an eight-fold division: Serbia; Old Serbia with Macedonia; Bosnia; Croatia, Slavonia and Medjomurje; Montenegro and Cattaro; Dalmatia; Syrmia and Vojvodina; and Slovenia.[137] Taken together these seemed to British observers to constitute a broad non-Serb consensus for provincial federalism: the only enlightened model for Yugoslavia, and a stark contrast to the Serb chauvinism which would focus the power of a centralised state in Belgrade.

The truth which this black-and-white picture contained, however, blinded Whitehall to its defects. For one thing, a glance at these various autonomist schemes should have shown them to be each as self-serving as those of Pašić or Protić were accused of being. The Croat Union proposal secured the long-held Croat ambition of reuniting the provinces of the triune kingdom. By instating Montenegro, Bosnia and even Vojvodina as distinct regions, moreover, it denied to the nationalists of Belgrade an expanded Serbia, and ensured the balance of power tilted towards Zagreb. The single difference in the Slovene scheme was significant: in not uniting the three majority Croat provinces it reflected a desire to limit the power of Croatian politicians resented by Slovenes for an arrogant and condescending manner towards their north-western neighbours. The Muslim scheme, meanwhile, no less plainly advanced Muslim interests. A province comprised of Old Serbia (Kosovo) and Macedonia, along with an autonomous Bosnia, ensured that Muslim populations could exert considerable influence in the provinces which they inhabited. To Muslim parties both the Croat and particularly the Slovene scheme (which by merging Bosnia with Dalmatia diluted Muslim clout in this heartland province) were not minor variants but were fundamentally unacceptable.

In the context of a Yugoslav political scene, furthermore, in which each national group sought to secure its own interests, it should scarcely have been surprising that the Serbs inclined to do likewise. Nor, given that this was the case, should it have been surprising that autonomist schemes retaining historical boundaries did not commend themselves to Serb interests. All of the above proposals left significant Serb populations stranded as potentially powerless minorities in provinces dominated by rival groups. In an atmosphere of increasing mutual suspicion (fostered, admittedly, by the insensitivity of Serb-majority governments) it was not unnatural for Serbian politicians to fear their Orthodox brethren in Croatia, southern Dalmatia or Bosnia might be left at the mercy of regional governments deaf to their concerns.[138] This was why Pašić insisted that the only form of federalism his party would contemplate was a 'racial' one in which a new and greatly enlarged Serb unit was carved out at the expense of separate and much diminished Croat and Slovene counterparts.

British analysts, however, did not ask for instance how Bosnia, an undeniably historic province, could be considered 'strong in racial prejudice and racial pride', with its impossibly intermingled Serb, Croat and Muslim population; nor how Serbs in Croatia were to be reconciled to inhabiting an autonomous province conceived explicitly as an ethnic Croatia; nor how Yugoslav Macedonia was to be integrated – as Adam at least seems to have imagined – into the province of 'Old Serbia' (by which it was conquered only during 1912-13) in the light of the hostility to Belgrade in that troubled region. ('Southern Serbia', the British consul in Skopje warned in February, was 'a Serbian colony rather than an integral part of the Serbian Kingdom', and as such could not 'with any hope of success be subjected to a form of administration framed for a homogeneous population, such as that of France').[139] By failing even to acknowledge these fundamental problems for any scheme based upon autonomy for the historic regions Whitehall overestimated the strength and cogency of the decentralist cause.

Unfortunately a lack of media and popular interest in the Yugoslav constitutional question meant that – unlike, say, in the case of Montenegro – officials were not subjected to external scrutiny and interrogation. Young himself remarked this lack of interest, and the reduced pressure on British officials which resulted (though it naturally seemed to him an advantage rather than otherwise). At the end of January 1921, a moment 'of decisive import for the tranquillity and prosperity of the new-born Southern Slav state', it seemed to him 'remarkable, and perhaps a cause for thankfulness, how little attention is being paid in the English or other Western press to the interesting situation now arising at Belgrade out of the hesitation of the more cultured races to lock themselves in the iron embrace of the untutored but forceful Serb'.[140] (A couple of months previously, in the last issue of *New Europe*, Seton-Watson had rather lamented this 'renewed indifference of the general public to foreign affairs').[141]

By late January 1921, however, Whitehall's complacency concerning the outcome of the assembly had finally given way. The continued refusal of Radić's party to participate left the Radical-Democrat bloc little difficulty maintaining the majority needed to secure its centralist vision. (On 31 January the deputies present elected a Constitutional Commission to examine the draft constitution on which a majority belonged to the NRS-DS coalition. Had Radić come to Belgrade, Young lamented, his five seats would have removed this government majority).[142]

The persistent talk of local autonomies by leading Radicals (Protić in particular) had gradually undermined officials' earlier view of the Radical agenda as centralist and Great Serbian, and reinforced the presumption of a decentralist outcome. But this rhetoric, it was belatedly recognised, was largely phoney. As Temperley noted in a detailed report early in March, Protić's December 1918 assurance that under State control existing autonomous institutions would be retained (an equivocal statement which Temperley rightly, if only with hindsight, considered 'vague') appeared 'not to have been carried out in any really intelligible sense'. The Croatian Diet had been abolished, and though the Ban had been granted the status of a Cabinet Minister, he seemed more the servant of Belgrade than a spokesman for Croatia. Elsewhere, government was effectively conducted by presidents of districts who were 'dependent on the Minister of the Interior at Belgrade, and consequently […] liable to be changed according to the party squabbles of the capital'.

Meanwhile in some regions – Montenegro, Bosnia, or Vojvodina – the Serb military commander, or the chief of police ('usually a Serb'), was 'more powerful or more important than the actual civilian governors'. The result, Temperley rightly sensed, was extreme centralisation of executive authority, even if this owed as much to administrative inexperience as political ideology. 'The meddling interference and delays caused by reference of minute details to Belgrade' had produced, he noted, 'endless irritation without any corresponding advantage'. And while Radicals had seemed ready to conciliate Croats and Bosnian Muslims in late 1919, their proposals 'received little practical application' when they came to power. Protić's draft constitution, 'intended to be forced on the Constituent Assembly *en bloc*', seemed to offer administrative devolution, but was in reality 'a species of disguised or camouflaged centralisation'.[143]

This element of subterfuge was now remarked in the rhetoric of Belgrade, where 'unitarism', Young noted, had become 'a blessed word […] more attractive than centralisation', but which (he implied) amounted in Radical usage to the same thing.[144] And this was a deception to which non-Serb groups were becoming wise. ('M.Pašić, like an old spider, is still alluring the Yugo-Slav flies to come into his parlour', Young observed wryly, 'but their coyness seems to be increasing').[145] That the Government's approach in early 1921 was 'Great Serbian' and so by definition *not* unitaristic (in the sense of believing in or aspiring to an undifferentiated Yugoslav identity) seemed evident from the preliminary debate over state nomenclature. During the 'considerable discussion' which the issue provoked Radicals, Young reported, insisted upon the unwieldy form 'Serbs, Croats and Slovenes', a determination whose underlying chauvinism he readily detected:

> I have frequently in private conversation protested humorously against the embarrassment caused to the Chanceries by the awkwardness of this cumbrous title, which lends itself to no adjectival variations, but I have found the Radical politicians most seriously insistent. They say their Serb constituents would never accept for their country a name which contained no allusion to the Serbs. They have also in their minds that, if 'Serbs, Croats and Slovenes' is awkward in common parlance, the tendency will be to drop the 'Croats and Slovenes' and the word 'Serbs' will in time gradually be used to designate the whole country.[146]

While officials preferred (and often used) the form 'Yugoslavia', and were contemptuous of the bigotry which sought to brand all Yugoslavs as Serbs, they had themselves clearly abandoned the 'unitarist' notion that Yugoslavs shared a monolithic national identity. 'The one real attempt to fuse the different races into one Yugo-Slav nation', Temperley wrote, 'was made by the Democrats under Pribićević'. But, he noted with hindsight, 'no one really believed' that their attempts to advance this goal by radical social and economic reforms could have succceeded against 'so many vested interests'.[147] By early 1921 British officials effectively agreed with the view of a Communist deputy reported by Young:

> The country is now further from unity than it was two years ago. The policy adopted during that period was fatal. It was an arbitrary centralist ordering of our State on the supposition that national unity and a centralist organisation are one and the same thing.[148]

Few in Britain yet followed this deputy to his conclusion that 'the Serbs, Croats and Slovenes are not spiritually ready for union in one State'. In fact, Temperley affirmed, 'the desire for some kind of unity is apparent in many directions, and even Radić is for it [...]'. Nevertheless, real concerns were now surfacing about what the future might hold if the struggle between obstinate Serb centralism and increasingly vociferous non-Serb autonomism continued on its current course. 'Old Serbians', Young reported, seemed still 'convinced that the Opposition has no dangerous character, and that after the fanciful schemes of the dissidents are sufficiently honoured the Centralist Constitution will force itself on the country'. But, he warned, 'it looks to me as though the Opposition is gaining strength', an opinion, Temperley thought, confirmed by other evidence and representing 'a serious prospect for the future'.[149] Temperley's conclusion in his March report displayed clearly this new pessimism:

> At the present moment the Radical-Democrats appear to have the power to drive through their programme, which is really a disguised centralisation. If they do they will be strenuously resisted by strong parties in Slovenia, Croatia and Bosnia, also by Radić and the Communists, though for different reasons. The Union is therefore in measurable danger because the arbitrary methods of the Government have already awakened universal suspicion outside the ranks of their own supporters, and further persistence in this course can only increase the separatising tendencies of the Federalists and the revolutionary violence of the Communists.[150]

At the end of March Temperley recorded that the scheme of dividing the state on non-historic lines had passed the constitutional committee: Bosnia would be divided into at least three provinces, Croatia-Slavonia into four, Macedonia into two, with Slovenia alone perhaps forming a single province. 'All historic divisions', he commented, 'are [...] quite clearly obliterated'.[151] This was a 'very far-reaching change' which was 'calculated to produce great discontent'.[152] The reformed state structure, along with the proposed aggressive measures against major landowners in Croatia and Vojvodina, amounted to a 'considerable revolution' showing 'marks of great violence and arbitrariness'. There was, Temperley concluded (displaying again the British tendency to demonise an individual rather than a wider body of opinion), 'an unmistakable taint of oriental intrigue, corruption and despotic method of which all are probably due directly to M.Pašić'.

Nevertheless, with changes to the ministry and Radić's abstention giving the government an effective two-thirds majority, the constitution's passage seemed 'assured'.[153] In fact over the subsequent weeks British observers suspected the centralisers were 'gaining ground slightly', while those for historical frontiers like Korošec and Drinković became increasingly 'cornered'.[154] On 12 May, amid reports of growing Radićist agitation, a large majority in the Assembly passed the constitution. It was, Temperley lamented, 'really an epoch-making decision', certain to increase autonomist opposition.[155] On 28 June (Vidovdan) 1921 the constitution was finally ratified, fundamentally unchanged.[156] Of 285 deputies in attendance, 223 voted in favour, 35 against. 161 deputies had either walked out or abstained. As Alexander left the formal ceremony in the temporary Assembly building, a bomb was thrown at him by a Communist agitator, an unsuccessful attack which boded ill for the future stability of the state.[157]

Reaction from British observers was glum. The situation in Zagreb, Maclean reported, was 'far from satisfactory'. The constitution was causing 'deep discontent'. Services to mark Vidovdan had been 'tinged with gloom'.[158] The provinces from which a majority of deputies had backed the constitution, Strang observed, were Serbia, Montenegro, Vojvodina and Bosnia: the first two purely Serb, the third largely Serb, the last result owing to the vote of Muslims who 'were paid their price'.[159] Of 27 Croatian deputies who had voted in favour, two thirds were Serbs. In general, he suggested, those who had voted against the constitution had seen some good in it, those who had abstained none:

> In the face of this it is impossible to argue that the Constitution has not been imposed on the country by the Serb majority, and the fact that the real opposition abstained from the vote as a

protest is a measure of the extent to which their claims have
been disregarded [...], and of the determination of the Serbs to
destroy everything, whether good or bad, that savours of the
bureaucratic, autocratic, aristocratic spirit of Austria-Hungary,
and to put in its place the simplicity and democracy of which
they are so proud, and the easy-going inefficiency which to
them is the mark of a free spirit.[160]

Perhaps no single quotation so succinctly captures official British attitudes
towards the Serbs in the aftermath of the war, as a poised ambivalence
(fruit of the country's martial gallantry) tilted decisively back towards the
wry denigration which had characterised pre-war assumptions. What a
damning weight of condescension and faint praise lies in those two final
clauses!

In London officials echoed this reaction. *The Times'* pessimistic
analysis, one noted, would displease the SCS Government but put the
situation 'admirably'. The desired compromise between centralists and
decentralists had not materialised. Pašić was 'the foster-parent' of a
constitution which was 'a triumph for centralisation', owing more to 'the
clever wire-pulling of a politician than to any considerations of
statesmanship'. The last-hour deal with the Muslims was 'typical of the
taint of intrigue and corruption that unhappily pervades the whole
construction of the Constitution'. Though the final vote seemed decisive,
the key to appreciating the situation lay in 'the ominous balance of [...]
abstentions'. This victory for rigid centralisation was 'in the opinion of
many the one event liable to throw the three peoples into discord and to
prevent them from settling down in unison'. And with even future
Radical-Democrat cooperation uncertain, the state seemed 'doomed to
political instability'.[161]

In his detailed annual report for 1921 Young provided a more
detailed analysis of voting patterns, and clearly highlighted the
constitution's polarising effect. While a majority in Serbia, Bosnia and
Vojvodina had been in favour, 70% of deputies from Croatia-Slavonia had
abstained, 60% from Slovenia and 55% from Dalmatia. Meanwhile,
considering deputies' religious background rather than provenance, it
transpired that 75% of those who voted for the Constitution were Serb-
Orthodox, while 70% of abstentions were by Catholics. 80% of Catholic
deputies had abstained.[162]

He also scrutinised for the first time the constitution's precise
definition of the relationship between local authorities and central
government. This was an issue, he noted, which since unification had
'never ceased to be the subject of the most acrid discussion'. And it was
one whose resolution emphasised the settlement's rigid centralism. At the
head of each region was to be a 'Lord Lieutenant' (*načelnik*) appointed by

the crown, and though local elective bodies were to be instituted, with limited decision-making authority, this official might refuse to promulgate any decree deemed to conflict with state policy. 'The object of the whole system of local administration', Young observed, 'is to grant as large a measure of autonomy as possible to local authorities while at the same time striking a blow at provincial particularism […] which is looked on as a danger to the existence of the young State'. If the common people could be trusted, the same could not be said of the governing classes of Zagreb, Sarajevo, Split or Ljubljana. These centres would therefore be reduced to 'provincial towns with no authority beyond their own particular small region or (in the case of Zagreb) beyond the limits of the city itself'. The 'millenary if somewhat mythical' triune Kingdom of Croatia, Slavonia and Dalmatia, as well as the 'Banovina' of Croatia, would receive 'their final death blow' and would in time 'find themselves administered by half-a-dozen nominees of the Ministry of Interior in Belgrade'.[163]

The Outlook for Yugoslavia

In November 1921, as the Assembly – now an official Legislative Chamber – turned to the law delimiting the State into twenty-six administrative districts, Nicolson rued a centralising policy which could 'only lead to trouble in the future'. The sooner the constitution was remade under a man like Trumbić (or even, he admitted, Protić) the better.[164] Pašić seemed, he wrote, to be governing Yugoslavia on the same lines and ('what is worse') with the same staff as he ran Serbia: 'in the end the Slovenes, the Croats, and the Dalmatians will stand it no longer, but […] the harm will have been done'.[165] Further instability late in the year – the Government's resignation, victory for Radić and the Croat bloc in the December municipal elections, Radić's demand for recognition within the state of a 'separate Croatian people, and a separate Croat state' – was lamented as 'the inevitable result of M.Pašić's policy'.[166] Only a report on the military offered any hope. The army, it suggested, was gradually losing the commanding position and political influence it enjoyed in old Serbia. If this 'backbone of old-Serbian hegemony', was losing political influence, then 'debalkanisation of the SCS State', Nicolson dared suggest, 'is nearer than we had hoped'.[167]

This oscillation between profound pessimism and unguarded optimism was more typical of Whitehall's idealistic junior officials than it was of Young, who was less squeamish about the use of government power in the interests of stability and more consistent in his mild, somewhat resigned pessimism. His 1921 report was less negative than much British analysis in the constitution's aftermath, no doubt because he had not shared the lofty hopes of younger colleagues. He noted the 'gigantic internal problem' facing a kingdom with component parts on such 'differing planes of civilisation'. But to understand this was implicitly, at least in part, to forgive the failings of the government confronted by it.

Clearly there was now no sympathy for Pribićević's ostrich-headed unrealism, which was seen to endanger the country's very existence. (Since the population were all Yugoslavs, Young quoted him with disbelief, 'the Croatian question does not exist' and anyone denying this was 'an enemy of the State'). Nevertheless, the need for legal standardisation, with twelve systems said to be in force, was 'obvious', and in some areas 'fair headway' had been made. And 'not all Democrats', Young added, were as rigid as Pribićević; even members of his own group had shown concern at the effects of an over-zealous centralism. Meanwhile the Radical party was, he thought, 'ready to swing if it sees profit in it'. This, allied to the fact that Trumbić and some Slovenes were trying to moderate the extreme autonomists, suggested, Young wrote, that future elections might empower a coalition open to constitutional reform. (Though quite how the Radicals, fiercely protective of Serb interests, were likely to approve any revision acceptable to Croat sensibilities is unclear in this too-sanguine analysis).

But the big question, Young was clear, was the mercurial Radić – a man whose 'high educational achievements' failed to disguise a 'somewhat unbalanced and idealistic mind'; who, while advocating a strict policy of non-violence, nevertheless 'sets no curb [...] on his tongue'. For all the increased sympathy for Croatian autonomism in Whitehall during 1920-21, Radić remained far too quixotic and temperamental a figure-head to appeal to cautious British diplomats: a 'dreamer' whose 'ideally Christian' tenets included 'no taxation' and 'no army'. He was, Young considered, 'as much a thorn in the flesh of the Belgrade authorities as Gandhi in that of the Viceroy of India' and whether to deal with him by violence or indulgence was a problem 'much exercising the Serb-Croat-Slovene Government'.[168] The comparison here (a recurrent one) displayed sympathy with the central authorities, and he praised their 'wise patience' in allowing Radić his say 'in spite of his provocative language'.[169] It was, he noted, 'difficult to say whether his influence is growing'. His success in the recent municipal elections showed an increasing urban influence. And some said his doctrines were spreading to Bosnia and Dalmatia, even perhaps among Serb peasants in Croatia. (He had himself recently warned that this Croatian 'poison' was 'working down through Bosnia and Hercegovina to Montenegro'). On the other hand the Government had pointed out that even in Radićist strongholds 'recruits come up well and taxes are readily paid'.

Much of the unrest among the Croatian peasantry could certainly be attributed, Young felt, to the arrogant and disrespectful manner of Serbian military administration. The Serbian Army 'from the beginning treated

Croatia (unlike Slovenia) as occupied enemy territory, indulged in flogging (which even the Hungarians never did), introduced martial law, overrode the civil power, punished infringements of regulations which had never been promulgated, and worked in Cyrillic script, [...] so that in time the Serbs appeared merely to have taken the place of the hated Magyar'. But such 'overbearing' conduct, he implied, was tactless and *ad hoc* rather than part of a centrally-orchestrated campaign. Violent incidents had been, he noted, 'a good deal less' in 1921 than in 1920. It was not surprising that such army brutality as persisted, combined with the penalties suffered by Croat peasants as a result of tax and exchange-rate reform (which may indeed have been skewed to favour the Serbian population), had lured Croats towards Radić's Edenic vision of a republic without army or tax-collectors. But, Young implied, these were in large part the inevitable teething problems of a newly-amalgamated state which might be expected to diminish.[170]

If this reassured officials, however, there soon followed Young's account of an interview with Trumbić which emphasised the latter's utter disillusionment with a regime of 'mere force'. Serbian misrule had, Trumbić argued, turned Radić's 'harmless faddist band' into 'an association of the Croat people suffering from a sense of real injury'. In part Young sympathised. Serbians who classed Trumbić as an enemy of state unity meant, he observed wryly, that he was 'an enemy to that unity under Serbian hegemony'. His charges of inefficiency, corruption and disregard of legal procedure and popular rights, Young noted, 'I never meet anybody inclined to dispute'. But he questioned autonomist tactics. Surely, he wrote, the new provinces 'had [...] the remedy within their own hands': by political participation Slovene, Muslim and Croat deputies would comprise at least 'a very important minority which, by its superior culture, could doubtless impose to a great extent its views on the governing class'. 'An oppressed people', he continued, 'could only hope to gain sympathy abroad if they could show that constitutional methods were denied them' (an argument which calls to mind once again British preoccupation with the Irish question).[171]

In London Trumbić's high standing gave this communication a considerable (and depressing) impact. Nicolson was particularly maudlin:

> This represents by far the most important and authoritative criticism of the Pašić system which we have as yet received. M.Trumbić is a man of high character, great learning, and courageous, if somewhat dour, patriotism [...]. He is a serious and slow-thinking man; he would not have made these statements [...] unless he was firmly convinced of their reality and importance. We can take it therefore that the selfish and blind policy of M.Pašić will lead to a disintegration of the

> Yugo-Slav Union. The Croatian question will become acute: the Muslim elements in Bosnia will join the movement: the Slovenes, who have been so badly treated by Belgrade will further embitter the issue; and the Montenegrin question, which we had hoped was settled, will revive with renewed intensity. From all this it will he Hungary and Italy who will reap the advantage.

'The outlook', he added in comically-understated conclusion, 'is not hopeful'.[172] Meanwhile in another minute written on the same day he continued his diatribe against the aged Yugoslav premier:

> Mr Pašić is a danger to Europe. Old, obstinate, venerable and ingratiating he combines all the futilities of a Balkan politician with the appearance and prestige of an elder statesman. The only hope for Yugo-Slavia is that he should disappear.[173]

This was, to be sure, a letting-off of steam which may not fairly represent the day-to-day mood of British officials dealing with Yugoslavia. And Nicolson was certainly one of those younger, idealistic officials whose great optimism for the post-war settlement paved the way for moments of corresponding disillusionment. ('I wonder', mused the older guard in the shape of Lord Curzon, 'if things are quite so bad').[174] But there is no doubt, nevertheless, that by the spring of 1922 most British observers were profoundly disappointed with the constitutional path Yugoslavia had taken since its formation in 1918 and regarded a significant revision in the direction of regional autonomy as indispensable to the country's future as a united entity.

Conclusion

The period of this study was claimed in the introduction as an important, formative one for British attitudes towards the Yugoslav peoples. It is certainly true that preconceptions about this region then became established which have proved tenacious in subsequent British discourse, as any brief perusal of the literature on Britain's involvement in and attitudes towards the Yugoslav wars of the 1990s will make clear.[1] But it will also have become apparent – indeed this has constituted one of the monograph's recurring themes – that attitudes towards the Yugoslavs as a whole, or towards one or more of their component elements, were capable on occasion of changing with great rapidity in response to contemporary events and perceived British interests.

During the war in particular, the altered shape of European geopolitics produced fundamental shifts in Britain not only towards south-east Europe's present and future, but also towards its past. Arnold Toynbee summoned each nation's ancestors – its 'host of unseen witnesses' – to testify to the world about the living generation and its future.[2] What he did not perhaps appreciate was the degree to which the interrogation and interpretation of these ancestral voices would be shaped, and subsequently reshaped, in accordance with particular contemporary circumstances. No doubt this mutability in the interpretation of South Slav history was assisted by the fact that the region was, in general, little known before 1914. It might be harder now for scholars to accept uncritically the sort of national myths which were often embraced during the First World War. But it would be implausible to suppose that the changes we have charted were the result simply of an influx of new information. For one thing, the altered circumstances of the immediate *post-war* period quickly brought, as we have seen, a revived emphasis on historical divisions, and a return to other pejorative stereotypes which had dominated the pre-war discourse.

Rather than viewing our period as one in which a single monovalent paradigm was established, therefore, it perhaps makes more sense to think of it as having provided and consolidated a set of alternative resources. Some (such as the view of the Balkans in general as turbulent, primitive and unstable) obviously predated the 20th century, but were further entrenched during that century's first quarter. Others were first established – or at least first became widespread – during the World War I era, though they were quickly provided with a long historical pedigree, dating back to that 14th century resistance against the Turks which proved such a rich source of precedent and analogy. Subsequent generations of British observers of the Yugoslavs have been able to draw upon these alternative stock images in a manner dictated substantially by contemporary contingency. Thus the Serbs have become brave, patriotic, democratic, egalitarian and anglophile in one prefabricated image, primitive, chauvinistic, 'oriental' in another; the Croats cultured, westernised and Yugoslav, or narrowly nationalistic, clericalist, and pro-Austrian; the Montenegrins brave, independent and instinctively poetic, or backward, violent and pro-Russian. And so on. At later moments of crisis – during the military coup of 1941 and the subsequent German invasion, for instance, or the 1948 expulsion of Yugoslavia from the Cominform – British commentators resorted freely to these stereotypes, shaped earlier in the century, selecting and employing them as they buttressed attitudes to contemporary events.[3]

If the distant and recent past of constituent Yugoslav peoples was in important respects reinterpreted in Britain during the war, perhaps the most significant conclusion of the monograph's early chapters concerns the manner in which the pre-unification relations of the Yugoslavs as a whole were re-assessed in the light of the apparent contemporary strength of the Yugoslav movement. Historians looking back on the creation of Yugoslavia in 1918 have often considered it a 'major historical surprise' – a development which could not be said to be obviously foreshadowed by the previous histories of the various Yugoslav peoples, but which was brought about by the highly unusual circumstances of the war.[4] It is pointed out that even those South Slav intellectuals who were enthusiastic about the notion of Yugoslav unity before the war nevertheless considered that any political unification would be the result of a long and gradual evolutionary process taking decades if not longer.[5] Even the most optimistic of such enthusiasts, it is now assumed, would have admitted that in 1918 no single Yugoslav nation yet existed to live in the new state.[6]

In Britain, however, the possibility that the apparent strength of pro-Yugoslav feeling – or the apparent precedence of Yugoslav feeling over other, narrower identities – might be the result of unusual short-term factors, and might therefore not prove enduring once the war was over and some sort of stability had returned, was barely considered. The emerging new state was not allowed to be a 'historical surprise'. Instead, the past was reinterpreted to allow it (the state) to appear the natural result of profound long-term trends, even if – as was widely acknowledged – these trends had accelerated significantly during the 20th century. The failure of the Yugoslavs to coalesce earlier than 1918 became ascribed not, as before, to acute internal divisions, but rather to the cynical manipulation of external imperialist powers – and the failure in Britain to appreciate the strength of pre-war Yugoslav sentiment and aspiration to the deliberate campaigns of misinformation orchestrated by these powers.

After the war, as we have seen, British observers were rapidly disillusioned of their belief in a single, existing Yugoslav nationality, as older traditions such as those centred on Croatian 'State Right' and 'Great Serbia' demonstrated a continued vitality, and new growths – Radić's republican movement in particular – grounded themselves upon sub-Yugoslav identities. In the space of the thirty months which separated the initial formation of the state and the ratification of its first constitution, the image of Yugoslavia in Britain shifted fundamentally, from being that of a new *national* state among the several which succeeded to the lands of the old, multinational Habsburg Monarchy, to being that of another multinational conglomeration (albeit one with strong linguistic and cultural ties) which suffered the same acute difficulties in managing its antagonistic national elements as had the Empire which preceded it. Under Serb dominance Yugoslavia came, as Austria-Hungary before it, to seem effectively a 'prison of the peoples'.

And just as most pre-war British analysts had assumed that some sort of federalisation of the Habsburg realm was ultimately the only way in which that power would overcome its internal ethno-linguistic tensions, so in the case of post-war Yugoslavia did they quickly conclude that a federal solution – or at least one that incorporated substantial regional autonomies – offered the only route to future stability. But as was also the case with the Monarchy before the war, observers failed to confront the difficult questions: for in post-war Yugoslavia, as in the Monarchy, 'historic' provinces and the boundaries of ethnic population were by no means coterminous, and any system of autonomy based (as Britons generally assumed) on the former raised intractable difficulties, particularly for a Serb population reduced to minority-status in several of the principal provincial units.

Broadly speaking, in fact, it may be said that while those British analysts enthusiastic about Yugoslav union during the war tended to judge the country's post-war problems as being more simple in origin than was in fact the case, those more pessimistic inclined to the opposite extreme. Thus while the former, as we have frequently seen, sought to pin all the blame on supposedly isolated individuals or groups, an interpretation premised at times upon a misreading of broader opinion, the latter saw in Yugoslavia's teething problems the expression of rivalries so ancient and complex as to defy either analysis or remedy. Increasingly, the deteriorating situation during 1920-21 seemed to corroborate the second view. For many of those in wartime Britain who had hoped, and believed, that the new state's western elements would 'raise up' the 'oriental' Serbs to the level of central Europe, it began to seem that the reverse had occurred. Instead of a stable, pro-western bulwark across the old Austrian-Ottoman frontier, Britain was faced with the fact that 'all Austria-Hungary' might now be considered part of 'the Balkans', a region defined less by geographical extent than by moral climate – one in which it could be assumed, as Harold Temperley predicted gloomily, that 'atrocities will take place in dark corners'.[7] The scene was set for a century in which the phrase 'national question' would seem to many western observers the central fact of Eastern Europe – as timeless and irremediable in its final quarter as it had been in its first.

Notes

Introduction

[1] This point was made by Lloyd-George in his *Memoirs of the Peace Conference* (New Haven, 1939), ii, 588-9. The question of the Habsburg Empire, R.G.D.Laffan noted in the official peace conference history, was 'decided by its own disruption': 'The Liberation of the New Nationalities: The Yugo-Slavs', in H.W.V.Temperley (ed.), *A History of the Peace Conference of Paris*, 6 vols. (London, 1920-4), iv, 204. 'The most solemn peace conference imaginable', one participant agreed, 'could not put [Austria-Hungary] together again': C.Seymour, 'The End of an Empire: Remnants of Austria-Hungary', in E.M.House and C.Seymour (eds.), *What Really Happened at Paris: The Story of the Peace Conference, 1918-1919* (London, 1921), pp.87-8.

[2] Quoted in Laffan, 'The Liberation of the New Nationalities', p.183.

[3] H.Hanak, *Great Britain and Austria-Hungary during the First World War* (London, 1962), pp.1,3.

[4] W.Miller, *Travel and Politics in the Near East* (London, 1898), p.xiii. Another who penetrated the realms of 'savage Europe' agreed that most Englishmen were more familiar with the geography of 'darkest Africa': H.de Windt, *Through Savage Europe* (London, 1907), p.15.

[5] N.Forbes, *The Southern Slavs* (Oxford, 1914-15), p.3.

[6] K.Calder, *Britain and the Origins of the New Europe 1914-1918* (Cambridge, 1976), p.214. A.H.E.Taylor complained during the war that the British public's traditional attitude towards Balkan problems had been 'one of indifference tempered with annoyance at certain small nations whose affairs are continually threatening to set other people by the ears', while that of the Foreign Office, 'if not actuated always by indifference, though indifference has largely been present, has constantly been based upon a misapprehension of the problems at issue' (*The Future of the Southern Slavs* (London, 1917), p.8).

[7] Markedly less information flowed back to London even from Vienna, Robin Okey has pointed out, than from regions of imperial concern – two extant volumes of general correspondence from the Vienna Embassy for 1911, the same number as for Abyssinia and Haiti/San Domingo, contrast with 19 for Morocco and 22 for Persia: R.Okey, 'British Impressions of the Serbo-Croat speaking lands of the Habsburg Monarchy – Reports to the Foreign Office 1867-1908', in R.Evans, D.Kováč and E.Ivaničková (eds), *Great Britain and Central Europe 1867-1914* (Bratislava, 2002), p.62.

[8] Quoted in H.Seton-Watson and C.Seton-Watson, *Making of a New Europe* (London, 1981), p.322.

[9] H.Seton-Watson and C.Seton-Watson (eds.), *R.W.Seton-Watson and the Yugoslavs: Correspondence 1906-1941*, 2 vols. (London; Zagreb, 1976), i, 265-7 (henceforward Seton-Watson, *Correspondence*).

[10] Quoted in Seton-Watsons, *Making of a New Europe*, p.227. No doubt a similar sentiment prevails among idealistic internationalists of our own age. Vernon Bartlett recalled a spoof bulletin circulated to British officials in Paris declaring that

serious trouble had broken out in Dalmatia between the Yugos and the Slavs: 'every one concerned initialled the news without a murmur'! (*Behind the Scenes at the Paris Peace Conference* (London, 1920), p.146).

[11] The future Israeli leader David Ben-Gurion estimated that perhaps a hundred people in interwar England, in and out of Parliament, interested themselves in Palestine. There is little reason to think Yugoslavia had a broader market (T.Segev, *One Palestine Complete: Jews and Arabs under the British Mandate* (London, 2000), p.398).

[12] See his *Great Britain and Austria-Hungary*.

[13] A number of works deal well with this subject. See, for instance, Harry Hanak, 'The Government, the Foreign Office and Austria-Hungary, 1914-1918', *Slavonic and East European Review*, XLVIII, no 108 (1969); W.Fest, *The Habsburg Monarchy and British Policy 1914-1918* (London, 1978), pp.88-115, 241-4; and Seton-Watson and Seton-Watson, *Making of a New Europe* (an excellent survey which, perhaps inevitably, gives a slightly exaggerated impression of Robert Seton-Watson's influence on British policy-making).

[14] The idea itself was not new, of course: the sense both of a shared South Slav heritage as well as of a broader Slavic affinity had a long history as well as a grounding in an objective linguistic kinship. In their early modern roots Yugoslav and pan-Slav ideas were the province of a tiny intellectual elite, but by the 19th century had become more widely disseminated, particularly in Austria-Hungary, where they found expression in the 'Illyrian' movement of the 1830s and 1840s. See I.Banac, *The National Question in Yugoslavia: Origins, History, Politics* (Ithaca and London, 1984), pp.70-115. My debt to this excellent work will be apparent. See also D.Djordjević, 'The Idea of Yugoslav Unity in the Nineteenth Century', in D.Djordjević (ed.), *The Creation of Yugoslavia 1914-1918* (Santa Barbara, Calif., 1980), pp.1-14; W.Vucinich, 'Croatian Illyrism: Its Background and Genesis', in S.B.Winters and J.Held (eds.), *Intellectual and Social Developments in the Habsburg Empire from Maria Theresa to World War I* (Boulder, 1975), pp.55-114.

[15] This point is made by D.Rusinow: 'The Yugoslav Idea before Yugoslavia', in D.Djokić (ed.), *Yugoslavism: Histories of a Failed Idea 1918-1992* (London, 2003), pp.4-5, 11.

[16] Journalists might perhaps be considered a discrete fifth group. In practice, however, the majority of analytical journalism drawn upon in this study was written by individuals who may fairly be considered within the first two categories. Such journalistic coverage of the South Slav region as contained more than a skeletal outline of events was scanty during the pre-war period, and when wartime developments created a rapid escalation of interest among the British public, the demand for information and first-hand accounts was met, often as not, by individuals who were not professional reporters but who had otherwise acquired personal experience or knowledge of the area. Of the many column inches written about the Serbs in particular during World War I, a substantial portion was written by individuals who had served in Serbia in a military or civilian capacity, had an active connection with the Serbian relief fund or other charitable organisations, or had an academic interest in the Yugoslav region.

[17] De Windt, working as a correspondent for the Westminster Gazette, admitted undertaking his journey with the haziest of preconceptions – of Cetinje as a

mountain stronghold 'swarming with armed men and bristling with fortifications', and Ragusa (Dubrovnik) as a 'squalid Eastern place' (*Through Savage Europe*, pp.15, 42, 70).

[18] P.E.Henderson, *A British Officer in the Balkans: The Account of a Journey through Dalmatia, Montenegro, Turkey in Austria, Magyarland, Bosnia and Hercegovina* (London, 1909), p.15. For other pre-war travel accounts, see, for instance, M.Holbach, *Bosnia and Herzegovina: Some Wayside Wanderings* (London, 1910), or F.K.Hutchinson, *Motoring in the Balkans: Along the Highways of Dalmatia, Montenegro, the Herzegovina and Bosnia* (London, 1910). Of the prospect of visiting Dalmatia, the latter wrote: 'Dalmatia! What strange magic in the name! How remote and Asiatic it sounded! What visions of mountain fastnesses and landlocked harbours, of curious buildings and primitive peoples, danced before my excited fancy!' (p.17).

[19] Omer Hadžiselimović (ed.), *At the Gates of the East: British Travel Writers on Bosnia and Herzegovina from the Sixteenth to the Twentieth Centuries* (New York, 2001), p.471.

[20] Miller, *Travels and Politics*, pp.xv-xvi.

[21] B.Korte, *English Travel Writing from Pilgrimages to Postcolonial Explorations* (London, 2000), pp.99-105.

[22] Representative examples of this genre include G.Gordon-Smith, *Through the Serbian Campaign: the great retreat of the Serbian Army* (London, 1916) and Douglas Walshe, *With the Serbs in Macedonia* (London, 1920).

[23] For the best brief survey of this relief work, and its impact upon British public opinion, see Hanak, *Great Britain and Austria-Hungary*, pp.64-80. First-hand accounts may be found in M.A.St.Clair Stobart, *The Flaming Sword in Serbia and Elsewhere* (London; New York; Toronto, 1916), C.Matthews, *Experiences of a Woman Doctor in Serbia* (London, 1916), C. and A.Askew, *The Stricken Land: Serbia as We Saw It* (London, 1916), and E.P.Stebbing, *At the Serbian Front in Macedonia* (London, 1917). Gordon-Smith, *Through the Serbian Campaign* (pp.239-92) also contains a detailed account of the relief effort.

[24] Mabel St.Clair Stobart was a prominent suffragette. Elsie Inglis and other initiators of the Scottish Women's Hospital for Foreign Service were members of the Scottish Federation of the National Union of Women's Suffrage Societies (Hanak, *Britain and Austria-Hungary*, p.66).

[25] *Ibid.*, pp.70-1.

[26] Of the names listed above, Brailsford and Durham were the only notable exceptions in this respect. One might also include Charles and Noel Buxton. The latter was supportive of the Serbian Relief Fund – indeed, he became a Vice-President. But in his *Contemporary Review* article 'The Future of Austria' (Jan 1918), he argued against the break-up of the Empire. Seton-Watson's article in the same journal, 'Austria-Hungary and the Federal Solution' (March 1918), was intended as a direct rejoinder (*Correspondence*, i, 312-3).

[27] See Hanak, *Great Britain and Austria-Hungary*, ch.6 for a discussion of those currents of opinion in Britain opposed to the dismemberment of the Habsburg realm.

[28] R.J.W. Evans, *Great Britain and East-Central Europe, 1908-48: A Study in Perceptions* (London, 2002), p.12.

[29] Seton-Watsons, *Making of a New Europe*, p.89.

[30] Such people found a congenial home within organisations like the Union of Democratic Control, and wrote for journals like the *Cambridge Magazine*. See Hanak, *Great Britain and Austria-Hungary*, ch.6.

[31] As Hanak points out, Brailsford's lack of familiarity with the politics of the Monarchy did not prevent him penning numerous articles on the subject, or hamper his reputation in left-wing circles as an expert (*ibid.*, p.144). Before the war in particular, Britons with a strong interest in the Balkans tended to be pro-Bulgarian in their outlook, and therefore unsympathetic to Serbia over the Macedonian issue.

[32] Toynbee – pupil of Alfred Zimmern – admitted his great debt to Seton-Watson in this respect (*Nationality and the War*, p.ix); James (Viscount) Bryce had been a founder member of the Balkan Committee in 1903, and a champion of the oppressed Ottoman Armenians, before becoming Ambassador to Washington between 1907 and 1913. J.H.Rose had made his name as a biographer of Napoleon and Pitt the Younger.

[33] Zimmern's paternal family were German Jews, and Namier's parents were Polonised Jews, though both men were brought up as Christians. (Norman Rose, *Lewis Namier and Zionism* (Oxford, 1980). See the article on Zimmern in H.C.G.Matthew and B.Harrison (eds), *Oxford Dictionary of National Biography* (Oxford, 2004)). Other writers on nationality, like Sidney Herbert and Bernard Joseph, displayed strong Zionist sympathies.

[34] Hanak, *Great Britain and Austria-Hungary*, pp.66-7.

[35] In his obituary of Seton-Watson R.R.Betts observed that his Scottish feeling 'perhaps made him the more sympathetic to the rights and sentiments of small nations' (quoted in L.Péter, 'R.W.Seton-Watson's Changing Views on the National Question of the Habsburg Monarchy and the European Balance of Power', *Slavonic and East European Review*, Vol.82, no.3 (July 2004), 656). In a pre-war speech in Split Seton-Watson told his audience that it was easier for the citizen of a small country like Scotland to sympathise with Dalmatia, and that he wished Dalmatia the same fate as Scotland (Seton-Watsons, *Making of a New Europe*, p.79). The empathy afforded by his Scottish nationality was a theme that arose frequently in his correspondence with Croats in particular: see, for example, *Correspondence*, i, 240, 269, 289.

[36] Zara Steiner, *The Foreign Office and Foreign Policy, 1898-1914* (Cambridge, 1969), *passim*. Technically, it may be noted, the Foreign Office and the Diplomatic Service remained distinct, but informal interchange increasingly took place at the higher levels of the two services (R.A.Jones, *The British Diplomatic Service, 1815-1914* (Gerrards Cross, 1983), p.196).

[37] Roberta M.Warman, *The Foreign Office 1916-1918: A Study of Its Role and Functions* (New York; London, 1986), p.59.

[38] One exception was the Magyarophile C.N.Knatchbull-Hugueson, whose history of Hungary was the best available in early 20th century Britain (*The Political Development of the Hungarian Nation* (London, 1908)).

[39] Okey, 'British Impressions', pp.63-4.

[40] See below pp.106-7.

[41] These points (and the increasing challenge to Foreign Office control of foreign policy formulation from other government organisations during the war) are further discussed below. See pp.115-18.

Chapter One

[1] R.Schlesinger, *Federalism in Eastern and Central Europe* (London, 1945), p.217.

[2] On Herder, see I.Berlin, *Vico and Herder* (London, 1976).

[3] E.Barkan, *The Retreat of Scientific Racism: Changing concepts of race in Britain and the United States between the world wars* (Cambridge, 1992), p.23. See also, for example, H.J.Fleure, 'The Racial History of the British People', *Geographical Review*, March 1918.

[4] E.T. Buckle, *History of Civilisation in England* (3rd ed; London, 1861), i, 36-7. T.H. Huxley, 'On the Methods and Results of Ethnology', *Fortnightly Review*, Vol I (1865), 257-77. For J.S.Mill, see footnote 7 below.

[5] R.R.Marett, *Anthropology* (London, 1912), p.92; S.Herbert, *Nationality and its Problems* (London, 1920), p.10.

[6] Herbert, *Nationality and its Problems*, pp.7-13. It was, J.Oakesmith remarked, 'difficult to refrain from impatient words in face of those who hold the racial theory of nationality' (*Race and Nationality* (London, 1919), p.38. For similar views see J.M.Robertson, *The Germans* (London, 1916), pp.3-18; W.B. Pillsbury, *The Psychology of Nationality and Internationalism* (New York; London, 1919), pp.11-17.

[7] Mill quoted in Robertson, *The Germans*, pp.109-10.

[8] A.H.Keane, *Man, Past and Present* (Cambridge, 1899), p.532.

[9] Lord Bryce, *Race Sentiment as a Factor in History* (London, 1915), p.5.

[10] A.Zimmern, *Nationality and Government* (London, 1918), p.84.

[11] Lord Acton, 'Mr Buckle's Philosophy of History', *Historical Essays and Studies* (London, 1907), p.341.

[12] Quoted in Oakesmith, *Race and Nationality*, p.40.

[13] C.A.Macartney, *National States and National Minorities* (London, 1934), p.132.

[14] R.W. Seton-Watson, 'Pan-Slavism', *Contemporary Review*, Oct 1916, 420.

[15] R.W. Seton-Watson, *Roumania and the Great War* (London, 1915), pp.7-8; quoted in Oakesmith, *Race and Nationality*, pp.42-6. Seton-Watson seemed happy to accept, despite a millennium of uncharted, large-scale population movements through the region, that the modern Romanian was the pure descendant of Trajan's Roman colonists (many of whom were of non-Roman origin in the first place).

[16] Oakesmith, *Race and Nationality*, p.2. For the largely unchallenged view of race as a natural biological category, divisible into observable hierarchies, until well into the interwar period, see Barkan, *Retreat of Scientific Racism*, pp.2-3 and passim, and J.Barzun, *Race: A Study in Modern Superstition* (London, 1938), chs. I, IX, X, XI.

[17] Joseph, *Nationality*, p.40.

[18] It was not long since races had been regarded in pre-Darwinian terms as products of divergent biblical descent, Noah's sons progenitors of eponyomous 'Semitic', 'Hamitic' and 'Japhetic' races. Such vague presumptions tended, as ever, to outlive the 'science' on which they were based (Robertson, *The Germans*, ch.1).

[19] And race is still, of course, considered a valid social, as opposed to a strictly scientific, category.

[20] J.Holland Rose, 'The National Idea', *Contemporary Review*, March 1916, 336.

[21] Oakesmith, *Race and Nationality*, pp.20-1; G.Le Bon, *The Psychology of Peoples* (London, 1899), p.19.

[22] Robertson, *The Germans*, p.12.

[23] Oakesmith, *Race and Nationality*, p.39.

[24] F.Hertz, *Nationality in History and Politics: A Psychology and Sociology of National Sentiment and Nationalism* (London, 1944), p.68.

[25] M.Mazower, *Dark Continent: Europe's Twentieth Century* (London, 1998), p.102.

[26] F.Fellner, 'George D. Herron and the Italian-Yugoslav rivalries during the final stages of World War I 1917-1919', in Djordjević (ed.), *Creation of Yugoslavia*, p.129.

[27] The anthropologist Arthur Kroeber complained of this tendency in his textbook *Anthropology*, cited in J.E.Terrel, 'The Uncommon Sense of Race, Language, and Culture', in J.E.Terrell (ed.), *Archaeology, Language and History* (London; Westport, Connecticut, 2001), p.27.

[28] The respected journalist and historian William Miller, for instance, could at once consider the South Slavs a single race 'split up into three distinct religions' and hail the Dalmatians as 'physically one of the finest races in the world': *Travel and Politics*, pp.xv-xvi; 19.

[29] K.J.Calder, *Britain and the Origins of the New Europe 1914-1918* (Cambridge, 1976), p.214.

[30] Forbes, *Southern Slavs*, pp.7-10; 14. (Neville Forbes was Reader – subsequently Professor – in Russian and other Slavonic languages at Oxford; he travelled widely and took a keen interest in the South Slavs). See also R.W.Seton-Watson, *The Southern Slav Question and the Hapsburg Monarchy* (London, 1911), p.2 and J.Cvijić, 'The Geographical Distribution of the Balkan Peoples', *The Geographical Review*, Vol V no 5 (May 1918), 345.

[31] R.G.D.Laffan did admit the apparent racial and religious similarities of Bulgar and Serb which had struck Britons before 1878, when it seemed 'probable that the Bulgars and Serbs would merge into one people': *The Guardians of the Gate: Historical Lectures on the Serbs* (Oxford, 1918), pp.42-3. (Laffan was an academic and army chaplain who served alongside Serbian forces on the Macedonian front, and who later became a Foreign Office specialist on Yugoslavia). For a post-war account playing down Serb-Bulgar racial differences, and advocating their political union, see H.Baerlein, *The Birth of Yugoslavia* (London, 1922), i, 24, 33-37.

[32] On the Turkic origin of the Bulgar elite, and their subsequent Slavicisation, see J.V.A.Fine, *The Early Medieval Balkans* (Michigan, 1983), pp.66-9; F.Fernández-Armesto (ed.), *The Times Guide to the Peoples of Europe* (London, 1997), p229. It was not then believed, as today, that Serbs and Croats were also non-Slavic tribes which had ruled and become assimilated by a Slav substratum. See below p.21.

[33] C.Mijatovich, preface to W.M.Petrovitch, *Hero Tales and Legends of the Serbians* (London, 1914), pp.v-vi.

[34] Forbes, *The Southern Slavs*, pp.8-11.

[35] Sir C.Eliot, *Turkey in Europe* (London, 1908), pp.322, 333. During his time in the diplomatic service Eliot had served in Belgrade, Sofia and Constantinople, as well as travelling widely in Russia and Central Asia.

[36] Seton-Watson, 'Pan-Slavism', p.420. On the pro-Bulgarian lobby in Britain during the war, see Hanak, *Great Britain and Austria-Hungary*. It is true, as William Miller pointed out, that Bulgarians assisted this racial redefinition, exaggerating to their German, Turkish and Hungarian allies their non-Slavic (and, in the case of the latter two, kindred) origins: Miller, 'The Rise and Fall of the First Bulgarian Empire 679-1018', in *The Cambridge Medieval History Volume IV: The Eastern Roman Empire 717-1453* (Cambridge, 1923), p.230.

[37] 'The Inter-Allied Commission's Report on Bulgarian Atrocities in Eastern Macedonia', *The Balkan Review*, Aug 1919, 79.

[38] Miller, 'Rise and Fall', p.230.

[39] Baerlein, *Birth of Yugoslavia*, i, 26-7.

[40] M.B.Petrovich, *A History of Modern Serbia 1804-1918* (2 vols., New York; London, 1976), ii, 635.

[41] During the 1917 Corfu negotiations the Serbian Government only reluctantly accepted the term 'Yugoslav' as a synonym for 'Serb-Croat-Slovene' to give an impression of unity. 'The very denomination "Yugoslav"', Ivo Lederer has commented, 'represented in 1918 a subterfuge designed to deemphasise the points of division between the component groups' ('Nationalism and the Yugoslavs', in P. Sugar, I. Lederer (eds.), *Nationalism in Eastern Europe* (Seattle; London, 1969), p.397). The Serbian Government rejected the name 'Yugoslavia', but not because of the absent Bulgarians: Petrovich, *History of Modern Serbia*, ii, 646.

[42] Stubborn, that is, on the part of the Yugoslavs themselves – particularly the Serbs – who refused to forsake their primary identity. Of the new states 'Czecho-Slovakia' and 'Jugo-Slavia', one British writer observed, 'their composite names prove their composite characters' (quoted in Baerlein, *Birth of Yugoslavia*, i, 10).

[43] In fact leading students of the Empire denied that it was moribund. 'The monarchy', wrote Louis Eisenmann, 'no longer rests on the power of the dynastic tie alone, but also on their [the various nationalities'] conscious desire for union. Herein lies its [...] mighty new strength' ('Austria-Hungary', in The Cambridge Modern History, vol.XII, *The Latest Age* (Cambridge, 1910), p.212). See also R.W. Seton-Watson, *The Future of Austria-Hungary* (London, 1907) and W.Steed, *The Habsburg Monarchy* (London, 1913). Eisenmann, like Seton-Watson and Steed, would revise his opinion during the war, and contribute to the journal *New Europe*.

[44] Some, it is true, hoped that a Slavic unit in a federal Monarchy might encourage Serbia for political and economic reasons to abandon its independence and seek national unity under the Habsburg umbrella.

[45] N.Buxton and C.Buxton, *The War and the Balkans* (London, 1915), pp.42-3.

[46] Hanak, *Great Britain and Austria-Hungary*, p.63.

[47] Constituted in July 1916 by Seton-Watson, Steed, Annan Bryce, Elsie Inglis and A.F.Whyte (Seton-Watsons, *Making of a New Europe*, pp.175-6).

[48] On the Committee's activities and influence, see G.Stokes, 'The Role of the Yugoslav Committee in the Formation of Yugoslavia' in Djordjević, *Creation of Yugoslavia*, pp.51-71.

[49] Balfour papers. Cited in Seton-Watsons, *Making of a New Europe*, p322.

[50] FO 371/3138/202583. That this usage later seemed an inappropriate suggestion of disunity is implied by Whitehall's emendation of the Serbian Minister's proposed address to the Mansion House meeting. The first two words of the phrase 'Serbs and Yugoslavs' were deleted (FO 371/3135/130170).

[51] A memo by Seton-Watson in October 1918 provides one of many examples of the confusing juxtaposition of different senses of the term, referring both to a need to recognise 'the Yugoslav Nation' as a belligerent ally (meaning clearly the Habsburg South Slavs in *contrast* to those in Serbia) and to the unification of foreign policy of 'all the Yugoslavs inside and outside Serbia': *Correspondence*, i, 357.

[52] For the sake of clarity subsequent use of 'South Slav' and 'Yugoslav' will refer only to those groups included within the 1918 Yugoslav state, and to all of those groups, unless the context implies otherwise.

[53] Seton-Watson, *Southern Slav Question*, p.2.

[54] The latter two states did, since the Balkan Wars, contain substantial non-Slavic minorities as well as the disputed Slavic population of Serbian Macedonia, but in Britain the significance of these was little heeded outside the Foreign Office. See below pp.84-5 and pp.105-7.

[55] Djordjević, 'Idea of Yugoslav Unity', p.3.

[56] W.Miller, *The Balkans* (London, 1896; 3rd edn 1923), p.512.

[57] Though it is true that the use of 'Croatian' in this narrow, regional sense continued for some time to coexist with the broader ethnic use.

[58] Some of whom were, of course, Serbs. But the reference was clearly to all South Slav groups (FO 371/3138/205290, 11 Dec 1918).

[59] Seton-Watson, *Southern Slav Question*, p.2.

[60] Taylor, *Future of the Southern Slavs*, p.250; Forbes, *The Southern Slavs*, pp.12, 17. Taylor's biographical details are obscure. His book, nevertheless, was highly regarded and influential, and not without justification. One reviewer considered it 'without exception the best on the subject in English' (S.P.Duggan, *Political Science Quarterly*, 33 (1918), 442); another – the American Yugoslav specialist Robert Kerner – thought it 'perhaps the [...] best general statement of the Yugo-Slav problem as a whole' (*Nation*, 20 December 1917).

[61] Seton-Watson, *Southern Slav Question*, p.2.

[62] Keane, *Man, Past and Present*, pp.548-9.

[63] F.S.Copeland, 'Who Are the Yugo-Slavs?', *The Balkan Review*, Feb 1919, 32-3.

[64] This gestation was accelerated by the increased exposure for the non-Russian Slavs during World War I. Seton-Watson, Ronald Burrows and others promoted the inauguration of the School of Slavonic Studies in October 1915 (*Correspondence*, i, 205; Seton-Watsons, *Making of a New Europe*, pp.153-4; R.W.Seton-Watson, 'The Origins of the School of Slavonic Studies', *The Slavonic and East European Review*, Vol XVII, no.50 (1939), 360-71).

[65] Those few medieval scholars who, like J.B. Bury, did take a specialist interest in this material tended to be Byzantinists for whom the South Slavs were a tangential question.

[66] R.W.Seton-Watson, 'Pan-Slavism', *Contemporary Review*, Oct 1916, 420. See also his eulogistic obituary of Jagić, *Slavonic Review*, Vol II, no 5 (Dec 1923), 417-23.

[67] Fine, *Early Medieval Balkans*, pp.49-59. This interpretation has since been undermined by sources supporting the fundamentals of Constantine's account.

[68] M.Stanoyevich, 'The Ethnography of the Yugo-Slavs', *Geographical Review*, Vol 7, no 2 (Feb 1919), 91-7.

[69] Modern anthropology, Traian Stoianovich notes, questions the validity of even these anthropological divisions, noting, for instance, significant diversity among supposedly homogeneous 'Dinaric' populations: *Balkan Worlds: The First and Last Europe* (New York; London, 1994), p.134.

[70] See above p.14.

[71] G.M. Trevelyan, for instance, thought the Serbians 'temperamentally averse to the German mind, its over-discipline, and its humourless precision', and more akin to 'the mixed English temperament': 'Serbia Revisited', *Contemporary Review*, March 1915, 274.

[72] Petrovitch, *Hero Tales*, p.13. *Encyclopaedia Britannica*, 11th edn (London, 1911), 'Serbia: Population, Government and Religion'.

[73] H.J. Fleure, *The Peoples of Europe* (London, 1922), pp.80-2.

[74] E.Durham, *Twenty Years of Balkan Tangle* (London, 1920), pp.12-13. (Though she was writing two years after the war). One modern scholar considers that Dalmatian Latin and Morlak elements were largely Slavicised by 1700 (Stoianovich, *Balkan Worlds*, p.133). It is interesting that almost no contemporary works referred to the migration of Orthodox Vlachs to the Ottoman frontier in modern Croatia and western Bosnia, most of whom subsequently acquired Serb consciousness: N.Malcolm, *Bosnia: A Short History* (London, 1994), pp.70-81.

[75] Durham, *Twenty Years*, p.15. The 'severe Serbizing' of 'wholly Albanian tribes' in Montenegro she argued further in a more scholarly study, *Some Tribal Origins, Laws and Customs of the Balkans* (London, 1928), p.51. See also pp.29-30 below.

[76] Ibid., p.141.

[77] Taylor, *Future of the Southern Slavs*, p.250.

[78] *Encyclopaedia Britannica*, 'Serbia: early history'. The term 'ethnic' was comparatively rare in this period, and here seems to relate purely to race. Today, though misused in this sense, it connotes a self-conscious group identity embracing (as relevant) history, culture, language or religion. See the helpful discussion in C.Renfrew, *Archaeology and Language: The Puzzle of Indo-European Origins*, (London, 1998), pp.214-17.

[79] H.W.V.Temperley, *History of Serbia* (London, 1917), pp.1-2. Temperley had begun his academic career as a student of 18th and 19th century British constitutional history, but travelled extensively in Austria-Hungary and the Balkans prior to 1914 and developed a profound sympathy for the 'subject peoples' of the region, especially the Slovaks and the Serbs. Retiring from active military service after contracting typhoid fever, he spent most of the war doing research and intelligence work for the War Office (J.D.Fair, *Harold Temperley: A Scholar and Romantic in the Public Realm* (London and Toronto, 1992)).

[80] Particular satisfaction was taken in the story that the Bosnian Governor, von Kállay, had felt obliged to ban his own book arguing the racial unity of Bosnian

groups. See, for example, H.A.Gibbons, *The New Map of Europe 1911-1914* (London, 1914), p.143.

[81] *Southern Slav Question*, pp.vii; 2 (emphasis added).

[82] *Correspondence*, i, 222.

[83] *The New Europe*, 28 Dec 1916; quoted in Seton-Watsons, *Making of a New Europe*, p.192.

[84] *Correspondence*, i, 310.

[85] These two similar forms were often used interchangeably. A sensible usage, however, followed here unless quoting from other sources, employs 'Serbian' to mean a citizen of Serbia or pertaining to Serbia, and 'Serb' as a label of ethnic identity. The forms 'Croat' and 'Croatian' operate similarly; likewise Slovenian/ Slovene (though there was no history of statehood in this case and the geographical expression 'Slovenia' scarcely predates the 19th century). The English vocabulary pertaining to other regions and identities – Montenegrin, Macedonian, Bosnian etc – does not permit such differentiation, a consequence perhaps of the purely regional (rather than 'ethnic') nature of these labels in British thinking.

[86] Laffan, *Guardians of the Gate*, p.20; see also, for example, Gibbons, *New Map*, p.149. Unless the context indicates otherwise, 'Bosnia' is used henceforward as shorthand for 'Bosnia-Hercegovina'.

[87] L.Dominian, *The Frontiers of Language and Nationality in Europe* (London; New York, 1917), p.182.

[88] S.Wilkinson, 'The Question of Servia', in S.Wilkinson (ed.), *August 1914: The Coming of the War* (London, 1914), p.11.

[89] Forbes, *The Southern Slavs*, p.12.

[90] D.H.Low, 'The Kingdom of Serbia: Her People and Her History', *Scottish Geographical Magazine*, June 1915, 308-9. Low had worked as a lecturer at the University of Belgrade, and was thus a pertinent example of the dominant influence among British writers of a Serb perspective.

[91] Gibbons, *New Map*, p.344.

[92] FO 371/3137/190445 (forwarded by Lord Derby, 17 Nov 1918).

[93] Lederer, 'Nationalism and the Yugoslavs', p.406.

[94] Forbes, *The Southern Slavs*, p.24; Seton-Watson, *The Emancipation of South-Eastern Europe* (London, 1923), pp.13-14 (Bosnian Muslims were of 'the purest Serbian blood'). Works published in Britain by respected Serb writers had routinely claimed all Bosnians, regardless of religion, as Serbs. See, for example, C.Mijatovich, *Servia and the Servians* (London, 1908), p2. It should be stressed that we are here talking purely about underlying racial rather than political or national identity.

[95] J.Bryce, *Essays and Addresses in Wartime* (London, 1918), p.145.

[96] Taylor, *Future of the Southern Slavs*, p.251 ('the "Croats" here are entirely Serb by race'). By implication, for Taylor, there was some racial distinction between these and the Catholics of Croatia and the Slovene lands. He referred also to the 'Muslim Serbs of Bosnia' (p.281).

[97] *Correspondence*, i, 264. Italy exploited this semantic confusion over Habsburg prisoners-of-war in Italy. Orlando, to British annoyance, interpreted the phrase

'Yugo-Slav prisoners of Serbian race' to apply only to Orthodox Serbs. See Hanak, 'The Government, the Foreign Office and Austria-Hungary', 195.

[98] This is something of a simplification since the principles of Karadžić and Starčević were not symmetrical and neither were true unitarists. The former defined a Serb by linguistic criteria enabling him to identify most Croats as such (language a corollary of race); the latter defined Croat identity in terms of the historical 'state right' of the Croatian race. Only Croats and Bulgars, Starčević claimed, were primary Yugoslav peoples, the 'Serb' a creation of 18th century pan-Orthodox propaganda designed to split the Croats by religion. He *was* forced to concede a Serb 'genetic' rather than 'political' identity, but his attempt to reconcile this with pan-Croatianism makes the head swim. For a detailed treatment see Banac, *National Question*, pp.70-115.

[99] B.Vošnjak, *A Bulwark Against Germany* (London, 1917), pp.217-18.

[100] The latter in particular enjoyed just renown for his work of linguistic standardisation.

[101] Banac, *National Question*, pp.98-102. For the development of the HSK see N.J.Miller, *Between Nation and State: Serbian Politics in Croatia before the First World War* (Pittsburgh, 1997), p.75 and ch.3 *passim*. See also Seton-Watson, *Correspondence*, *passim*.

[102] Seton-Watson, *German, Slav and Magyar: A Study in the Origins of the Great War* (London, 1916), p.48.

[103] W.Gordon, *A Woman in the Balkans* (London, 1918), p.38. One critic noted that: 'in ordinary times the art of Meštrović might be too alien to England [...], but in these times of stress [...] we can see and feel the message of his terrible images and the deep pitifulness, too, that lies within them. His heroic art, indeed, is almost the only art that does not seem alien to these mighty days' (ibid.).

[104] Hanak, *Great Britain and Austria-Hungary*, p.74.

[105] James Bryce was unusually circumspect in cautioning that exiled leaders 'naturally tend to attribute their own ardent convictions to their fellow-countrymen at home, many of whom may be but faintly interested in nationalistic aspirations': *Essays and Addresses*, pp.162-3, quoted in A.J.May, 'R.W. Seton-Watson and British Anti-Hapsburg Sentiment', *American Slavic and Eastern European Review*, XX, no 1, (1961), 43.

[106] The formula 'three-named people' (*troimeni narod*) was adopted by Yugoslav representatives in Corfu keenly aware of their interest in presenting an impression of unity: Petrovich, *History of Modern Serbia*, ii, 645-6. See also the example in L.Marcovitch, *Serbia and Europe 1914-1920* (London, 1920), p.98.

[107] Vošnjak, *Bulwark*, p.11.

[108] I.Žolger, 'Concerning the Slovenes', *The Balkan Review*, July 1919, 442.

[109] Temperley, *History of Serbia*, p.2. By the time he wrote an official report on the Yugoslav problem in June 1918 he had, it should be said, shifted his priorities. While the 'Bosnians' were out, replaced by 'Serbs of Bosnia-Hercegovina', the Slovenes were now in (FO 371/3135/116831).

[110] Minutes of EPD meeting, 27 May; quoted in Seton-Watsons, *Making of a New Europe*, p.281.

[111] Taylor, *Future of the Southern Slavs*, pp.249-50.

[112] FO 371/3133/48743 (7 March 1918).

[113] *Correspondence*, i, 184. For an account of the genesis of Yugoslav feeling among the Slovene intelligentsia largely confirming this picture, see C.Rogel, *The Slovenes and Yugoslavism, 1890-1914* (New York, 1977).

[114] See the situation report on Austria-Hungary by the War Office, no 2, May 1918, in FO 371/3136/98080.

[115] FO 371/3137/174611 (8 Nov 1918).

[116] Baerlein, *Birth of Yugoslavia*, p.38.

[117] Linguistic questions will be dealt with in the next chapter.

[118] Mijatovich, *Servia and the Servians*, p.1. This 1908 account, it is true, was uninfluenced by Slovene pro-Serb feeling during and after the Balkan Wars.

[119] Forbes, *The Southern Slavs*, p.7.

[120] Banac, *National Question*, pp.44-5.

[121] Laffan, *Guardians of the Gate*, p.20.

[122] Bryce, *Essays and Addresses*, pp.142-3. This statement is puzzling given that in the same essay Bryce declared nationality not a factor simply of race (pp.128-9). This sort of *non-sequitur*, however, was common in British writing on nationality.

[123] A.Devine, *Off the Map - The Suppression of Montenegro: the Tragedy of a Small Nation* (London, 1921), pp.vii-viii.

[124] Private letter (21 March 1931), cited in N.Malcolm, *Kosovo: A Short History* (London, 1998), pp.358-9.

[125] de Windt, *Through Savage Europe*, p.29. See also *Encyclopaedia Britannica*, 11th ed., 'Montenegro: Population and Government': 'The physical type contrasts with that of the northern Serbs: the features are more pronounced, the hair is darker, and the stature is greater. The men are tall, [...] muscular and wonderfully active'. Curiously, Montenegrin men seemed a contrast to their animals: the former tall, strong and primitive, their horses 'diminutive, wiry and intelligent'!

[126] 'In the past', Gladstone had remarked, 'Montenegro was the beach on which were thrown up the remnants of Balkan freedom' (quoted in Gordon, *Woman in the Balkans*, p.271).

[127] Gordon, *Woman in the Balkans*, pp.271, 279.

[128] Eliot, *Turkey in Europe*, pp.336-8, 347.

[129] Durham, *Twenty Years*, p.16.

[130] As Dragovan Šepić noted with reference to the Serbs and Habsburg Yugoslavs: 'Macedonia was discussed in 1915 as a Serbo-Bulgarian problem; but after the entry of Bulgaria into the war on the side of the Central Powers nobody raised the Macedonian question; if and when it was mentioned it was not treated as a separate problem': 'The Question of Yugoslav Union in 1918', *Journal of Contemporary History*, III, no 4 (1968), 35.

[131] E.A.Freeman noted in 1877 that all Orthodox subjects of Turkey had until recently been considered Greek in most European eyes, quoted in M.Mazower, *The Balkans* (London, 2000), pp.2-3. See also M.Todorova, *Imagining the Balkans* (New York; Oxford, 1997), p.98.

[132] For a contemporary treatment of the Balkan Vlachs see A.J.B.Wace and M.S.Thompson, *The Nomads of the Balkans* (London, 1914). Modern accounts

support the idea of a link between Romanian and Vlach populations, the product, it is generally assumed, of a common Dacian ancestry. See T.J. Winnifrith, *The Vlachs: The History of a Balkan People* (London, 1987); Fine, *Early Medieval Balkans*, p.10. On the successful 'Serbianising' and 'Albanianising' of Vlachs in regions of the future Yugoslavia and Albania see Malcolm, *Bosnia*, pp.202-5.

[133] Taylor, *Future of the Southern Slavs*, p.254; Eliot, *Turkey in Europe*, p.338;

[134] Eliot, *Turkey in Europe*, pp.337-8.

[135] 'The Balkan Atrocities', letter to *The Nation*, 6 Sept 1913, Vol XIII no. 23, 844-5.

[136] Miller, *Travel and Politics*, p.378.

[137] A.Goff and H.A.Fawcett, *Macedonia: A Plea for the Primitive* (London, 1921), p.xiv.

[138] H.N.Brailsford, *Macedonia* (London, 1906), p.101. A staff member of the *Nation* between 1907 and 1922, Brailsford travelled widely and earned a reputation as an authority on Russia, Egypt and the Balkans, becoming an influential member of the Balkan Committee. See F.M.Leventhal, *The Last Dissenter: H.N.Brailsford and His World* (Oxford, 1985).

[139] A.H.E.Taylor, 'the Serbo-Bulgarian Situation', in C.Price, *Light on the Balkan Darkness* (London, 1915), p.100.

[140] Eliot, *Turkey in Europe*, p.332.

[141] Ibid, pp.337-8; Durham, *Twenty Years*, p.48.

[142] Eliot, *Turkey in Europe*, pp.337-8. The 'vilayet of Kossovo' indicates the Ottoman province of that name, extending considerably beyond the modern region to include the Sanjak of Novi Pazar and part of north-west Macedonia: see the map in Malcolm, *Kosovo*, p.xxii. The area comprehended by the classical label 'Macedonia' was not demarcated by any existing administrative borders in the early 20th century.

[143] Brailsford, *Macedonia*, pp.274-5.

[144] *The Nation*, 'Great Britain and the Future of Turkey', 17 May 1913, Vol XIII no 7; 'No More War in the Balkans', 31 May 1913, Vol XIII no 9.

Chapter Two

[1] H.F.Pelham, *The Reciprocal Influence on each other of National Character and National Language* (Oxford, 1870), p.7.

[2] We will discuss shortly perceptions of the relationship between language and 'nationality'.

[3] T.H. Huxley, 'On the Methods and Results of Ethnology', *Fortnightly Review*, Vol I (1865), 257-8. In his essay 'Ethics and Evolution' in *Evolution and Ethics and Other Essays* (London, 1894), pp.1-45, he demonstrated why there could be no necessary correlation.

[4] Bryce, *Essays and Addresses*, pp.3-4. A.Lefèvre, *Race and Language* (London, 1894) is an example of a work infused with the idea that language classification offers a direct guide to civilisational success.

[5] Robertson, *The Germans*, p.4. Bryce's assurance was premature. Attempts to link social characteristics with linguistic groups continue, if in more sophisticated, less

value-laden form. See, for instance, Stoianovich, *Balkan Worlds*, p.121 and the cogent critique in Renfrew, *Archaeology and Language*, pp.15-19, 86-94.

[6] R.Handler, cited in S.May, *Language and Minority Rights: Ethnicity, Nationalism and the Politics of Language* (London, 2001), p.58. The anthropological study of ethnicity has gradually moved, Michael Herzfeld notes, 'from the analysis of bounded groups to a focus on constitutive process', *Anthropology Through the Looking Glass: Critical Ethnography in the Margins of Europe* (Cambridge, 1987), p.219 note.

[7] Quoted in B.Anderson, *Imagined Communities*, (London; New York, 1983, 1991), p.70.

[8] We are dealing invariably, of course, with the 'mother tongue', whose role in reflecting and shaping patterns of perception was considered vastly more significant than any subsequent linguistic facility.

[9] Quoted in May, *Language and Minority Rights*, p.57.

[10] Barkan, *Retreat of Scientific Racism*, p.19.

[11] F.Boas, *The Mind of Primitive Man* (New York, 1911), p.127; ibid. (New York, 1938; 1965), p.19, cited in Terrel, 'Uncommon Sense', p.16.

[12] Joseph, *Nationality*, pp.60-1. The Norman conquest of Britain seems only the most obvious counter-example.

[13] Zimmern, *Nationality and Government*, p.69.

[14] Morant, *Races of Central Europe*, p.142.

[15] Joseph, *Nationality*, p.54.

[16] This point was made by the Greek philologist Ioannis Psykharis; see S.Skendi, 'Language as a Factor of National Identity in the Balkans of the Nineteenth Century', *Proceedings of the American Philosophical Society*, Vol 119, no 2 (April 1975), 186.

[17] See, for example, Lord Acton, 'Nationality', p.289ff; Zimmern, *Nationality and Government*, pp.65-9.

[18] Seton-Watson, *German, Slav and Magyar*, p.41.

[19] H.A.Gibbons, *The Foundation of the Ottoman Empire 1300-1403* (Oxford, 1916), p.196.

[20] The term 'national group' was often used instead of 'nation' or 'nationality' to suggest peoples with shared outward characteristics but no feeling of political community.

[21] A.Toynbee, *The New Europe* (London, 1915), p.56.

[22] Herbert, *Nationality and its Problems*, p.49.

[23] Pillsbury, *Psychology*, p.17. Pillsbury was American, but much read and respected by British theorists.

[24] How satisfied, it might have been asked, would independent Irish or Welsh states have been with boundaries drawn purely with reference to linguistic data? See Fleure, *Peoples of Europe*, pp.80-1.

[25] Herder quoted approvingly in Joseph, *Nationality*, pp.67-8.

[26] J.H. Rose, *Nationality as a Factor in Modern History* (London, 1916), p.13.

[27] Oakesmith, *Race and Nationality*, pp.47-50.

[28] Joseph, *Nationality*, pp.55-6.

[29] Pelham, *Reciprocal Influence*, p.7.

[30] Joseph, *Nationality*, pp.61, 67-8.

[31] Hertz, *Nationality in History and Politics*, p.78.

[32] Preface to Dominian, *Frontiers*, p.xvii.

[33] Joseph, *Nationality*, p.61.

[34] FO 371/44346/19436. FORD paper on the Austro-Yugoslav frontier.

[35] Toynbee, *The New Europe*, p.56. See also his *Nationality and the War* (London, 1915), pp.14-15, and A.Cobban, *National Self-Determination* (Oxford, 1945), p.24. Ultimately, adhering to the 'psychological school', Toynbee accepted only 'the ascertained wish of the living population actually concerned'. Consultations in southern Carinthia and upper Silesia (and the striking case of the Lutheran Masurians of Poland) supported this belief by violating the dictates of linguistic identity. But the widespread use of plebiscites was a logistical impossibility, a certain cause of unrest and presented problems of principle of its own.

[36] Hertz, *Nationality in History and Politics*, p.96.

[37] Djordjević, 'Idea of Yugoslav Unity', p.2.

[38] Seton-Watson, *Southern Slav Question*, p.339.

[39] Seton-Watson, *German, Slav and Magyar*, pp.85-6.

[40] Taylor, *Future of the Southern Slavs*, p.82.

[41] R.G.D.Laffan, *Jugoslavia since 1918* (London, 1929), p.5.

[42] Laffan, *Guardians of the Gate*, pp.20-1.

[43] H.Vivian, *Servia: The Poor Man's Paradise* (London, 1897), pp.29-30.

[44] de Windt, *Through Savage Europe*, p.87.

[45] Forbes, *The Southern Slavs*, pp.27-8.

[46] M.Macmillan, *Peacemakers* (London, 2001; repr 2002), p.120.

[47] Seton-Watson, 'Vatroslav Jagić' (obituary), *Slavonic Review*, Vol II, no 5 (Dec 1923), 419.

[48] Seton-Watson, *Southern Slav Question*, p.335.

[49] Seton-Watson, *The Spirit of the Serb* (London, 1915), p.22.

[50] H.A.Gibbons, *Europe Since 1918* (New York; London, 1923), p.274.

[51] Dominian, *Frontiers*, p.191.

[52] C.Jelavich, 'Milenko M.Vukićević: From Serbianism to Yugoslavism', in D.Deletant and H.Hanak (eds.), *Historians as Nation Builders: Central and South East Europe* (Basingstoke, 1988), p.120.

[53] Toynbee, *Nationality and the War*, p.168.

[54] FO 371/4355/68. Paget headed the South Eastern Europe section, which included Leeper and Nicolson.

[55] A.Stead, 'General Characteristics', in A.Stead (ed.), *Servia by the Servians* (London, 1909), p.3.

[56] Eliot, *Turkey in Europe*, p.335.

[57] Ibid, p.338.

[58] Vivian, *Servia*, pp.29-30.

[59] Taylor, *Future of the Southern Slavs*, p.82.

[60] Forbes, *The Southern Slavs*, p.30.

[61] Durham, *Twenty Years*, pp.13-14; Seton-Watson, *Correspondence*, i, 205.

[62] There was also, in southeastern Serbia and Macedonia, a dialect known as Torlak (Prizren-Timok), classified in the eastern South Slavic group. On this linguistic background see R.Katičić, 'The Making of Standard Serbo-Croat', in R.Picchio and H.Goldblatt (eds.), *Aspects of the Slavic Language Question Vol I: Church Slavonic-South*

Slavic-West Slavic (New Haven, 1984), pp.261-95, and Banac, *National Question*, pp.46-9, 77-81, 209, especially the map of dialectal distribution on p.48.

[63] On the development of the Croat language question, see I.Banac, 'Main Trends in the Croat Language Question', in Picchio and Goldblatt, *Aspects of the Slavic Language Question*, pp.189-259; P.Herrity, 'The Problematic Nature of the Standardisation of the Serbo-Croatian Literary Language in the Second Half of the Nineteenth Century', in R.Bugarski and C.Hawkesworth (eds.), *Language Planning in Yugoslavia* (Columbus, Ohio, 1992); W.Vucinich, 'Croatian Illyrism', passim; and A.B.Wachtel, *Making a Nation, Breaking a Nation: Literature and Cultural Politics in Yugoslavia* (Stanford, 1998), pp.24-31.

[64] Gibbons, *New Map of Europe*, pp.139-40; Seton-Watson, *German, Slav and Magyar*, p.87.

[65] This view did not, though, *override* the equation of Serbdom and Orthodoxy, which remained strong. 'Linguistic Serbianism' was concerned only to undermine the notion that a Catholic or Muslim from Bosnia, Croatia or elsewhere was necessarily *not* a Serb. Cake was had and eaten. Karadžić's linguistic grounding of Serb identity was more successful among the Serb diaspora in Vojvodina, Vienna and elsewhere than in Belgrade itself: J.B.Allcock, *Explaining Yugoslavia* (London, 2000), p.327.

[66] C.Jelavich, *South Slav Nationalisms: Textbooks and Yugoslav Union before 1914* (Columbus, 1990), p.175 and ch.4, passim.

[67] Jelavich, 'Milenko M. Vukičević', p.108.

[68] See, for example, Forbes, *The Southern Slavs*, p.17.

[69] See above pp.25-6.

[70] Such thinking was not limited to a marginal intellectual clique. Karadžić's theories were embraced by the Serbian Radical Party. Linguistic Serbianism, Banac argues, was accepted among a Radical intelligentsia whose least supremacist elements, like Stojan Protić, took it for granted that štokavian was inherently Serbian. Even formerly-kajkavian Croats who had recently adopted it were, by a tortuous casuistical process, claimed as genuine Serbs (*National Question*, pp.156, 161). During the constitutional debates after 1917 Pašić told Croat federalists that a Croatian federal unit would be defined on the assumption that only kajkavian and čakavian speakers were Croats. An appreciation of these questions would thus have greatly benefited British analysis.

[71] To take one example, 'flower' is rendered in ekavian as 'cvet', in ijekavian as 'cvijet' and in ikavian as 'cvit'. These differences are discussed in T.F.Magner, *Introduction to the Croatian and Serbian Language* (Pennsylvania, 1991; revised edn 1998), pp.211-14.

[72] A.Pavković, *The Fragmentation of Yugoslavia: Nationalism in a Multinational State* (Basingstoke, 1996), pp.11-12.

[73] Banac, *National Question*, p.210.

[74] As well as structural and orthographic differences, alternative vocabularies were maintained and developed as symbols of national identity. (Peter Herrity notes, indeed, that lexicon proved the main distinction between the variants: 'Problematic Nature', 173). Curiously, in Croatia, traditionally proud of its Western orientation, neologisms have often been Slav calques or inventions, while Serbs have borrowed directly, often from French.

[75] M.Ekmečić, 'The Struggle for Nation States and Modern Society, pp.295-6, 306-7, in V.Dedijer et al (eds.), *History of Yugoslavia* (London; New York, 1974). If full unity was ever realised, Bernard Joseph commented in 1929, it would be a 'remarkable exemplification of the unifying power of language as a factor of nationality' (*Nationality*, p.60).

[76] A.Djilas, *The Contested Country: Yugoslav Unity and Communist Revolution 1919-1953* (Cambridge, Massachusetts; London, 1991), p.3.

[77] A.D.Smith, *The Ethnic Origin of Nations* (Oxford; New York, 1986), p.27. Smith is generally unpersuaded by language's primary role in the creation of 'ethnic' identities.

[78] G.Szépe, 'Central and Eastern European Language Policies in Transition', in S.Wright and H.Kelly (eds.), *Ethnicity in Eastern Europe: Questions of Migration, Language Rights and Education* (Clevedon; Philadelphia; Adelaide, 1994), p.44.

[79] G.Schöpflin, 'Yugoslavia: State Construction and State Failure', in S.Bianchini and G.Schöpflin (eds.), *State Building in the Balkans: Dilemmas on the Eve of the 21st Century* (Ravenna, 1998), p.242.

[80] Ibid.

[81] H.Birnbaum, *Language, Ethnicity and Nationalism: On the Linguistic Foundations of a Unified Yugoslavia*, in Djordjević (ed.), *The Creation of Yugoslavia*, p.162.

[82] R.Auty, *Language and Nationality in East-Central Europe 1750-1850* (unpublished manuscript), pp.64-5.

[83] Hertz, *Nationality in History and Politics*, p.96.

[84] Katičić, 'Making of Standard Serbo-Croat', p.295.

[85] E.Haugen, 'Dialect, Language, Nation', *American Anthropologist*, Vol 68, 4 (Aug 1966), 922. Logically, Haugen notes, 'every dialect is a language, but not every language is a dialect' (ibid, 923).

[86] R.Auty, *History of the Serbo-Croat Language* (unpublished lecture notes, 1973). There are though, as Rado Lencek points out, symbolic sociolinguistic functions attached to the possession of a literary 'standard': 'The Modern Slovene Language Question: An Essay in Sociolinguistic Interpretation', in Picchio and Goldblatt, *Aspects of the Slavic Language Question*, p.314.

[87] May, *Language and Minority Rights*, pp.150-1. A language, it has been more pithily put, is 'a dialect with an army'.

[88] On recent linguistic developments and controversies in the Serbo-Croat area see R.Lučić (ed.), *Lexical Norm and National Language: Lexicography and Language Policy in South-Slavic Languages after 1989* (Munich, 2002).

[89] A.Nečak Luk, 'The Linguistic Aspect of Ethnic Conflict in Yugoslavia', in P.Akhavan and R.Howse (eds.), *Yugoslavia: The Former and Future: Reflections by Scholars from the Region* (Geneva, 1995), p.119.

[90] J.R.Lampe, *Yugoslavia as History* (Cambridge, 1996), p.299; Pavković, *Fragmentation*, p.63. The protests were led by the Croatian writer Miroslav Krleža, no ethnic exclusivist.

[91] Nečak Luk, 'Linguistic Aspect', pp.114-15. Official Communist policy after 1945 was federalist in national if not in economic terms, but had backed linguistic unitarism rather than Serbian or Croatian philologists who seemed excessively nationalistic in their commitment to regional peculiarities.

[92] Lederer, 'Nationalism and the Yugoslavs', p.409. Tension caused by the political exploitation of Croatian and Serbian language varieties Lederer dates to 1849 with the subsiding of the Hungarian linguistic threat.

[93] B.Anzulović, *Heavenly Serbia: From Myth to Genocide* (London, 1999), p.113.

[94] Freud, cited in Stoianovitch, *Balkan Worlds*, p.301.

[95] Haugen, 'Dialect, Language, Nation', 932.

[96] This key distinction, Haugen notes, has been neglected in English-language studies lacking the terminological resources provided in French, for example, by the differentiation of 'patois' and 'dialecte' (ibid, 924).

[97] Gibbons, *New Map*, pp.139-40.

[98] Ekmečić, 'Struggle for Nation States', p.306.

[99] See, for example, Bryce, *Race Sentiment*, pp.33-4. Race and language, he argued, would suffer this fate together: 'Everything points to a reduction of the number of human stocks and languages. The weaker will disappear [...]'.

[100] W.A.Morison, 'The Serbo-Croat language', pp.269-76, appendix to H.D.Harrison, *The Soul of Yugoslavia* (London, 1941). Morison was lecturer in Comparative Slavonic Philology at the School of Slavonic and East European Studies.

[101] Harrison, *Soul of Yugoslavia*, pp.36-7; H.M.Chadwick, *The Nationalities of Europe and the Growth of National Ideologies* (Cambridge, 1945), p.23. The latter noted that Serbo-Croat rivalry was probably the only European example of a national dispute *not* bound up with language (p.2).

[102] Miller, *Travel and Politics*, pp.xv-xvi.

[103] Forbes, *The Southern Slavs*, p.30.

[104] Seton-Watson, *Spirit of the Serb*, p.22.

[105] Taylor, *Future of the Southern Slavs*, pp.302-3.

[106] See I.J.Lederer, *Yugoslavia at the Paris Peace Conference: A Study in Frontier Making* (New Haven; London, 1963), pp.24-6; Stokes, 'The Role of the Yugoslav Committee', pp.58-60.

[107] Miller, *The Balkans*, pp.510-11.

[108] Seton-Watson, *Correspondence*, i, 162-4.

[109] FO 371/3135/116831. Namier minuted that he agreed with 'every single point' of this memorandum.

[110] FO 371/4355/68.

[111] Banac, *National Question*, pp.211-13.

[112] Ibid, pp.79, 213.

[113] H.Seton-Watson, *Nations and States: An Enquiry into the Origins of Nations and the Politics of Nationalism* (London, 1977), p.134.

[114] H.J. Fleure, *The Treaty Settlement of Europe: Some Geographic and Ethnographic Aspects* (London, 1921), p.77. American Balkan specialist Archibald Coolidge, a strong influence on both US and British conference delegations, was another who, with a little hindsight, emphasised religious and alphabet divergence between Serb and Croat: introduction to H.Fish Armstrong, *The New Balkans* (London; New York, 1926), pp.12-13.

[115] J.A.Fishman, *Language and Ethnicity in Minority Sociolinguistic Perspective* (Clevedon; Philadelphia, 1989), p.7: 'The ever-present link between language and religion (what would religion be without language?) not only sanctifies "our language" but

helps raise language into the pale of sanctity even in secular culture'. See also J.A.Armstrong, *Nations before Nationalism* (Chapel Hill, 1982), pp.203-4.

[116] Katičić, 'Making of Standard Serbo-Croat', p.273; see also Malcolm, *Bosnia*, pp.101-2.

[117] This vile imposition by 'Bohemian Hussites and Lutherans' he referred to with disgust as 'stercora muscarum' (fly droppings)! See R.Auty, 'Orthographical Innovations and Controversies among the Western and Southern Slavs during the Slavonic National Revival', *Slavonic and East European Review*, vol.xlvi, no.107 (1968), 328.

[118] G.C.Arnakis, 'The Role of Religion in the Development of Balkan Nationalism', in C.Jelavich and B.Jelavich (eds.), *The Balkans in Transition: essays on the development of Balkan life and politics since the 18th century* (Berkeley; Los Angeles, 1963), p.119.

[119] Anderson, *Imagined Communities*, pp.73-4.

[120] R.Auty, 'The Formation of the Slovene Literary Language against the Background of the Slavonic National Revival', *The Slavonic and East European Review*, vol.xli, no.97 (June 1963), 393; R.L.Lencek, 'Modern Slovene Language Question', pp.297-8.

[121] Auty, 'The Formation of the Slovene Literary Language', p.395.

[122] Banac, *National Question*, p.113.

[123] V.S.Mamatey, *The United States and East Central Europe 1914-1918* (New York; London, 1957), pp.91-2.

[124] Banac, *National Question*, p.49.

[125] FO 371/44346/10006. FORD paper on Yugoslavia's political structure, July 1944. 'Such a language does not, in point of fact, exist' ('The Jugo-Slav Constitution', *The Slavonic Review*, III, no.7 (June 1924), 173-4).

[126] Miller, *Balkans*, p.511.

[127] Forbes, *The Southern Slavs*, p.12 and passim.

[128] N.Buxton and T.P.Conwil-Evans, *Oppressed Peoples and the League of Nations* (London; Toronto, 1922), pp.7-8; Gibbons, *New Map*, p.135. In a later work Buxton similarly described both Croats and Slovenes as 'identical in race and language with the Serbs': *Travels and Reflections* (London, 1929), p.115.

[129] Seton-Watson, *German, Slav and Magyar*, pp.118-19. Privately, as we have seen, he mooted a separate Slovene edition of *New Europe*, an indication of the conscious simplification in his propagandistic writing.

[130] Seton-Watsons, *Making of a New Europe*, pp.131-2.

[131] Vošnjak, *Bulwark*, pp.70, 216, 229.

[132] Toynbee, *Nationality and the War*, pp.168, 248.

[133] Joseph, *Nationality*, p.78; Laffan, *Guardians of the Gate*, p.20.

Chapter Three

[1] Oakesmith, *Race and Nationality*, p.51.

[2] Strictly, of course, 'historical tradition' was an overarching category incorporating language, religion and other elements. In practice religion, like language, was treated separately.

[3] Joseph, *Nationality*, p.75.

[4] Toynbee, *Nationality and the War*, p.14.

[5] C.D.Burns, *The Morality of Nations: An Essay* (London, 1915), p.20.

[6] Brailsford, *Macedonia*, pp.22, 61.

[7] Miller, *Travel and Politics*, p.32.

[8] Joseph, *Nationality*, p.76.

[9] Ibid, p.71.

[10] Hertz, *Nationality in History and Politics*, p.108.

[11] Ibid, p.82.

[12] Herbert, *Nationality and its Problems*, p.51.

[13] *Nationality and Government*, p.73.

[14] Seton-Watson, *Correspondence*, i, 237.

[15] FO 371/4366/283 (Percy, 22 Aug 1918).

[16] Hertz, *Nationality in History and Politics*, p.78.

[17] Seton-Watson, *Southern Slav Question*, p.2. To this, he stressed, there were 'virtually no exceptions'. This Catholic-Orthodox division afflicted also, he noted, the broader pan-Slav movement, for which antipathy between Catholic Poles and Orthodox Russians had been a perennial obstacle ('Pan-Slavism', 426-7).

[18] Todorova, *Imagining the Balkans*, p.98; L.Namier, *Vanished Supremacies* (London, 1958), p.168. See also p.236 note 131 above.

[19] Seton-Watson's early study, *Absolutism in Croatia* (London, 1912) was a groundbreaking work on this theme; Allcock, *Explaining Yugoslavia*, pp.329-30.

[20] Miller, *Travel and Politics*, p.32.

[21] A.Fortescue, *The Orthodox Eastern Church* (London, 1907), p.281.

[22] FO 371/599/7133 (Howard, 8 Feb 1909); FO 371/599/5137 (Cartwright, 1 Feb 1909).

[23] FO 371/1575/7514 (15 Feb 1913).

[24] Buxton, *Travels and Reflections*, pp.52-3.

[25] Miller, *Travel and Politics*, pp.118-19; 128-9.

[26] Temperley, *History of Serbia*, pp.111-12.

[27] Todorova, *Imagining the Balkans*, pp.124-5.

[28] Seton-Watson, *Southern Slav Question*, p.2.

[29] A.Goff and H.A. Fawcett, *Macedonia: A Plea for the Primitive* (London, 1921), p.xiv. (This refers, in fact, to the Orthodox-Muslim division in Macedonia).

[30] Seton-Watson, *Emancipation of South-Eastern Europe*, p.7.

[31] Adolf von Harnack, cited in Hertz, *Nationality in History and Politics*, p.113.

[32] G.C.Arnakis, 'The Role of Religion in the Development of Balkan Nationalism', in Jelavich and Jelavich, *Balkans in Transition*, p.117.

[33] Todorova, *Imagining the Balkans*, p.101.

[34] Fortescue, *Orthodox Eastern Church*, pp.280-2.

[35] Marcovitch, *Serbia and Europe*, p.117.

[36] FO 371/3135/116831 (report on 'The Jugo-Slav Problem', June 1918).

[37] Brailsford, *Macedonia*, p.62.

[38] Fortescue, *Orthodox Eastern Church*, pp.324-5. 'If one were to grant all their wishes', he noted, 'there would be no end to the disintegrating influence of Orthodox jealousies, till each diocese became an autocephalous Church'.

[39] Fleure, *Peoples of Europe*, pp.82-3.

[40] Forbes, *The Southern Slavs*, p.26.

[41] Encyclopaedia Britannica, 'Serbia', p.168.

[42] Seton-Watson, *Spirit of the Serb*, p.26.

[43] Brailsford, *Macedonia*, p.68.

[44] Hertz, *Nationality in History and Politics*, p.110. Herbert Vivian discusses the mutual sympathies existing between Anglican and Serb Orthodox Church hierarchies in *The Servian Tragedy With Some Impressions of Macedonia* (London, 1904), pp.211-13.

[45] FO 371/3025/217193.

[46] W.J.Sparrow Simpson, 'The English Church and the Orthodox East', *The Balkan Review*, Vol IV No 6, Jan 1921, 394.

[47] Sir G.Young ('A Diplomatist'), *Nationalism and War in the Near East* (Oxford, 1915), p.22. This respected work was produced under the aegis of the Carnegie Commission, G.P.Gooch hailing it as a classic study (*Contemporary Review*, Nov 1915, 663-4).

[48] Brailsford, *Macedonia*, pp.70-1.

[49] J. and C.Gordon, *Two Vagabonds in the Balkans* (London, 1925), p.79; Sparrow Simpson, 'English Church', 393. For a study of changing British attitudes to the Balkans and the 'East', see Todorova, *Imagining the Balkans*. On the British sense of Ottoman stasis, see R.Schiffer, *Oriental Panorama: British Travellers in 19th Century Turkey* (Amsterdam; Atlanta, GA, 1999), p.198 and *passim*.

[50] Vivian, *The Servian Tragedy*, p.227.

[51] Forbes, *Southern Slavs*, p.22; Forbes, 'Serbia', p.104, in N.Forbes, A.Toynbee et al (eds.), *The Balkans: A History of Bulgaria, Serbia, Greece, Rumania, Turkey* (Oxford, 1915). J.A.R. Marriott, *The Eastern Question: An Historical Study in European Diplomacy* 2nd edn (Oxford, 1918), p.315. The role of the revived Patriarchate of Peć between 1557 and 1766 seemed particularly important.

[52] *Encyclopaedia Britannica*, 'Serbia', p.176.

[53] Cited in FO 371/1472/34881.

[54] Seton-Watson, *Southern Slav Question*, p.339. Seton-Watson, to be fair, was not one of those persuaded by Serb nationalist propaganda to regard large groups of Catholic South Slavs as 'really' Serbs.

[55] Ivo Banac provides examples of these exceptions: *National Question*, p.58.

[56] Ibid, p.221. The centralised structure faced internal dissent, especially from Bosnia and Vojvodina: see R.Radić, 'Religion in a Multinational State: the case of Yugoslavia', pp.196-7, in Djokić (ed.), *Yugoslavism*.

[57] *Encyclopaedia Britannica*, 'Montenegro', p.125.

[58] FO 371/3140/17406, (7 Jan 1918).

[59] FO 371/827/10301 (Esmé Howard, 19 March 1910).

[60] See below pp.94-5 and pp.189-90.

[61] C.Jelavich, 'The Croatian problem in the Habsburg Empire in the Nineteenth Century', *Austrian Yearbook*, III, Part 2 (1967), p.96. On the stimulus provided by Hungarian nationalism in particular to the development of Croat identity, see Vucinich, 'Croatian Illyrism', pp.68-73. Ivo Banac points out that Croat nationalists had themselves not identified Croatdom with Catholicism (*National Question*, p.108). It is true, however, that British observers in Bosnia did accord much more emphasis to Serb-Croat confessional tensions.

[62] FO 371/2862/137019 (July 1917).

[63] FO 371/2862/239280 (Dec 1917).

[64] See above p.28.

[65] Banac, *National Question*, p.113.

[66] Ibid. Since 1905 the clericalist party had been known as the Slovene People's Party. Carole Rogel's claim that that during the two decades before World War I, 'nearly all [Slovenes] came to focus on Southern Slav unity', however, is scarcely plausible.

[67] Bosnia remained technically under Ottoman suzerainty until 1908 but was effectively administered as a Habsburg territory from the Congress of Berlin in 1878.

[68] Durham, *Twenty Years*, p.35.

[69] William Miller, *Travel and Politics*, p.89.

[70] R.M. Brashich, *Land Reform and Ownership in Yugoslavia, 1919-1953* (New York, 1954), p.13.

[71] Eliot, *Turkey in Europe*, p.344. 'Beys' (or 'Begs') were the Muslim landlords.

[72] For a precise social breakdown of the provinces' population by religion, see Donia and Fine, *Bosnia and Hercegovina: A Tradition Betrayed* (New York, 1994), pp.76-9. Under Habsburg rule, which had not outlawed serfdom, some 6,000 Bosnian Muslim peasants had become enserfed by 1910.

[73] R.J. Donia, *Islam Under the Double Eagle: The Muslims of Bosnia and Hercegovina, 1979-1914* (New York, 1981), p.5. The early 20th century British view of the Orthodox population as wholly peasant also overlooked a growing body of urban, middle-class Serbs, critical to the province's growing nationalist movement (ibid., p.4).

[74] PID Memo on the formula of the 'Self-Determination of Peoples' and the Muslim World, FO 371/4353/25 (10 Jan 1918).

[75] Donia, *Islam under the Double Eagle*, pp.91-2. 'Fanaticism' was commonly noticed in Muslim centres other than Sarajevo, notably Mostar (where the traditional forms of dress seemed particularly sinister). As Donia notes, the quiescence of Sarajevan Muslim leaders owed much to the fact that they were courted by the Habsburg authorities in a manner not extended to their brethren elsewhere: ibid., pp.35-6.

[76] Seton-Watson, *Emancipation of South-East Europe*, pp.13-14.

[77] FO 371/4352/PC 25.

[78] Ibid.

[79] Todorova, *Imagining the Balkans*, p.109. David Cannadine (*Ornamentalism* (London, 2001)) highlights the prevalence of a similar class-based empathy, transcending racial and religious boundaries, between British and indigenous elites in the Empire.

[80] Eliot, *Turkey in Europe*, p.345.

[81] W.Denton, *The Christians in Turkey* (London, 1863), p.1.

[82] G.Gaillard, *The Turks and Europe* (London, 1921), pp.106-8.

[83] FO 371/3508/59385 (Oman report, Oct 1918).

[84] Taylor, *Future of the Southern Slavs*, p.87.

[85] FO 371/4356/172.

[86] On the genesis of this organisation, see Malcolm, *Bosnia*, pp.163-4.

[87] Seton-Watson, *Southern Slav Question*, p.8.

[88] Forbes, *The Southern Slavs*, p.31.

[89] On the attitude of Bosnian Muslims to Serbs and Croats, and to the Yugoslav idea, see Xavier Bougarel, 'Bosnian Muslims and the Yugoslav Idea', in Djokić (ed.), *Yugoslavism*, pp.100-14.

[90] See, for instance, Malcolm, *Bosnia*; R.J.Donia and J.V.A.Fine, *Bosnia and Hercegovina: A Tradition Betrayed* (New York, 1994). The latter work asserts that, prior to 19th century nationalist agitations, 'Bosnians [...] had not described themselves as either Serbs or Croats' (p.73).

[91] Such a line of thinking might have developed from Stjepan Radić's suggestion that Yugoslavia only looked like one nation from the outside (cited in E.J.Woodhouse and C.G.Woodhouse, *Italy and the Jugoslavs* (Boston, 1920), p.127).

[92] FO 371/3136/98080 (May 1918).

[93] See, for instance, his *Religion and Nationality in Serbia*.

[94] Preface to Petrovitch, *Hero Tales*, p.v. (If written in 1917 instead of 1914 it seems unlikely that it would have spoken of 'nations' rather than 'nation').

[95] Preface to Velimirović, *Religion and Nationality*, p.3.

[96] Seton-Watson, *Spirit of the Serb*, p.29.

[97] Taylor, *Future of the Southern Slavs*, pp.267, 303.

[98] Price, *Light on the Balkan Darkness*, p.119 note.

[99] FO 371/4355/68.

[100] FO 371/3138/207115.

[101] FO 371/3133/88314 (Rumbold, Berne, 10 May 1918).

[102] FO 371/4358/21 (July 1918). See also *The Jugo-Slav Movement*: handbook no.14 (March 1919), pp.25-6. Historians have confirmed the strength of wartime Yugoslavism among the Slovenes, while noting that it coexisted with genuine loyalty to the Monarchy, and was motivated as much by the Italian nationalist threat as by South Slav sentiment: M.Cornwall, 'The Experience of Yugoslav Agitation in Austria-Hungary, 1917-1918', in H.Cecil and P.Liddle (eds.), *Facing Armageddon: The First World War Experienced* (London, 1996), pp.662-7.

[103] FO 371/3508/59385 (15 Oct 1918).

[104] FO 371/3138/213164 (15 Dec 1918).

[105] FO 371/3135/116831.

[106] See, for instance, the Amery report in FO 371/3136/177223.

[107] FO 371/3138/204655.

[108] FO 371/3135/116831.

[109] Termperley, *History of Serbia*, p.3.

[110] *The Jugo-Slav Movement*, p.5 (citing uncritically the Yugoslav proverb 'a brother is dear, whatever his faith').

[111] Ramet, 'Religion and Nationalism', pp.306-7.

[112] See below pp.94-5 and pp.189-90.

[113] F.M.D.Berry, *Austria-Hungary and her Slav Subjects* (London, 1918), p.35.

[114] Price, *Light on the Balkan Darkness*, pp.11-12. Price was *The Times*' correspondent in Serbia during the early part of the war. See also Woodhouse and Woodhouse, *Italy and the Jugoslavs*, p.131, citing T.R.Gjorgjević, 'Religious Toleration among the Southern Slavs', *New Europe*, vol. X, p.61.

[115] Laffan, *Guardians of the Gate*, pp.30-1.

[116] 'The Yougoslav Patriarch', *Balkan Review*, Jan 1921, 413-14.

[117] The phrase was Lloyd George's. Cited in M.Beaven, *Austrian Policy since 1867* (London; Edinburgh; New York, 1914), p.5.

[118] Miller, *Travel and Politics*, pp.97,116-19. This tendency is noted in Andrew Hammond, 'The Uses of Balkanism: Representation and Power in British Travel Writing, 1850-1914', *The Slavonic and East European Review*, Vol.82, No.3 (July 2004), 604-9.

[119] Holbach, *Bosnia and Herzegovina*, pp.15-16. Holbach did, it should be said, wonder if Western opinion had not 'painted [the Turk] blacker than he deserved'.

[120] de Windt, *Through Savage Europe*, p.81.

[121] Vivian, *Servia*, pp.36-7. Benjámin von Kállay was Austro-Hungarian Finance Minister from 1882 until 1903.

[122] A.F.Pribram, *Austria-Hungary and Great Britain 1908-1914* (London; New York; Toronto, 1951), pp.98-9.

[123] Murray Beaven, *Austrian Policy since 1867* (London; New York, 1914), pp.8-9. F.R.Bridge suggests, however, that in diplomatic circles disillusionment with Austrian rule did grow after the annexation crisis: *Great Britain and Austria-Hungary 1906-1914: A Diplomatic History* (London, 1972), pp.38-9.

[124] Sir H.Johnston, *Commonsense in Foreign Policy* (London, 1913), *passim*.

[125] Taylor, *Future of the Southern Slavs*, pp.86-7, 89.

[126] Seton-Watson, *German, Slav and Magyar*, p.92.

[127] Gibbons, *New Map*, p.140. See also, for instance, W.E.D. Allen, *The Turks in Europe* (London, 1919), p.214, and Laffan, *Guardians of the Gate*, p.97.

[128] Forbes, 'Serbia', p.135, 106.

[129] Marriott, *Eastern Question*, p.345. Only now, Marriott noted late in the war, did Britons perceive the division and strangulation of the Yugoslav race as the necessary precursor to a German drive to the East (p.391).

[130] Cornwall, 'Experience of Yugoslav Agitation', p.670.

[131] F.S.Copeland, 'Who are the Yugo-Slavs?', p.40.

[132] Berry, *Austria-Hungary*, pp.30, 35. Laffan even denied any economic benefits. The region, he claimed, 'was not allowed to develop', its poverty so wretched that peasants had to drag their own ploughs (*Guardians of the Gate*, pp.97-8).

[133] Speech reported in *The Times*, 'An End to Austrian Tyranny', 26 July 1918.

[134] Laffan, *Guardians of the Gate*, pp.30-1.

[135] R.W.Seton-Watson, 'Serbia's Need and Britain's Danger', *Contemporary Review*, Nov 1915, 579.

[136] Taylor, *Future of the Southern Slavs*, p.88.

[137] See, for instance, the appendices in the War Office report on the 'Yugo-Slav problem', FO 371/3138/207115.

[138] See below p.96.

[139] Cornwall, 'Experience of Yugoslav Agitation', pp.669-71.

[140] See below chs. 7 and 8.

[141] Quoted in J.Hanly, *The National Ideal: A Practical Exposition of True Nationality Appertaining to Ireland* (London, 1932), pp.9-10.

[142] FO 371/4366/559.

[143] FO 371/4366/281 (1 Aug 1918).

Chapter Four

[1] Herbert, *Nationality and its Problems*, p.33.

[2] J.K.Bluntschli, quoted in Joseph, *Nationality*, p.22.

[3] L.Fawcett, *Religion, Ethnicity and Social Change* (London, 2000), p.9.

[4] The oft-cited phrase is Benedict Anderson's.

[5] P.Berger and T.Luckmann, *The Social Construction of Reality* (London, 1967) exemplifies the modern constructivist approach. See also P.Jackson and J.Penrose, *Constructions of Race, Place and Nation* (London, 1993).

[6] E.Renan, quoted in Herbert, *Nationality and its Problems*, p.40.

[7] J.Mazzini, quoted in Joseph, *Nationality*, pp.105-6.

[8] J.R.Muir, *Nationalism and Internationalism* (London, 1916), p.43.

[9] Hertz, *Nationality in History and Politics*, p.10.

[10] *The Basis of Ascendancy*, pp.78-80, cited in Joseph, *Nationality*, pp.33-4.

[11] Thus, for instance, the common perception that the Slavic race was innately poetic, and politically fissiparous (a racial explanation for the circumstance that the Slav peoples, Russians apart, had owned no independent state since the partition of Poland). The Celtic blood of the Irish, English writers similarly claimed, made them innately unfit to self-govern. For instances and criticism see J.M.Robertson, *The Saxon and the Celt* (London, 1897).

[12] Joseph argued that such tradition 'moulds the national character and forms the groundwork of the national sentiment'; and also that it was 'the expression of the soul or spirit of the nationality' (*Nationality*, pp.103-5).

[13] The Zionist cause, dear to many British theorists, was pertinent here.

[14] On this theme see E.Hobsbawm, 'Introduction: Inventing Traditions' in E.Hobsbawm and T.Ranger (eds.), *The Invention of Tradition* (Cambridge, 1983), pp.1-14.

[15] A.Zimmern, 'Nationalism and Internationalism', *Foreign Affairs*, June 1923, 121.

[16] Laffan, *Jugoslavia since 1918*, p.5.

[17] Banac, *National Question*, pp.222-3; Allcock, *Explaining Yugoslavia*, p.55; J.R.Lampe, 'Unifying the Yugoslav Economy, 1918-1921: Misery and Early Misunderstandings', in Djordjević (ed.), *Creation of Yugoslavia*, p.143.

[18] Cited in E.Goldstein, *Winning the Peace: British Diplomatic Strategy, Peace Planning, and the Paris Peace Conference, 1916-1920* (Oxford, 1991), p.134.

[19] Lederer, 'Nationalism and the Yugoslavs', p.397.

[20] J.B.Hoptner, *Yugoslavia in Crisis 1934-41* (New York, 1962), p.2.

[21] Lederer, *Yugoslavia at the Paris Peace Conference*, pp.81-2.

[22] Herbert, *Nationality and its Problems*, p.22.

[23] Ibid, pp.24, 27-8.

[24] Marriott, *The Eastern Question*, p.36.

[25] M.Newbigin, 'The Problem of the South Slavs', *The Scottish Geographical Magazine*, Jan 1919, 2-3.

[26] Forbes, *Southern Slavs*, pp.19-20.

[27] Taylor, *Future of the Southern Slavs*, pp.32-3.

[28] On Montenegro see, for instance, Eliot, *Turkey in Europe*, p.347. On Dalmatia, see Dominian, *Frontiers*, p.186; T.H.Holdich, *Boundaries in Europe and the Near East* (London, 1918), p.66; M.I.Newbigin, *Geographical Aspects of Balkan Problems in their Relation to the Great European War* (London, 1915), pp.37,43.

[29] 'Unity has never been a feature of the Southern Slavs', one influential pre-war writer had observed, 'except at rare intervals, under the sublime influence of some great man, whose successors were unable to hold his heritage together' (Miller, *Travel and Politics*, pp.118-19).

[30] Seton-Watson, *German, Slav and Magyar*, p.52.

[31] Temperley, *History of Serbia*, p.2; *Balkan Review*, 'Editor's Causerie', Aug 1920, p.10.

[32] Seton-Watson, *Southern Slav Question*, pp.335-6.

[33] Dominian, *Frontiers*, pp.186, 338.

[34] Temperley, *History of Serbia*, p.2.

[35] Forbes, 'Serbia', p.82.

[36] In 1918 no rail links connected Serbia and the western Yugoslav lands. Arteries in the west converged on the major Habsburg cities. (See V.Rogić, 'The Changing Urban Pattern in Yugoslavia', in F.W.Carter (ed.), *An Historical Geography of the Balkans* (London, 1977), p.414). 19th century Serbian communications had improved very slowly, in part due to international rivalry over the transcontinental routes through Belgrade. And in 1918 existing networks were often incompatible and badly damaged (Lampe, 'Unifying the Yugoslav Economy', pp.144-5; D.Turnock, *Eastern Europe: an historical geography, 1815-1914* (London, 1989), pp.147-62).

[37] Temperley, *History of Serbia*, pp.1-2.

[38] T.Judah, *The Serbs: History, Myth and the Destruction of Yugoslavia* (New Haven; London, 1997), pp.17-28.

[39] J.Rives Childs, 'Sight-Seeing in Serbia', *Balkan Review* (September 1920), 134.

[40] 'Serbia: Population, Government and Religion', p.166.

[41] Miller, *Travel and Politics*, p.47.

[42] Miller, 'The Balkan States I: the Zenith of Bulgaria and Serbia 1186-1355', in J.R.Tanner, C.W.Previté-Orton and Z.N.Brooke (eds.), *The Cambridge Medieval History Vol IV: The Eastern Roman Empire 717-1453* (Cambridge, 1923), p.550.

[43] Taylor, *Future of the Southern Slavs*, pp.126-7.

[44] Miller, *Travel and Politics*, pp.91, 378.

[45] Brailsford, *Macedonia*, p.98.

[46] The name derives from *duša* (soul/ spirit) rather than from *dušiti*. Taylor (*Future of the Southern Slavs*, p.26) corrects this widespread tendency. Dušan's bloody record rendered the claim plausible, of course.

[47] Temperley, *History of Serbia*, pp.viii, 87.

[48] Taylor, *Future of the Southern Slavs*, pp.46-51.

[49] Allen, *The Turks in Europe*, p.2.

[50] Miller, 'The Balkan Peninsula for the Balkan Peoples', *Balkan Review*, December 1920, 317.

[51] Copeland, 'Who are the Yugo-Slavs?', p.37; Laffan, *Guardians of the Gate*, p.15.

[52] M.Mügge, *Serbian Folk Songs, Fairy Tales and Proverbs* (London, 1917), p.19.

[53] On the Serbian kings conscious aping of Byzantine ritual, see D.Milošević, quoted in Judah, *The Serbs*, p.22.

[54] Forbes, 'Serbia', p.95.

[55] Temperley was one: *History of Serbia*, pp.91-2. And Edith Durham's hostility to Serbia (as well as her critical mind) made her resist such specious romanticism. In truth, she wrote, Dušan's Empire 'was an incoherent mass of different and hostile races, and it broke to pieces immediately on his death' (*Twenty Years*, p.64).

[56] Joseph, *Nationality*, p.106. See also Bryce, *Essays and Addresses*, p.129; Muir, *Nationalism and Internationalism*, p.43; Pillsbury, *Psychology*, p.89.

[57] Temperley, *History of Serbia*, p.92.

[58] Forbes, 'Serbia', p.97.

[59] This phrase, recurrent in British discourse, was used by Lloyd George, and by Laffan as the title for his influential romanticised account of Serbian history. (Lloyd George quoted in Seton-Watsons, *Making of a New Europe*, p.225).

[60] Velimirović, *Religion and Nationality in Serbia*, p.8.

[61] Allcock, *Explaining Yugoslavia*, pp.315-18.

[62] H.T.Norris, *Islam in the Balkans: Religion and Society between Europe and the Arab World* (London, 1993), p.261. Ironically, Norris observes, contemporary Western documents damned the Serbs as an ally of the infidel.

[63] Taylor, *Future of the Southern Slavs*, p.54.

[64] Count de Salis, FO 371/2409/313 (annual report on Montenegro 1914).

[65] Seton-Watsons, *Making of a New Europe*, pp.174-5; Hanak, *Great Britain and Austria-Hungary*, pp.75-7 and ch.4. The response to the 'Kosovo day agitation' Seton-Watson considered 'extraordinarily satisfactory' (*Correspondence*, i, 270).

[66] On this retreat, see Fry, *Destruction of Serbia*, pp.91-104, 113-125.

[67] G.K Chesterton, 'The Thing Called a Nation', in *The Lay of Kossovo: Serbia's Past and Present (1389-1917)* (London, 1917), pp.32-5. On the potency of themes of fatalism and suffering in national mythologies, see G.Schöpflin, 'The Functions of Myth and a Taxonomy of Myths', in G.Hosking and G.Schöpflin (eds.), *Myths and Nationhood* (London, 1997), pp.29-30.

[68] S.K.Pavlowitch, *Serbia: The History Behind the Name* (London, 2002), pp.97-8. 'A nation that can sing about its defeats and not lose heart', Lloyd George observed in 1917, drawing a parallel with his native Wales, 'is immortal; and that is why Serbia is immortal [...]' (quoted in Seton-Watsons, *Making of a New Europe*, p.224).

[69] Malcolm, *Kosovo*, ch.4.

[70] Eliot, *Turkey in Europe*, pp.341-2.

[71] Temperley, *History of Serbia*, p.viii. A romantic fascination with Serbian culture coexisted always with Temperley's more scholarly instincts; the diaries he kept of his travels in the region at the end of the war were, as his biographer notes, instinct with his love of South Slavic culture and national traditions (Fair, *Harold Temperley*, pp.126-7).

[72] Dominian, *Frontiers*, p.322: 'the geographer, in search of Serbian boundaries, tries in vain to discover a surer guide to delimitation. For Serbia extends as far as her folk-songs are heard'.

[73] Mügge, *Serbian Folk Songs*, p.17.

[74] *Balkan Review*, July 1920, 471. Chadwick drew extensive parallels between the Kosovo poems and the Iliad (*The Heroic Age* (Cambridge, 1912), p.309ff, while admitting the former lacked the same rarified elevation.

[75] 1903 Austrian statistics for the Ottoman sançaks of Priština, Peć and Prizren put the Orthodox Serbs at 25% of the population, Ottoman statistics of 1912 at 21% (Malcolm, *Kosovo*, p.230).

[76] Zimmern, *Nationality and Government*, p.91 ('Shrines of nationality').

[77] Toynbee, *Nationality and the War*, p.203; L.F.Waring, 'Kosovo', *Slavonic Review*, Vol II no 4 (June 1923), 62; Brailsford, *Macedonia*, pp.100, 274-6. As historians have pointed out, growth in the Muslim population in Kosovo and Macedonia during the 19th century was largely due to expulsions by the independent Serbian state from lands gained in 1877-8 (Malcolm, *Kosovo*, pp.228-30; J.McCarthy, *Death and Exile: the Ethnic Cleansing of Ottoman Muslims, 1821-1922* (Princeton, NJ, 1995)).

[78] Todorova, *Imagining the Balkans*, pp.101-9.

[79] Pribram, *Austria-Hungary and Great Britain*, p.97 (Young Turk revolution); Protić reply to Seton-Watson, *Correspondence*, i, 331-3.

[80] B.Lewis, 'Some Reflections on the Decline of the Ottoman Empire', in C.M.Cipolla (ed.), *The Economic Decline of Empires* (London, 1970), p.215.

[81] Forbes, *Southern Slavs*, p.26; Low, 'The Kingdom of Serbia', 309; Taylor, *Future of the Southern Slavs*, p.44; Holland Rose, 'The National Idea', 337; Laffan, *Guardians of the Gate*, pp.22, 26. For the British hostile Eastern armies were always 'hordes', with that term's intimations of barbarism and anarchy.

[82] Marriott, *Eastern Question*, p.3. Of course the Habsburgs believed their rule, unlike the Ottoman, originated in dynastic right. But Marriott claimed that the Turk was 'akin to the European family neither in creed, in race, in language, in social customs, nor in political aptitudes and traditions', which overlooked both differences within this 'European family' and the fact that local Ottoman governors were often natives of their region (Malcolm, *Bosnia*, p.46, note 10; P.F.Sugar, *Southeastern Europe under Ottoman Rule* (Seattle; London, 1977), p.58).

[83] Allen, *The Turks in Europe*, pp.1-2.

[84] Baerlein, *Birth of Yugoslavia*, i, p.49.

[85] Miller, *The Ottoman Empire 1801-1913* (Cambridge, 1913), p.503. Turkish rule, he later wrote, 'meant complete paralysis of national life', with no form of progress: 'The Balkan Peninsula for the Balkan Peoples', pp.316-17. On the 19th century view of the Ottoman legacy as an 'alien imposition' upon medieval Christendom, see Maria Todorova, 'The Ottoman Legacy in the Balkans', in L.Carl Brown (ed.), *Imperial Legacy: The Ottoman Imprint on the Balkans and the Middle East* (New York, 1996), pp.46-7.

[86] Allcock, *Explaining Yugoslavia*, p.334.

[87] Temperley, *History of Serbia*, pp.110-12, 120-2. See also G.Gaillard, *The Turks and Europe* (London, 1921), translated from French.

[88] Ibid, p.103.

[89] L.von Ranke, *The History of Servia and the Servian Revolution* (London, 1853; tr. A.Kerr), p.207.

[90] Forbes, *Southern Slavs*, p.4.

[91] Serbian history, unlike the Greek, Forbes suggested, 'had not been sufficiently brilliant to produce a Byron' (*Southern Slavs*, p.5).

[92] Zimmern, *Nationality and Government*, p.71.

[93] Young, *Nationalism and War in the Near East*, p.31.

[94] Miller, *Balkans*, p.496; Editorial, 'Great Britain and the Future of Turkey', *The Nation*, 17 May 1913 (vol XIII, no 7); Brailsford, *Macedonia*, p.319.

[95] Ibid.

[96] Miller, *Travel and Politics*, pp.118-19.

[97] Seton-Watson, *Southern Slav Question*, pp.336-8; see also his letter of 17 Oct 1909, *Correspondence*, i, 50-4. He later admitted this fear of an 'oriental' culture among the Serbs had been 'unduly coloured by the Viennese point of view' (though he continued to decry 'old oriental tendencies' in uncongenial individuals): Ibid., i, 20-1, Appendix no 3; ii, 92-3.

[98] Allcock, *Explaining Yugoslavia*, pp.262-3. Of course Serbian politics did also, as Allcock points out, own a less salubrious militaristic undercurrent, represented by organisations like the Black Hand.

[99] G.Stokes, *Politics as Development: the Emergence of Political Parties in Nineteenth Century Serbia* (Durham, 1990), *passim*.

[100] Allcock, *Explaining Yugoslavia*, p.263; Petrovich, *History of Modern Serbia*, ii, 441-3.

[101] Todorova, *Explaining the Balkans*, p.110.

[102] Miller, *Travel and Politics*, pp.118, 279.

[103] Sir V.Chirol, *Serbia and the Serbs* (London, 1914), p.8.

[104] On English reactions to the regicide, see W.S.Vucinich, *Serbia Between East and West 1903-1908* (Stanford; London, 1954), pp.105-12. Of course the fact that pre-war British relations with Serbia 'owing to the absence of any close point of contact in their interests' were 'always more or less perfunctory' (Ralph Paget, 6 June 1913, FO 371/1748/28340) made such a principled stand an uncomplicated one for Britain.

[105] Seton-Watson, *Correspondence*, i, 52 (17 Oct 1909).

[106] E.J.Dillon, 'Servia and the Rival Dynasties', *The Contemporary Review*, 84, July-Dec 1903, 143.

[107] The same year's Macedonian revolt served further to shore up such assumptions.

[108] Brailsford, *Macedonia*, p.xi.

[109] D.Walshe, *With the Serbs in Macedonia* (London; New York, 1920), p.231. Chirol doubtless had this in mind in observing that before the war it was 'the worst pages of [Serbia's] history which chiefly clung to people's memory' (*Serbia and the Serbs*, p.3). See also Rebecca West's testimony to the murder's impact in *Black Lamb and Grey Falcon: A Journey Through Yugoslavia* (London, 1942; Edinburgh, 1993), pp.10-12. Further examples of outrage are given in Todorova, *Explaining the Balkans*, p.118.

[110] de Windt, *Through Savage Europe*, p.144.

[111] Marriott, *Eastern Question*, p.314.

[112] J.Berry, F.M.D.Berry, W.L.Blease et al, *A Red Cross Unit in Serbia* (London, 1916), pp.5-6.

[113] For positive pre-war views of Alexander see, for example, de Windt, *Through Savage Europe*, p.133; Vivian, *The Servian Tragedy*, passim.

[114] C.Price, *Serbia's Part in the War Vol I: The Rampart against Pan-Germanism* (London, 1918) p.3.

[115] Gordon, *Woman in the Balkans*, p.69. By the assassination, claimed Price, Serbia not only rid herself of the 'mentally irresponsible' Alexander, but also 'checkmated' Austria's plans to secure control of the country (*Serbia's Part in the War*, p.12).

[116] *The War and the Balkans*, pp.46-7. See also the similar assessment by Forbes, 'Serbia', p.129.

[117] Gibbons, *New Map of Europe*, pp.154-5. Both quotations were taken, he noted, from the same British newspaper. (See E.Crankshaw, *The Fall of the House of Habsburg* (London, 1963), pp.377-8). Paul Fussell suggests that the shift in British usage from 'Servia' to 'Serbia' was itself indicative of a change in attitude – an end to the old pejorative etymological association with 'servant' and 'servile' (*The Great War and Modern Memory* (Oxford; New York, 1975;2000), p.175). But in fact this change was requested by the Serbian embassy. M.T.Seleskovic noted in 1919 a similar shift, prompted by the war, in German attitudes to the Serbs: 'La Serbie dans l'opinion Allemande Contemporaine' (Doctoral thesis, University of Paris, 1919), pp.7-8 and *passim*.

[118] Young, *Nationalism and War*, p.13. 'Every Serbian peasant is a poet', agreed M.St.Clair Stobart (*The Flaming Sword*, p.28).

[119] Taylor, *Future of the Southern Slavs*, p.70; Admiral Troubridge, preface to Laffan, *Guardians of the Gate*, p.2. See also Noel and Charles Buxton, *The War and the Balkans*, p.46; Forbes, 'Serbia', p.120.

[120] G.Trevelyan, 'Serbia's Fight for Freedom', *Nash's & Pall Mall Magazine*, June 1915, 392.

[121] W.F.Bailey, *The Slavs of the War Zone*, (London, 1916), pp.252-3. This work is, in general, a typically romanticised wartime account of the South Slavs, and the Serbs in particular.

[122] Price, *Light on the Balkan Darkness*, pp.11-12.

[123] Even though the Yugoslav idea appealed to some Serbian intellectuals during the war, it remained for older politicians a disposable addition to the Great Serbian agenda. As Charles Jelavich points out, nearly all Serbs in responsible positions in the post-war state had been educated before 1912 and 'been indoctrinated in the tradition of Serbianism and not Yugoslavism' ('From Serbianism to Yugoslavism', p.121). See also J.Udovički, 'Nationalism, Ethnic Conflict and Self-Determination in the Former Yugoslavia' in B.Berberoglu (ed.), *The National Question: Nationalism, Ethnic Conflict, and Self-Determination in the 20th Century* (Philadelphia, 1995), p.283. On the lack of a clear idea of what Great Serbia represented, spatially, and the shifting phases of preoccupation, see Allcock, *Explaining Yugoslavia*, pp.343-6. In suggesting that the idea of Great Serbia was wholly abstract and divorced from specific territorial associations, he seems to overstate this point.

[124] Marriott, *Eastern Question*, pp.313-14.

[125] Todorova pp.118-19; Pribram, *Austria-Hungary and Great Britain*, p.220.

[126] Bridge, *Great Britain and Austria-Hungary*, p.214.

[127] Grey to Sir Maurice de Bunsen (British ambassador at Vienna), 27 July 1914, printed in *War 1914: Punishing the Serbs* (London, 1915; 1999), pp.80-4. British public opinion, Grey had written to Sir George Buchanan two days previously, would not sanction going to war 'over a Serbian quarrel' (ibid, pp.53-4).

[128] Hanak, *Great Britain and Austria-Hungary*, pp.150-1.

[129] Wilkinson, *Question of Servia*, p.12.

[130] Low, 'The Kingdom of Serbia', 314.

[131] Chirol, *Serbia and the Serbs*, p.18.

[132] Bailey, *Slavs of the War Zone*, p.252. Already by October 1914 G.K.Chesterton remarked that anyone reading the papers would become 'bored with the cant about Serbia' (quoted in W.M.Klimon, 'Chesterton, "Kossovo of the Serbians", and the Vocation of the Christian Nation', *The Chesterton Review* (Feb1994), 42).

[133] Dickinson Berry, *Austria-Hungary*, p.47.

[134] Seton-Watson, 'Serbia's Need and Britain's Danger', *Contemporary Review*, Nov 1915, 576-9. See also his 'The Pan-German Plan and its Antidote', *Contemporary Review*, (April 1916), 422-8. A cartoon in Harper's Weekly illustrated the clearing of Serbia's responsibility for the war: T.D.Hadjich (ed.), *The World's War Cartoons: The Balkans in Caricature* (London, 1916), p.44. For a similar French argument that any negative view of the Serbs had been cynical misinformation on the part of Vienna, see P.de Lanux, *La Yougoslavie: la France et les Serbes* (Paris, 1916), p.234. For a French work drawing the same parallel between Serbia's supposed historic role as 'rampart of Christianity against the Turks' and her wartime obstruction of Germany's drive east, see Paul Labbé, *L'Effort Serbe* (Paris, 1916), p.4.

[135] A. and C.Askew, 'Kossovo Day Heroes', in *The Lay of Kossovo* (London, 1917), pp.29-31; Chirol, *Serbia and the Serbs*, p.3.

[136] E.Christitch, 'Letters from Serbia', *Contemporary Review*, Jan 1915, 85.

[137] de Windt, *Through Savage Europe*, p.143; Balkan Review, 'Editor's Causerie', Aug 1920, 8. Amnesia quickly set in. The present war had proved, Noel and Charles Buxton wrote, '*more strikingly than ever* the brilliant military quality of the Serbs' (*The War and the Balkans*, pp.45-6, my emphasis).

[138] Laffan, *Guardians of the Gate*, pp.260.

[139] M.A.St.Clair Stobart, 'With the Serbian Army in Retreat', *Contemporary Review*, April 1916, 437.

[140] Mügge, *Serbian Folk Songs, Fairy Tales and Proverbs*, p.6; Seton-Watsons, *Making of a New Europe*, pp.178, 189, 311. But see Norman Stone on the Austrian army's inadequacy in 1914 (*The Eastern Front* (London, 1975), pp.71-2). Hew Strachan notes the genuine improvement of the Serbian army during the early 20th century (*The First World War: A Call to Arms* (Oxford, 2001), p.341). For accounts of Austria's failed assault, see ibid, pp.335-47, and C.E.J.Fryer, *The Destruction of Serbia in 1915* (Boulder; New York, 1997). A graphic first-hand account of Serbia's wartime sufferings, from typhus above all, is in J.Reed, *The War in Eastern Europe* (London, 1916), pp.29-108.

[141] T.A.Emmert, 'Kosovo: Development and Impact of a National Ethic', in I.Banac et al (eds), *Nation and Ideology: Essays in Honor of Wayne S.Vucinich* (Boulder, 1981), pp.77-8. Emmert gives examples of similar American enthusiasm, as does

Stevan Pavlowitch for France (*Serbia: History Behind the Name*, p.98). On the pronounced enthusiasm in France for Serbia before and (particularly) during the war, see M.Pavlović (ed.), *Temoignages Français sur les Serbes et la Serbie 1912-1918* (Belgrade, 1988), pp.22-32.

[142] Gordon-Smith, *Through the Serbian Campaign*, p.1.

[143] Laffan, *Guardians of the Gate*, p.15. The near-universal acclaim in the British media may be contrasted with the strongly hostile opinion of a British military representative with the retreating Serbian army (FO 371/2603/263), though in general the Foreign Office did consider the Serbs had fought a 'heroic campaign' (Oliphant, 371/1901/83097). For a recent account of the Serbian defeat see Fryer, *Destruction of Serbia*.

[144] St.Clair Stobart, *The Flaming Sword*, pp.203, 309-10. The enthusiasm of these accounts cannot simply be explained with reference to the bond between 'brothers-in-arms'. It is significant that the account of a medical relief worker who served in Serbia forty years previously evinces none of the same romantic attachment. 'We could not admit', wrote Emma Pearson and Louisa McLaughlin, 'that the nation was far on the path of progress [...]. The people were no better than those of other lands' (*Service in Servia under the Red Cross* (London, 1877), pp.347-8).

[145] C.and A.Askew, *The Stricken Land*, p.358.

[146] Quoted in T.Judah, *Kosovo: War and Revenge* (New Haven; London, 2000), pp.xvi-xvii.

[147] Schlesinger, *Federalism in Eastern and Central Europe*, p.16.

[148] Fine, *Early Medieval Balkans*, pp.284-8. Croats sometimes considered the 1102 union analagous to the 1867 'Ausgleich'. In some respects, as historians have observed, this claim to state continuity was no less mythic than Serbian Kosovo traditions. It was anachronistic to assume the *judicial* Croatian identity represented in the feudal nobility's claim to customary rights *vis-à-vis* the Hungarian crown equated to the modern ethno-linguistic idea of a Croat. Nobles of the 15th or 16th centuries claiming the traditional rights of a Croatian aristocracy may, ethnically, have been German or Hungarian (see Allcock, *Explaining Yugoslavia*, pp.317-23).

[149] On relative French ignorance of the Croats as opposed to the Serbs, see Kovač, *La France, la creation du royaume 'yougoslave' et la question croate*, pp.110-12, which notes Frano Supilo's amazement at the widespread assumption that Dalmatia was Italian.

[150] Seton-Watson, *Southern Slav Question*, p.342. A.J.May has remarked of Seton-Watson before the war that he had 'a decided preference for the westernized Croats under the Magyar yoke rather than for the Serbs' ('R.W. Seton-Watson and British Anti-Hapsburg Sentiment', *American Slavic and East European Review*, Vol.XX, no.1 (1961), 46).

[151] Temperley, *History of Serbia*, p.3.

[152] See below ch.8.

[153] Lloyd George, *Memoirs of the Peace Conference* (New Haven, 1939), ii, 514; quoted in M.Almond, *Europe's Backyard War: The War in the Balkans* (London, 1994), p.72. See also W.F.Lofthouse, 'Serbia: A Study in Nationality', *The Holborn Review*, April 1920, 148. On the pro-Hungarian strain in Britain, even during the war, see Hanak, *Britain and Austria-Hungary*, pp.2-4, 161-3; Bridge, *Great Britain and Austria-Hungary*,

pp.36-7. Seton-Watson had himself been firmly Magyarophile. As his sons note, 'the name of Kossuth, and the version of events of 1848 generally accepted in Britain, caused the name of Hungary to be especially dear to British persons of liberal outlook', *Correspondence*, i, 13.

[154] Hanak, *Britain and Austria-Hungary*, pp.195-7 gives examples.

[155] On Dalmatia's separate administrative history since the early 13th century (continuously since the mid-15th), and also on the spatial inconstancy of regional labels like 'Croatia' and 'Slavonia', see P.R.Magosci, *Historical Atlas of East Central Europe* (Seattle; London, 1993), p.17 and *passim*.

[156] *Correspondence*, i, 180-6 (letter to Foreign Office, 1 Oct 1914).

[157] Toynbee, *Nationality and the War*, pp.213-15.

[158] See extract in Seton-Watsons, *Making of a New Europe*, pp.131-2.

[159] Josip Frank was a lawyer who adapted Starčević's programme to suit his allegiance to the Habsburg dynasty, campaigning for a Croat unit within the imperial framework. He died in 1911. (See Banac, *National Question*, pp.94-5).

[160] Okey, 'British Impressions', p.66. What Okey terms the 'Britishness of coverage' entailed in general a greater empathy with 'moderation' than with 'extremism' (*ibid*, p.75).

[161] FO 371/825/904.

[162] FO 371/1047/44966 (Grant Duff, Budapest, 7 Nov 1911). All other parties, and public opinion, Max Müller observed, accepted the Croat-Hungarian 'Ausgleich' of 1868 (FO 371/1576/57517 (Budapest, 8 Dec 1913)). A similar emphasis on the Party of Right as 'the extreme Left' and as 'noisy and troublesome agitators' had been made by Sir Arthur Nicolson in his late 19th century reports which were among very few to deal at any length with the Croatian situation (Okey, 'British Impressions', pp.69-70).

[163] *Correspondence*, i, 50-4 (17 Oct 1909).

[164] FO 371/827/10301 (Budapest, 19 March 1910).

[165] FO 371/599/7133 (Budapest, 8 Feb 1909). The Pure Right Party's hatred of Serbs, he noted elsewhere, was 'less a matter of nationality than religion' (FO 371/827/10301). In fact, as Banac points out, Croat ideologists had generally resisted the equation of Catholicism and Croatdom, often claiming Bosnian Muslims and the Orthodox of Croatia and Bosnia as Croats (*National Question*, p.108).

[166] Seton-Watson, *Slav, German, Magyar*, p.92.

[167] Seton-Watson, *Southern Slav Question*, p.339.

[168] For further discussion of British attitudes to these Croatian groups, see below pp.189-90.

[169] While Croatia-Slavonia possessed a degree of autonomy under Hungary, Vojvodina was ruled directly by Budapest; meanwhile Dalmatia and the part-Slovene provinces of Carniola, Styria and Carinthia were under different forms of Austrian administration, while Bosnia-Hercegovina was from 1878 ruled as an 'independent' crown land.

[170] M.Gross, 'Social Structure and National Movements Among the Yugoslav Peoples on the Eve of the First World War', *Slavic Review*, Dec 1977, 628-9; Allcock, *Explaining Yugoslavia*, pp.27-8. Not before the rise of Radić in the early

1920s, Ivo Banac has noted, did the majority of Croats feel unified under a common national leadership (*National Question*, pp.236-7).

[171] Brashich, *Land Reform and Ownership in Yugoslavia*, p.17; Allcock, *Explaining Yugoslavia*, p.331; Djordjević, 'Idea of Yugoslav Unity', pp.4-5.

[172] Seton-Watsons, *Making of a New Europe*, p.33; Djordjević, 'Idea of Yugoslav Unity', p.10.

[173] Allcock, *Explaining Yugoslavia*, pp.280, 326, 332.

[174] Seton-Watson, *Spirit of the Serb*, p.17.

[175] Newbigin, *Geographical Aspects*, p.62.

[176] Forbes, *Southern Slavs*, p.30; Temperley, *History of Serbia*, p.4. As we have seen British writers commonly regarded southern Dalmatia as natural 'Serb' territory.

[177] Toynbee, *Nationality and the War*, p.173.

[178] FO 371/2711/57457 (Count de Salis report on Montenegro for 1915).

[179] Allcock, *Explaining Yugoslavia*, pp.254, 279.

[180] In a pamphlet entitled *The Balkans, Italy and the Adriatic* (London, 1915), Seton-Watson claimed Dubrovnik had been 'a centre of Slavonic culture and aspirations for many centuries' (p.35), a claim rejected by de Salis ('whatever the future may give the Slavs, the past was not theirs', FO 371/2711/57457).

[181] FO 371/2862/210519 (19 Nov 1917).

[182] Miller, *Travel and Politics*, pp.510-11.

[183] Bosnian Serbs, under Habsburg rule only since 1878, are not considered here. Roughly a third of Serbs lived outside the borders of 1913 Serbia (Allcock, *Explaining Yugoslavia*, p.220).

[184] Taylor, *Future of the Southern Slavs*, p.59.

[185] Temperley, *History of Serbia*, p.122; Lederer, 'Nationalism and the Yugoslavs', p.408.

[186] Young, *Nationalism and War in the Near East*, pp.17-18.

[187] Laffan, *Guardians of the Gate*, pp.23-4.

[188] Temperley, *History of Serbia*, pp.170-1.

[189] FO 371/1472/34881; Lederer, 'Nationalism and the Yugoslavs', p.407.

[190] Pavlowitch, *History behind the Name*, pp.113-14.

[191] Djordjević, 'Idea of Yugoslav Unity', p.11; Banac, *National Question*, p.65.

[192] Allcock, *Explaining Yugoslavia*, p.332. In general the voting patterns in 1920 support this assertion, though not all prečani Serbs preferred the Democrats. In Vojvodina – whose Serb population outnumbered their Croat neighbours, felt less isolated from Serbia, and wished to preserve their regional identity and economic advantages – the Radicals prevailed (Banac, *National Question*, p.389 table 5.2). 'In order to assert itself', Banac remarks, 'the periphery often argues for an identity that is more integrated than the identity of a metropolis' (ibid., p.59).

[193] Seton-Watson, *Southern Slav Question*, p.2.

[194] Vošnjak, *Bulwark*, p.44.

[195] Zholger, 'Concerning the Slovenes', pp.442, 445-6.

[196] Vošnjak, *Bulwark*, p.258; what this meant, if not that the Slovenes *were* imbued with the German influences these writers argued had for centuries been resisted, is difficult to say.

[197] A leading US official also argued in 1917 that Slovene bonds with Austria were too old to disrupt (Mamatey, *United States and East Central Europe*, pp.91-2). Toynbee's judgement is striking given that Carniola was the only Slovene majority province. As often in East-Central Europe, the Carniolan Germans dominated economic life. Namier noted that though only 5% of the population, German capitalists owned a quarter of the land, all the mines and most of the industry: FO 371/3135/116831 (24 June 1918).

[198] Indeed, they were ignored in Serbian teaching of South Slav history as they were in Britain: Jelavich, 'From Serbianism to Yugoslavism', p.120.

[199] Toynbee, *Nationality and the War*, pp.248-58.

[200] Taylor, *Future of the Southern Slavs*, pp.249-50.

[201] Laffan, 'Liberation of the New Nationalities', p.188.

[202] FO 371/3135/116831; FO 371/3133/48743; FO 371/3508/59385.

[203] FO 371/3508/59385 (C.Oman, 15 Oct 1918). Given that Slovenes boasted the highest literacy rates of any Yugoslav group, this view seems rather unfair.

[204] J.Velikonja, 'The Quest for Slovene National Identity', pp.251-5, in D.Hooson (ed.), *Geography and National Identity* (Oxford, 1994). We have noted before the dialectal variation which reflected this regionalism. Slovene emigrants usually identified themselves by region ('Carniolan', 'Carinthian' etc) rather than as Slovenes.

[205] Allcock, *Explaining Yugoslavia*, pp.347-8. Strangely, Toynbee regarded the unity of Slovenia as 'primarily geographical rather than racial' (*Nationality and the War*, pp.257-8).

[206] Allcock, *Explaining Yugoslavia*, pp.278-9.

[207] Vošnjak, *Bulwark*, p.71.

[208] L.Valiani, *The End of Austria-Hungary* (London, 1973), p.41. Only in 1911 did the revived Croatian Party of Right agree to cooperate with the Slovene Catholic Popular Party. The HSK consistently refused during the war to depart from the dualist framework which entailed loyalty to Budapest and a refusal to cooperate with Austrian Slovenes (see J.Pleterski, 'The Southern Slav Question', in M.Cornwall (ed.), *The Last Years of Austria-Hungary: A Multi-national Experiment in Early Twentieth-Century Europe*, 2nd edn (Exeter, 2002), pp.141-5).

[209] Seton-Watsons, *Making of a New Europe*, p.139.

[210] Toynbee, *Nationality and the War*, p.213. And Montenegrins anyway shared in the lustre of Serb medieval history.

[211] de Windt, *Through Savage Europe*, p.24.

[212] Forbes, *Southern Slavs*, p.6.

[213] E.M.Tappan (ed.), *The World's Story: A History of the World in Story, Song and Art* (Boston, 1914), vol. VI: *Russia, Austria-Hungary, The Balkan States, and Turkey*, p.420.

[214] *Encyclopaedia Britannica*, 'Montenegro: Population and Government'.

[215] de Windt, *Through Savage Europe*, pp.28-9.

[216] Gordon, *Woman in the Balkans*, pp.284-6. Nicholas enjoyed some familiarity in Britain for that success in forging dynastic links through his children which saw him nicknamed 'father-in-law of Europe'.

[217] Laffan, *Guardians of the Gate*, p.46.

[218] *Encyclopaedia Britannica*, 'Montenegro: History'; 'Montenegro: Population and Government'.

[219] See ch.6 below.

[220] Allcock, *Explaining Yugoslavia*, pp.388, 390.

[221] Laffan, *Guardians of the Gate*, p.25.

[222] Temperley, *History of Serbia*, p.105.

[223] *New Statesman*, 12 April 1913: the journal's first issue, here voicing majority opinion rather than its own.

[224] FO 371/2409/313. 'As late as the Congress of Paris in 1856', he added, 'the Turkish representative asserted without contradiction that the Porte regarded Montenegro as part of the Ottoman Empire'. In the early 18th century Montenegrins had rid themselves of Ottoman overlordship under their prelates (who governed only a small district around Cetinje), but as recently as 1852-3 and 1861 Ottoman armies had compelled subordination to Constantinople. Not until the 1878 Congress of Berlin was independence formally recognised by the European Powers: Banac, *National Question*, p.44; Magosci, *Historical Atlas*, p.84.

[225] For centuries St.Petersburg had kept it solvent; while British Near-Eastern policy was governed by hostility towards Russia, Montenegro was denigrated as a minor outpost of Tsardom.

[226] Suspicion that Nicholas sought an understanding with Austria to protect his regime from Serbian domination surfaced sporadically in the West. *The Times*, on 6 February 1912, suggested he had cast in his lot with Vienna. Whitehall understood secret talks had stuck over access to the fortress of Lovćen (FO 371/2711/57457).

[227] FO 371/1748/28340 (Paget report on Serbia for 1912, 6 June 1913).

[228] Austria's occupation of the Sanjak (technically still Ottoman) represented a serious barrier to amalgamation.

[229] FO 371/2041/24154 (2 Feb 1914). Ultimate union was often forecast in terms of Nicholas' life-expectancy, his issue considered incompetent to succeed. For more on Montenegro, see below ch.6.

[230] For the early history of the region, see Malcolm, *Bosnia*, chs.1 and 2.

[231] Between 1463 and 1580 the 'sandžak' of Bosnia had formed part of the larger *eyalet* of Rumelia, which covered most of the Balkans (Malcolm, *Bosnia*, p.50).

[232] Forbes, *Southern Slavs*, p.24. Seton-Watson later noted strong traditions of local autonomy among the Bosnian begs: *The Role of Bosnia in International Politics (1875-1914)* (London, 1932), p.7.

[233] Forbes, 'Serbia', p.135. During the war Austria was accused both of inventing Bosnian identity and of fomenting division among Bosnia's confessions. The extent of Bosnian consciousness before the rise of Serbian and Croatian nationalisms is unresolved. Some historians (Robert Donia and Noel Malcolm, for example) have attempted to demonstrate such a consciousness; but see Allcock, *Explaining Yugoslavia*, p.323 for a more sceptical view.

[234] Taylor, *Future of the Southern Slavs*, p.87. There was, as Malcolm notes, a strand in pre-war Bosnian Muslim culture inclined to be pro-Serb. But its rapid disappearance in the Yugoslav state suggests that it was no more than a superficial political alliance. In practical terms, he concludes, they were already a separate community: *Bosnia*, pp.163-6.

[235] Taylor, *Future of the Southern Slavs*, p.89. To Serbs, it was noted (with apparent sympathy), this claim seemed 'an unprovoked attack upon their legitimate aspirations'.

[236] Seton-Watson, *The Spirit of the Serb*, p.17.

[237] FO 371/3508/59385 (Oman, 15 Oct 1918). Emphasis added. (This was despite noting Dušan's failure to terminate medieval Bosnian independence).

[238] See above pp.69-72. For historical treatments of Habsburg economic policies in Bosnia, broadly positive about their motivation and outcome, see P.F.Sugar, *Industrialization in Bosnia-Hercegovina* (Seattle, 1963), and M.Palairet, *The Balkan Economies c.1800-1914: Evolution without Development* (Cambridge, 1997), pp.203-42. As Sugar shows, the failure to create infrastructural links with other South Slav territories resulted more from rivalry between Budapest and Vienna than from a unified policy of 'divide and rule' in the Monarchy's South Slav lands (p.219).

[239] A.J.Evans, *Through Bosnia and the Herzegovina on Foot during the Insurrection, August and September, 1875* (London, 1876), p.139. 'Old Serbia' here refers to Kosovo and the Sanjak while 'the free Principality' was Serbia, technically under Ottoman suzerainty until 1878.

[240] Miller, *Travel and Politics*, pp.91, 118-19.

[241] FO 371/1296/9024 (Freeman, Sarajevo, 26 Feb 1912).

[242] Bailey, *Slavs of the War Zone*, pp.9-10.

[243] Vošnjak, *Bulwark*, p.216.

[244] See above p.27.

[245] *Correspondence*, i, 277.

[246] 'In truth', Banac notes, 'there was no unitary Yugoslav culture', only a brief 'trend in the Croat artistic colony', 'a hopeless quest', largely limited to Meštrović's evocation of Serbian myths (*National Question*, pp.203-7). With hindsight Meštrović himself admitted that he had much overestimated the psychological readiness for Yugoslav union ('The Yugoslav Committee in London and the Declaration of Corfu', in A.F.Bonifačić and C.S.Mihanovich (eds.), *The Croatian Nation* (Chicago, 1955), pp.173-4).

[247] FO 371/3135/116831.

[248] FO 371/3508/59886 (Memo on Croatian politics, 31 March 1919).

[249] *Travel and Politics*, p.377.

[250] Laffan, *Guardians of the Gate*, p.64. Some who served in Macedonia were struck by the syncretism of beliefs and customs. See, for example, Walshe, *With the Serbs*, pp.186-7.

[251] Banac, *National Question*, pp.308-9. See the map showing the extent of medieval Serb and Bulgarian states in the 14th and 15th centuries in Magosci, *Atlas*, p.29.

[252] Seton-Watsons, *Making of a New Europe*, p.132-3. The Minister was Matija Bošković.

[253] Lederer, *Yugoslavia at the Paris Peace Conference*, p.248.

[254] FO 371/1748/28340 (report for 1912).

[255] FO 371/1748/53104 (Dayrell Crackanthorpe, 18 Nov 1913; Vansittart, 25 Nov; Crowe, 25 Nov).

[256] FO 371/2099/4614 (28 Jan 1914).

[257] FO 371/1748/57490 (Skopje, 14 Dec 1913).

[258] FO 371/1748/53800 (Charles Greig, Monastir, 14 Nov 1913). See also his letter in FO 371/2098/4617, dated 19 Jan 1914, for detailed charges against the Serbian administration of systematic persecution of the Muslims, destruction of minarets, seizure of local revenues and so on. For the Carnegie Commission's conclusion that a systematic policy of murder and expulsion had been applied by the Serbs in Kosovo, see Malcolm, *Kosovo*, pp.253-6. For a report of Montenegrin brutality towards Albanians in Kosovo, one of very few such to appear in the British media, see Durham's letter to *The Nation* (no 17), 26 July 1913.

[259] FO 371/2099/16241 (4 April 1914). Metohia referred to the western half of the district now known as Kosovo (which referred originally just to the eastern half). See Malcolm, *Kosovo*, pp.3-4.

[260] FO 371/1748/55169 (16 Nov 1913).

[261] FO 371/1748/57490; 55163; 56441 (Vansittart, 23 Dec 1913; 10 Dec 1913; 16 Dec 1913).

[262] FO 371/2098/20793 (11 May 1914); Paget recalled an alleged massacre in August 1912 in which, initial reports claimed, 3,000 Serbs had been killed by the Turks: 'on closer enquiry this number fell to 300, then to 30, finally to only 1 individual' (FO 371/1748/28340, 6 June 1913).

[263] FO 371/1748/57489; 53800 (24 Dec 1913; 30 Nov 1913).

[264] FO 371/2099/4614 (4 Feb 1914).

[265] FO 371/1748/55482; 55169 (10 Dec 1913; 9 Dec 1913); Greig's 'sense of proportion', Lancelot Oliphant concurred, was 'very faulty': FO 371/2098/66980 (4 Nov 1914).

[266] FO 371/2099/16239 (Crowe, 16 Apr 1914). Even Crowe suggested laying reports before Parliament at one stage but Grey rejected the idea (FO 371/1748/56441). Representations were made to Belgrade, but with little expectation.

[267] FO 371/2098/2438 (14 Jan 1914).

[268] FO 371/2098/11574; 25498 (18 March 1914; 11 June 1914). Arthur Nicolson noted his agreement.

[269] Šepić, 'The Question of Yugoslav Union in 1918', p.35.

[270] J.Headlam Morley, *A Memoir of the Paris Peace Conference 1919* (A.Headlam Morley et al (eds.); London, 1972), p.136. In fact officials did later assume the treaty applied in Macedonia, but they did not wish to foster unrest by enforcing it; on the contrary, forced Serbianisation was assumed, in the long run, to be the best solution to the region's instability: see P.B.Finney, '"An Evil for All Concerned": Great Britain and Minority Protection after 1919', *Journal of Contemporary History*, 30, 3 (July 1995), 535-40.

[271] Quoted in Banac, *National Question*, p.185.

272 Lederer, 'Nationalism and the Yugoslavs', p.401.

273 FO 371/826/29123 (Freeman, 6 Aug 1910). A little later Fairfax Cartwright, British ambassador in Vienna, predicted similar jealousies would re-emerge in the Croatian Diet. And whatever the brotherly feelings of race, he insisted, there was 'no doubt of the strong ties of loyalty and veneration which bind all parties and races to the person of their august Sovereign' (FO 371/1046/855 (annual report for 1910)).

274 FO 371/827/13171 (Howard, 13 Apr 1910; Orde, 19 Apr 1910).

275 FO 371/1297/13711 (Vice-consulate report, 29 Dec 1911; Clerk minute (undated)). This view is supported by modern accounts emphasising the 'multi-centred' nature of the pre-war Yugoslav movement: Pleterski, 'Southern Slav Question', p.133.

276 FO 371/1472/17911 (Paget, 24 Apr 1912; Nicolson, undated c.29 Apr).

277 FO 371/1576/57517 (Oliphant, 22 Dec 1913).

278 *Correspondence*, i, 183.

279 FO 371/2041/14874 (general report on Montenegro for 1913, 10 March 1914).

280 FO 371/1575/7514 (Annual report for 1912).

281 FO 371/3135/116831 (June 1918). See numerous similar examples in previous chapters.

282 Reported by Lord Derby in FO 371/3137/183200 (3 Nov 1918).

283 W.E.D.Allen, *The Turks in Europe*, pp.214-15.

284 Toynbee, *Nationality and the War*, p.220. In three years between Kumanovo and the fall of Serbia, the American Balkanist Robert Kerner commented in 1918, 'religious differences, political rivalries, linguistic quibbles and the petty foibles of centuries appeared to be forgotten [...]. The Yugo-Slav movement had ended in the formation of a nation which is neither a doctrine, nor a dream but a reality' (R.J.Kerner, *The Jugo-Slav Movement* (Cambridge, Mass., 1918), pp.81-95.

285 G.MacAdam, 'Jugo-Slavia: The New Great State of the Balkans', *World's Work*, Dec 1918, 325-30.

286 Supilo quoted in Stokes, 'The Role of the Yugoslav Committee', p.57.

287 Temperley, *History of Serbia*, p.3.

288 FO 371/3507/16797 (25 Jan 1919).

289 *Correspondence*, 'Introduction', i, 36. Of his wartime writing this is dubious. His manifesto for the Yugoslav Committee proclaimed the Yugoslavs 'a single nation, alike by identity of language, by the unanswerable laws of geography and by national consciousness'. But he did, particularly before the war and near its end, emphasise cultural differences, and express the hope that union would prove a symbiotic 'diversitas in diversitatae', as in the case of the Scottish and the English since 1707. It seems testimony to his optimism, as well as his heritage, that he chose Scotland as an analogy rather than the less auspicious, but more compelling, Irish case.

290 M.B.Petrovich, 'Russia's Role in the Creation of the Yugoslav State, 1914-1918', in Djordjević (ed.), *Creation of Yugoslavia*, p.73; M.Gross, 'Croatian National-Integrational Ideologies from the End of Illyrism to the Creation of Yugoslavia', *Austrian History Yearbook*, XV-XVI (1979-80), 4-5 and passim.

[291] 'Idea of Yugoslav Unity', p.4.

[292] Lederer, 'Nationalism and the Yugoslavs', p.398. The argument of Ivo Banac's *National Question* also denies that Yugoslavia had in 1918 any sound basis in popular feeling. See also Šepić, 'The Question of Yugoslav Union in 1918', p.33. Valiani (*The End of Austria-Hungary*, p.311 note 15) cites the experience of Baron von Musulin who, on returning to his native Croatia in 1913, found Croat intellectuals had become pro-Serbian while the mass of the peasantry remained firmly loyal to the Empire.

[293] 'Experience of Yugoslav Agitation', pp.669-70. See also Kovač, *La France*, p.108.

[294] FO 371/3136/98080 (report on situation in Austria-Hungary no 3, Aug 1918).

[295] On the unlikely claims of widespread hostility to the Monarchy made by Slav exiles, see R.J.W.Evans, 'The Habsburg Monarchy and the Coming of War', in R.J.W.Evans and H.P.von Strandmann (eds.), *The Coming of the First World War* (Oxford, 1988), pp.43-53. As Kosta St.Pavlowitch notes, far from the Yugoslav insurrection feared by Vienna, the initial period of the war was characterised by smooth mobilisation and political stability: 'The First World War and the Unification of Yugoslavia', in Djokić (ed.), *Yugoslavism*, pp.29-30.

[296] Allcock, *Explaining Yugoslavia*, pp.211, 229. Italian publicists, by contrast, urged repeatedly that Yugoslavism was narrowly confined to the intelligentsia and middle-class (often, of course, for self-interested reasons): Lederer, *Yugoslavia at the Paris Peace Conference*, p.72.

Introduction to Part II

[1] Steiner, *Foreign Office*, p.212.

[2] Goldstein, *Winning the Peace*, p.10.

[3] Steiner, *Foreign Office*, p.211.

[4] Quoted in Goldstein, *Winning the Peace*, p.65. The increasing role played during the war and after by experts from outside the government service is considered in Dimitri Kitsikis, *Le Rôle des experts à la Conference de la Paix de 1919* (Otttawa, 1972).

[5] Seton-Watsons, *Making of a New Europe*, p.105.

[6] Harold Nicolson, for one, recalled that he 'never moved a yard' in Paris without consulting 'experts of the authority of Dr Seton-Watson' (*Peacemaking*, pp.125-6).

[7] Robert Evans, *Great Britain and Central Europe, 1908-1948: A Study in Perceptions* (London, 2002), p.6.

[8] 'Caviar to the general' was the borrowed maxim he applied to the last issue of his journal *New Europe* in October 1921 (Seton-Watsons, *Making of a New Europe*, p.410). It is of course true, as Dimitri Kitsikis points out, that the final decision on all questions that mattered remained with the Council of Four (*Le Rôle des Experts*, p.209). But this does not dispute the real influence which such experts exerted on British – and French and American – attitudes and policies.

[9] Temperley himself noted in his diary that 'the basis of the whole British Peace Conference appears to have been the papers – prepared under my supervision – in MI2E which supplied the groundwork of solid information to reach our delegates', a verdict with which his biographer does not take issue (Fair, *Harold Temperley*, pp.125-32).

[10] MI2(e) had close links with the Foreign Office's PID – a fact not surprising, as Erik Goldstein points out, given the number of Oxford and Cambridge historians employed in these departments (*Winning the Peace*, p.53). Laffan went on to collaborate with Temperley on the official history of the conference, and to become the Foreign Office Research Department's historical expert on the Balkan region.

[11] Steed's close relationship with Lord Northcliffe, in particular, allowed him access to Lloyd George and his immediate entourage. When Northcliffe was made director of propaganda, A.J.A. Morris notes, 'it was Steed who defined the policy followed' (*DNB* entry on Steed).

[12] E.H. Carr, *From Napoleon to Stalin and Other Essays* (London, 1980), p.166.

[13] Goldstein, *Winning the Peace*, p.86.

[14] Evans, *Great Britain and Central Europe*, p.8. Some of those within the Foreign Office who were closest to these newer elements – men like Sir Eyre Crowe and Sir James Headlam-Morley – were, as Evans points out, often outsiders themselves. Nine of the ten founder members of PID had Oxford connections, but this belied their varied backgrounds. See Alan Sharp, 'Some Relevant Historians – the Political Intelligence Department of the Foreign Office, 1918-1920', *The Australian Journal of Politics and History*, Vol 34 (1989), 360-1.

[15] Sharp, 'Some Relevant Historians', 363.

[16] Goldstein, *Winning the Peace*, p.4; Maisel, *The Foreign Office and Foreign Policy*, p.2. The decline of Foreign Office influence under Lloyd George is well treated in Warman, *The Foreign Office 1916-1918*, which discusses the exclusion of the Foreign Secretary from membership of the War Cabinet, the increasing influence of both Cabinet and Prime Ministerial Secretariats, and Lloyd George's 'lack of respect for traditional institutions [...] and [...] preference for private rather than official advice' (p.23; pp.5-42). Warman stresses, however, the significant victory over Lord Beaverbrook's rival Ministry of Information represented by the effective transfer of the Intelligence Bureau to the Foreign Office as the 'new' PID (*ibid.*, pp.58-65). Individuals like Seton-Watson and Wickham Steed were, in any case, never confined to exerting their influence through Foreign Office channels, but were able to make contact directly with the Prime Minister and his closest personal adviser, Philip Kerr. (In general, indeed, the division of the PID between Paris and London meant that its influence was often exercised 'through the activities of its individual members rather than as a corporate whole' (M.Dockrill and Z.Steiner, 'The Foreign Office at the Paris Peace Conference in 1919', *International History Review*, 2, vol.1 (Jan 1980), 55-96)).

Chapter Six

[1] FO 371/3580/124889 (21 Aug 1919). The others were Serbians, one an official who had been coordinating Serbian propaganda in Montenegro. De Salis had been sent in mid-1919 to investigate the situation on behalf of the British Government.

[2] Reports of Major Furlong, cited by de Salis.

[3] Of the 168 (subsequently 176) elected, only nineteen had sat in the old Skupština. More than half the members of the previous (technically undissolved) skupština were abroad and unable to participate.

[4] Proceedings were irregular. One witness, considered impartial by de Salis, reported: 'There was no voting; the resolutions were declared to be carried by unanimity. Anyone who attempted to object was howled down [...]. All this was under the shadow of the bayonet'.

[5] Quoted in Petrovich, *History of Modern Serbia*, ii, 682.

[6] FO 371/3579/204823 (on behalf of the Foreign Secretary, 26 June 1919).

[7] H.Nicolson, *Peacemaking* (London, 1934), pp.148-9.

[8] FO 371/3149/77441 (Leeper, 4 May 1918).

[9] FO 371/3582/208009 (H.Nicolson, 30 June 1920).

[10] FO 371/3581/142846 (16 Oct 1919).

[11] FO 371/2099/11576 (Crackanthorpe, annual report on Serbia for 1913).

[12] FO 371/2041/10053 (Akers-Douglas, Cetinje, 6 Feb 1914). *Figaro* on 1 July 1914 claimed full union was to have been announced on 28 June before events in Sarajevo, but de Salis was sceptical (FO 371/2409/313).

[13] *Correspondence*, i, 174 (22 July 1914). See H.Heilbronner, 'The Merger Attempts of Serbia and Montenegro, 1913-1914', *Journal of Central European Affairs*, XVIII (July 1958), 111-33, and M.Cornwall, 'Between Two Wars: King Nikola of Montenegro and the Great Powers, August 1913-August 1914', *The South Slav Journal*, 9, 1-2 (1986), 60-71. For a general survey of pre-war Montenegrin relations with Austria see J.D.Treadway, *The Falcon and the Eagle: Montenegro and Austria-Hungary, 1908-1914* (West Lafayette, Indiana, 1983).

[14] FO 371/2409/313 (annual report for 1914).

[15] In simple numerical terms – of soldiers and armaments – Montenegro was of course 'of little value' to her Serbian ally (D.Stevenson, *1914-1918: The History of the First World War* (London, 2004), p.72).

[16] FO 371/2711/57457 (de Salis report for 1915).

[17] FO 371/2254/57113 (8 May 1915).

[18] Britain did deliver food aid in October 1914, planned to transport Montenegrin reservists from Canada and the US, and sponsored relief work by British organisations. In March 1915 a loan of up to £10 million was agreed by Britain, France and Russia, but dropped two months later, with no sign of intent on the Austrian front, and in the light of flagrant Montenegrin provocation in Albania.

[19] FO 371/2262/108054 (de Salis to Grey, 18 July 1915).

[20] FO 371/2262/86999 (Grey to des Graz, 28 June 1915). Grey denounced an action 'not merely rash, but essentially stupid'. It would be difficult, Radović was told, for Britain to have any further confidence in his government's assurances.

[21] FO 371/2262/112939 (de Salis to Grey, 14 Aug 1915), reporting the view of the Serbian Acting Chief of Staff with which he evidently sympathised.

[22] While Whitehall was totally disillusioned with the Montenegrin Government, continued support in the media was accompanied by the claim that Italy had failed to counter the Austrian fleet: see Sir Arthur Evans' letter, cited in Woodhouse and Woodhouse, *Italy and the Jugoslavs*, pp.96-7. French reports of Montenegrin capitulation may well have been deliberately overstated: Fryer (*The Destruction of Serbia*, p.108) talks of 'determined opposition'.

[23] FO 371/2262/108054 (de Salis to Grey, 18 July 1915).

[24] Ibid (Harold Nicolson, 7 Aug 1915; Oliphant, 7 Aug 1915).

[25] FO 371/2245/87024; FO 371/2262/94459 (Oliphant, 1 July 1915; 14 July 1915).

[26] FO 371/2262/89700 (Oliphant, 6 July 1915).

[27] FO 371/2262/96947 (Clerk, 18 July 1915).

[28] FO 371/2268/108972 (Grey, 10 Aug 1915).

[29] FO 371/2262/112939 (Harold Nicolson, 10 Aug 1915).

[30] FO 371/2272/145517 (8 Oct 1915).

[31] FO 371/2268/180724 (Lord Eustace Percy, 30 Nov 1915).

[32] FO 371/2268/182057 (de Salis to Grey, 30 Nov 1915; Clerk, 2 Dec 1915). De Salis was probably right, one official noted, but Britain was not on sure enough ground. The perfidy of the French Minister in Cetinje would become a recurring refrain.

[33] FO 371/2608/7401 (13 Jan 1916). The fact that Montenegro, along with Serbia, was now facing a concerted assault temporarily undermined the conviction that she had reached a clandestine agreement.

[34] FO 371/2274/180595 (Grey to de Salis, 25 Dec 1915).

[35] On lack of fighting see, for example, Taylor to War Office, 29 Dec 1915 (FO 371/2608/1403); the Serbian General assured the Allies that, while Nicholas' Government favoured Austria, his army would resist the invasion (FO 371/2608/3812 (de Salis to Grey, 6 Jan 1916)).

[36] FO 371/2608/1403 (de Bunsen to the Secretary to the Army Council, 11 Jan 1916).

[37] Ibid (Grey to Rendell Rodd, 6 Jan 1916).

[38] Ibid (de Bunsen, 11 Jan 1916).

[39] FO 371/2608/5969 (Percy, 11 Jan 1916).

[40] FO 371/2262/105071 (Grey to Rodd, 31 July 1915). See below pp.162,169.

[41] In Whitehall Nicholas' 'unedifying role' entirely displaced his positive pre-war image. 'No one', Percy remarked after Lovćen had fallen, 'will say a good word for King Nicholas' (FO 3712608/14973).

[42] FO 371/3154/47217 (24 March 1916).

[43] FO 371/2804/180510; quoted in Lloyd George, *Memoirs of the Peace Conference*, i, 15.

[44] FO 371/2608/44744 (Hugh O'Beirne, undated). A similar enquiry from Sir J.Roper Parkington, head of the Montenegrin Relief Fund, met the sublimely non-committal response that Montenegro's rehabilitation was a question 'which will always engage the earnest consideration of His Majesty's Government' (FO 371/2624/166490).

[45] FO 371/2890/154799 (question tabled by Mr King, 17 July 1917).

[46] FO 371/2608/122906 (Durham letter 14 June 1916; Nicolson, 26 June).

[47] FO 371/2881/34053 (13 Feb 1917). This sentiment was initialled by Cecil and Hardinge.

[48] FO 371/2617/97227 (Report from Alex Devine, acting Commissioner for the Montenegrin Red Cross, dated 5 May 1916; Harold Nicolson, 23 May 1916).

[49] FO 371/2871/184331 (14 Sept 1917); Italy was excluded from the 'allies' in this context because of its presumed emotional engagement with the Petrović dynasty, related by marriage to the Italian royal family.

[50] Quoted in Seton-Watsons, *Making of a New Europe*, p.191.

[51] Sir George Grahame reported that mention of Montenegrin restoration in a Lloyd George speech on war-aims had been 'greatly appreciated by the King and Government': FO 371/3579/13170 (19 Jan 1918). That the *New Europe* camp had more reason to feel reassured, over Montenegro at least, is shown by a document drawn up in February summarising British obligations. While note was made of promises to Serbia, in terms of restitution, reparation and territorial compensation, and of those to the Yugoslav Committee, Montenegro was passed over in silence (FO 371/4357/10).

[52] 'Under cover of the general war', he alleged, 'an underground war [is] going on between Montenegro and Serbia', in which the latter held the advantage, and which would 'no doubt come to a head and be settled one way or the other when the general war ends' (FO 371/3579/13170 (19 Jan 1918)).

[53] FO 371/3154/47217 (Tyrrell, 28 March 1918).

[54] FO 371/3157/88970 (21 May 1918).

[55] FO 371/3159/187666 (Balfour, Nov 1918); FO 371/3149/130733 (Nicolson, 2 Aug 1918).

[56] FO 371/3149/77441 (Grahame to Oliphant, 19 Apr 1918). The Committee was headed by Andrija Radović, a former prisoner of King Nicholas as well as briefly, in 1916, his Prime Minister.

[57] FO 371/3154/58211 (8 Apr 1918).

[58] FO 371/2884/104400 (Dept of Info weekly report, 23 May 1917). The phrase 'tiny clique' was substituted for the first draft's much weaker 'certain number', describing the strength of the 'reactionary' element.

[59] FO 371/2890/141823 (IB Report, 6 July 1917).

[60] Lord Derby had wondered, late in 1917, how much could be reliably gleaned from Radović's statements beyond his bitter hostility to King Nicholas (FO 371/2871/219996 (19 Nov 1917)).

[61] FO 371/2889/162723 (20 Aug 1917).

[62] FO 371/3149/77441 (3 May 1918).

[63] FO 371/3149/123820 (Derby to Grey, 13 July 1918; Nicolson, 23 July). Derby had telegraphed sympathising with Montenegrin complaints against the French (who had ceased paying their share of the Anglo-French grant to the Petrović Government and were obstructing communication between Neuilly and Paris). Nicolson's draft did also claim that Britain would not want to commit 'until such time as the wishes of the Montenegrin people can be ascertained'. But it is hard to believe in a desire to gauge Montenegrin opinion when this was so clearly prejudged.

[64] Ibid (FO to Derby, 30 July 1918, emphasis added). Nicolson's draft had read '[...] renders it *most unlikely, if not undesirable* that a separate Montenegrin Dynasty *will* survive the settlement' (emphasis added).

[65] FO 371/3158/126841 (enclosed by Grahame, 18 July 1918; Leeper, 24 July).

[66] FO 371/3149/130733 (2 Aug 1918).

[67] The *Encyclopaedia Britannica* had noted in 1911 that some 77% of the Montenegrin population was illiterate ('Montenegro: Population and Government'). Most Montenegrins educated or 'progressive' in a Western sense had been educated abroad, largely in the USA, where the majority had remained as an influential émigré group.

[68] Where, likewise, in the opposition between a reactionary 'clique' and the majority of *younger* opinion, were most middle-aged and elderly Montenegrins considered to stand?!

[69] FO 371/3157/85253 (14 May 1918).

[70] FO 3149/175679 (Leeper, 14 Nov 1918).

[71] FO 371/3149/205017 (Laurence Collier, 13 Dec 1918). There was, it was argued, a desperate need for impartial observers not just in Montenegro but across the collapsing Austrian Empire (FO 371/3149/191504).

[72] FO 371/3149/131553 (undated, 29 July-6 Aug 1918).

[73] FO 371/3149/191504 (Collier, 20 Nov 1918).

[74] FO 371/3149/205017 (Paget, 16 Dec 1918).

[75] FO 371/3138/198773 (Capt.H.Edwards, Cattaro, to Commodore of British Adriatic Force, 21 Nov 1918). Sir Arthur Evans, a trusted witness and campaigner for South Slav union, reported on 4 December that the assembly had 'solemnly' deposed the King and confirmed Montenegrin union with Serbia. 'All this', he assured Derby, 'was inevitable and the démentis being put forward by the ex-King have no value whatever. For some considerable time it was certain that the Montenegrins would never allow either King Nikola or any of his family to set foot in the country again' (FO 371/3138/202583).

[76] FO 371/4356/62549 (16 Dec 1918). The 'national committee' was Radović's provisional government.

[77] FO 371/3137/163724 (Leeper, 5 Oct 1918).

[78] FO 371/3149/197334 (3 Dec 1918).

[79] FO 371/3149/201905 (Leeper, 12 Dec 1918).

[80] FO 371/3149/200446 (Grahame, 4 Dec 1918).

[81] FO 371/3149/212313; 212705 (undated, *c*.25 Dec 1918).

[82] FO 371/3570/13815 (General Phillips). On a point of pedantry this 'ancient Monarchy' was eight years old; only in 1910 had Nicholas elevated himself to the position of King.

[83] FO 371/4356/199 (report undated, probably late December).

[84] This development will be examined fully in the following chapter.

[85] See, for example, F.Grumel-Jacquignon, *La Yougoslavie dans la stratégie française de l'Entre-deux-Guerres (1918-1935)* (Berlin etc, 1999), p.35 and J.Adler, *L'Union forcée – la Croatie et la creation de l'état yougoslave, 1918* (Geneva, 1997), p.156.

[86] FO 371/3149/212705 (Grahame, 24 Dec 1918).

[87] FO 371/3149/213092 (Grahame, 27 Dec 1918).

[88] FO 371/3149/212705.

[89] Ibid. (Oliphant, 28 Dec 1918; Collier, 28 Dec 1918). On the rapid re-emergence of antagonism and suspicion between Britain and France after the armistice, see D.R.Watson, 'The Making of the Treaty of Versailles', in N.Waites (ed.), *Troubled Neighbours: Franco-British Relations in the Twentieth Century* (London, 1971).

[90] FO 371/3149/212705 (28 Dec 1918).

[91] FO 371/3159/187666 (Oliphant, 14 Nov 1918; Balfour, undated).

[92] 'There seems little doubt', Collier noted on 24 December, 'that if King Nicholas did return, he would be deposed; but if he likes to expose himself to that humiliation and if care is taken to keep him to his promise to go if the people wish him to, it is difficult to see how we can, in justice, avoid accepting this proposal

and pressing it on the French Govt' (FO 371/3159/210792). A report from Cattaro said the Montenegrins there would shoot Nicholas at once (FO 371/3149/209980 (21 Dec 1918)). British officials, who had often mused wistfully that the old king's demise might resolve the Montenegrin problem, could scarcely have felt alarmed at such a possibility. (Union on Nicholas' death, Graham had observed in July, would be 'the best consummation'. 'Yes', agreed a colleague, 'but when will he die?' (FO 371/3149/131553)).

[93] FO 371/3137/190845 (Derby to Balfour, 16 Nov 1918).

[94] Rather more so: while Montenegro had sued for peace under Serbian pressure, Romania had not only capitulated but had also accepted as reward a province of her Russian ally. She was granted two delegates at the Conference.

[95] FO 371/3159/189336 (16 Nov 1918).

[96] In fact Montenegro was allocated a seat but it remained empty, Nicholas and Radović's rival claims unresolved. The situation as regards Montenegrin representation, Nicolson remarked, was 'not a situation at all, but merely a haze'. It was eventually dropped on the assumption that 'as far as external questions are concerned [...] the Serbian Representatives [...] may be trusted to defend Montenegrin interests': FO 371/3590/31514 (22 Feb 1919).

[97] FO 371/4355/68. The document was drafted by Paget, Nicolson and Leeper and printed as a cabinet paper on 13 Dec 1918 (CAB 29/2/P51).

[98] FO 371/3137/190845 (16 Nov 1918). Nicholas' confederal proposal, by which both dynasties would be retained in a loose Yugoslav grouping, was, understandably, dismissed as quite unfeasible.

[99] 'Montenegro', an official statement conveyed to Whitehall in late December had declared, 'is reunited to Serbia under the Karadjordjević dynasty and, *ipso facto*, thus enters the Kingdom of Serbians, Croatians and Slovenes' (FO 371/3579/2884 (des Graz, 26 Dec 1918)).

[100] FO 371/3149/212705 (Collier, 28 Dec 1918, emphasis added).

[101] Ibid (28 Dec 1918).

[102] FO 371/3590/31514 (22 Feb 1919).

[103] Banac, *National Question*, pp 285-7. Autonomists became known as 'Greens', Radovićists as 'Whites', after the colour of their candidate lists for the November 'election', a colour symbolism which endures to this day.

[104] FO 371/3565/1057 (Rodd, Rome, 1 Jan 1919; Collier, 2 Jan).

[105] FO 371/3580/16689.

[106] FO 371/3579/5503 (9 Jan 1919).

[107] FO 371/3570/13815 (Phillips to Gribbon, 11 Jan 1919).

[108] FO 371/3579/5503 (George Warner, 10 Jan 1919).

[109] FO 371/3579/5503.

[110] FO 371/3580/16689.

[111] FO 371/3579/5503 (Warner, 10 Jan 1919).

[112] FO 371/3565/9622 (Grahame, 14 Jan 1919); FO 371/3565/3581 (Derby, 5 Jan 1919). The final communication is in FO 371/3578/4380. It stated simply that the Allied Governments could not, prior to the peace conference, recognise such a political transformation as Serb-Croat-Slovene unification.

[113] FO 371/3565/6331 (Derby, 12 Jan 1919).

[114] Ibid.

[115] FO 371/3580/16689.

[116] FO 371/3565/9622 (letter dated 25 Dec 1918, forwarded to London 14 Jan).

[117] FO 371/3579/5503.

[118] FO 371/3565/24822 (13 Jan 1919).

[119] FO 371/3579/11210 (12 Jan 1919).

[120] FO 371/3579/7957 (14 Jan 1919). Thwaites was the Director of Military Intelligence (DMI).

[121] FO 371/3565/6325. FO files were routinely headed 'Reunion of Montenegro with Serbia', attaching a sense of inevitability to the process – an unconscious acceptance of the Serbian nationalist presentation.

[122] FO 371/3579/13215. The majority of the country, the French General Venel had similarly reported, was for Yugoslavia but did not recognise annexation to Serbia (FO 371/3579/13170).

[123] FO 371/3580/16689 (Temperley); FO 371/3570/13815 (Brodie, 9 Jan 1919). In one district, General Bridges reported on 1 February, about eighty men from some four thousand had apparently voted, and there existed 'real dissatisfaction' about how the election's conduct (FO 371/3580/26859).

[124] FO 371/3590/31514 (22 Feb 1919).

[125] FO 371/3580/17343 (Warner, 1 Feb 1919).

[126] FO 371/3579/13170 (undated, c.24 Jan 1919).

[127] FO 371/3580/35124 (Plunkett, Belgrade, 12 Feb 1919; Warner, 5 March 1919); FO 371/3565/24822 (Plunkett, 2 Feb 1919). Plunkett suspected Temperley's advice was too concerned with ethnographical and historical factors; in our own interest, he urged, 'we should back the union for all we are worth' (FO 371/3565/50990).

[128] FO 371/3565/48066 (Warner, 27 March 1919).

[129] FO 371/3580/21524.

[130] FO 371/3149/213092.

[131] FO 371/3579/3254 (Warner, 7 Jan 1919); on 9 January the French General Franchet D'Esperey had cabled that the situation in Cetinje was not serious enough to necessitate the despatch of troops.

[132] FO 371/3580/26859 (1 Feb 1919).

[133] FO 371/3579/13170.

[134] On Wilson's sympathy, see S.Bonsal, *Suitors and Suppliants: The Little Nations at Versailles* (New York, 1946), pp.85-6 (based on diaries of Colonel Bonsal, a member of the US conference delegation).

[135] FO 371/3579/5503 (27 Jan 1919).

[136] FO 371/3565/18001 (1 Feb 1919); FO 371/3565/22913 (2 Feb 1919).

[137] FO 371/3565/14476 (31 Jan 1919).

[138] 'From what I hear from Americans in Paris', Grahame warned, 'the United States Government are more and more chary of new commitments in Europe, as public opinion in America has in no way been converted to the principle of active intervention in European affairs' (FO 371/3580/27399 (16 Feb 1919)).

[139] FO 371/3579/16417 (forwarded 29 Jan). The French were quick to second this proposal.

[140] Ibid (Warner, 30 Jan 1919; Graham, 31 Jan; Curzon 31 Jan).

[141] FO 371/3580/21558 (7 Feb).

142 FO 371/3580/27399 (16 Feb).

143 FO 371/3580/24283 (DMI, 12 Feb).

144 FO 371/3590/32139 (Warner, 27 Feb 1919).

145 Having already stated that Britain did not recognise the Podgorica decisions, the Under-Secretary of State for Foreign Affairs Cecil Harmsworth assured Parliament on 13 February that the best method of gauging Montenegrins' true wishes was 'engaging the attention of the Allied and Associated Powers' (*The Times*, 29 Apr 1919).

146 FO 371/3580/21715 (6 Feb 1919).

147 FO 371/3580/33898 (4 March 1919). Quite how this course of action would protect Montenegro from Serbian coercion was left unclear.

148 FO 371/3580/42885 (Warner, 19 March 1919).

149 FO 371/3580/55391.

150 FO 371/3580/64368 (de Graz, 23 Apr 1919; Warner, 26 Apr).

151 FO 371/3580/60289 (Warner, 18 Apr 1919).

152 FO 371/3580/71011 (de Salis, Scutari, 1 May 1919).

153 Ibid.

154 FO 371/3580/73717 (14 May 1919).

155 The Americans, Grahame asserted, had 'recognised the new triple title of the King of Serbia but that does not mean that they recognise the annexation of Montenegro to Serbia'. The French Government had certainly gone too far, Warner agreed (FO 371/3580/61893 (Grahame to Graham, 19 Apr 1919; Warner, 24 Apr)).

156 FO 371/3578/85372 (Hansard, 5 June 1919).

157 Bonsal, *Suitors and Supplicants*, p.93.

158 FO 371/3580/71011 (Howard-Smith, 10 May 1919; Graham, 10 May).

159 FO 371/3580/78065 (21 May 1919).

160 FO 371/3580/81372 (27 May 1919).

161 FO 371/3580/92881 (26 June 1919).

162 FO 371/3580/86030 (Phillips to DMI, 24 May 1919). The pejorative term 'yoke', commonly attached to the Ottoman regime, suggests rising contempt for Serbian administration. The chief of the British Food Mission reported that scarcity in Montenegro was being exacerbated by Serbian obstruction and by the distribution of supplies on political lines. In Nikšić, he said, few supported the Serbophil party while outspoken opponents were imprisoned in deplorable conditions (FO 371/3571/101649 (20 June 1919)).

163 FO 371/3580/93328 (26 June 1919).

164 FO 371/3580/92881 (24 June 1919).

165 FO 371/3580/124889 (21 Aug 1919).

166 For instance in his pamphlet 'the Question of Montenegro', written for the Paris conference. 'Serb people' of course included the Montenegrins.

167 FO 371/3580/111557 (Spicer, 4 Aug 1919).

168 FO 371/3580/124889 (Howard-Smith, 6 Sept 1919; Oliphant, 6 Sept).

169 FO 371/3581/131285 (Adam, 19 Sept 1919).

170 The schoolmaster Alex Devine was a persistent thorn in the Government's side. Though his views were initially received with some sympathy, his increasingly pro-Nicholas propaganda soon grated, and he was dismissed in Whitehall as an

'agent [...] probably in the pay of King Nicholas' (FO 371/3580/95252 (Balfour to Curzon, 27 June 1919)). He regurgitated his views relentlessly, but they may be found in his books *Montenegro in History, Politics and War* (London, 1918) and *Off the Map – the Suppression of Montenegro: the Tragedy of a Small Nation.*

171 FO 371/3578/85372 (McNeill, Hansard, 5 June 1919).

172 FO 371/3581/131045 (Howard-Smith, 22 Sept 1919; FO to Crowe, 29 Sept). The Peace Delegation must 'take up this matter vigorously <u>at once</u>' (ibid., 1 Oct 1919).

173 FO 371/3590/119478 (Minutes undated, 3 Oct or soon after).

174 FO 371/3581/142846 (16 Oct 1919).

175 Ibid. On the general constitutional question in Yugoslavia at this point see below ch.8.

176 FO 371/3581/147825 (Adam, 29 Oct 1919). Although a draft was produced to lay before Parliament, the report was not, in the end, presented.

177 FO 371/3581/142846 (20 Oct 1919).

178 FO 371/3581/151200 (Hansard, 10 Nov 1919).

179 FO 371/3576/150648 (8 Nov 1919).

180 Ibid (12 Nov 1919).

181 FO 371/3576/123170 (Victor Wellesley to Treasury, 5 Sept 1919).

182 Since the discontinuance of the subsidy was, Spicer argued, 'undoubtedly creating the impression in South Eastern Europe that His Majesty's Govt have a considered policy of prejudice against the former institutions of the Montenegrin people, Lord Curzon is at a loss to understand the reluctance of Their Lordships to re-consider their decision' (FO 371/3576/171709 (19 Jan 1920)).

183 Ibid [171709]. On the strained relations between Foreign Office and Treasury in this period, see Ephraim Maisel, *The Foreign Office and Foreign Policy, 1919-1926* (Brighton, 1994), pp.14-17.

184 FO 371/3576/147429 (7 Nov 1919).

185 FO 371/3576/150648 (13 Nov 1919).

186 FO 371/3581/160278 (Howard-Smith, 10 Dec 1919); FO 371/3590/157197 (*c.*3 Dec 1919).

187 FO 371/3576/152107 (17 Nov 1919).

188 FO 371/3590/157197 (Adam, 3 Dec 1919; Hardinge, undated).

189 FO 371/3581/164456 (19 Dec 1919).

190 FO 371/3581/168350 (7 Jan 1920).

191 FO 371/3582/194950.

192 FO 371/3582/197235 (Hansard, 6 May 1920).

193 FO 371/3582/197235 (Adam, 6 May 1920). In July the Prime Minister insisted that Montenegro could not be separated from a general Adriatic settlement (FO 371/4660/2132 (Hansard, 22 July 1920)).

194 FO 371/4703/4846 (27 Aug 1920). The point is illustrated by a seemingly trivial debate the previous August over whether Whitehall should continue forwarding mail to Nicholas as King of Montenegro. Pending the de Salis report, Howard-Smith had concluded, it should 'consider King Nikita as sovereign of Montenegro, and thus should send the letters'. Since that report, far from approving the Serbian occupation or the Podgorica assembly, had cast further

doubt on their legitimacy, it had hardly altered the situation (FO 371/3597/69664, 10 Aug 1919).

[195] FO 371/3582/205949 (23 June 1920).

[196] FO 371/3582/208009 (30 June 1920).

[197] See Nicolson, *Peacemaking*, pp.148-52.

[198] FO 371/4660/4115 (14 Aug 1920). Nicolson admitted having been greatly influenced in Paris by the impressive personage of Sir Eyre Crowe, and the latter's influence is manifest here (*Peacemaking*, pp.210-11).

[199] FO 371/4660/4115 (Curzon to Lord Gladstone, 17 Aug 1920). Gladstone had assumed his forbear's interest in Montenegro.

[200] FO 371/4668/4789 (16 Aug 1920).

[201] FO 371/4668/7029 (25 Sept 1920). Sir Alban Young, he noted, could provide first-hand information.

[202] FO 371/4695/1489 (16 July 1920).

[203] FO 371/4668/7029 (18 Sept 1920).

[204] FO 371/4669/9142 (16 Oct 1920); FO 371/4688/4785 (21 Aug 1920).

[205] FO 371/4668/4789 (*c*.16 Aug 1920). As ex-viceroy of India Hardinge had had ample chance to study the habits and predilections of the 'oriental'!

[206] FO 371/4668/7029 (25 Sept 1920).

[207] FO 371/4668/4789 (7 Sept 1920).

[208] FO 371/4668/7029 (Curzon to Young, 28 Sept 1920; Curzon internal minute, 26 Sept 1920).

[209] FO 371/4661/11368 (Hansard, 10 Nov 1920).

[210] D.Šepić, 'Question of Yugoslav Union', p.35. Croats and Slovenes, with no desire to antagonise Belgrade over this issue, were happy to accept.

[211] In fact he provided a preliminary report on 12 October and another on 24 November: FO 371/4669/9142; FO 371/4661/12217.

[212] Unlike diehard Yugoslav enthusiasts like Leeper, Temperley did admit the unrepresentative nature of 'intellectual' opinion: it was difficult, he noted, especially for a foreigner, 'to gauge the opinions of a people of conservative instincts as distinguished from its intellectual leaders'.

[213] Macmillan's claim (*Peacemakers*, p.127) that Italy had been 'quite content to see Montenegro swallowed up by Serbia, hoping that the mouthful would be particularly indigestible' is misleading. Italian opposition to a seat for Montenegro was based on the assumption that it would be filled by Radović, reinforcing the Yugoslavs. Italy continued to support pro-Nicholas activists while there seemed hope of undermining the Yugoslav state.

[214] FO 371/4670/13829 (30 Nov 1920).

[215] FO 371/4662/13982; 14090 (Hansard: Harmsworth, 14 Dec 1920; Lord Sandhurst, 15 Dec).

[216] FO 371/4669/12824 (Temperley, 3 Dec 1920). At least, he noted, the Communist success confirmed Bryce's belief in the freedom of the elections (FO 371/4662/12576, quoted by Adam, 30 Nov 1920).

[217] FO 371/4662/13982 (10 Dec 1920).

[218] FO 371/4670/13311 (3 Dec 1920); FO 371/4670/13890 (11 Dec 1920).

[219] FO 371/4670/13815 (Adam, 14 Dec 1920).

[220] FO 371/4670/14517 (report dated 16 Dec 1920).

[221] While this level did compare well with other regions, Bryce failed to note that in core areas of Old Montenegro, the heartland of Green insurgency, the rate was much higher – 50.38% among the Cetinje tribe, 48.18% among the Ćeklići and Bjelice. According to Banac, 'in two out of three electoral districts of Old Montenegro more than half of the eligible voters did not participate in the balloting' (*National Question*, pp.391, 287). Average voter abstention by region ranged from 26.48% in Slovenia to 43.87% in Dalmatia. Banac's statement that 'electoral absenteeism in Montenegro was exceptionally high' thus seems unwarranted for Montenegro as a whole. Bryce's attribution of many abstentions to logistical difficulties, inability to appreciate subtle party differences, and a tribal culture in which a family member spoke for the extended unit, seems plausible.

[222] In Serbia proper the KPJ polled 15.49% of the vote, much less than half the Montenegrin level. Even in the unsettled region of Macedonia the Communists polled only 27.16%: see tables of voting figures, ibid., pp.388-9. This Macedonian figure includes the neighbouring (and also unsettled) regions of Kosovo, Metohia and Sandžak.

[223] Djilas, *The Contested Country*, p.63. See also Banac, *National Question*, p.330.

[224] Banac, *National Question*, p.391.

[225] FO 371/4670/14517 (Adam, 24 Dec 1920; Nicolson, 24 Dec).

[226] FO 371/4680/5243 (Nicolson, record of conversation with Trumbić, 2 Sept 1920).

[227] FO 371/4670/14517 (26 Dec 1920).

[228] Temperley report: HoC: Cmd 1123 1921 vol.xliii; Bryce report: HoC: Cmd 1124 1921 vol.xliii. The general proceedings of this Assembly, and British observations thereof, are dealt with in ch.9.

[229] FO 371/6200/3221 (14 Feb 1920).

[230] FO 371/6200/3692 (22 Feb 1920).

[231] FO 371/4662/13229 (6 Dec 1920).

[232] FO 371/4670/13167 (7 Dec 1920).

[233] Montenegro had been granted 10 deputies instead of the 14-15 to which her pre-war population entitled her, Nicolson had noted, but as so small a proportion of the whole this made 'little real difference' (FO 371/4668/7490, 30 Sept 1920). The consequences of this insight for Montenegrin self-determination were not developed.

[234] FO 371/4669/12186 (conversation with M.Cambon, 24 Nov 1920). Emphasis added.

[235] FO 371/4662/12481 (Hansard, 25 Nov 1920; the term 'confederation' was presumably used loosely here). It had, as officials had expressed it in August, 'always been an axiom of the Balkan settlement that when this federation was once achieved Montenegro would take her place with Croatia and the Slovenes within the body of the Union' (FO 371/4697/4545 (unsent letter to Grahame, c.20 Aug 1920)).

[236] FO 371/4662/14502 (18 Dec 1920).

[237] Ibid (24 Dec 1920). On misguided British assumptions about the nature of the constitutional settlement, see below ch.8.

[238] FO 371/6194/6414.

[239] FO 371/6194/22132 (24 Nov 1921).

[240] FO 371/6194/8448 (26 Apr 1921).

[241] FO 371/6193/6413 (Temperley, 1 Apr 1921).

[242] 'We get very little from Belgrade about affairs in Montenegro', one official complained in December 1922 (FO 371/7681/16756).

[243] FO 371/7682/5643 (11 Apr 1922).

[244] Young talked of 'a spread of the Radić poison' (FO 371/7675/2481: 16 Feb 1922); see also the memorandum prepared for the Duke of York's visit to Yugoslavia (FO 371/7679/8016: June 1922).

[245] FO 371/7681/10484 (Miles Lampson, 26 July 1922).

[246] FO 371/7681/16356 (Hansard, 29 Nov 1922; Troutbeck minute, 28 Nov 1922). Ironically, the junior minister who told Parliament that Montenegro was an integral part of the SCS Kingdom and that no opinion could be expressed as to the disposition of troops within that State, was Ronald McNeill, who for several years had denounced British policy on Montenegro, and admitted privately that his views were unchanged.

[247] Ibid.

[248] See Young's report of increasing anger at the sacrifice of Yugoslav interests to Western 'imperialistic designs' (FO 371/4668/2980: 4 Aug 1920).

[249] FO 371/4689/13542 (12 Dec 1920).

[250] FO 371/4669/9420 (Curzon to Young, 29 Oct 1920).

[251] FO 371/3581/160278 (Howard-Smith, 10 Dec 1919).

[252] *Peacemaking*, pp.151-2.

Chapter Seven

[1] FO 371/2261/83042 (24 June 1915).

[2] Quoted in Seton-Watsons, *Making of a New Europe*, pp.101-2. He specified explicitly the inclusion of Croatia and Dalmatia as well as Bosnia.

[3] On the Yugoslav Committee see G.Stokes, 'The Role of the Yugoslav Committee in the Formation of Yugoslavia', in Djordjević (ed.), *Creation of Yugoslavia*, pp.51-71.

[4] FO 371/2241/4404. It was circulated to King and Cabinet: CAB 37/123.

[5] FO 371/2257/48283 (22 April 1915).

[6] FO 371/2258/76671 (12 May 1915). This state, the manifesto declared, would bear the name 'Yugoslavia', 'Serbia' ceasing to exist as the name of a European state.

[7] Seton-Watson, *Correspondence*, i, 251 (29 Oct 1915). Many propagandistic works, like Bogumil Vošnjak's *Bulwark against Germany*, laboured this point.

[8] Ibid., i, 213-14 (26 April 1915). Yugoslavia, the Serbian Society similarly impressed on Lloyd George in June 1917, would be 'the strongest barrier against the Prusso-Austrian design of mastery over the Near and Middle East' (ibid., 298-300; see also ibid., 265).

[9] Ibid., i, 239 (17 Sept 1915). Such arguments only increased as the war went on. See Taylor, *Future of the Southern Slavs*, pp.56-7 and ch.10. By July 1918 Steed was claiming that unless independent Polish, Czechoslovak and Yugoslav states were created, 'London, Paris, Milan and Rome would not be habitable a generation hence' (speech to the inauguration meeting of the Serbian (Yugo-Slav) National War Aims Committee, *The Times*, 26 July 1918).

[10] FO 371/2265/112839 (Drummond, 14 Aug 1915).

[11] FO 371/599/14552 (19 April 1909).

[12] Hanak, 'The Government, The Foreign Office and Austria-Hungary', 173-4; May, 'R.W.Seton-Watson', 42.

[13] FO 371/2862/97435 (11 May 1917). French thinking – astutely encouraged by Pašić – was on precisely these lines: an independent or federal Croatia must fall under German influence, and only a Yugoslav state firmly centralised in Belgrade could serve as an effective bulwark. (Grumel-Jacquignon, *La Yougoslavie*, pp.40-1 and *passim*).

[14] FO 371/2257/54094 (Letter counter-signed by Pašić and addressed to Jovan Cvijić in Britain, 1 May 1915; the conversation with Grey took place on 11 January).

[15] FO 371/2258/90173 (2 July 1915).

[16] FO 371/2241/4404 (13 Jan 1915).

[17] For a detailed treatment of this diplomacy, see K.Robbins, 'British Diplomacy and Bulgaria 1914-1915', *Slavonic and East European Review*, 117 (Oct 1971), 560-85.

[18] FO 371/2261/83042 (24 June 1915).

[19] Alexander had told Seton-Watson he would cede Bosnia before Macedonia (Seton-Watsons, *Making of a New Europe*, p.113); similarly for a nationalist like Bošković, Serbian Minister in London, the gains of 1912-13 were Serbia's proudest achievement, sacred, non-negotiable, and independent of her claims in the west (ibid., p.132). French politicians were more informed about (as well as in sympathy with) Serb nationalism on this point. See É.Haumant, *La Formation de la Yougoslavie* (Paris, 1930), pp.683-4, which cites Clemenceau's argument that offering Macedonia to Bulgaria would be a betrayal of the Serbs.

[20] FO 371/2268/116675 (Percy, Aug 1915).

[21] FO 371/2263/105071 (Grey to Rodd, 31 July 1915).

[22] FO 371/2241/4404 (13 Jan 1915).

[23] FO 371/2257/53757.

[24] FO 371/2241/4404 (Arthur Nicolson, 15 Jan 1915).

[25] Seton-Watson suspected that Italian 'efforts to emphasise the difference between Serb and Croat' had been responsible for '[impressing] on the mind of Sir E[dward] G[rey] the fact that the Croats are an element in the situation which deserves to be reckoned with' (*Correspondence*, i, 225-6).

[26] FO 371/2265/108843 (9 Aug 1915); FO 371/2265/112839 (Eric Drummond, 14 Aug 1915); FO 371/2265/112838 (15 Aug 1915).

[27] FO 371/2257/53757 (undated); FO 371/2263/105071 (31 July 1915). In private Britain and Russia promised Pašić not to object if Croatia desired union with Serbia at the end of the war. Pašić had requested Slovene territories too, but these were little considered by British analysts, who were reluctant to commit. While Sazonov supported the request, Britain and France demurred (Seton-Watsons, *Making of a New Europe*, p.139).

[28] Sir Arthur Nicolson had advised against promising to facilitate Serbo-Croatian unity as being unfair to Italy (FO 371/2265/112839 (recorded by Percy, 14 Aug 1915)). The idea that Slavonia's future too be 'subject to wishes of inhabitants' was dropped in view of the need to match Russian promises to Serbia (FO 371/2265/112838).

[29] FO 371/2507/34053; 28275 (23 March 1915).

[30] In fact Russia obliged Italy to drop its claim to Fiume and reduce its claims in Dalmatia. It did so, however, on economic and strategic grounds. Her claim to the Straits and Constantinople precluded any appeal to ethnicity.

[31] Nicolson, *Peacemaking*, pp.137-8.

[32] See, for example, ibid, pp.159-161. The terms were, Nicolson declared, 'wholly indefensible'.

[33] 'Deserve to be hanged' comment reported by Steed, 29 April 1915 (cited in Seton-Watsons, *Making of a New Europe*, p.130 note 26).

[34] FO 371/2376/37639 (31 March 1915).

[35] FO 371/2241/41098 (9 Apr 1915). All aspirations could never be realised, Sir Arthur Nicolson agreed.

[36] Record by Seton-Watson of conversation with Grey, 4 May 1915 (Seton-Watsons, *Making of a New Europe*, p.130).

[37] FO 371/2257/53757 (draft telegram Grey to des Graz, May 1915).

[38] FO 371/2261/83042 (Percy, 24 June 1915).

[39] FO 371/2258/90173 (27 June 1915).

[40] FO 371/2265/109491 (10 Aug 1915).

[41] FO 371/2266/122256 (31 Aug 1915).

[42] FO 371/2281/200194 (29 Dec 1915). Grey signified his approval.

[43] Even for a tireless campaigner like Seton-Watson, 1916 saw a marked decline in correspondence on the subject. His collected correspondence contains less than half the number of items for 1916 than for 1915.

[44] FO 371/2615/58989 (30 March 1916).

[45] Since the condition attached to the guarantee to Serbia of Austro-Hungarian territories (cession to Bulgaria of the 'uncontested zone') was unfulfilled, it was deemed 'not contractually valid', though it should be borne in mind, a later memo on British obligations noted, along with Grey's verbal assurance in May 1915 that Allied victory would secure for Serbia Bosnia, wide access to the Adriatic 'to say nothing of what Montenegro and Croatia would have' (FO 371/4358/10 (Feb 1918)). While Grey had told Supilo post-war Croatia should decide her own fate, this too was considered non-binding.

[46] In *New Europe* he excoriated Grey, urging a more professional approach and clear war aims. When Balfour took over the Foreign Office, Seton-Watson advocated dismembering Austria-Hungary, urging the Government to deny it had 'some dark purpose' of preserving it ('The Failure of Sir Edward Grey' (1916); 'Wanted – A Foreign Policy' (1917), reproduced in R.Seton-Watson, *Europe in the Melting Pot* (London, 1919), pp.86-120 and 121-36). Seton-Watson's highly critical view of the performance of Grey and the Foreign Office at this stage was echoed more privately by his friend Harold Temperley, working for the War Office's Military Intelligence Department. Jibes at the Foreign Office's general ignorance of Balkan affairs were 'a constant theme in his diaries' (Fair, *Harold Temperley*, p.119).

[47] Rodd, quoted in Seton-Watsons, *Making of a New Europe*, p.181. The problem, he later lamented, was that Italians wrongly assumed Seton-Watson, and Steed with his position at *The Times*, strongly influenced British policy (FO 371/2627/231670, 10 Nov 1916).

[48] FO 371/2804/180510.

[49] Hanak, 'The Government, the Foreign Office and Austria-Hungary', pp.168-70, 174; the Paget-Tyrell memo, it is pointed out in C.A.Macartney and A.W.Palmer, *Independent Eastern Europe: A History* (New York, 1966), p.64, was not even discussed in Cabinet until the following year. And other memoranda, such as that by the Chief of the Imperial Staff, General Robertson, were much more conservative (Goldstein, *Winning the Peace*, pp.10-12).

[50] Seton-Watsons, *Making of a New Europe*, p.191.

[51] On the impact of the Russian Revolution, see A.J.Mayer, *Political Origins of the New Diplomacy 1917-1918* (New Haven, 1959), p.163ff. The collapse of Russian power, some argued, ended the 'balance of power' argument for Austria's existence: 'so far from restoring a balance against Germany, an Austrian federation under German leadership would merely increase the difficulties caused by the collapse of Russia' (FO 371/3136/177223, Nicolson and Namier minute, 7 Nov 1918).

[52] V.Rothwell, *British War Aims and Peace Diplomacy, 1914-1918* (Oxford, 1971), p.119.

[53] Seton-Watson, 'Special Memorandum on the Question of a Separate Peace with Austria', *Correspondence*, i, 292-4. Cecil and Balfour denied that the Allied reply pledged Britain to the form liberation of the subject nationalities would take (Seton-Watsons, *Making of a New Europe*, p.222). Eric Drummond's February 1917 memo had acknowledged Paget and Tyrrell's formula as ideally desirable, but proposed instead a federal Monarchy with Czech and Yugoslav units as well as German and Hungarian. It was keenly endorsed by Hardinge and Cecil (Rothwell, *British War Aims*, p.81).

[54] FO 371/2890/140532 (16 July 1917).

[55] G.Bátonyi, *Britain and Central Europe, 1918-1933* (Oxford, 1999), p.11.

[56] Hanak, *Great Britain and Austria-Hungary*, pp.143, 248-50.

[57] Memo on general situation in Austria, 23 June 1917, quoted in Seton-Watsons, *Making of a New Europe*, pp.211-12.

[58] Though many Foreign Office officials were also kept largely in the dark about this.

[59] Quoted in Seton-Watsons, *Making of a New Europe*, p.211.

[60] Since 1915 Pašić had been wary of the Yugoslav Committee and of enhancing its independent status. But with the collapse of his Russian ally, American intervention, and pressure from domestic opponents, he felt compelled to propose a conference to discuss common aims. (Trumbić, in turn, was motivated to regain the initiative after the 'May declaration' had suggested that Habsburg South Slavs, contrary to Committee claims, could speak for themselves). The Corfu Agreement was announced on 20 July, declaring that a united state would be known as 'the Kingdom of the Serbs, Croats and Slovenes', and would guarantee equality to the three faiths, two alphabets and three 'national designations'. The state structure was reserved for decision by a Constituent Assembly.

[61] FO 371/2889/119339 (c.16 June 1917). Rodd reported Italian scepticism at Trumbić's claim to speak for all Croatians and Slovenes (FO 371/2889/165368 (13 Aug 1917)).

[62] FO 371/2889/180815 (15 Sept 1917). He thus downplayed the change of Serbian Government during the negotiations as a result of the Salonica controversy (see p.284 note 152 below).

[63] FO 371/2889/235396.

[64] FO 371/4353/55.

[65] FO 371/4355/68: Paget, Leeper, Nicolson, 'South Eastern Europe and the Balkans'. We have seen how factors of race and language seemed, during the war, to outweigh those of history and tradition: see above chs.1 and 2.

[66] FO 371/4354/64. Leeper and Zimmern, 'The Principle of Self-Determination and its application to the Baltic Provinces'.

[67] Rothwell, *British War Aims*, pp.145-53. Rothwell calls this speech, 'the most important single British statement on war aims in the Great War'. The break-up of Austria-Hungary, Lloyd George had affirmed, was 'no part of our war aims' (M.Cornwall, 'Disintegration and Defeat: The Austro-Hungarian Revolution', in Cornwall (ed.), *The Last Years of Austria-Hungary*, p.177; D.Stevenson, *The First World War and International Politics* (Oxford, 1988), p.193).

[68] FO 371/3149/6573 (9 Jan 1918).

[69] FO 371/3149/16711 (28 Jan 1918); FO 371/3149/16712 (28 Jan 1918). If it was an unrealisable aim, Seton-Watson responded, officials should realise that the alternative was the absorption of Serbia in Central Europe. She could no longer stand alone; 'in one form or other unity must come' (15 Feb 1918).

[70] FO 371/4362/60 (Monitored by the Uncommon Language Dept, 12 May 1918; 18 March 1918).

[71] Seton-Watsons, *Making of a New Europe*, pp.259-60. For a first-hand account of this debate, and of the propaganda war in general, see Sir C.Stuart, *Secrets of Crewe House: The Story of a Famous Campaign* (London etc, 1920), pp.20-49. See also M.Cornwall, *The Undermining of Austria-Hungary: the Battle for Hearts and Minds* (Basingstoke; London, 2000), pp.174-85.

[72] FO 371/3135/89828 (FO to Derby, 21 May 1918). Hardinge likewise wrote to Rumbold: 'I fear all our attempts to detach Austria have come to nought [...]. We now face the prospect of fighting it out, while doing all we can to encourage the subject races to revolt' (Hardinge papers, cited in Seton-Watsons, *Making of a New Europe*, p.288 fn 16).

[73] CAB 28/4, IC 66. Sonnino, Balfour told Steed and Northcliffe, had rejected his original draft 'which would [...] have satisfied the strongest advocate of Yugo-Slav aspirations' (FO 800/329 (8 June 1918)).

[74] FO 371/4358/212 (July).

[75] CAB 23/42, IWC 30. Stevenson, *First World War and International Politics*, p.220.

[76] Seton-Watson's *New Europe* articles, such as 'Twilight in Austria' on 8 August, reflected this view.

[77] FO 371/4356/159 (18 Dec 1918).

[78] EPD memo for an Inter-Allied Propaganda Conference, Aug 1918: *Correspondence*, i, 329-31.

[79] Historians have often pointed this out, but the notion of Yugoslavia as a Versailles creation endures. Even Margaret Macmillan suggests misleadingly that 'Yugoslavia and Nauru both owed their existence as independent states to the

Paris Peace Conference' (*Peacemakers*, p.3; her account on pp.119-20 is more accurate).

80 FO 371/2257/53757 (draft telegram to Niš, May 1915).

81 FO 371/2263/105071 (31 July 1915). It is noteworthy that the Slovene lands were excluded from consideration at this stage.

82 FO 371/2804/180510. It spoke also of a '*federation*' of States: the terms 'federation'/ 'confederation' were used loosely.

83 FO 371/2241/4404 (Supilo, 'Memorandum Respecting the Southern Slavs', 7 Jan 1915; Clerk, 13 Jan 1915).

84 FO 371/2258/123158 (Clerk, 30 Aug 1915).

85 Ibid.

86 FO 371/2241/147119.

87 Seton-Watson to Foreign Office, 1 Oct 1914, *Correspondence*, i, 180-6. His insistence now that the Slovenes 'must share the fate of their Croat and Serb kinsmen' is noteworthy.

88 Ibid. The local diets of Dalmatia, Istria and Carniola would likely merge, he noted, in a Parliament at Zagreb, while Montenegro, Cattaro and probably Bosnia would merge in the Serb Parliament at Belgrade.

89 *Correspondence*, i, 237-40 (17 Sept 1915).

90 FO 371/2252/13146 (30 Dec 1915).

91 FO 371/2258/125871 (6 Sept 1915).

92 *Correspondence*, i, 233-4 (22 Aug 1915).

93 FO 371/2884/95788 (9 May 1917). This might be managed, he suggested, by discussions in the existing Diets of Croatia, Dalmatia, Istria and elsewhere, which could then be confirmed by referenda.

94 FO 371/2889/180815 (15 Sept 1917). For the sharp disputes over 'basic concepts' which did in fact take place before and during the Corfu negotiations, see Meštrović, 'The Yugoslav Committee in London' pp.174, 186-91.

95 FO 371/4355/68. Hardinge applauded this 'excellent memo'. On the idea that Yugoslav differences were 'artificially created', see above p.71.

96 FO 371/3133/88314 (Berne, 10 May 1918).

97 Ibid (22 May 1918). Rumbold referred erroneously to a Corfu Declaration distinct from the Corfu Agreement.

98 FO 371/3135/116831. Croatian feeling, he noted, was 'specially anxious to prevent the political extinction of Agram [Zagreb]'; unlike the Slovenes Croatians had some autonomy to lose.

99 FO 371/3138/207115.

100 It is possible that by 'federated Yugoslavia' he and others understood at this stage a loose (what we would term 'confederal') arrangement – the voluntary cession by states of circumscribed functions to a central body; and that Corfu seemed a compromise, with Serbian nationalists and Croatian (con)federalists agreeing to respect local traditions and autonomies within a unitary state.

101 FO 371/3135/111985 (25 June 1918). 'I do not fully see why they wish for a "national" army', he wrote.

102 Those like the Frankists who rejected union with Serbia were considered, as the Yugoslav Committee claimed, 'an insignificant and pitiful clique' (FO

371/3135/107968: a communication from the Committee, dated 15 June 1918, hailed by Leeper as excellent and quite accurate).

[103] FO 371/3140/108493 (19 June 1918).

[104] FO 371/3154/126161 (6 July 1918).

[105] See his famous article 'Serbia's Choice' of late August 1918 (*Correspondence*, i, 385-91).

[106] 'Serbia's Choice'. Seton-Watson's criticisms of Pašić's regime were, in any case, questioned by des Graz, who sympathised with Protić's rebuttal (FO 371/3154/158256, 3 Sept 1918).

[107] FO 371/3137/169690 (Oct 1918). Since Supilo's death in the summer of 1917 Trumbić was unrivalled as the leading international figure among the Austrian Yugoslavs.

[108] *Correspondence*, i, 350-5.

[109] Pašić admitted to Seton-Watson's friend and ally Wickham Steed that the Corfu declaration had been issued merely to make an impression on European public opinion (Steed, *Through Thirty Years*, II, 236).

[110] FO 371/3154/169142 (c.4 Oct 1918).

[111] Since April, Seton-Watson observed, the Serbian Opposition had withdrawn from parliament, removing the Government's quorum. Serbia had 'been under an unconstitutional regime ever since' ('The Policy of Mr Pašić').

[112] FO 371/3154/169142.

[113] As Yugoslavs knew, Britain had recognised the unelected Czechoslovak National Council. Given the importance of this body's control of a national army, officials were slow to appreciate why the Yugoslav Committee wanted a Yugoslav army (memo on Czechoslovak sovereignty in FO 371/3135/132422).

[114] FO 371/3137/169690 (Leeper, 8 Oct 1918).

[115] FO 371/3137/154848 (9 Sept 1918).

[116] FO 371/3154/169142; FO 371/3137/171759. If necessary, Leeper wrote, 'friendly pressure' should be applied to secure this outcome. The positions in the Serbian Cabinet Yugoslavs should hold were not specified.

[117] FO 371/3137/171114. On the Austrian collapse and the creation of Czechoslovak and Yugoslav states, see L.M. Namier, 'The Downfall of the Habsburg Monarchy', in Temperley (ed.), *History of the Peace Conference*, iv, 89-119.

[118] FO 371/3137/172539 (c.18 Oct 1918).

[119] FO 371/3154/179908 (19 Oct 1918).

[120] FO 371/3149/171789 (16 Oct 1918).

[121] FO 371/3137/171114 (15 Oct 1918). In the *Morning Post* Pašić had dismissed any sort of federalism. It was impossible, he argued, to draw frontiers between branches of the nation 'inextricably intermingled'. Politically, furthermore, a unitary kingdom would provide the strongest guarantee against foreign intrigue. At the time this position provoked no adverse comment in Whitehall (FO 371/3137/174278).

[122] FO 371/3137/179472 (29 Oct 1918).

[123] FO 371/3137/176378 (Nicolson, Graham, 2 Nov 1918).

[124] FO 371/3138/182475 (Acton, 2 Nov 1918; Nicolson, 4 Nov); PID Memo, see p.171 above.

125 Kovač, *La France*, pp.148, 151. The Italians assumed a Serb-dominated state would be more flexible regarding the disputed territories in Istria and Dalmatia than one in which the Habsburg Yugoslavs exerted a strong influence. A Yugoslavia dominated by a strong Serbia, and a strong Pašić, was the consistent French objective (see *ibid.* and Grumel-Jacquignon, *La Yougoslavie*, pp.24-7) – an attitude which led to growing anti-French feeling in Croatia (Grumel-Jacquignon, *La Yougoslavie*, p.42). The French Foreign Minister, Stephen Pichon, was – according to Raymond Poincaré (himself greatly interested in the Yugoslavs) – the principal agent of French politics in relation to the Yugoslav question. Pichon was a firm supporter of Pašić and was (so the French Senator Ernest Pezet alleged): 'totalement ignorant des questions yougoslaves et, plus généralement, danubiennes' (see Kovač, *La France*, pp.186-91).

126 FO 371/4356/12 (War Office Memorandum on the Unification of the Yugoslavs, 16 Dec 1918).

127 Seton-Watsons, *Making of a New Europe*, pp.319-20.

128 FO 371/3137/190445 (forwarded by Derby, 17 Nov 1918).

129 FO 371/3137/189073 (19 Nov 1918).

130 FO 371/4354/52 ('Memorandum Respecting Austria-Hungary: Legal Factors Replacing the Dual Monarchy', 25 Nov 1918; printed for the British Peace Conference delegation, 13 Dec).

131 FO 371/3137/190285 (25 Nov 1918).

132 FO 371/3137/193384.

133 Banac, *National Question*, pp.134-5.

134 FO 371/3137/196814 (25 Nov 1918). Meštrović recalled Pašić's admission that he had found himself completely isolated in Geneva, but had never intended to adhere to the agreement (quoted in Kovač, *La France*, p.191).

135 FO 371/3138/202583.

136 FO 371/3138/206375 (21 Dec 1918).

137 FO 371/3578/1709; 1819; 2882 (des Graz reports, 21, 22 Dec 1918).

138 FO 371/3578/4380 (13 Jan 1919).

139 FO 371/3137/195820 (Balfour to Rodd, 23 Nov 1918).

140 FO 371/4356/159 (Memo on the Relations between the Yugo-Slavs and the Entente, 18 Dec 1918).

141 Kovač, *La France*, p.201. G.Krivokapić, 'Politique Intérieure de Royaume des Serbes, Croates et Slovenes vue par les Français à l'Époque de sa constitution en 1918-1921', in L.Aleksić-Pejković (ed.), *Rapports Franco-Yougoslaves* (Belgrade, 1990), 255-6.

142 PID Memo, FO 371/4353/55.

143 D.Dutton, 'The Balkan Campaign and French War Aims in the Great War', *The English Historical Review*, 370 (Jan 1979), 97-8.

144 FO 371/3586/6784 (14 Jan 1919).

145 FO 371/3138/206375. This was the argument Pašić had long pressed in order to deny the Yugoslav Committee independent recognition. The correct analogy, he argued, was not the Czecho-Slovaks or the Poles, neither of whom had 'Piedmonts' – free states outside the Monarchy to represent their interests. Serbia had rather 'the same position among our allies as Italy [he might have said Romania], which, in the unification of its brothers, represents its countrymen from

Austria' (quoted in Banac, *National Question*, p.132). In reality neither Italy nor Romania provided a plausible parallel. In purely quantitive terms, Serbia was not a majority matrix state: Serbia's population was some four million, while twice that number of South Slavs lived in the former Habsburg lands. Moreover, there was a qualitative difference. While the Romanians of Transylvania and the Italians of Tyrol and Gradisca had developed cultures and traditions distinct in some respects from those of their fellow nationals, they could not (and did not) claim the separate identity and heritage possessed by Croats and Slovenes.

146 FO 371/3138/213162 (DMI, 28 Dec 1918).

147 FO 371/3507/16797 (Plunkett, Belgrade, 25 Jan 1919).

148 This, of course, was precisely what Serbian Radicals hoped in rejecting the name 'Yugoslavia'. While increasingly insensitive to the state's internal situation, 'Serbia' seemed adequate in an international context.

149 FO 371/3160/200994 (7 Dec 1918).

150 See, for example, Seton-Watson, 'The Policy of Dr Pašić and the Yugoslav Problem', *Correspondence*, i, 352.

151 The geographer Jovan Cvijić, for instance, who applauded Seton-Watson's criticism of Pašić in 'Serbia's Choice' (*Correspondence*, i, 347-8); for similar support from Pašić's political enemies, see the letters from Milorad Drašković, Milutin Stanojević and Ljubomir Stojanović, ibid., 336-45.

152 In June 1917 the trial by tribunal and execution of Serbian officers accused of plotting to assassinate Prince Regent Alexander provoked a political crisis as Independent Radical and Progressive leaders withdrew from Pašić's coalition, accusing him – apparently with justification – of rigging the trial in pursuit of his own objectives (see D.Mackenzie, *The 'Black Hand' on Trial: Salonica, 1917* (Boulder, 1995)).

153 *National Question*, p.133. Dragoslav Janković, the authority on Serbian wartime policy, described the Serbian Opposition as the Committee's 'least reliable ally'; having backed Trumbić six months earlier, it assured Alexander that Serbians could administer 'our several times larger Serb-Croat-Slovene Kingdom' (cited in ibid.).

154 FO 371/3137/172539 (*c.*18 Oct 1918, emphasis added).

155 'The Policy of Dr Pašić and the Yugoslav Problem'.

156 FO 371/3137/169690 (Oct 1918).

157 FO 371/3137/171759 (9 Oct 1918).

158 FO 371/3137/195820 (23 Nov 1918).

159 FO 371/3137/171759 (Balfour, 9 Oct 1918). It was also to disregard an earlier insight by Sir Valentine Chirol. Serbs, he had observed, drew a 'marked distinction between the Kingdom of Serbia and the Serb "nation" of which it considers itself the trustee', always giving precedence to the interests of the latter (FO 371/2262/128346).

160 Banac, *National Question*, pp.130-1.

161 *Correspondence*, i, 364.

162 Stokes, 'The Role of the Yugoslav Committee', pp.64-5; Banac, *National Question*, p.135. Pribićević's group had assumed leadership of the HSK after Supilo's departure in 1910.

163 At least, that is, until his famous U-turn of 1925.

[164] Banac, *National Question*, pp.170-3. He later frankly boasted as much.

[165] The only condition attached to the declaration of loyalty accepted by Alexander was that the (ex-Habsburg) Yugoslavs were guaranteed representation in the joint Government.

[166] FO 371/3138/213164 (Temperley, 15 Dec 1918).

[167] FO 371/3507/3222 (Temperley, 15 Dec 1918). Belief in this implausible alliance testifies, perhaps, to the vague sense of menace which Bolshevism exerted over Europe in the aftermath of the war and of events in Russia.

[168] 'We Croats', Radić had told the National Council's Central Committee, 'do not want any state organisation except a confederated federal republic' (M.Biondich, *Stjepan Radić, the Croat Peasant Party, and the Politics of Mass Mobilisation, 1904-1928* (Toronto, 2000), pp.138-9).

[169] FO 371/3507/3222; FO 371/3138/213164. See below pp.198-9.

[170] FO 371/3138/213164.

[171] The remaining Frankist movement *was* acknowledged in Britain to be pro-Habsburg and anti-Serbian, but was accorded no significance during 1917-18.

[172] Quoted in Banac, *National Question*, p.99.

[173] FO 371/3137/171114 (Leeper, 15 Oct 1918). The feeling existed, if rarely voiced explicitly, that while Britain was entitled to ratify the Yugoslav project, and set the state frontiers, constitutional questions were for the Yugoslavs themselves. Seton-Watson protested with justice, but in vain, that financial support for Pašić's Government already constituted an intervention in internal politics, and one which angered opposition groups ('The Policy of Mr Pašić and the Yugoslav Problem', *Correspondence*, i, 350-5).

[174] The same was true of the declaration of union guaranteeing Austro-Hungarian Yugoslavs representation in the national Government.

[175] FO 371/4356/172. 'Confederal' and 'confederation' were often used loosely as synonyms for 'federal' and 'federation'.

[176] 'The Policy of Mr Pašić and the Yugoslav Problem'.

[177] FO 371/3154/171702 (8 Oct 1918).

[178] FO 371/2889/180815.

[179] Banac, *National Question*, p.124.

[180] On the widespread unrest in Croatia in late 1918, see Biondich, *Stjepan Radić*, pp.145-8, and I.Banac, '"Emperor Karl has become a Comitadji": The Croatian Disturbances in the Autumn of 1918', *Slavonic and East European Review*, 70, no.2 (1992), 284-305.

[181] FO 371/4356/172 ('The Unification of the Yugo-Slavs'), p.5. See also Laffan, 'Liberation of the New Nationalities', p.201. Alexander himself had told the British Minister in Belgrade that Italian action had hastened and consolidated the union (FO 371/3138/205290 (des Graz, 11 December 1918)).

Chapter Eight

[1] Ivo Lederer, *Yugoslavia at the Paris Peace Conference* (New Haven; London, 1963), pp.64, 119; Andrej Mitrović, 'The Yugoslav Question, the First World War and the Peace Conference, 1914-1920' in Djokić (ed.), *Yugoslavism*, pp.54-5.

[2] Recognition was effectively accorded by the Allied and Associated Powers on 1 May 1919 when credentials were exchanged with the German delegation in the

name of the SCS State. Britain and France made their recognition public on 2 and 6 June respectively. On 28 June the Versailles Treaty (also signed by Italy of course) contained a full acknowledgement (Laffan, 'Liberation of the New Nationalities', p.207).

3 Greece was the exception, Albania, Bulgaria, Romania, Hungary, Austria and Italy the rule.

4 Quoted in Lederer, *Yugoslavia*, p.96, the standard work for the Conference's treatment of Yugoslavia. For a contemporary British account of the Adriatic problem, see Woodhouse and Woodhouse, *Italy and the Jugoslavs*.

5 Harold Nicolson recalled 'the corrosive influence of that problem upon the moral and diplomatic basis of the Conference of Paris' (*Peacemaking*, p.158). Italian 'Fiume' was preferred in Britain to Slavic 'Rijeka'.

6 Lederer, *Yugoslavia*, p.ix.

7 'Regrettable': Balfour to President Wilson (Lederer, *Yugoslavia*, p.39). Crowe, FO 371/3510/136009 (30 Sept 1919). British favour was little help: in November 1920 the Rapallo treaty granted Italy all the London treaty had promised *plus* Fiume (which was declared independent and lived an artificial existence as such until occupied by Italian troops in March 1922 and annexed by Mussolini in January 1924). Overall, however, Yugoslavia didn't fare badly. Some 720,000 Yugoslavs were left outside, but the state's 12 million inhabitants included nearly 2 million non-Slavs (Macartney, *National States*, pp.518-42).

8 FO 371/3154/211722 ('less obnoxious', Collier, 27 Dec 1918); FO 371/3579/198962.

9 Semantically, the label 'Old Radicals' (distinguishing them from 'Independent Radicals' among the Serbian opposition) distanced them from those liberal attitudes associated with the younger generation. (On the use of such epithets, see T.Stoianovich, 'The Social Foundations of Balkan Politics, 1750-1941', in Jelavich and Jelavich, *Balkans in Transition*, p.318).

10 See above pp.94-5.

11 FO 371/3581/142846 (16 Oct 1919).

12 FO 371/3579/180059 (21 Feb 1920).

13 FO 371/3579/185929 (27 March 1920).

14 FO 371/4670/14076 (10 Dec 1920).

15 On the genuine radicalism of Pašić's early career, see A.N.Dragnich, *Serbia, Nikola Pašić and Yugoslavia* (New Brunswick, N.J., 1974), pp.11-60. In his *Memoirs of the Peace Conference* (pp.525-6) Lloyd George recalled Pašić with veneration as a unifying force among the Yugoslavs. Protić's hostility to the DS's centralism and autocratic tendencies would lead, by August 1920, to his resignation and a period of principled opposition. When Nicolson lamented in September that the Government was 'under the influence of the Crown Prince and the "Greater Serbia" party', he meant the Old Radicals, associating them not only with chauvinism towards non-Serbs but also with the Regent's autocratic instincts (FO 371/4688/5243 (2 Sept 1920)). In fact in his ideals, and his willingness to impose them dictatorially, Alexander was closer to Pribićević.

16 FO 371/3578/63208 (des Graz, 17 April 1919). This Assembly had been convened the previous month.

[17] FO 371/3578/60126 (7 April 1919). The party's one representative had resigned over references in the Regent's inaugural speech to the future internal development of the state.

[18] See above pp.118-9.

[19] FO 371/3594/43979 (Feb 1919).

[20] FO 371/3509/103989 (9 July 1919).

[21] FO 371/3507/3222 (15 Dec 1918).

[22] Ibid. A dismissive reference to 'this separatist movement […] which the Italians are running for all they are worth' implied foreign intrigue rather than native sentiment underlay Croatian nationalism (FO 371/3508/43950).

[23] FO 371/3508/59886 (31 March 1919). On the similar blindness of Yugoslavist liberals to the strength of the Croatian state right movement on the eve of war, see Pleterski, 'The Southern Slav Question', pp.131-2; on Rightist ideology's greater social penetration, and more decisive influence on pre-war Croatian national integration, than that of Yugoslavism, see Gross, 'Croatian National-Integrational Ideologies', pp.5-6.

[24] Having initially promised the DS would not operate in Serbia, Pribićević seemed in Belgrade to represent 'Croat' opinion, considered thereby as firmly unitarist and centralist (Banac, *National Question*, pp.172-4).

[25] FO 371/3578/31098 (15 Feb 1919). He admitted also his 'very slight acquaintance with the pre-war politics in Croatia'.

[26] FO 371/3509/103989 (11 July 1919). Temperley (the sole British official with post-war experience in Zagreb), was alone in inclining immediately to identify the grouping rather with Serbia. Their agrarian reformism had, he noted, 'a definite chance of winning [the Croatian peasants] and turning them away from Croat separations and Radić towards Serbia and the new Democratic party' (FO 371/3508/59886 (31 March 1919)).

[27] FO 371/3578/63208 (17 April 1919).

[28] FO 371/3578/43988 (des Graz, 14 Mar 1919).

[29] FO 371/3578/63208.

[30] FO 371/3508/59886.

[31] FO 371/3578/63208. It was Pribićević, Alex Dragnich remarks, who set 'the tone and style' of day-to-day administration during the state's first year (*The First Yugoslavia: Search for a Viable Political System* (Stanford, 1983), p.15).

[32] FO 371/3511/149375, 155966; FO 371/3578/140518, 143033 (*Times* article, 20 Oct 1919).

[33] FO 371/3579/180059 (21 Feb 1920).

[34] FO 371/3579/198962 (Hope Vere, interview with an unnamed Democrat, 10 May 1920).

[35] It was fairly noted that conflicting forces in Montenegro resembled those elsewhere. But it was overlooked that for many Serbians Montenegro *was* a special case, not analogous to those of Croatia or Slovenia. Montenegrins had not been guaranteed equality at Corfu because they were considered not a separate people but merely Serbs isolated from the national body. See above pp.149-50.

[36] Banac, *National Question*, pp.383-4. The party had also secured the appointment of Pribićević's protégé Ivan Palaček as Croatian ban (ibid., 218-19). With Alexander's authority to dissolve the Assembly and call elections if denied

Parliamentary support, the Democrats were able to force measures past bitter opposition.

[37] FO 371/4668/7029 (18 Sept 1920).

[38] FO 371/3581/164456 (19/12/1919). An agreement for Croatia alone to have special commissioners to oversee certain areas of policy had been brokered by the Radicals, but it was clear, Athelstan Johnson reported, that they would remain firmly subordinate to Belgrade and that there was 'no question of the creation of an autonomous state' (FO 371/3578/145509 (18 Oct 1919)). It is unlikely that it was this status that was referred to.

[39] The fact that some of these politicians may indeed have rejected such an idea is not, here, quite the point.

[40] As we have seen, many British observers at this stage attached more significance to 'ancient provinces' like Dalmatia or Croatia-Slavonia than to what we now call 'ethnic' identities. Though terms like 'autonomy' and 'federalism' were often used interchangeably in Britain, we should be clear about the distinction. 'Federalism' denoted a division of legislative authority between a central parliament and subsidiary regional parliaments, the nature of the division to be defined by constitution and unalterable except by amendment. 'Autonomy' indicated a system of local administrative independence in which legislative authority remained with the central parliament. 'Devolution' (though the term was less frequently used) referred to an intermediary position, by which legislative authority in certain limited spheres was voluntarily *transferred* from central to regional parliament, subject to recall without constitutional amendment. These points are discussed in an article by the Serbian jurist and historian Slobodan Jovanović, enclosed in FO 371/6194/9607.

[41] FO 371/3580/73717 (14 May 1919).

[42] FO 371/3581/142846 (16 Oct 1919).

[43] 'The outlook', Leeper lamented, 'is not promising' (FO 371/3579/180059).

[44] FO 371/4668/2436 (Francis Jones, Sarajevo, 7 June 1920).

[45] FO 371/3579/189400;184539 (Young, 2 March 1920; 26 March 1920); FO 371/3603/145102 ('daily less certain', Bridge, 20 Sept 1919).

[46] FO 371/4687/2431 (Young, 23 July 1920).

[47] FO 371/3579/180059.

[48] FO 371/3579/184539; FO 371/3579/189400 (26 March 1920).

[49] Ibid.

[50] Ibid. (Leeper, 1 April 1920; Temperley, 13 April). By contrast Joseph de Fontenay, the French Minister in Belgrade, remained strictly loyal to the Belgrade line, treating all unrest in the non-Serb provinces – and Radić's electoral success – as expressions of separatism and pro-German intrigue. Would Paris, he simply asked, dream of supporting Irish agitation against Britain? See Kovač, *La France*, pp.223-4. (A few French officials – and many French soldiers on the ground in Croatia – did hold, it should be noted, a different and often more nuanced view).

[51] Strictly, Davidović headed two ministries during this period. The first fell after a month but a second was quickly formed. Protić's return had seen moves to relax the centralistic trend, in fulfillment of promises to autonomist groups in his coalition (Banac, *National Question*, p.384).

[52] FO 371/3607/198110 (26 May 1920).

[53] FO 371/3579/198115 (1 May 1920). Elsewhere he reported the indignation of Bosnian Muslim landlords, 'whose political influence was dangerous and who were threatening to cause a Mussulman rising if their lands were confiscated in favour of their Christian tenants' (FO 371/3604/206758, 20 June 1920).

[54] FO 371/4668/307 (25 June 1920).

[55] Banac, *National Question*, pp.352-3.

[56] Ibid, pp.354-7.

[57] There was, Leeper observed, 'no one else of his calibre and knowledge' (FO 371/3579/180059).

[58] FO 371/3579/180059 (Leeper, 21 Feb 1920); FO 371/3581/142846 (Crowe, 16 Oct 1919).

[59] FO 371/4668/307 (7 July 1920).

[60] FO 371/4669/11466 (20 Nov 1920).

[61] On British attitudes to Kun, see Bátonyi, *Britain and Central Europe*, pp.88-100.

[62] FO 371/3578/31098 (15 Feb 1919). The idea of Serbia as an anti-communist heartland would become particularly important in British thinking during World War II, with the rise of Tito's partisan movement. In France too Serbia was regarded as a crucial bastion against the Bolshevik threat. The influential General Franchet d'Ésperey urged that every Serb (or Romanian) soldier armed would save a French soldier, while the French Minister in Belgrade echoed the need for a barrier against Russian influence (Grumel-Jacquignon, *La Yougoslavie*, pp.41-4).

[63] FO 371/3508/59886 (Temperley, 31 March 1919). Some historians have echoed this view (Lederer, *Yugoslavia*, p.93). But Banac notes the HPSS assembly in Zagreb in February 1919, attended by 6,000 activists, and the petition to Paris demanding a Croat constituent assembly which raised 115,167 signatures in 6 weeks. 'Official estimates of the effects of Radić's republicanism in the Croat countryside', he writes, 'had assumed alarming proportions in the spring of 1919'; 'Proposed agrarian reforms [*pace* Temperley] interested the peasantry far less than the promises of Radić's movement' (*National Question*, pp.239-43). See also, in particular, Biondich, *Stjepan Radić*, which stresses strongly the alienation of the Croatian peasant majority from traditional, bourgeois politics and the – at least potential – strength of Radić's support (p.144 and *passim*).

[64] FO 371/3578/53298 (des Graz, 30 March 1919); FO 371/3507/3222 (Temperley, 15 Dec 1918). A little later Temperley admitted that the label 'Bolshevik' was inaccurate for a party that was 'older and more exclusive than that' (FO 371/3138/213164). For communists, as Mark Biondich points out, Radić's peasantism was thoroughly bourgeois and reactionary, offering no solutions to Croatia's or Yugoslavia's social ills (*Stjepan Radić*, p.157).

[65] Radić's pre-war popularity had not before been acknowledged. Seton-Watson had corresponded with Radić, sympathised with his 'trialist' aspiration, and drawn attention to his persecution, but Whitehall had shown scant interest in a group making little electoral impression (despite the fact that its primary constituency, 90% of the population, was unenfranchised, meaning full democracy must increase his influence).

[66] FO 371/3579/184539; FO 371/3579/189400 (26 March 1920). Radić had been rearrested (on 22 March) and held until the amnesty of 28 November, so his *direct* part in subsequent unrest was not great.

[67] FO 371/3607/198110 (26 May 1920).

[68] FO 371/3607/194689 (29 April 1920). Whether by his own pen or another is unclear.

[69] FO 371/3607/194759 (29 April 1920).

[70] This hesitancy contrasted with an Austrian police report received by Whitehall which noted that while Slovene communism had been largely confined to industrial centres, in Croatia the movement was 'purely national' (FO 371/4658/38, 28 May 1920).

[71] FO 371/4689/6254 (13 Sept 1920); FO 371/4689/7510 (14 Sept 1920). See also Banac, *National Question*, p.248ff.

[72] FO 371/4689/7510 (29 Sept 1920).

[73] Ibid.

[74] FO 371/4689/6254.

[75] A similar conclusion followed from the recognition of the DS, by provenance not specifically *Serbian*, as a *Serb* party. Thus Adam characterised the forthcoming electoral battle as 'between older Serb parties and "autonomists" of the new provinces' FO 371/4669/11466 (20 Nov 1920).

[76] The vitriolic rivalry which had seemed to indicate a fundamental divergence of principles was largely personal. Though Democrats, unlike Radicals, believed in a Yugoslav nation, Radicals could reconcile this with a Greater Serbian inclination. In their view, after all, Yugoslavs *were* largely uniform: the great majority were Serbs and the remainder, by a process of linguistic and cultural assimilation, could become so. (The sophistry required to argue at once that Catholics were racial Serbs without knowing it, and that Croats or Slovenes could *become* Serbs by an acculturative process, proving no barrier).

[77] FO 371/4669/11466 (20 Nov 1920).

[78] FO 371/4668/307 (25 June 1920).

[79] 'Slovenia', of course, was not a historic province at all, though British officials often treated it as if it were; but the amalgamation of Slovene-inhabited regions within the Conference-defined borders of Yugoslavia did not present the obstacles which any 'Croat' or 'Serb' amalgamation would have done.

[80] FO 371/4668/307 (7 July 1920).

[81] Ibid. This, of course, was Belgrade's perspective, but given the balance of power no less important for that. In general it was insufficiently appreciated in Britain that the experiences of French history, and more recently of Italian, had strongly equated centralism with the liberal, 'progressive' tide in modern history. Radović had written to Harmsworth that, while some Yugoslavs espoused federalism for the SCS State, others wanted the state ordered 'after the pattern of Italy or France because those countries likewise evolved from several small states' (FO 371/3580/111497, 27 July 1919).

[82] FO 371/4668/307 (7 July 1920).

[83] FO 371/4669/10883 (Young, 5 Nov 1920; Temperley, 15 Nov 1920; Strang notes undated).

[84] FO 371/4669/11466 (Temperley, 20 Nov 1920). Though he admitted to feeling unsure about Vojvodina and Bosnia which were, he wrote, 'always mysterious'.

[85] FO 371/4697/4545 (18 Sept 1920).

[86] FO 371/4669/12186 (24 Nov 1920).

[87] FO 371/4662/12576 (30 Nov 1920).

[88] FO 371/4662/12481 (25 Nov 1920).

[89] FO 371/4670/13669 (7 Dec 1920).

[90] FO 371/4670/13412

[91] FO 371/4670/13311. Save a brief earlier mention of censorship in Croatia (on Communist papers primarily) officials were also uncritical of the preceding campaign (FO 371/3607/198110, Maclean 21 April 1920).

[92] FO 371/4668/7029 (18 Sept 1920).

[93] FO 371/4668/7490 (Young 25 Sept 1920; Nicolson 30 Sept).

[94] Thus Nicolson, for instance, noted Montenegro's population had been underestimated, while J.J.McMalkin's detailed analysis was concerned principally with non-Yugoslavs: ibid. But British officials were over-sanguine. The ratio of deputies to voters varied by region in a manner favouring the centralist parties; and contrary to the state's treaty obligations, Germans, Magyars and Jews were excluded (Banac, National Question, pp.387-91).

[95] FO 371/4670/13311 (subsequent quotes from this source unless stated). This illustrates too, of course, the shift in the way Democrats were viewed in Britain which we noted above.

[96] Soon after the election, on 8 December, Radić changed the party's name to Croat Republican Peasant Party (HRSS). The party was alone in securing an overall majority in a particular region.

[97] Biondich, Stjepan Radić, p.140. Young's 'scarcely half a dozen' therefore undersold the extent of the collapse. In association with the Croat Husbandmen, who won 7 seats in Bosnia-Hercegovina, the 'National Club' amassed only 11 seats.

[98] Muslims, Young reported, had 'a strong representation' of nearly 30 members. The correct figures were 24 for the JMO and 8 for the Cemiyet in Kosovo, Metohia, Sandžak and Macedonia. The Slovene People's Party (SLS) was deemed to have suffered a 'reverse', and its leaders were unhappy. But it won 37% of the Slovene vote, and with its Bosnian Catholic ally, the Croat People's Party, controlled 27 seats.

[99] His declared intention to abstain called to mind again the Irish comparison: 'like the Sinn Feiners', Young observed (FO 371/4670/13311 (3 Dec 1920)).

[100] Initially the KPJ supported the idea of Yugoslav 'national oneness' and favoured a firmly centralistic structure, though it later supported disruptive internal nationalisms likely to foster revolution (Djilas, The Contested Country, chs.2 and 3).

[101] FO 371/4670/13311 (9 Dec 1920). Such an outcome, Adam concurred, was 'both in our interest and that of the Serbs themselves' (ibid).

[102] FO 371/4662/13229 (24 Dec 1920).

[103] FO 371/4670/13587 (11 Dec 1920).

[104] FO 371/4670/13669 (7 Dec 1920). The Government must remember, Young warned, that comments regarding Montenegro 'may be misapplied by Croatians' to their 'more or less analogous case' (FO 371/4670/13424;13669).

[105] FO 371/4670/13587;13888 (Young, 10 Dec 1920; 11 Dec 1920).

[106] Historians give a much higher figure: Banac (National Question, p.393) claims 100,000, Dragnich (The First Yugoslavia, p.21), 80,000.

[107] FO 371/4670/13888 (16 Dec 1920).

[108] FO 371/4670/13815 (15 Dec 1920).

[109] FO 371/4670/13815;14953 (14 Dec 1920; 29 Dec 1920).

[110] FO 371/4670/14953 (19 Dec 1920).

[111] Banac, *National Question*, pp.104-5. And only now did the party incorporate the word 'Republican'.

[112] FO 371/3138/213164 (15 Dec 1918). As Mark Biondich illustrates, 'republicanism' appealed to the Croat peasantry at the end of the war as entailing liberation from all forms of fiscal and social restraint: overbearing landlords, taxes, conscription, requisitioning, usury, and so on. It was not simply, or even chiefly, a matter of a crowned head of state (*Stjepan Radić*, pp.150-1 and *passim*).

[113] FO 371/4670/14954 (30 Dec 1920). Communists, National Club, Republicans, JMO and Social Democrats all initially rejected the standing orders as illegal, while Radić's party, which also rejected the pledge, refused to attend at all. By canny bargaining, however, the centralist bloc secured majority acquiescence. (The JMO, for one, was considered reliably monarchist by inclination, and malleable once its fears over land reform were assuaged). In fact this question was more significant than Whitehall allowed since it raised the fundamental question of the Assembly's sovereignty. The 'difficulties' included also the election as Assembly president of Ivan Ribar, a prominent Democrat, by 'only 243 out of 419 deputies', a result 'not satisfactory from the Serb point of view'. In fact Ribar's support was narrower even than Adam allowed: 192 votes from the *243 representatives in attendance*, a figure well under half the total membership (Banac, *National Question*, p.395).

[114] FO 371/6193/1414 (14 Jan 1921).

[115] FO 371/4670/13888 (16 Dec 1920). The use of the term 'Black-Yellows' in Serbia to describe inhabitants of the new provinces who hankered after Austrian rule (a black eagle on yellow ground being the Habsburg symbol) was, Young remarked a little later, 'ominously like Black and Tans' (18 Feb 1921: FO 371/6193/3773).

[116] FO 371/4670/13888. The connection between the Croatian cause and that of the Irish was not one that escaped the Croats: see Young (18 Feb 1921, FO 371/6193/3773).

[117] FO 371/4670/13311 (3 Dec 1920).

[118] FO 371/4670/13424 (10 Dec 1920). Radić's Republican movement, Adam agreed, was 'probably an immature expression of a trend in Croatia in a federal direction' (FO 371/4670/13815).

[119] FO 371/6193/4669 (7 March 1921).

[120] FO 371/4670/13815 (14 Dec 1920).

[121] Ibid.

[122] FO 371/6193/374 (31 Dec 1920); FO 371/6193/25 (Adam, 3 Jan 1921).

[123] FO 371/6193/1414 (14 Jan 1921). The JMO's principal concern was reckoned to be to prevent major agrarian reform in Bosnia. But Francis Jones reported nevertheless instances of oppression of Croats and Muslims by Serb officials in that province, and the growing feeling that Croats and Slovenes must be guaranteed an equal say with Serbs in the constitutional question: ibid. (7 Jan 1920; 12 Jan 1920).

[124] FO 371/6193/2340 (22 Jan 1921).

[125] FO 371/6193/374. The discovery of a Communist conspiracy, and consequent far-reaching restrictions imposed on Communists, credited this picture of clandestine Comintern machination.

[126] FO 371/6193/2 (1 Jan 1921).

[127] FO 371/6193/1414 (14 Jan 1921).

[128] FO 371/6193/25 (31 Dec 1920).

[129] FO 371/6193/2340 (29 Jan 1921)

[130] Ibid.

[131] FO 371/4670/13815 (14 Dec 1920).

[132] FO 371/6193/1414.

[133] FO 371/4670/13311 (Young, 3 Dec 1920).

[134] FO 371/4670/13815.

[135] As we saw in chapter 1, use of the 'race' concept was often vague. Nevertheless, talk of 'racial' differences *within* the Yugoslav group is clearly indicative of the rapid shift in attitudes towards Yugoslav nationality.

[136] Ibid. He misrepresented Trumbić's attitude: his constitutional proposal broke up these 'ancient provinces'. As a Dalmatian, Trumbić began more enthusiastic about Yugoslav unitarism than most Croatians, and recognised a need to erode provincial identities. In any case, Adam's praise for Trumbić as 'the only Yugoslav statesman whose views are broad and moderate' makes his faith in an ultimate broad and moderate settlement puzzling.

[137] FO 371/6193/3773 (Young, 18 Feb 1921).

[138] Though the Orthodox were numerically the largest community in Bosnia, they did not constitute an absolute majority, and were vulnerable to a Croat-Muslim political alliance.

[139] FO 371/6193/4351 (Stonehewer-Bird, 16 Feb 1921).

[140] FO 371/6193/2340 (29 Jan 1921).

[141] Seton-Watsons, *Making of a New Europe*, pp.410-11. Similarly in November 1919 he had complained of a 'conspiracy of silence and considerable indifference and ignorance' in relation to the Fiume dispute (ibid., p.383). One can understand his frustration, but a period of introversion after a drawn-out international conflict seems natural and not (on Occam's principle) requiring conspiratorial explanation. (Part of the problem, he suggested more plausibly, was the lack of Yugoslav representation in Britain before January 1920: ibid., p.390 footnote 82).

[142] FO 371/6193/2828 (2 Feb 1921). The KPJ, another troublesome opposition group, was weakened by strong measures to ban Communist agitation. (Vesnić's cabinet resigned on 23 December. On 1 January a new Democrat-Radical coalition cabinet was confirmed. Headed by Pašić, it was free of the commitments to autonomist partners which had hampered Protić and Vesnić: Banac, *National Question*, p.396).

[143] FO 371/6193/4669 (7 March 1921).

[144] FO 371/6193/3773 (18 Feb 1921).

[145] FO 371/6193/2340 (29 Jan 1921).

[146] FO 371/6193/4846 (4 March 1921). Temperley agreed, attributing the decision to Pašić: 'a reactionary of the "Greater Serbia" school' (9 March 1921).

[147] FO 371/6193/4669. Some British officials certainly had done. Temperley later remarked a statement by Trumbić to the effect that while Serbs and Croats were

racially similar, their divergent mentalities resulted from a distinct history. These remarks, Temperley commented, 'explain much' (6 May 1921, FO 371/6194/9143).

[148] FO 371/6193/3773. This line was untypical of the KPJ, which tended towards centralism and unitarism, while protesting indifference to the 'national question' in its quest for radical socio-economic change. But as a conglomeration of old leftist groups it remained prone to inconsistencies.

[149] FO 371/6193/4351 (Young, 18 Feb 1921; Temperley, 24 Feb 1921).

[150] FO 371/6193/4669.

[151] FO 371/6194/6414 (31 March 1921).

[152] FO 371/6194/7548 (16 April 1921). An article limited the administrative areas to a population of 700,000, Young reported, 'finally dissipating the hopes of the Slovenians and Croatians for the preservation of the identity of their countries' (31 March 1921, FO 371/6194/6967). The Croat Parliamentary Union, Temperley noted, had denounced the constitution, claiming it would make Yugoslavia a police-state, and vowing permanent opposition.

[153] FO 371/6194/7548.

[154] FO 371/6194/8560 (Temperley, 27 April 1921).

[155] FO 371/6194/10175 (20 May 1921). Young reported the view of one 'enlightened' Bosnian Croat that Radić's influence was spreading, among Muslims in Bosnia as well as Catholics.

[156] The Government did agree at the last minute to increase the regional population limit to 800,000, and to grant the JMO a compromise which looked likely to secure Bosnia's basic outline within the Yugoslav regional map.

[157] A month later, on 2 August, Communist gunmen again tried in vain to assassinate Alexander, instead killing former minister Milorad Drašković. The KPJ was formally banned, known Communist leaders arrested, and the party forced underground. (Alexander was crowned king on 16 August).

[158] FO 371/6194/14658 (29 June 1921).

[159] That the Bosnian Muslim community at large, far from sharing the Radical vision, was 'bitterly disillusioned' at events since the liberation, was suggested by British observers shortly afterwards. Strang recorded the view of 'an Englishman who has lived and travelled much in Bosnia' that, whereas eighteen months earlier the Muslims were proud of their place in the new State, they could no longer be considered 'an element [making] for unity and consolidation' and had 'regrets for the days of the Austrian regime' (8 Sept 1921, FO 371/6194/17935).

[160] FO 371/6194/14658.

[161] The Times, 20 July 1921. Enclosed with emphases in FO 371/6194/14606. Protić's rift with Pašić and the Radical majority (who had combined with his enemy Pribićević), and his demand for constitutional revision, added to the feeling of instability; as did the fact that both Serb parties had internal troubles: Vojvodina Radicals, for instance, rejecting Pribićević as Interior Minister (Strang 29 Sept 1921, FO 371/6194/19039).

[162] FO 371/7686/5308 (annual report for 1921).

[163] Agnes Headlam-Morley later concurred that Yugoslavia's was a 'completely centralised administrative system' (The New Democratic Constitutions of Europe (London, 1929), p.59). With the help of hindsight she observed that federalism

had 'from the first seemed doomed to rejection' (p.68). Interestingly, given the British view that considered decentralism progressive politics, her comparative study of new constitutions in Germany, Czechoslovakia, Poland, Finland, the Baltic States and the SCS Kingdom observed the 'general tendency' to strengthen the unity of the state 'even at the risk of arousing violent opposition amongst certain sections of the people' (p.88). See also the analysis in Banac, *National Question*, pp.398-9, and that (based on the work of Serb jurist Slobodan Jovanović), in 'The Jugo-Slav Constitution', *Slavonic Review*, III, no.7 (June 1924), 166-78.

[164] FO 371/6194/22132 (24 Nov 1921).

[165] FO 371/6195/22500 (30 Nov 1921). Young's observation in December that a centralised state facilitated representations concerning British interests in the non-Serb provinces was, Nicolson annotated, 'a very narrow point of view' (Young, 13 Dec 1921; Nicolson undated; FO 371/6195/23650).

[166] FO 371/6195/24027 (Nicolson, 21 Dec 1921).

[167] FO 371/7674/81 (Report on Politics in the SCS Army by military attaché James Blair, 26 Dec 1921; Nicolson, 4 Jan 1922).

[168] FO 371/7684/2476 (15 Feb 1922).

[169] FO 371/7686/5308. Given that Radić had been imprisoned from March 1919 to February 1920, and from March 1920 to the amnesty of 28 November 1920, in the first case without trial and in spite of his immunity as member of the Croatian Sabor, this view might seem puzzling; but he had campaigned relatively freely during 1921.

[170] This view was, however, at odds with his verdict in a February report that 'the schism between the Croats and the Serbs appears to be widening' (FO 371/7684/2476). On Serb-Croat relations within the military, see Mile Bjelajac, 'The Military and Yugoslav Unity' in Djokić (ed.), *Yugoslavism*, pp.208-21 (though his attempt to refute Istvàn Deàk's claim of anti-Croat discrimination in the Yugoslav army is unconvincing).

[171] FO 371/7684/3588 (7 March 1922). Trumbić admitted, he reported, that Radić's abstention had been 'from some points of view a mistake', though it was the illegal exaction of the oath that had held them aloof.

[172] FO 371/7684/3688 (16 March 1922).

[173] FO 371/7685/3689 (16 March 1922). Unfortunately, a colleague responded, he was 'precisely the sort of character that does not disappear'.

[174] FO 371/7684/3688.

Conclusion

[1] See, for example, B.Simms, *Unfinest Hour: Britain and the Destruction of Bosnia* (London, 2002), pp.12-13, 241-3 (Simms notes the 'neuralgic associations' the words 'Sarajevo' and 'Bosnia' have had for diplomats and statesmen since 1914); Almond, *Europe's Backyard War*, p.xvii

[2] See above p.75.

[3] I have discussed some of these British attitudes to the newly established Tito regime in 1945 in an article 'Britain and the Yugoslav General Election of November 1945', in A.Hammond (ed.), *The Balkans and the West: Constructing the European Other, 1945-2003* (Aldershot, 2004), 1-15.

⁴ J.Allcock, 'Aspects of the Development of Capitalism in Yugoslavia: The Role of the State in the Formation of a "Satellite" Economy', in Carter (ed.), *Historical Geography*, p.547.

⁵ See L.Trgovčević, 'South Slav Intellectuals and the Creation of Yugoslavia' in Djokić (ed.), *Yugoslavism*, pp.224-9. She points out that Stojan Novaković's 1911 essay 'After One Hundred Years: Belgrade, 15 May 2011' predicted a united Yugoslav state a century hence.

⁶ See A.B.Wachtel, 'Ivan Meštrović, Ivo Andrić and the Synthetic Yugoslav Culture of the Interwar Period', in ibid., p.238.

⁷ FO 371/3578/133811 (Temperley, 24 Sept 1919).

Lightning Source UK Ltd.
Milton Keynes UK
UKHW022243240620
365497UK00007B/266